AWAKENING *The* UNIVERSAL HEART

ABOUT THE AUTHOR

Serge Beddington-Behrens, M.A.(Oxon.), Ph.D is an internationally respected spiritual educator, psychotherapist, couples counsellor and life coach who has worked in the area of healing and transformation for most of his life. He teaches a deeper approach to life based on recognising the importance of 'growing' our heart life which in turn enables people more easily to integrate spiritual practice with psychological self-inquiry into a concrete and fundamental transformation of their lives.

Serge works with individuals, couples and groups via individual sessions, seminars and week-long spiritual retreats. Currently, the main focus of his work is exploring how people may best use their newly emerging psychological and spiritual health to become more effective change agents or spiritual activists and how corporations may transform themselves to promote a truly sustainable future for our world.

For a calendar of future seminars, retreats and talks, to make a booking and for information on how to download his CDs, either visit Serge's website on www.spiritual-activism.com, contact him on infosergebb@gmail.com or ring Serge Beddington-Behrens Seminars on 07787 474283.

AWAKENING *The* UNIVERSAL HEART

A Guide for Spiritual Activists

Serge Beddington-Behrens

UMBRIA PRESS

Copyright © Serge Beddington-Behrens 2013

Serge Beddington-Behrens has asserted his right
under the Copyright, Designs and Patents Act 1988
to be identified as the author of this work.

Umbria Press
London SW15 5DP
www.umbriapress.co.uk

Printed and bound by
Ashford Colour Press, Gosport

ISBN: 978-0-9541275-8-9

Serge Beddington-Behrens
www.spiritual-activism.com

For my darling daughter Irena

Foreword

Serge is a lovely man with a big heart and a correspondingly wide circle of friends. I have known him for nearly thirty years, first meeting him in 1984 when he lived in California and I was passing through promoting my new book. We went out to dinner in his open-top VW Beetle and I stayed for a few days in his house, where we had many engaging conversations. He had just completed his PhD in psychology and had co-founded an Institute for Conscious Evolution. He told me he was thinking of writing a book, and what you hold in your hands is the fruit of many years of living and reflecting on the role of the heart in spiritual and psychological practice – how we can heal both ourselves and the planet to which we have done so much damage.

Two years later, I moved into his spare cottage in Gloucestershire. As Serge lived next door, over the five years I spent there we were in very close contact. I remember us both talking about how important it was to take a stand for a new way of life and of looking at the world, and both of us have tried to honour our intentions ever since. With Serge, this primarily took the form of his working as a transpersonal psychotherapist, giving inspirational lectures and teaching spiritual retreats for business executives who wanted to find their heart. In the autumn of 1986 we co-chaired the celebrations for the eightieth birthday of Sir George Trevelyan, whose writings and teachings have inspired us both and who founded the Wrekin Trust, with which we are also both closely associated. We often used to meet him for lunch in those days. It was from Sir George that Serge got the idea of a 'rising tide of love' in the world, which is central to the theme of this important book.

In 2009, another friend, Iain McGilchrist, published his seminal book *The Master and His Emissary*, in which he proposed that our culture suffered from an imbalance, with too much emphasis placed on left-hemisphere analytical thinking at the expense of the right hemisphere, responsible for imaginative and creative activity. Serge's diagnosis follows a similar pattern, but it is written from a much more experiential angle. With great honesty and openness, he weaves many of his own experiences and life challenges involved in trying to become himself what he calls an 'activist of the heart' into a book greatly needed in these troubled times. His basic theme is that our planet is in great crisis today and that humanity urgently needs to grow up. We are therefore called to shift from a mindset of selfish operation based on the illusion that we are separate from our world, to one of operating holistically, so that our lives can begin to revolve around serving a deeper evolutionary purpose. Serge's view is that we can only 'do' this work effectively if we learn to open or awaken our hearts, and the book shows us how this can be done. He suggests we need to shift from being what he calls a caterpillar (old-style man) to becoming a butterfly (activist/heart man). In discussing the role that he feels the universal heart plays in this, he is building upon the work of the visionary UN assistant secretary general Dr Robert Muller, whom he also knew, and who also referred to the awakening of the Global Heart.

Serge told me he wanted to write about the universal heart because he believes that the emergence of this heart is an idea whose time has come and that more people should be introduced to it. Up until now we have heard a lot of talk about global brains and global minds, and now is the time for 'the world of heart' to come into its own. Indeed, if we look around at certain world events that have taken place in the last decade, we can see that this is in fact the case. For instance, readers will remember the worldwide tide of sympathy for the victims of the 2004 tsunami, the millions of people who protested against the Iraqi war, the passion of the Occupy movement and the many strands of environmental activism working towards the regeneration of nature. As Paul Hawken pointed out in his book *Blessed Unrest*, there is an enormous amount of work being carried out by NGOs around the world, which forms a counterweight to widespread apathy, despair and hopelessness. Most recently, many of us will recall the extraordinary 'heart spirit' of London 2012, which carried with it an enormous sense of hope, possibility and optimism. Our challenge, Serge suggests, is to learn not to close down our hearts again once the awakening moments have passed.

The first part of this fascinating book explores why the heart is so important and the huge price we pay if our hearts are closed or wounded, which leads us to feel cut off from experiencing what he calls the basic goodness of life. In the second section, Serge draws on his experiences as a shaman, healer and psychotherapist and looks at what we need to do to heal our hearts. He suggests that this is crucial if we wish to prepare ourselves for the next stage, the further cultivating of the 'garden of our hearts', which he explores in the third section of his book. Here it is not simply a question of awakening, but also of working at deepening our humanity, the essence of which he sees as residing inside our hearts. In this part there are fascinating chapters on how

FOREWORD

we may conduct our relationships more consciously, work more effectively with crisis and learn to forgive those who may have wounded us in some way. He also refers to the existence of 'spiritual help forces', and outlines ways and means that we can align ourselves with them and so receive an extra 'leg up' in our evolutionary endeavours. Of particular interest are his personal experiences with certain spiritual masters and his experiences with ayahuasca.

Perhaps the most significant part of this book is the last section, where Serge not only looks at challenges that might lie ahead for the human race, but also at what we can all concretely do to create a better world for ourselves and our children. Here, he has a chapter on what we can do to end war and find better ways of resolving conflicts than killing each other. In a fascinating chapter on how the activist might approach the whole topic of evil, he distinguishes between 'obvious' and 'non-obvious' evil, suggesting that the second kind is more deadly as it doesn't initially appear to be evil and therefore we often cannot see it for what it is. He also notes that it is essential to work at integrating our own personal Shadow sides if we are to integrate marginalised and disowned areas of our society. In his last chapter, exploring the awakening of the corporate heart, he suggests that the 'rising tide of love' is also occurring in the business world and that a new 'capitalism with heart' is steadily arising, phoenix-like, out of the ashes of corporate corruption.

This book cannot be rushed. It is long and needs to be read slowly and carefully. It is full of little gems and is written from a place of great hope and joy, being based on Serge's strong-felt sense that our world is changing for the better, that great goodness abounds and that the universal heart is awakening among increasing numbers of people, empowering them to move forward and confront those forces in the world that resist change. In these uncertain times, we need practical visionaries to show us the way towards a culture of love and of the heart. Serge is one such visionary and his book provides an invaluable roadmap if we have the courage to follow it. I welcome the fact that he plans to start an institute to teach the ideas presented in it, and I wish him all success with his venture and look forward to being on board.

David Lorimer, Fife, Scotland,
February 2013

David Lorimer is programme director of the Scientific and Medical Network, president of the Wrekin Trust and chief executive of Character Scotland. His website can be found at www.davidlorimer.net.

Acknowledgements

I want to thank the following people for having taught me so much about the heart.

Thank you, Irena, my beautiful mother. Thank you too, dear Averill Gordon, for also being a wonderful mother and for having given me a wise and beautiful daughter, Irena. Thank you, my old friend Peter Adler, for always making me laugh, and Peter Kyte for the consistency of your friendship and bless you, Joanna and Michael Brown, for your kindness and generosity at all times. Huge thanks to you, dear Michael Cowdray, for your generosity of spirit. I am so grateful to dear Alice Friend and lovely Monica Godwin, for the contribution that your big, loving hearts have made to my life, and also to Charles Montagu, Mark Collins, Chris Dreyfus and Chris Campbell-Carter, for the enormous gift of warmth which your buddy-hood always offers me. A big thank you to Lynne McGregor, Michael McIntyre, Simon Dermody and Yola Jerzykowski for having offered such wonderful support to me when I so needed it.

A very special thanks also goes to Alan Gordon Walker. No words can describe my gratitude to you for your kindness, love and support over the years and the many ways you have contributed to my life, and this is as true for your lovely wife Louise, who has also been such a loving and loyal friend. Thank you, too, my dear friend and fellow sacred activist David Lorimer, and bless you, Pragito Jackson, for having taught me so much about love and mindfulness. Carinthia West, I also want to acknowledge your big heart and generous spirit and I say a big thank you, too, to my old friend John Whitmore, for having turned me on all those years ago to the idea that the world is not always the way we see it. Huge gratitude also flows out to Roger Woolger, Larry Spiro, Papaji and Ram Dass. Your big, wise enlightened hearts have been invaluable to me at different stages of my soul journey. I am also grateful to you, dear Elisabet Sartouris, for having gone over this manuscript and for your many encouraging suggestions. Huge thanks to you, also, Johnnie Reed, for all your support and support over the years. We have been on so many important journeys together and I love you like the beloved brother I never had. Last, but in no way least, a vast thank you to Martina for being one of the kindest and most special women I have ever been privileged to meet and who, every day, teaches me more and more about the beauty, tenderness and generosity of the heart.

Thank you Ervin Laszlo, Elisabet Sartouris Susan Campbell, Stan Grof, John Welwood and Scylla Elworthy for giving me permission to quote from you. I have made every effort to contact those who I have quoted from, and I particularly regret being unable to thank Ken Wilber and Paul Hawken for the immensely valuable contributions which their works have made to the arguments put forward in this book. I will of course be happy to thank anyone who makes contact.

Contents

	Foreword by David Lorimer	vii
	Acknowledgements	000
	Invitation	1

Part One: Understanding the Heart

Chapter 1	The Significance of the Heart	9
Chapter 2	The Treasures of the Heart	20
Chapter 3	Understanding the Wounded Heart	29
Chapter 4	Opening to the Healing Heart	41
Chapter 5	The Challenges of Being an Activist	55

Part Two: Heart Work

Chapter 6	Eastern and Western Perspectives on Self-healing	69
Chapter 7	Investigating Ego Wounds	81
Chapter 8	Healing the Universal Heart	88
Chapter 9	Understanding the Shadow	99
Chapter 10	Integrating the Shadow	108

Part Three: Cultivating the Garden of the Heart

Chapter 11	Opening to the Spiritual Heart	121
Chapter 12	Opening to the Meditative Heart	131
Chapter 13	Awakening the Heart of Prayer	141
Chapter 14	Cultivating the Heart of Love	154
Chapter 15	Embracing the Virtues of the Heart	168
Chapter 16	Entering into the Heart of Relationship	177
Chapter 17	Working with the Sacred 'Help Forces'	189
Chapter 18	Exploring the Heart of Forgiveness	209
Chapter 19	Understanding the Crises of the Heart	222

Part Four: The Great Heart Work

Chapter 20	Looking to the Future	243
Chapter 21	Exploring the Path of the Spiritual Activist	260
Chapter 22	The Many Faces of The Activist of Heart	269
Chapter 23	Healing Evil	283
Chapter 24	Transforming War	298
Chapter 25	Awakening the Corporate Heart	314
	Epilogue	329
	Notes	333
	Index	336

Out of the confusion of a crumbling society will emerge individuals who are touched by higher guidance. These will inevitably flow together with others of like inspiration, and a new quality of society will begin to form. This is the true adventure of our time –
SIR GEORGE TREVELYAN

The movers and shakers on our planet aren't the billionaires and the generals. They are the incredible people around the world filled with love for thy neighbour and for the earth, who are resisting, remaking, restoring, renewing, revitalising –
BILL McKIBBEN

Invitation

Coming on a journey

I invite you to come on a journey with me into one of the most important, yet often most neglected, dimensions of yourself, namely your inner heart. I want to help you discover, as I have gradually been discovering over the course of my life, that this part of ourselves not only holds the key to our being able to live a fuller, happier and more authentic existence, but, if properly activated, will enable us to play a major role in helping create a happier and healthier world.

I believe that trying to focus on the creation of such a world is very important at this time and that as many of us as possible should start thinking seriously about this. We are living in enormously challenging times, and I think that those of us who are lucky enough not to be ill, destitute or incapacitated in some way have a certain responsibility to support those of our fellow human beings who may not be in such a fortunate position.

Our planet is in great crisis today and an enormous struggle is going on between two hugely conflicting worldviews. On the one hand, we are surrounded everywhere by outmoded behaviours and values, which are both holding us back and destroying our planet and therefore need to die off, yet are often fighting furiously to maintain their positions. On the other hand, we are seeing many movements for change going on all over the world, which are being led by people who are totally committed to working for a new and healthier future. These people are aware, as Erik Assadourian put it, that 'salvaging our society requires nothing less than a wholesale transformation of dominant cultural patterns, a dramatic shift in the very design of human societies'.

Being an activist

So if you are someone who envisions themselves as a 'redesigner' and who wants to be part of this wholesale transformation, that is, someone who wants their life to make a difference; if you are perhaps interested in campaigning for human rights, going on marches to protect the environment, saving jaguars from extinction or whales from being slaughtered, ending war, taking a stand for organic food or, indeed, engaging in any other similar 'difference-making' activity; then you are a potential activist, and I hope this book will encourage you to bring more Heart force into whatever it is that you choose to commit to.

As the word implies, activists are active. They are doers. They not only have a vision of how a better world might look and how it might come into being, but they are also unafraid to get their hands and feet dirty in the process of working to realise their vision. Furthermore, they know that in order to be truly effective in their work, they 'need to *be* the change that they wish to see happen', as that great activist and change agent Gandhi once put it. This means that we need actually to *embody* those new societal values that we wish to see unfurl in the world, so that they don't merely reside inside our heads as good ideas or concepts.

Opening to Heart

This is very important. Knowing *about* what is wrong with our planet and having the willingness and capacity to do something concrete about it are two entirely different things. Many people who are intellectually aware of many of civilisation's discontents (and have even written books about them) nonetheless continue being part of them, because they haven't yet made the necessary transition *within themselves* that would enable them to be part of the solution. Therefore, if we wish to be an activist in a true sense, we may be challenged to make certain *inner* shifts. This is where Heart comes in, which is why I believe it is so important and why many of us may have a lot of initial transformational work to do on ourselves.

If we would like our lives in some way to be about 'making a difference', we will need to have access to a lot of our humanity, and as the place where our humanity resides is inside our hearts, we will need to have an open heart if we wish to uncover it. However, an open heart is not a 'given'. Many of us, for many different reasons, have hearts which are blocked or closed down and therefore not properly activated, and this means that we do not have access to that part of ourselves which enables our love and grace and integrity and compassion to be present, which in turn would let us be the change we wish to see happen. I am arguing that only if we 'come from' or live out of our hearts do we possess the capability not only of *truly* appreciating what is amiss with our world, but at the same time having the willingness and capability to produce the necessary 'reordering energy' to do something positive about it.

The universal heart

But we need to go even further. In order to be an effective healer or transformer of society (which, essentially, is what the activist is), it is not only essential that we work from the perspective of an open heart, but that we also are able to connect into that dimension of our hearts which is universal.

Our universal heart is the sum total of all our individual hearts. It is the heart of our species. It is that 'one heart' which all of us human beings share and are connected into, and it contains the joys and fears and happy and sad memories of our species through the ages. We will know that we are beginning to connect to this universal heart when we observe ourselves being moved to support causes where there is no direct personal gain to ourselves, or when we begin feeling very angry about world injustice. We will sense the universal heart opening inside us when we notice that we care deeply about what happens to people whom we have never met, or when we feel moved to take a strong stand for a particular cause which we feel passionately about. We are tapping into this heart when we start feeling deeply connected to our fellow human beings and sometimes experience strong intimations of everyone on the planet being our brother and sister! The more we can begin to operate out of such a worldview, the more effective our activism is going to be.

One of the main differences between someone who is universally hearted and most of us today is that they possess a *qualitatively bigger heart*, that is, one that is larger in its dimensional attributes. People who have access to the universal heart are able to hold more of the world 'out there' inside themselves. They tend to be more understanding, more intuitive, more sensitive. They are much less fettered by boundaries and therefore able to embrace more surfaces of life and place more emphasis upon what it is that unites us, as opposed to what divides us. Despite coming from entirely different cultures, races or parts of the planet, when universally hearted people encounter one another, there is always the experience of a shared human unity. This is why being the possessor of an open heart is absolutely essential for effective activism. When Robert Muller, who served as assistant secretary general to the United Nations for most of his adult life, wrote that 'in order to model a happy and beautiful world, we must believe in it; we must be in love with it; we must reach out for the highest levels of peace, justice, beauty and happiness; we must encourage each other in this task, individual to individual, nation to nation, race to race, culture to culture, continent to continent', his words flowed directly out of an awakened universal heart.

I have invented a word: 'enheartener'. An enheartener is someone who has begun to live out of their heart and who therefore seeks to model Muller's world. To be effective as activists, we need to be enhearteners; we need to be able to move through life in a wakeful, tender, gentle, wise, loving, honest and strong way, so that wherever we go and whatever we do, wholesome energy naturally flows out of us and into whatever part of the world we happen to be engaging with. What enhearteners do is that they 'enhearten'. Regardless of how or where we work – be we a politician or a postman, a diplomat, banker, housewife or dustman – we become what I call a natural 'raiser' of life, in that in our presence the world around us starts to become elevated and ennobled.

How to read this book

This book is divided into four parts. The first section focuses on explaining what the heart is and what it means and how we can learn to connect more fully with this most intrinsic or core part of ourselves. The second part explores the whole issue of how our hearts have become wounded and what we can do to heal them. Here, I talk a lot about the ego and, I hope, correct a few misunderstandings that exist. The third part specifically looks at the world of the spiritual heart and at how we may awaken the heart's spiritual dimensions, while the last part explores some of the many different ways that our desire to be of service can be concretely embodied, thus enabling us to honour what Albert Schweitzer believed was our true task on Earth. In his words:

> *We who are heirs of a complex civilisation are charged with one major historical task: to aid the world in achieving true culture. It is up to us to make the light of a truly humanitarian culture shine throughout the world.*[1]

Heart, religion and spirituality

One cannot write about the heart and humanity without also looking at spirituality, since a 'Heart person' cannot help also being a spiritual person. At another level, therefore, this book may also be seen as a kind of basic 'spiritual primer'.

I need to make it clear that being spiritual does not necessarily require us to be religious. While I have experience of different religions and at various times in my life have studied and benefited enormously from my connection with shamans, Buddhists, Sufis and Christians, encountering along the way many religious people with enormous hearts and learning much from them, I have never felt myself drawn to be part of any particular religion. I am not in any way anti-religion; I have the greatest respect for people of all faiths and I know that religious traditions offer millions of people enormous comfort. It is simply that it is not my way or therefore the path I offer here. The word 'religion' comes from the Latin *religio*, meaning 'reconnection', and my experience is that if we can find our *own way* of reconnecting to the deeper parts of ourselves, we are already a large part of the way there. In this context, I would like to quote from what a very big-hearted friend who loves horses once said to me:

> *Serge, riding is my sacred occupation. It makes me feel fully alive, and on horseback I feel far more connected to my heart or to my spiritual self or whatever you want to call it, together with the whole glory of nature all around me, than I ever do inside a church.*

Eric Clapton, the great blues musician, feels the same thing about music and his way of reconnecting to himself comes through playing the blues. His music never ceased to 'hold him' as he was going through some pretty challenging experiences in his life. In his insightful autobiography, he tells us: 'For me, the most trustworthy vehicle for spirituality had always proven to be music. It cannot be manipulated or politicised.' Again, this is not to decry religion, churches or any other place of worship, so much as to suggest that there are many ways that we may connect to the sacred, some of which we will be exploring here, and that each of us is challenged to find what works best for us. I am, therefore, wholly in accord with a recent pronouncement about spirituality by His Holiness the Dalai Lama:

> *Spirituality I take to be concerned with qualities of the human spirit – such as love, compassion, tolerance, forgiveness, contentment, a sense of responsibility, a sense of harmony – which brings contentment both to self and others. And there is no reason why the individual should not develop these, even to a high degree, without recourse to any religious or metaphysical system. This is why I sometimes say that religion is something we can do without. What we cannot do without are these basic spiritual qualities.*

Moving into deep spaces

For the great visionary thinker and pioneer Stan Grof, 'spirituality is an intrinsic property of the psyche that emerges spontaneously when the process of self-exploration reaches sufficient depth'. It is my hope that this book will help you ask many new questions and, in trying to answer them, will take you to deep places. However, it is not one that you can rush through. It is long and quite detailed and I know people today like short books that they may easily whip through. So if you are a 'whip through' kind of person, I offer you my apologies. Due to my own limitations, I have not been able to go to the depths I felt were warranted without using a lot of words.

However, it is possible for you to skip about if you want to. Every chapter is self-contained and may be read individually. For example, if you would like to discover more about prayer or forgiveness or about the nature of evil, or if you want to see how you may work to try to end war or weather crises better or bring more sacredness into your relationships or learn how business may transform the planet, you can jump straight to the relevant chapter.

However you approach this book, please know that it has been written from a place of great hope and joy, based on the knowledge that our world *is* changing, that the universal Heart awareness *is* awakening among increasing numbers of people, and that, as we will be seeing, the forces of resistance or of heartlessness are being powerfully confronted. As I write, millions of people from all over the planet, are coming together to protest – to say 'no' to corruption and dishonesty, 'no' to manipulation and limitation, 'no' to despotic regimes, 'no' to dishonest bankers and large corporations that pollute the planet, and this gladdens me enormously.

What has particularly inspired me is my great love for my beautiful fourteen-year-old daughter. She is a wise soul. I want a better world for her and other young people to grow up in. I don't want her to have to censor the joy inside her heart or feel she has to sacrifice her innate sacredness in order to 'fit in' to the requirements of a soulless society – become some diminutive little cog on a vast faceless wheel. I also want the many wise young people who are being born today to grow up in a wholesome society where there is peace and good heart. If this book can help in a minuscule way towards achieving that objective, it will not have been written in vain.

ONE

Understanding the Heart

Man becomes great not by birth but by heart –
A NOTICE IN A TIBETAN REFUGEE CAMP

The present threat to mankind's survival can be removed only by a revolutionary change of heart in individual human beings –
ARNOLD TOYNBEE

Chapter 1
The Significance of the Heart

Without the heart, the human would be sinister ...
All feeling is born in the heart – JOHN O'DONOHUE

Civilisation gets its basic energy not from its resources but from its hopes. The tragedy of life is not death, but what we let die inside us while we live – NORMAN COUSINS

The importance of the heart

The world of the heart is deeply significant As the poet John O'Donohue put it:

> *Without the heart, the human would be sinister. To be able to feel is the great gift. When you feel for another, you become united with that person in an intimate way; your concern and compassion come alive, drawing some of the other person's world and spirit into yours ... Without the ability to feel, friendship and love could never be born. All feeling is born in the heart. This makes the human heart the true jewel of the world.*[1]

Our hearts, then, connect us feelingly, not only to ourselves, but also to the hearts of others and to the heart of our world, and, as I hope to show, they are our *greatest weapon of mass construction*. The great Catholic visionary theologian Pierre Teilhard de Chardin, writing in the 1940s, understood this. He postulated that *there was more power inside our human hearts than inside the atomic bomb*. The mistake that we often make is to believe that the mind is the boss and that we may only think clearly when our minds are 'uncontaminated' by our 'mushy hearts'. In actuality, it is the other way round. Osho puts the record straight:

> *The mind is only a servant. The master is the heart, because all that is beautiful grows in the heart; all that is valuable comes out of the heart – your love, your compassion, your meditation. Anything that is valuable grows in the garden of the heart. The heart is the only*

possibility for you to be bridged with your being, with existence. It is the only possibility for songs to arise, for stars to descend in you, for your life to become a rejoicing ... When you have a heart that is alive, your mind's quality will also change. Then you can go to the mind; you can function through the mind. Then the mind will become just an instrument: you can use it ... Then you are not obsessed with it ... The heart will give you a feeling that you are a master.[2]

This corresponds to the view of Chinese medicine, which regards the heart as the 'Emperor' or the 'Supreme Controller'. While every organ in the body is regarded as an 'official' with a specific piece of work to do, the heart is always seen as the 'director' in charge of them all. Most importantly, the heart is the centre of our emotional life. It is the core of who we are and the Latin word for heart is *cor*. Daniel Goleman argues that the pervading view of human intelligence as essentially being intellectual is far too narrow and hence he coined the term 'emotional intelligence', which is based on qualities such as self-awareness, altruism and compassion. He regards a high EQ (emotional quotient) as being more important than a high IQ, and as being a key ingredient in all people who excel in the face of life's challenges.[3]

Our heart is essentially our affective centre or the seat of our emotional life. It is through the heart that we feel things and digest our emotions, and so it connects our body, mind, emotions and spirit together. In the words of Doc Childre, founder of the Institute of HeartMath: 'Since emotional processes can work faster than the mind, it takes a power stronger than mind to bend perception, override emotional circuitry and provide us with intuitive feeling instead. It is the power of the heart.' He goes on to suggest that

when the heart rhythm patterns are coherent, the neural information sent to the brain facilitates its cortical function, and the effect is often experienced as heightened mental clarity, improved decision-making and increased creativity ... The consistent and pervasive influence of the heart's rhythmic patterns on the brain and body not only affects our physical health, but also significantly influences our perceptual processing, emotional experience and our intentional behaviour.

Put simply, with Heart, *we feel better, think much more clearly and act much more effectively*. Inside our hearts is also the place where, metaphorically speaking, Heaven and Earth converge, that is, where the 'downflow' of involution encounters the 'upflow' of evolution, and thus where agape (divine love) blends with eros (erotic love). It is inside our hearts where our spirituality meets with our materiality. In Sufism, the heart is always seen as being winged because it is rooted in the heart of our Creator, and thus is regarded as being the doorway into our deeper, sacred self. Indeed, all the great inventors, explorers, writers, poets, activists and visionaries who in their various ways have contributed to our culture have all done so on the wings of their hearts. I therefore believe that one of our great challenges at this time is for us to learn how to harness our Heart power, which we can then use to propel ourselves forward as a species. In the process, we may create a new and improved world for ourselves – a world that 'works', a world that is more compassionate, sustainable and humane.

The loss of heart

Sadly, what is most 'wrong' with our society – what underlies so many of the problems and crises that we see all around us today – is that as a species, we seem to have lost touch with our hearts. In Thomas Merton's words: 'We have lost Dante's vision of that love which moves the sun and all the stars and, in so doing, we have lost the power to find meaning in the world.' The novelist Ben Okri believes that 'our material success has brought us to a strange spiritual and moral bankruptcy, where the more our society has succeeded, the more its heart has failed'.[4]

This is a profound observation. Our problem in the world today is that not enough of us think with our hearts, feel with our hearts or act through our hearts. Particularly if we are male, we may believe that only so-called 'manly things' that are hard, concrete and pragmatic are of 'real importance', and that the softer, more poetic domains of life, connected to qualities such as awe, wonder, beauty and mystery are somehow of less significance. As a result, many of us men may relegate our hearts to the basement of our being, where, shut away, they gradually shrivel up through neglect. Many of the distortions in our modern lifestyles, which include our tendencies to overconsumption, overwork, superficial and narcissistic lifestyles, self-destruction and addiction, and the devaluation of beauty, emanate from an insufficiently lived Heart life.

This lack of emotional heart is particularly visible in the world of politics and economics. Too many mistakes occur as a result of complex situations being improperly grasped or misread. In the recent Iraq war, for example, had even a modicum of Heart been present in the decision-making, not only would we never have gone to war in the first place, but all the many subsequent mistakes that took place, including the heartless treatment of the Iraqi people, and the enormous costs all round that resulted from this, would never have occurred.

At a relational level, our loss of Heart is especially destructive, because it is only through our hearts that we can effectively connect to 'the heart' or true essence of another human being. If we are closed off to this dimension of ourselves, we won't be able to relate intimately; we won't be able to sense how others see the world, and thus intuitively know the right way to be with them. This means that we can never know another person deeply, empathise properly with them or fully enjoy or appreciate them, all of which is so important if we are to understand and love them.

If we wish to be effective activists, where we are seeking to be instrumental in creating a happier, more harmonious and workable world, many of us need to learn to bring our hearts back in from the cold and have them become a central factor in the way we live. A better world will come into being only when sufficient numbers of us will have learned to eat our meals with Heart, raise our children with Heart, make love with Heart, go to the office with Heart, cook with Heart, surf the internet with Heart, and play all our sports with Heart.

An inability to experience the goodness of life

The reason we experience this devaluing of Heart is that many of us have learned from an early age only to live out of the left hemisphere of our brain – only to utilise and trust that part of ourselves which perceives life through a rational lens. As a result, we are forever trying to understand our world and respond to its problems, not by trusting in our intuition or by looking at life as a whole, but rather by coldly dissecting it – breaking it down into small pieces and reducing and analysing each part separately. From this perspective, the domain of feelings and senses becomes regarded as (a) 'unscientific' and therefore not dependable, and (b) irrelevant in the larger scheme of things. Recently, a Brandeis University biochemist, on being asked to dissolve his humanities programmes due to budget cuts, challenged this rational approach, proclaiming that 'science unleavened by the human heart and the human spirit is sterile, cold and self-absorbed'.

He was so, so right. Indeed, had even a modicum of Heart been present among those scientists who had been working on the atom bomb, this monstrosity would never have seen the light of day, nor would all the newest weapons of mass destruction that are currently being invented. The insane doctrine of 'perpetual war for perpetual peace', which not too many years ago was a cornerstone of American foreign policy, could only have been invented by men whose hearts were cold as iron.

Hearts need to be employed

The point about our hearts is that they need to be used. They are not like a machine, where the less it is employed, the newer it remains. With our hearts, it is the direct opposite. Underuse makes them contract and wither, rendering it difficult for us to bring passion or grace into our lives. Not only does this incline us to live numbed and sometimes robotic lives, but it inevitably disconnects us from life's inherent joy and abundance. Life's magic is there, sure enough, but in our underused Heart state, we cannot properly experience it. This is why so many of us 'rationals' are so enamoured with our struggling and feel that if we were only to 'have' more, 'do' more or 'achieve' more, we would be happier. Deep down, we all know what an illusion this is. The main point I want you to understand at this stage is that all our imbalances and injustices and disorders and inequalities basically have the same root, which is an insufficiently utilised heart. When we learn to step forward into our integrity and balance, which is a by-product of reconnecting with our hearts, we will all naturally and wholeheartedly feel moved to create a better world for ourselves, one that doesn't simply favour the privileged few but works for the benefit of all.

Heart work

To have a world that functions properly, then, requires that we all have hearts that function properly. This does not happen just by magic. The process of awakening our hearts involves work. However, it is not the kind of work that many of us ordinarily associate with this word. We are used only to understanding work as being something external, as when, say, we 'go *out* to work'. Here, we must learn that there is another 'living' to be earned, namely an inner one, and that if we want to enjoy a richer inner life where we can be of real service to our fellow human beings, that attention must also be directed to the idea of 'going *inside* ourselves to work'. The poet Rumi understood this: 'If you wish your heart to be bright, you must do a little work. If metal can be polished to a mirror-like finishing, what polishing does the mirror of the heart require?'[5]

As we begin to work on our hearts in this way, and as they slowly start to open, we may find that many of life's absurdities which our rational mind had accepted as being 'normal' now start revealing themselves to us more clearly. We may gradually come to see how absurd it is to look for happiness by following the path of materialism and power, or how insane it is that one of the main ways we try to keep the peace is by channelling most of our funds (that could go to help the poor) into designing ever more grotesque weapons to destroy ourselves with.

Lack of education for the heart

Once we start to 'work on' our hearts, we may become increasingly aware that ordinarily, we focus little attention on them (unless we suffer from heart disease, and then only on their physical aspects), and that most of our focus goes on our minds. Of all the many courses available designed to 'improve ourselves', 99 per cent are directed towards developing ourselves mentally – becoming more efficient, more effective and so on. Our educational system also primarily only addresses our minds. At my old school for example, our motto was *'mens sana in corpore sano'*: 'a healthy mind in a healthy body'. No mention of the heart!

Similarly, at our universities, all the emphasis is on the developing of our cognitive faculties. We learn *about* things, not how to experience them directly. In all the classes I attended in my student days, I only ever learned to amass factual knowledge. No one ever pointed out to me that there might be knowledge *inside* me and that the place where it resided might be my heart. In this context, Jung once said something very important: 'Any part of ourselves that we do not own becomes our enemy.' It is therefore perhaps not surprising that our culture today is one that is very prone to heart attacks – especially among men – as perhaps attacking us is one of the few ways that our poor, underused and repressed little hearts can gain our attention and remind us that they exist! So long as we do not learn to activate the 'peacemaker' inside our hearts, we will always be liable to require a pacemaker!

The need for heart/mind integration

Please don't get me wrong. I do not wish to suggest that heart is *superior* to mind, nor that the domain of thinking and analysing is not important and is not a key ingredient of life. Of course it is. I have enormous respect for the mind. My concern is simply about what happens to it when it becomes separated from heart, for when this occurs, it so often turns into a suppressor of it. In Ian McGilchrist's words:

> *The left brain is tyrannous. It's a ratchet mechanism, difficult to reverse. This arrogant left hemisphere behaves like a brain in a vat. It doesn't see us as integrated minds and bodies ... In the madness of our left-brain lives, it is not other people with whom we empathise but machines.*[6]

This is especially true today in the way that we are all being swamped with left-brain technology. Yes, I like it that I can send emails on my mobile phone. Yes, it is wonderful that I can instantaneously access information by going onto the internet (our global brain). However, I never want to be a slave to this technology or be under the illusion that greater efficiency necessarily adds to the *quality,* as opposed to the convenience, of my life. While I agree that the Arab Spring could never have been as successful as it was were it not for the new technologies enabling people to link up, I feel that far too many of us are becoming far too dependent on them. New data suggests that long hours on the internet actually begin to rewire our brains and are starting to create a whole new list of psychiatric disorders. So however useful Facebook may be at one level, reminding us how many 'friends' we have, we must never pretend that 500 cyberbuddies are any substitute for the kind of real Heart work that goes into the making of a handful of genuine flesh-and-blood ones. In other words, merely possessing a technology that enables us to link up with others guarantees neither that we feel moved to utilise it nor that we are capable of connecting to another person in a genuine way. The truth is that if our technology is to be effective, we need something more than that technology alone. We need to have both the desire and the capacity to connect, which is only possible through the awakening of our emotional and spiritual intelligence which is only to be located inside our hearts.

The truth is that mind needs heart as its partner, in exactly the same way that heart needs mind to be its friend. If we are to function effectively, love and logic need to fuse inside us, and the more we learn to feel with our minds as well as think with our hearts, the more our humanity will grow and the wiser we will become.

The empowering force of whole-heartedness

When we feel really good about something, we can say that we feel 'whole hearted' about it, which means that many of the functions of our heart are being activated. What is significant, however, is that this expansive experience does not occur just for us. It may also be sensed by those who, in some way, are included in our experience. Let me give you two examples of what I mean, as they beautifully demonstrate the power of the heart.

I am a tennis player. I love the game, which is to say that my heart is in it. And I have just watched the final of the Australian Open, and the reason I particularly love watching Rafa Nadal play, and also the reason he is so good, is that he always plays with his full heart. He does not hold himself back from sharing his emotions and putting his all into every stroke, so that one feels that it is his heart that is coordinating his body and his mind, and that this is what enables him to be so effective – to always seem to produce the right shot for the occasion. The fact that he plays with heart also uplifts me, as something of his joy and enthusiasm is able to convey itself to me – to touch and inspire me. Indeed, my own tennis game becomes that little bit better after I have watched him at work. Through his deep connection to the 'heart' of tennis and through my watching him play, I am also helped to become more connected to the heart of tennis.

I will give you another example. A few days ago, I watched a performance on TV of three people all singing the same song to qualify to represent the United Kingdom in the upcoming Eurovision Song Contest. Two people sang the song very well, but the third contestant put something extra – a certain magic – into it. One could say that she put her whole heart into it and in so doing, got into the true heart of the song, which was something that neither of the other contestants had managed to do. The consequence of this was that she enabled the deeper essence or the full-heartedness of that song to be conveyed directly to me.

The effect was extraordinary. When this woman sang, my heart felt deeply touched, which is another way of saying that it also sang. Not only did I feel that the real essence of the song had emerged, but – and this is the key point – so did the beauty and sweetness of the singer emerge along with it. Singer and song – the heart of both essences had converged. In singing her heart out – quite literally – this woman not only revealed the beauty of the song but added the beauty of her own heart and voice to it as well. As I listened to her, I became aware of a powerful force of goodness being present, of a light streaming out of her and into me, and as a result, I felt more connected to my own heart and I think I temporarily became a slightly better person. It felt as if a beautiful little gift had just been given to me. This is the power of the enheartening presence. And we may connect to it in so many different ways.

So if, for whatever reason, we become disconnected from our hearts, or worse, if we have never learned to link into them in the first place, it will be hard for Heart presence to touch us. Beauty will not be able to reach us. We will feel distanced from love. The result will often manifest itself as a nagging sense that there is something intrinsically wrong with us, that something is radically lacking in our lives. As a consequence, we may feel marooned on life's surfaces, alienated, envious, suspicious, unhappy with our lot. If we cannot see through our hearts, speak from our hearts, feel with our hearts, listen with our hearts, act from our hearts, process life through our hearts, we will not be open to the heart of life communicating to us in all the many ways that it is continually trying to do. And this will give us pain. The tragedy is that many of us live every day in this state and feel it is normal because we have never known anything else. I also believe there is a strong connection between an absence of heart and a fear of change, which is a theme we will explore later.

The power of Heart presence

I will tell you a little true story. A robber broke into a woman's house in the middle of the night, and when she woke up and found him there, she told him in a loving way where her main jewellery was to be found. 'Obviously,' she said to him, 'you are in dire need.' In the face of such kindness, the robber felt disarmed. He dropped everything and ran away. The next day, she found a letter in her letterbox telling her that he hadn't been able to bear her kindness and love and so had had to leave!

Nelson Mandela is a great example of someone with Heart presence. I think the main reason that he was able to lead his people out of the darkness of apartheid and into the light of a new and more integrated society without a single drop of blood being shed was that *his heart was big enough to carry his entire nation within it*. Tenderness and compassion ooze out of his every pore. There is something about this extraordinary, sweet and open man, who bore no grudges against those who had jailed him for so many years, that makes us instinctively love and trust him, which in turn also brings out the best in us. Mother Teresa was another big-hearted person. She would always stress that the true measure of effectiveness of any action is not how big it is or how many people it will affect, but how much heart is being put into it.

In my small way, I have always tried in my role as a psychotherapist and consultant to bring Heart into my work, and if I have ever been a little bit helpful to anyone, it has probably been due to an ability to hold that person inside my heart, and not through any 'clever interpretations' I may have been able to spout out as to what I felt may have been amiss with them. An Indian chief once said: 'Never judge another person until you have walked ten miles in their moccasins.' This is a beautiful idea, but we can't embrace it unless we know how to connect with our heart to another person's heart. Heart power, we must understand, is soft power. It is not power over anyone or anything. It doesn't want to control or dominate. Rather, it is a subtle kind of cooperative force that both enables and ennobles whomever or whatever it happens to be directed upon at any time.

Variations of Heart

There are many different variations to our hearts, and this needs to be borne in mind, especially if we have particular ideas about what characterises a 'Heart person'. We may, for example, feel that 'Heart people' should all be gentle, warm and fuzzy, and that if they are not, they don't have Heart. Nothing could be further from the truth. While many people of Heart are this way, many are not. It certainly was not Mother Theresa's way, who by all accounts had a side that would not suffer fools gladly. The truth is that no one person enheartens in exactly the same way as anyone else, as all our hearts are different.

How we may manifest Heart is not only affected by the situation we face, or by how awake our hearts are, but also by the kind of temperament we have. Some people, for example, have very fiery and passionate hearts – a lot of Sufi teachers are like this – while other hearts are much cooler, quieter and detached. I learned much about the detached heart through my experience with Buddhist meditation teachers during my years living in California. Some people like to wear their hearts more on their sleeves, while others prefer to keep them more under wraps and will only reveal them when deemed appropriate. Also, each of us tends to embody a different quality or different qualities of Heart. For example, I can contrast my 'brave-hearted' friend Danaan, who lived his life with enormous passion (he used to work in the field of conflict resolution) with my more tender and kind-hearted friend Pragito. In Danaan's presence, I would feel uplifted and inspired; with Pragito, I would feel connected to my inner gentleness.

Conversely, I can think of the beautiful, soothing and totally non-judgemental 'listening heart' of my dear friend Louise, in whose calming presence I always feel seen and heard, or the practical and very incisive heart of her husband Alan, who is one of my oldest friends, and who, throughout my life, has always been there to assist and support me in those many areas where I am deficient. I also think of the 'forgiving heart' of my friend Larry, whose presence always brings up compassion inside me, and then, of course, there is the jolly, merry heart of my old friend Sue, whose humour, laughter and generosity of being are so infectious that whatever anxieties I might be carrying soon get despatched after just a few minutes in her presence. I also think of the tender and generous heart of beautiful Carinthia, who, despite a very busy life, is always there to love and support her many friends. I have never met anyone who does not adore her.

As I contemplate the various kinds of Heart qualities of some of my friends, I also think very tenderly of a special friend, Roger, who, sadly, has just died and who also taught me so much. I miss him hugely. His heart was vast and brave and kind, and to the end, he never lost touch with his inner child and a sense of mischief. He was one of the best examples I know of a great scholar with a great intellect, yet whose mind was continually being leavened by the influence of his awakened heart. All his ideas flowed out of him on the wings of love, which was both what gave them their power and enabled them to be so palatable. When in his company, my heart would always be stretched and would never be allowed to be lazy, and for this I am eternally grateful.

Without Heart, there can be no poetry in our lives, and we need poetry to balance us. President J. F. Kennedy recognised this only too well: 'When power leads man towards arrogance,' he told us, 'poetry reminds him of his limitations. When power narrows the area of man's concern, poetry reminds him of the richness and diversity of existence. When power corrupts, poetry cleanses.' Genuine poets are always Heart-ful human beings. Even if we have never written a line of verse in our entire lives and never will, the more we are able to access the richness inside our hearts, the more spontaneously poetic we will naturally become in all areas of our lives.

Chapter 2
The Treasures of the Heart

For where your treasure is, there will your heart be also –
MATTHEW 6:21

The treasure chest inside our hearts

Our hearts are a veritable treasure trove. Inside each of them lives the full spectrum of virtues or qualities which both determine our humanity and serve as antidotes to the many different kinds of deficiency that exist out in the world. For example, the reason there is so much indifference to human suffering is that the quality of love has not been sufficiently generated inside us. Similarly, we allow for injustices to occur because the 'justice factor' that also lives inside our hearts is not yet strong enough, while we often turn a blind eye to evil because we lack the courage to live as our truth and stand up for what we truly believe.

We must understand, however, that these qualities existing inside what I will now call the 'treasure chest' of our hearts (and later will refer to as 'the garden of our hearts') are only seed potentials. If we do not do what is necessary to activate them – if we don't work to try to stir them to life – they will remain hidden inside us and it will be *as if they do not exist*. Heartless people are not people without heart. They are people whose Heart potential, for whatever reasons, remains suppressed and has never been effectively 'outed'. We will now look at a few of our hearts' major qualities.

Love

Love is perhaps the most central, as well as the most mysterious of the many Heart qualities. We all yearn for it, yet secretly, we often fear it. One of the problems we face is that in a culture where many people's hearts are still very closed, love often gets used in a debased way. Either we tend to fixate love solely onto its romantic aspects, or, conversely, we load it with all kinds of conditions and say we will only love someone if they behave in a particular way towards us. When this happens, our love is not, of course, the 'genuine article'. Rather, it is a watered-down expression of the real thing, Thomas à Kempis describes the real thing as follows:

> *Love is eager, sincere and kind. It is glad and lovely; it is strong, patient and faithful and it never seeks its own ends ... It knows no measure but burns white-hot beyond all measure. Love feels no burden and counts up no toil; it aspires to do more than its strength allows. So it finds strength for anything; it completes and carries through great tasks where one who does not love, would fall and fail. Love is vigilant; it sleeps without losing control; it is wearied without exhaustion, cramped without being crushed, alarmed without being destroyed.*[1]

Just imagine how our world would be, if our hearts were all so big that we were able to love along those lines, or along those suggested by Thomas Merton, where

> *love may be seen as the bond between man and the deepest reality of his life. Without it man is isolated, alienated from himself, alienated from other men, separated from God, from truth, wisdom and strength. By love man enters into contact first with his deepest self, then with his brother, who is his other self, and finally with the wisdom and power of God, the Ultimate Reality.*[2]

If our hearts are closed, we cannot connect to this level of love, which is why so many of us may find it hard to care properly for the poor and destitute in our society or why we can be so indifferent in the face of human suffering. Sadly, many of us believe love to be a scarce commodity, available only if someone 'loves us'. When our hearts begin to open, however, we start to realise that this is a myth, and that love actually comes from inside us, and is, as Mother Teresa once put it, 'a fruit that is ripe in all seasons, and within range of every hand'. As the great Bulgarian spiritual master Peter Deunov said: 'Everything in the world lives in love and by love ... Life is meaningful only when our hearts are full of love.'

Compassion

Compassion is the tender face of love. If we have compassion for ourselves, it means we hold ourselves in our hearts and do not make ourselves wrong for our imperfections. If we have compassion for others, then we do the same for them and we understand why they are as they are, and from that place, we do not judge them as lacking. If the compassionate side of our hearts begins to open, it allows us to care for life more fully and to be more open to the suffering and struggles of other people, thus weaning us away from our own selfish inclinations.

Here is what the Tibetan Buddhist master Tarthang Tulku says about it.

> *Until the positive energy of compassion flows through our hearts, we accomplish little of real value. We may simply be occupying our minds with hollow words and images. We may master various sciences or philosophy, but without compassion, we are just empty scholars trapped in vicious circles of craving, grasping and anxiety. There is little real meaning or satisfaction in our lives ... But when this energy is awakened, relationships with others become healthy and effortless – we have no duty or obligation ... Like the sun, which emits countless rays, compassion is the source of all inner growth and positive action ... So, at this time, when man has the power to completely destroy the earth, it is especially important to develop whatever is beautiful, beneficial and meaning ... and to practise compassion. In the beginning our compassion is like a candle – gradually, we need to develop compassion as radiant as the sun. When compassion is as close as our breath, as alive as our blood, then we will understand how to live and work in the world effectively and be of help to both ourselves and others.*[3]

Kindness

The Dalai Lama believes kindness to be one of the most important of all human qualities and that if we were simply to practise being kind – which includes, of course, being kind to ourselves –our world would change. Mother Teresa's advice to us was also to

> be kind and merciful. Let no one ever come to you without feeling better and happier. Be the loving expression of God's kindness; kindness in your face, kindness in your eyes, kindness in your smile, kindness in your warm greeting.

Kindness brings warmth into the world. If we are feeling sad or alienated and have lost heart for some reason, if someone is kind to us, they take us into the embrace of their heart and, in so doing, help reconnect us to our own source of hope and belief in ourselves. Kindness is therefore a powerful reconnecting force; it helps us feel that we belong; it enables us to realise that we have a right to be and that we have value in ourselves. It is therefore a very important 'food', which, as activists of the heart, we may be called to dole out when dealing with people who have been oppressed, marginalised or excluded in some way from mainstream society.

Beauty

Beauty is another very important Heart quality, but one which is seldom given its due and, if related to at all, primarily only at a superficial level. In actuality, beauty has great healing potential and I believe that if we only recognised the importance of our own capacity to do things in life more beautifully – do our politics more beautifully, bring more beauty into the way we manage our relationships or educate our children, etc. – we would have a very strong defence against our tendencies to being seduced by so many of our society's uglinesses.

A friend of mine who suffered from cancer felt she healed herself by meditating daily on beauty, surrounding herself with beautiful things and beautiful friends, reading beautiful literature and listening only to beautiful music by the great composers. Beauty so filled her heart that there was no space for anything else. Similarly, a client who, for years, used to steal from shops because she felt so empty inside gradually healed herself of this addiction as a result of long meditations on beauty.

As with all Heart virtues, beauty connects us to many other qualities, as Keats knew when he reminded us that 'beauty is truth, truth beauty, that is all we know and all we need to know'. The great Russian visionary artist and philosopher Nicholas Roerich saw beauty as a sacred weapon when he told us: 'Through beauty we pray. With beauty we conquer.' It is so true. Beauty is a powerful transformational force.

Vision

Vision is so important today, because it enables us to see the world through the expanded eye of our heart and allows us to apply our new perceptions in whatever field or area of life we feel moved to operate in. In a world which is breaking down and where so many of us are slaves to 'tunnel vision' (that is, living our lives out of a box – only looking directly ahead!) and where so many difficult problems exist in need of a solution, people of vision, who are able both to see old issues in a new light and to inspire others to 'lift up their eyes unto the hills, from whence cometh our help', have never been more needed.

The power of the visionary was beautifully embodied by that great Heart warrior Martin Luther King, who dreamed that one day all African Americans would be free. The realisation of his dream has now manifested itself in the fact that, half a century later, America now has a black President who also has a vision for freedom.

Gratitude

Gratitude serves as a significant antidote to our tendency to feel dissatisfied with our lot, whereby we either believe that in order to be happy, we need more of what we already have, or conversely, that we must get what we don't have. This dissatisfaction, which can also take the form of a fear of loss, lies behind much of our greed and materiality and hence our tendency to spend time and energy engaging in the kinds of activities that have little relevance to what will either advance our own well-being or that of the larger community around us.

If our hearts are full of gratitude, we will be much more able both to accept and to be content with our lot, and we will therefore not feel envious of others who we believe possess what we lack. If gratitude floods into our hearts, our glass at once becomes half full, enabling us to more easily appreciate ourselves and thus be more open to allowing ourselves to let in life's many blessings. This in turn enables us to connect to life's inherent abundance and even to appreciate the many gifts contained in our difficulties, which may then permit us to confront them in a good spirit.

Courage

Courage is a quality which, in our rapidly changing world, all activists need in abundance. Chögyam Trungpa Rinpoche, in his book on the path of the spiritual warrior, suggested that the prime kind of courage we need is to not be afraid to be who we truly are.[4] This is so important and is something which, sadly, so many of us fear and which often takes the form of our preferring to conform and be part of the herd, in case we might not be liked or approved of.

Yet if our world is to change, it will require millions of us to stand in our full activism and stop compromising and selling our souls to the nearest company store! Being courageous means that we are continually willing to ask new questions of ourselves and that we are not afraid to do things in new ways. If we have courage, it doesn't mean that all our fears vanish; it implies rather that we are much more willing and therefore able to confront them in the spirit of our moving forward. The moment St George faced his dragon, as opposed to running away from it, he discovered that it no longer was that fearsome thing that he once believed it to be.

I had a friend whom I considered to be rather a timid person, until one day he told me that he had jumped onto a railway line, a split second before a train whizzed by, in order to rescue a small child who had fallen onto it. I remember saying to him: 'Goodness, that was fantastic! I never knew you were so brave!' His reply was: 'I didn't either, but'– and this is the important point, not only about this quality but also about all Heart qualities – 'I discovered my courage the moment that I made the split-second decision that I had to save this child's life. *At the precise moment when I jumped down onto the tracks, with a train coming towards me, was when courage entered me, and it was as if I found I had all the time and all the strength in the world to do what I needed to do.*' He told me that he felt as if he existed in a different dimension, and that everything was happening in slow motion.

It probably was. This is one of the extraordinary characteristics of all Heart qualities. When strongly activated, they transport us into wholly different worlds of being, where the laws of space and time and what is possible for us begin to shift. Choosing courage allows us to live much more on the edge, which is where transformations always occur. In this way, we are moved out of our old comfort zones that conspire to keep us unaware.

Courage also connects us to our capacity for commitment and endurance, which are other important Heart attributes required by the activist today. All too often, we give up on things because we lack these two abilities. When our hearts open to this quality, we become empowered to be so much more than we ever believed we could be.

Joy

Another very tangible expression of an awakened heart is the capacity to feel joy. Pierre Teilhard de Chardin suggested that 'joy is a sign of the presence of God'. I so agree. When I am privileged enough to be in the presence of truly joyful people, there is always something deeply radiant, holy, playful and abundant about them that always rubs off on me. Joy, like beauty, also heals. It serves as a kind of inoculation that can protect us against so much of the negativity that is all around us. When our hearts fill with joy, we are so much stronger and resilient and it also becomes easier to find peace in our hearts, and for our various 'deficiency holes' to start filling up.

With joy, it becomes easier to recover the vision we had as a small child, when we were still naturally connected to life's magic and mystery, in the days before our societal conditioning came in to blur everything. Joy also enables us to experience the sacred within the mundane, and as a result, we may find ourselves being moved to live a simpler, and therefore a healthier and more sustainable, lifestyle, without seeing it as any burden.

Peace

Few of us are truly at peace with ourselves, and this of course is reflected in our personal lives and our relationships, and is then projected into international relationships. And without peace there is no antidote to the virus of war. Peace, like joy, may only be discovered inside our hearts, as we have the courage to detach ourselves from the fear and conflict-producing effects of our society which, via our media and news channels, are continually broadcasting to us how dire everything is, and that if the terrorists or the economic downturn don't 'get us', then a tsunami or a pandemic or global warming will!

What peace requires is that we learn to distance ourselves from all our dramas by being less inwardly restless. Many spiritual teachers tell us that unless we find the key to open the room marked 'peace' inside our hearts and spend as much time as we can there, we will never make much progress in discovering the many other qualities that also reside there.

Wisdom

In a world where so many dumb mistakes continue to be made by our legion of clever, left-brained experts and specialists, wisdom is an important quality that is urgently needed. It is especially required by those in positions of authority who need to make important political, economic, scientific and social decisions which directly affect all our lives. Wisdom emerges when head and heart converge, when we are able to feel and intuit as well as think and sense our way through life, when the totality of who we are becomes increasingly linked into the totality of our world.

When we have wisdom, our decision-making is always informed by deeper considerations, and what defines the wise person is that they can much more easily intuit the next step of our human evolution, and how best to cooperate with its emergence in whatever field they happen to work in. Unlike clever people, who are often moved to try to control things – to fit life into their own agendas of what they deem is best (which is generally what serves the intentions of their own egotism) – wise people are aware that life itself is intelligent and will, if listened to, guide them into making the most appropriate decisions.

Justice

If our hearts were to awaken to justice, there is no way that we would continue to countenance ethnic cleansing, torture, one law for the rich and another for the poor, or genocide. If a sense of justice burns strongly inside us, we will feel moved to take stands towards honouring and respecting everyone's fundamental human rights. If our sense of justice is strong, we will find that we will naturally possess a strong reverence for all of life.

Nobody or nothing will be felt either as less than us, or conversely, as more than us, and whenever we will encounter injustice we will spontaneously feel impelled to do something about it. As such, this quality is closely associated with all the other qualities which we have explored. Not only do we need to love justice, but, if it is to prevail, we may at times need to stick our necks out in order to consolidate it – and doing this requires courage.

Comments on the heart virtues

Our planet sorely lacks and is in great need of these virtues, none of which live 'inside our heads' or are directly accessible through our intellects. So long as we continue primarily to identify with our minds and place insufficient credence on our hearts as having any importance, these qualities or virtues will never be given a chance to emerge and ripen. Yes, we may know a lot *about*, say, wisdom and may have read what all the great philosophers have had to say about it, and we may even be capable of quoting long passages from their writings and discussing their thoughts very intelligently. We may know too that there are many injustices in the world and that we need more justice. But if we are not actually able to *embody* any of these qualities – that is, if wisdom or justice simply remain as concepts in our head and do not blossom inside our hearts and so are not in any way being embodied through our activities out in the world – then in no way can we say that we possess them.

However, if we *do* choose to commit to trying to embody some of these virtues, what we will discover is that they will definitely start showing up in our daily lives, only they will do so in their own time and in their own way and when we are ready to receive them. As we are all different and have different life challenges, not all of us will develop the same qualities at the same depth or in the same way. Some may never grow inside us because they are not relevant to us and embracing them may not be part of our path, while others may even show up in our lives without our having intentionally gone looking for them.

While there are many specific things that we can do – and indeed need to do – to create the most favourable environment inside ourselves for these virtues to begin sprouting, one of the most important factors is the way we choose to live our everyday lives. If we do not try to live in a balanced way and to treat those whom we encounter with kindness, or remember to take stands for what we believe in, we will not create a conducive atmosphere inside our hearts for these qualities to blossom. I remind you once more that none of them come from outside. They all exist inside us as beautiful possibilities. Indeed, the more deeply these qualities emerge from within us, the purer of heart we become, and, as the Dalai Lama put it, 'with a pure heart, you can carry on any work – farming, engineering, working as a doctor, as a lawyer, as a teacher – and your profession becomes a real instrument to help the human community'.

Chapter 3
Understanding the Wounded Heart

Let the scar of the heart be seen, for by their scars are known the men and women who are in the way of love – FARID UD-DIN ATTAR

A thorn in the foot is hard to find.
What about a thorn in the heart?
If everyone saw the thorn in his heart,
When would sorrow gain the upper hand? – RUMI

Understanding the wounded heart

To be an effective activist, we need to know that most of us have hearts that are wounded in some way, and it is important that we understand how and why. This is not only for our own well-being and 'peace of heart', but also because our wounds always get exteriorised into our society – the world outside ourselves being very much a reflection of the one inside us.

Many of us, however, have a resistance to looking inside our hearts. As our wounds hurt, and as we don't like feeling pain, the best way to avoid it, is to repress our hearts and take refuge in the safety of our heads, where we are not compelled to feel. If we wish to be whole hearted, however, this is no way to live, and thus it is important that we devote some time and energy first towards discovering, and then towards addressing, our wounds. In this chapter, we will explore some of the most common wounds that block or constrict us.

A wounded heart will reveal its symptoms in different ways, depending upon our overall nature, the way we are wounded, and how deeply. Some of us have hearts that have become so withered and dry that they simply cannot bleed; everything is held in and repressed. Others of us have wounds that cause our hearts to be so liquid that they never stop suppurating. Whatever form our wounds take, what I have learned is that just as our limb grows stronger in the area where the breakage occurred (here we remember that Achilles, the Greek god, who was the fastest runner, had been wounded in his heel), so it is often those of us with the severest heart wounds and facing the biggest tests in life who end up with the biggest and purest hearts. Therefore, as good activists, we must try never to view our emotional wounds as our enemies, but rather endeavour to be mindful of Jung's words to the effect that 'anything that touches me deeply, be it something painful or joyful, I know has come from God'.

If we can approach our wounds from this angle, we begin to understand that they are there to test us, to help us grow. Often, the moment that we begin to embark on our quest for Heart, our blockages and fears begin revealing themselves. I learned many things about the heart during my time spent studying with a Sufi master. One of the most interesting things he told me was that unless our hearts have been broken, they are not capable of properly opening. At the time, I didn't believe him or quite understand how this could be so. It was only later, when I underwent a severe 'heartbreak' (over a woman), that I realised the truth of his words. I found that as my heart cracked open in its anguish, not only was it able to release a lot of old pain that had been stored there, but it also allowed for an old 'skin' to be discarded, thus allowing space inside for something new and much deeper to emerge.

So just as we saw earlier that the uncovering of a sacred quality may serve as the antidote to a particular negative behavioural trait, so the reverse is equally true. Often love chooses to reveal its presence inside us by illuminating what makes us fear or resist it. Interestingly, since many of our blessings lie hidden in the darkness, one of the main ways that we may access the deeper reaches of our humanity is to try to confront and work with those aspects of ourselves that are scarred and damaged. Thomas Mann understood this. In one of his novels, he made a character tell us that 'if a way to the better there be, it lies in our taking a full look at the worst!' Jung said much the same thing: 'We do not become enlightened by sitting in the light,' he told us, 'but by going into our darkness.'

So while at one level we can say that our wounds initially seem to act as barriers preventing us from accessing the life of our hearts, if faced and worked with, they can also serve to bring us much closer to them. Recognition of this fact is found in an old Tibetan Buddhist prayer.

Grant that I be given appropriate difficulties and sufferings on this journey, so that my heart be truly awakened and my practice of liberation and compassion be truly fulfilled.

Different responses to the wounding in our hearts

Different hearts respond to different kinds of wounding in different ways. Sometimes, they simply shut down. They turn to stone and become rigid, petrified and impenetrable, so we cannot feel the pain any more. This, however, causes additional grief, for then we do not feel anything – including joy. At the other end of the spectrum are those hearts that are too open for too much of the time, and consequently let too much in. These bleed too much, as they lack the capability to filter out negativity. In acupuncture, there is a point called the heart protector, which, if not in balance, means we are insufficiently defended, and most overly open people tend to be vulnerable in this area. Yes, the aim is to have an open heart, but not all the time. Indeed, the more open it is, the more we also need to be able to protect it. A Zen master gives us good advice: 'Have an open heart but keep it under your kimono.'

The wounded heart and dysfunctional relationships

One of the main ways we can observe the wounded heart is in the area of dysfunctional relationships. In my own case, for many years, I would only fall in love with wounded 'ice-queeny' kinds of women – that is, with women unable to give their hearts – as this reflected how my mother, whose heart had been deeply traumatised as a tiny baby, had related to me. (She had been born in the full trauma of the 1917 Russian Revolution and escaped from Russia in a battleship that was being bombed.) Despite being an exceptional human being, my dear mama could never allow me truly to come close to her, and I would then act out this 'unhealed relationship' over and over again in my life, manifesting in my continually trying to get close to wounded, emotionally unavailable women with patterns similar to my mother's.

Needless to say, I would often feel deeply unnourished and unappreciated, as the many defences around my partners' hearts also meant that I would never be 'allowed in', and so the love I was trying to give could not be received. Of course, the fact that I would attempt intimacy with the kind of woman terrified of it indicated a similar fear inside myself. It also meant that I could 'stay safe'. This is the way that many of our neurotic love patterns operate, namely, that we 'go for' people carrying a corresponding wound to our own. In those days, I found that I would not be attracted by women whose hearts were freer and who were capable of letting me in and loving me at a deeper level. That 'pattern' didn't 'turn me on'! Because of my relationship with my mother, love for me had become 'wired up' to coldness and to my not getting the emotional warmth that my heart most desired.

Sometimes, in those days, I would also have relationships with women of the 'bleeding heart' ilk, that is, with hearts devoid of balance and who were always more adept at giving than receiving. These relationships would also be unsatisfactory, because our hearts long to give as much as to receive, and here I would tend not to be permitted any opportunity to give, and generally would end up being accused of being emotionally stingy.

The pattern of 'overgiving' and finding it hard to receive in return can often be traced back to our having had an unconscious bond with a parent to 'take on their suffering' as a condition for being 'looked after', as in 'I will carry your pain if you will protect and support me'. Such an 'agreement' is, of course, never made conscious, never verbalised. But a certain pattern can be set in stone at a very early age, namely, that the only way to be loved is to serve as a repository for our parent's toxicity. Later in life, this gets projected into our relationships, and, until recognised and worked with, may continue long after our actual parent is dead.

In my psychotherapy practice, I have worked with many people who have felt so wounded in this area that they have chosen to not be in a relationship at all, and as a result close themselves off from one of the best ways available to enable us to grow our Heart life. Just as we can suffer if our physical diet is deficient in core nutrients, so the same thing applies to our emotional diet, and today many people suffer from severe emotional and spiritual malnutrition. If we cannot relate empathically to our partner, or cannot connect to our own needs and verbalise them, if we do not feel strong enough to stand up to difficult people, or lack the confidence to speak our truth, or if we fear allowing ourselves to be spontaneous, it is always because there is some kind of damage to our emotional hearts.

Giving our hearts away

The song 'I Left My Heart in San Francisco' gives us another clue as to why we can be vulnerable in a relationship. Many of us have never learned how to take care of our hearts, and when in a relationship, we may give too much of it away to our partner to do the caring for us. This means that we give them the responsibility not only for making us feel good, but also for looking after our pain for us. This makes us extremely vulnerable, as it implies not only that there is little heart left in reserve for ourselves, but also that if our partner were to leave us, they would do so taking a large part of ourselves away with them, a part which we may not know how to reclaim.

This pattern of 'giving away' our hearts, then, only 'works' so long as that other agrees to take care of it. If, for whatever reason, they stop doing so – and this often occurs because being made to be responsible for how another person feels is experienced as burdensome – we can end up in deep trouble, for now we are without our core as well as being bereft of that part of ourselves that can help us deal with our suffering and metabolise the source of our loss.

This can also be difficult for the person who is left holding our heart, as it can feel like a huge imposition. Not only are they left carrying pain that is not theirs and which they don't want, but they also may not know how to release it. In other words, just as the heart giver may not know how to retrieve their heart, so the heart receiver may not know how to return it. Sometimes, the one who has done the 'hurting' by leaving the relationship may unconsciously atone by still remaining bound to their old partner and so will continue to hold their pain. It follows that neither party will feel sufficiently free, unless they recognise what has transpired and find ways and means of cutting the ties that still unconsciously bind them to one another.

Case histories of wounded hearts in relationships

The above pattern holds true between lovers but it can also exist between parents and their children. Sometimes the parent holds their child's pain and cannot allow that child to get on with their own life. Sometimes the situation is reversed. As in all these matters, these patterns can be invoked unconsciously with neither party having any awareness of what is going on. Quite recently, I worked with a depressed young man and we were making little progress, until in one session, he stumbled onto the fact that he had had a 'secret contract' with his father, whereby his father agreed to 'look after him financially' so long as he 'took on his father's feeling of inadequacy'. As a result, neither of them could properly move on with their lives.

I once worked with a woman who longed to draw closer to a particular man who was gentle and kind, and who she instinctively felt was the right partner for her. But somehow she found herself unable to. Each time he tried to come near, she found new ways to push him away. As we dug deeper, we discovered that she had been treated very harshly by her stepfather, who came onto the scene when she was very young. This deeply harmed her self-esteem. She saw how this had led her always to go for the 'wrong kind of man'. 'I now see why I have always gone for bad guys and avoided the kind and loving ones,' she told me. 'It is because I see myself as a bad person and not deserving of this kind man who has come into my life.' A lot of untangling at many levels was required before this woman's heart became free enough and she was ready to believe that she deserved something better, and felt able to love in a more mature way. Happily, this man waited patiently for her, and his love was able to deepen the healing that she and I had embarked upon. 'For the first time,' she told me, 'I have met someone who is willing to see the real me and who does not treat me like dirt. I cannot tell you how much this helps me to be the real me and to realise that I deserve to be loved.' These words are a beautiful example of the healing power of Heart.

Another case history of a young woman who came to me for help, again over her relationships with men, also illustrates this. Though basically stable and well integrated, she had a habit of marrying men and then finding her love tailing off towards the end of the third year of marriage. She had left three husbands in twelve years and was terrified of this happening again. During one therapy session, she suddenly relived a memory where, as a child of three, she had had to witness her father, whom she loved deeply, going off to fight in the Vietnam War while she screamed at him, 'Daddy, don't leave me! Please don't leave me!' Daddy did leave her, and he never returned. She realised how this fear of loss had been deeply buried and would surface again, but not until the magical number of three years approached. So in order to protect herself against the imagined fear of loss, she would always find reasons why her marriages were not working, which would therefore justify her to find reasons to reject her husbands before – in her imagination – they abandoned her. As she came to realise what she was doing, and as I gave her the space to work with the unbearable pain of the death of her father, which, as a small child, she had completely blocked out, she was gradually able to free herself. She is now into the fifth year of her current marriage.

To be the possessor of a whole heart is, of course, important for all of us, but it is especially so for those of us who wish to serve as an enheartening force in the world. In my own case, I find that I can be in no position to support those I work with unless my own heart feels clear and strong, unless

I am also continually working with my own process. This does not mean that my heart should never feel pain or that I can only be effective if I am 'fully healed' or that if I am personally going through a difficult patch, I need to close down to my own feelings. On the contrary, it means that I need to be in touch with my pain and consciously allow my own heart to get to work with my troubles, as this puts me in the best position to honour my clients' challenges. Again, I can truly say that I am grateful for my own heart wounds, as they have enabled me to explore many different healing methodologies as well as having helped me be more understanding towards others with similar scars.

The dangers of the unhealed heart

Another reason why it is so important to address the wounds inside our hearts is that there is often an unconscious tendency to want to hurt others in the same way that we ourselves were damaged. It is well known that those who were badly abused as children often go on to abuse others and choose victims of the same age as they were when the original damage occurred. A deep heart wound is always present in all abusers, tyrants and sadists. Saddam Hussein, for example, suffered much trauma as a child. Firstly, he was illegitimate, which was a source of shame in his culture, then he was introduced to the world of murder and torture by his violent stepfather, who beat him regularly. By the time Saddam was in his teens, he had already carried out several murders, and the gradual hardening of heart that this encouraged made possible the further maturing of his psychopathic tendencies, which blossomed more fully when he became ruler of Iraq. He could allow mass murder to occur because his own heart had been effectively assassinated.

Sources of heart wounding

Our hearts generally carry all sorts of wounds or scars that emanate from many different sources. The main source, which we are most familiar with, is of course what happened to us in our early childhood. Most traditional psychiatrists believe that the primary reason behind most of our emotional difficulties is to be found in what transpired in the early years of our growing up.

While of course our hearts will have been damaged if we have had abusive or unloving care givers, I believe there are other, deeper sources of wounding which also need to be taken into consideration. Some of our wounds may relate to our having had a traumatic birth; some may be the result of particular 'spirit attachments', which may have fixed themselves in our hearts, while other wounds are those of the society which we belong to. As a Western male, I know I that I carry particular splits inside my own heart – particularly between my spirituality and my sexuality.

Ancestral wounds

Just as we are connected to our existing family, so we are also linked into our ancestors and may therefore be affected by past events that took place within our lineage and which have never been healed or resolved. For instance, if there was some form of 'dishonour' in our family past – perhaps some dire family secret, such as insanity, murder, suicide, criminality, financial loss, incest, rape or war experiences where the dead were not properly mourned – this pattern can be 'handed down the line' and we can actually come into 'this life' with it lingering inside our hearts. For example, a psychotic child could possibly be holding the pattern of the insane uncle who was packed off to the asylum and whom everybody was too ashamed ever to mention. Similarly, the 'black sheep' of the family could have inherited some ancient, unresolved family pattern around being a victim that goes back for many generations and which still lies lodged inside the ancestral memory.

Wounds due to spirit attachments

Sometimes the source of emotional pain and trauma in our lives is due to the attachment to us of an earthbound entity: that is, the spirit of someone who has died but does not yet realise it and, failing to 'move on', instead clings to someone still living, 'entering' them where there is some 'hole' in their psyche or some area of vulnerability. When such attachments occur – very often the spirit will limpet itself to our hearts – its presence is always negative and it can prevent us from being ourselves and from being able to move on in our lives.

Often, when we say 'I don't quite feel myself today', this may be evidence that such an attachment has occurred. Recent research into heart transplants, for example, has shown that those receiving a new heart may inherit many of the characteristics of the donor. One recipient of a new heart suddenly became obsessed with sex and alcohol, and subsequent research showed that the donor had been an alcoholic and a sex addict. Spirit attachments can come about in many different ways. They can occur as a result of traumatic events having taken place in prior incarnations, which means that a baby may be born with a pre-existing condition which may incline it to be perpetually upset, ill or hyperactive.

Many people working in this field believe that the disordered emotional lives of many addicts make them very susceptible to attachments by negative spirit entities, and that releasing them ought therefore to be an integral part of all drug and alcohol rehabilitation. An attachment can also happen with someone whom we have known. To give two examples: let us say there are twins who are very close, and one dies. It may not want to abandon its sibling. Thus, it may attach itself to the live twin's heart centre, unaware of the interference that this will cause. Conversely, one may have a situation where someone who has promised to take care of another dies, feeling that they have failed in their mission, and as a result may refuse to let that other go, still remaining limpeted to them by guilt and sorrow.

Birth trauma
The way we are actually born also has an influence upon the health of our heart. For example, if our mother was heavily anaesthetised during our birth, we may absorb some of the drug, which may predispose us later in life towards seeking similar states of numbness. Conversely, if we were pulled out roughly with forceps by uncaring doctors more intent on congratulating the mother than considering the feelings of the baby, the effect can also be traumatic and may lead us to believe that the world is an unsafe place or, at worst, if the trauma was very great, that life is against us. If we believe this, we won't be particularly motivated to want to open our hearts to life and allow its magic in.

Heart/soul wounds in early childhood
When we are born, we are still very open and tender, with our souls still connected to our source, our hearts being extremely vulnerable. Therefore, the way we are actually 'received' into the world and cared for by our parents or primary care givers – that is, how little or how much real heart they show us – plays a very significant role as to how healthy our hearts are going to be. For our connection with Heart to remain so that our Heart life may continue to evolve and blossom, we will need to have had parents or care givers who were themselves open hearted and connected to their soul life, so that they could subtly 'mirror' this linkage to us.

If, as tiny babies, we were not 'received' in this way – that is, not exposed to Heart light – what can happen is that we gradually learn to turn away from our own inner light, and as we grow up, we begin increasingly to close down to this most sacred and precious dimension of ourselves. Put another way, when we are a baby, among the many important ingredients needed for our health and wholeness is that of our being loved unconditionally. If those who bring us up lack this capability and instead let us know that we will only be loved if we behave in ways that are pleasing to them, we gradually learn to close off to those many precious parts of ourselves not contained within this remit. The result is that we may grow up closing much of our hearts down and thus come not only to believe that we are not good enough, but also that there is something inherently flawed about us. Wordsworth understood this heart/soul wounding only too well when he reminded us:

> *... trailing clouds of glory do we come*
> *From God, who is our home ...*
> *Shades of the prison-house begin to close*
> *Upon the growing Boy.*[1]

If there was little joy or spontaneity present in the world of our parents during the time of our growing up, our own capacity to manifest these qualities may also remain suppressed. One of the consequences is that it may scare us to 'open up' and explore spirituality in any depths. Many people drawn to embrace the inherently heartless religiosity that, for example, characterises many forms of fundamentalist religions tend to carry these kinds of heart wounds. If, on top of this, we were also criticised, marginalised and abused in some way, our wounds will be deeper and we will lose touch even more with the deeper ground of our being and thus with any potential access to the treasure chest inside our hearts.

Wounds due to past lives

Certain heart wounds may also be due to 'unfinished business' or unresolved issues lingering over from prior incarnations. For example, we may have 'come into' this life carrying a deep memory of having been badly betrayed by someone whom we loved, leading us to find it difficult to trust those whom we are close to.

Through past-life psychotherapy I discovered that I came into this life carrying a memory of having been an unorthodox preacher in a past life, which resulted in me having been hanged, drawn and quartered for speaking my truth. Suffice to say that until this old memory had been allowed to surface and had been appropriately worked through or exorcised, I always found myself burdened with an irrational fear of speaking out and walking my talk. This shows that if such hidden memories are not surfaced, worked on and gradually integrated, they may continue to operate as traumatic blockages deep inside our hearts, obscuring our way forward and haunting us like ghosts at the very core of our being.

Morphogenetic field resonance theory

If the idea of past lives does not appeal, we may view our past from a different perspective. The biologist Rupert Sheldrake has posited the existence of what he calls the morphogenetic field resonance theory, arguing in a series of books that the individual members of every species are networked into a 'group mind' that constitutes the dynamic blueprint of that species. He suggests that this 'field' not only contains the blueprint of the species' physical form, but that it also collects and incorporates into itself the new experiences of its individual members. Thus, this morphic field mediates between the parts and the whole of a species, as well as between its past and its present. He suggests that the mental and emotional processes which we see operating within a human being might therefore be paralleled by similar processes operating in the species mind (and, I would also suggest, the species heart), and that in the same way that we remember our individual experiences, so the species mind and heart remembers its collective experiences.

So just as undigested problematic experiences can collect at a personal level and block the healthy functioning of our personal hearts, similar blockages may also occur at a collective or universal level and have exactly the same effects. In a recent lecture, the historian Chris Bache suggested that 'the unresolved anguish of human history may be active within the species mind, burdening its life just as individual unresolved anguish burdens our individual life'. To relate this to my experience of having been hanged, drawn and quartered, one could say that what I had been tapping into may not necessarily have been the result of anything that happened to me personally in a prior incarnation. It may also have been a species memory which, for reasons unbeknownst to me, I happened to be carrying.

Whatever way we approach these kinds of issues, I think we need to reflect upon how vast must be the 'unfinished business' or the undigested suffering of world man, and how deeply, therefore, our species or universal heart must still be troubled and in need of healing. Certainly, if we cast our hearts and minds back in history and reflect upon the brutality and the inhuman and destructive ways in which for aeons we have treated one another, and if we also reflect upon how little we human beings have ever really sought to resolve the deep wounding resulting from this, it surely follows that our species heart must be in a state of considerable turmoil. Of course, this affects us. So long as our species patterns remain unhealed, we will merely continue to repeat them and so persist in treating our fellow human beings inappropriately. This is again why it is so important that, as activists, we devote time and energy towards the healing of our hearts.

Chapter 4
Opening to the Healing Heart

Don't curse the darkness, but light a light – MOTHER TERESA

Through love, all pain turns to medicine – RUMI

The alchemy of the heart

One of the many remarkable aspects of our hearts is not only the essential multi-dimensionality of their nature, but also how it is that, while at one level a part of them may be very wounded and in need of being healed, at a whole other – much deeper – level they also possess extraordinary healing and regenerative capabilities. If we examine the many treasures that reside inside them once more, we see that their one common denominator is that they all contain healing or 'whole-making' attributes of one kind or another. We saw how kindness is able to uplift a depressed spirit and how wisdom expands us, while compassion enables us to be gentler with ourselves and how, if we tune into beauty, it is able to fill the hole of our deficiency. The power of love to heal pain and to expand our awareness, emotionally, mentally and spiritually, is common knowledge. Rumi understood this very well: 'Through love, all pain turns to medicine.'

Just as our stomachs enable us to digest and metabolise our food, so our hearts, if 'invited', allow us to process and metabolise our suffering. There is a verse in the poem 'Last Night' where Antonio Machado beautifully describes this whole process:

Last night, as I was sleeping,
I dreamt – marvellous error! –
that I had a beehive
here inside my heart.
And the golden bees
were making white combs
and sweet honey
from my old failures.

Our hearts are our personal alchemical processors and serve as a 'transmutational laboratory' inside us. The more we feed them the 'base metal' of our pain or anguish or our less admirable characteristics – say, our vanity or our envy, our resentments or our fears and hatreds – the more they are able to digest and recycle them into the true gold of our emerging Heart self. This is an enormous accomplishment even if it may sometimes take time. I have particularly found that if I give my heart my anxiety, so long as I remain connected to my feelings – the alchemical process absolutely demands this of us – it will gradually transform that anxiety into the experience of a greater loving concern. Similarly, my heart can turn my despair into hope and my indifference into compassion. I have found over the years that I have fed my heart a lot of my own pain and fears, and that it really has been able to gobble them up! That is its magic.

Also, whenever I consciously bring my heart into the solving of my problems, I find that I am given a much wider perspective with which to view them, thus helping me decide the wisest course of action to take. I often find that when I can see clearly into the 'heart' of something that may be troubling me (which requires that I be connected to my heart), it ceases to cause me pain. Just as the flames of a fire will flare up the more logs we throw onto it, so the more we feed our hearts our thorny issues for them to grapple with, the brighter they will glow. Our hearts are always happy to do the work intended for them.

Our challenge as spiritual activists, then, is for us to grow increasingly into our 'heart-centredness', that is, to learn increasingly to live from, or 'come from', our hearts. The more we are able to do this, the better equipped we become, not only to confront our personal wounds and work through them more effectively, but also – so very important – to face and concretely address the wounds that exist in the larger heart of our society. We cannot effectively do one thing without the other. The more whole we are as human beings, the more capable we are of bringing wholeness into our society.

Living appropriately

As our hearts start to open, a natural sense of what is right and appropriate slowly emerges, and we may start asking ourselves important questions about the way we live. A deeper understanding of what is harmonious and what works for us comes into play, and we find ourselves gradually moved to evolve new habits that are increasingly life-affirming and to shed old ones that are not. It is of particular importance that the healing qualities of the heart be brought into play if we have a serious illness, for without such a perspective, illness can all too often be viewed as an enemy come from outside to attack us, and which we therefore need to fight back against and eliminate. When we are connected to our hearts, however, illness starts being recognised as an ally emerging from deep inside us to reveal to us where we have become off balance and informing us where we need to make changes in our lives to bring us back to health.

If a politician comes from Heart, if a scientist looks at how his achievements can be used to benefit the world, if all of us try to work with, and from, Heart, a whole new spirit of wholeness, which is integrally healing, is naturally injected into our environment. This is so important. Governments can't 'force' us to change our diets or lighten our carbon footprints or save more and spend less. However, when a sense of our own global responsibility starts emerging – and this happens naturally as our hearts begin opening wider – we naturally feel impelled to relate to other people and our planet in a wiser way, to want to live more organically and holistically and tread more delicately on Earth's surfaces.

Heart as a reconciler of conflict

The heart is also a key ingredient in the way we work with conflict, which is not 'bad' as many believe, but an integral part of life. Carl Jung believed 'conflicts exist to increase consciousness'. If we lack the wherewithal to resolve them, which is so often the case if our hearts are closed, we become, as he put it, 'crucified between the opposites and delivered up to torture until the reconciling third takes place'. What he is suggesting is that if a resolution is to take place, we need a 'third force' or a reconciliatory capability to come into play, and I believe this occurs as we learn to open up to the naturally integrative and synthesising presence of our hearts. Put simply, our hearts are that reconciling third force. Pseudo-resolutions can occur without Heart and we often see this in the various peace treaties initiated between nations after wars. However, I maintain that there can be no genuine or long-lasting reconciliation without the involvement of Heart.

Wordsworth understood this. In his 'Ode: Intimations of Immortality', he wrote that inside us there exists 'a dark, inscrutable workmanship' that has the ability to 'reconcile discordant elements' and gather them in a whole, making them 'cling together in one society', but – and this is the key point – this integrating capability can *only* operate when 'we feel worthy of ourselves'. In other words, this reconciliatory presence can only really work or come into its own when we are connected to the deeper abundance that naturally grows inside us, as a by-product of our being increasingly attuned to the world of our hearts.

Certainly, my own experience is that if I can be more fully aware of the reconciliatory power inside my heart, the many conflicting parts of myself that are often wont to wage outright war with one another begin to calm down and may even begin celebrating each other's existence. As my heart deepens, I observe less and less separation between those parts of me that like to contemplate life and those that like action. I can also much more easily integrate the pragmatic side of myself with the more mystical me, and the male, initiating part of myself can bond more intimately with my feminine side, with all these reconciliations occurring quite naturally without me trying to *make* anything happen.

On those occasions when I face particularly conflicted situations in my life, I find that if I am able to embrace them with my heart, a much larger picture opens up for me and I can often sense the deeper meaning of what is going on, and as a result, much of the sting often goes out of the conflict's tail! I can start recognising (a) that opposites need each other and are actually contained within one another, and (b) what it is that I need to learn from the conflict. From this place, I can much more easily intuit the right way to proceed.

We can learn a lot about how to relate to our conflicts from a reconciliatory perspective if we study the martial arts. There, our opponent is never seen as the enemy, but as our friend, and the more skilful they are, the more skill they will elicit from us. A worthy adversary, therefore, has an important gift to offer us and we need to thank them. This is why in all contests, both sides always begin by bowing to each other's deeper Heart essence, in order to affirm the respect they have for each other. If we could only learn to do the same with all our oppositions – be they conflicting sides of our nature or conflicts we have with other people or conflicts out in the world – our world would be a very different place. Just imagine what it would mean if members of Parliament behaved in this way during parliamentary debates, or if Israelis and Palestinians could more easily view each other through the lens of the heart of forgiveness and so 'walk in each other's moccasins'.

Activating the healing capacity of our hearts

It is so important that we realise what a powerful 'secret weapon' our hearts are, for if we do, we will want 'with all our heart' to utilise it as fully as possible. One excellent way to strengthen them is to engage intentionally in activities that we enjoy and which give us pleasure and make us feel whole, as these activities always have a stimulating and healing effect on our hearts. Much of our ill health, I maintain, is connected with our not allowing ourselves to do this (our Puritanical mindsets making us feel guilty if we experience pleasure). In my case, my heart delights in playing tennis, listening to music, hanging out with close friends, playing my guitar, playing the fool, swimming in warm waters, being with a woman I love and teaching my groups, and I do my best to ensure that all these activities are factored into my 'diet'. Whenever I am engaging in activities that delight me, I feel that my heart is getting an aerobics workout and that the more it does, the more its healing capacity grows.

My daughter

Whenever I am with my daughter, my heart especially 'lights up' and fills me with joy as I so adore her. I will never forget the effect that her birth had on me. When the midwife handed her to me, still attached to her mother's umbilical cord, and as I clutched this miraculous little creature to my chest, tears of joy just exploded out of me. In that precious moment, my heart catapulted open so strongly and I felt so much love that I felt it would burst! And it did. And I let it. It burst wide, wide open. And that felt so good.

I mention this as so many of us are ordinarily so used to restraining our hearts, keeping them reined in, afraid of ever showing emotion, as if it is something to be ashamed of. This is also a particular British trait. We no longer wear stiff collars but we still can't let go of our emotional uptightness! This attitude needs to fall away. Our hearts need to be bursting open with excitement all the time, over many more issues, as this is one of the chief ways that they heal and grow and come into their own.

I always thank God for the gift that the birth of my daughter has brought into my life, and I think of those powerful words of Wordsworth telling us that when a new baby is born, it comes 'trailing clouds of glory ... from God, who is our home'. This is why newborns are so precious. They remind us how close each of us really is to our own divine self, from which, sadly, in the process of our 'growing-up' and becoming socialised, we increasingly learn to distance ourselves.

Activating the remembering heart

We now need to ask ourselves what happens to the healing capacities of our hearts when we are *not* doing things we specifically love – when we need to be engaging in so-called mundane, 'uninteresting things' (which, after all, often constitutes the major part of life). What happens, for example, when we are doing our accounts, travelling to work or cleaning the car? Do we have to forsake Heart or can we still engage in life with Heart? My answer is 'Yes we can', and we need to try our best to do so, only here, we generally have to *remember* to do so, and therefore we need consciously to bring in the ingredient of *remembrance*. If we *remember* to have our hearts present and open when we are engaging in activities that may not naturally stimulate or touch us, then they become imbued with a new spirit and as a result, we can begin seeing and relating to them in a new light. This is because when Heart is present, other dimensions of a situation which were not visible before now start coming into view. If one of the great tragedies of life is that, in our heartlessness, we have sucked a lot of the sacredness out of it, reconnecting with our hearts in this way offers us a beautiful opportunity to bring sacredness back into the world.

This happens when we start choosing to bring Heart into ordinary activities, as gradually their ordinariness starts becoming extraordinary, which in turn leads to the realisation that all of life – even those parts of it that don't initially seem so interesting to us – is precious, profound, mysterious and beautiful. If we can come from a space that enables us to feel and to see this, then we may also find that we do not need all the various bells and whistles which we are continually grasping after and trying to inject into our lives in order to compensate for our failure to experience this. When we start living more and more out of a sacred space – and the more we do so, the more natural it becomes and the less we need to remember to do it – whole new dimensions of meaning begin springing up for us out of nowhere.

Mundane life as an adventure of Heart

Since I have not the time, finances, inclination or ability to spend my days doing 'exciting things' all the time, such as climbing Everest, crossing the

Sahara or exploring the bottom of the ocean in a submarine, I try to make the ordinary little things of my life into an adventure of Heart. I try to make them special. One way I tried to put this into practice was in my journeying to and from London twice a week to see my clients, which would involve a long train journey with plenty of bus rides in between.

I realised I could either succumb to treating this as an ordinary, boring routine, where I would 'fall asleep' into its mundanity, or, if I brought my heart into play, I found I could imbue it with aliveness and give it new meaning. Then, everybody I encountered, from the ticket office clerk or newsagent to the person I sat next to on the bus or train, I'd choose to hold in my heart in an affirming way. I would either engage with them personally – perhaps say something complimentary, or make a little joke – or, and only if I felt it appropriate (I would always respect people's space if I sensed they wished to be left alone), engage them in deeper conversation. This process would always give me a great deal of pleasure even if some of my 'sacred little encounters' only lasted for a minute.

The importance of being in 'present time'

As I said, one of the reasons we so often need the excitement and stimulation of 'new things' – a new relationship, a fantastic holiday, a new car, etc. – is that we fail to do this kind of thing often enough, that is, we fail to bring enough Heart-ful awareness into our ordinary, everyday experiences. We therefore find them monotonous because we are experiencing 'what is, right now', not as it is at all, but as it once was, filtered through the memory of how we remembered things in the past. Thus, we live a lot in our past, and one of the consequences is that it brings in a deadening energy.

Intentionally choosing to bring in Heart awareness, on the other hand, introduces a revitalising presence. If I see something or someone through the lens of my heart, it means that I allow its or their core freshness to emerge. In other words, if my heart is present, it can evoke the heart of whatever or whoever I am choosing to be present to. So, as I said, wherever I go, whatever I do, I always try to engage in life in as alive and as interested a way as I can. As I also travel abroad a lot in my work, I find that airports are great places to practise this, as they offer one the opportunity to interact with people from wholly different backgrounds and cultures. As Heart-ful communications with fellow human beings are such exquisite and delicious experiences, many of my so-called 'mundane journeys' have turned out to be wonderful little sacred adventures.

Opening to the universal heart

Earlier, I defined the universal heart as being our species heart or the 'one heart' which we all share and are all potentially connected into. I say potentially, for we need to be in touch with our own heart in order to connect with it, as it is through our personal hearts that this 'greater heart' is able to make its presence known. If our own individual hearts are closed or contracted, we will have no way of making that deeper connection and therefore no way of experiencing that we are all part of something much vaster and much more encompassing than just 'little old us'.

Just recently, I had a powerful experience of this bigger heart, as I was at the ceremony to celebrate the end of the 2012 Olympics. It was an extraordinary feeling. A huge 'Heart field' had opened up, having been created over the last fortnight by thousands of athletes from all over the world, all of whom had been putting their all into trying to expand the parameters of their athleticism. One felt the power of collective excellence strongly in the air. When we become included in an energy field that has been built up by courageous men and women engaged in seeking to extend the boundaries of their possibilities, it is a highly inspiring and enheartening experience. During that time, I felt that I also wanted to be the best that I could be, and that I wanted to take myself to the very edge of my possibilities, if no longer through athletic feats, then through feats of Heart of some kind. Let me become the Usain Bolt of Heart, I thought to myself! I also thought: wouldn't it be wonderful if all of these great Olympians were to take their energy of personal excellence and use it to make a difference to the world?

Actually, some *are* doing exactly this, and here I think in particular of the great Mo Farah, who won two gold medals, and what he is doing to inspire his Somali community, and the wonderful Jessica Ennis – who won a gold medal in the heptathlon – and her work in inspiring disadvantaged kids to take up sport. Sport can be so healing and unifying, and many athletes do have very big hearts and go on to become activists.

This, then, is the experience of the universal heart. Yes, we access it through our personal hearts, but it is not personal. In fact, it allows us to transcend the boundaries of our 'skin-encapsulated me-ness' and experience that we are part of a much larger and all-encompassing whole. The universal heart always has a distinct presence, and sometimes when linking with it, we may find ourselves gaining access to particular Heart treasures that we do not ordinarily connect with. In addition, because we are becoming more naturally attuned to a much larger spectrum of what it means to be a human being, we may also find that we can relate much more easily and effectively with all sorts of different kinds of people who, in our normal state, we might experience difficulty with.

When the universal heart becomes activated, many things begin to change. Young people can better understand how old people feel; Christians can relate to Muslims much better; people who have wealth can more easily enter the lives of those who are poor and start seeing the world through their eyes. All the many boundaries of class, race, colour, nationality and religion which conspire to keep us so separate from one another begin dissolving. We are no longer the 'me' we thought we were and used to be identified with. Rather, we have expanded into a truer, fuller, more genuine and universal 'us', where many of our old fears and prejudices, predicated upon the belief that we are only 'individuals', begin dissolving. Yes, we are still a citizen of a particular country, but more and more we are coming to experience ourselves to have a much more significant identity, that of *citizen of the planet*. As such, we realise that there is a real need on our part to give up our attachments to our old nationalistic mindsets and also start viewing our country from the perspective of its existence within the larger world community.

Another area where we can experience this 'bigger heart' very powerfully is at international conferences which have been organised around themes of how we may work together in some way to enhance the well-being of our planet. I have attended many such conferences in my life, and they are always extremely uplifting and joyful occasions. Life becomes much more abundant when we are connected with what unifies us as opposed to what separates us, as the latter mindset means we are always engaged in a series of undercurrent dramas. If we look at those people, for example, whose main *raison d'être* is to wish for the state of Israel to be obliterated from the face of the earth, one thinks of how painful it must be to live, day in day out, in such a miserable and violent state of mind.

The death of Princess Diana as a universal heart trigger

There are many catalysts that can trigger the temporary emergence of universal heart. Pain is one such. The grief many people around the world felt as a result of the death of Princess Diana, the 'Queen of Hearts', in a tragic car crash, was a classic example of this. Perhaps Diana achieved more for people by her death than she ever achieved in her life. The fact that she was young, beautiful and vulnerable, as well as being a famous flesh-and-blood princess, struck a deep archetypal chord inside many of us, and resulted in the opening of many millions of hearts all around the world – many for the very first time. I had the distinct sense that a profound 'collective heart of mourning' had come into being.

When something like this occurs, it is always very healing, for whenever hearts open strongly, either a lot of grief is released, or some particular heart virtue starts to emerge. In Diana's case, she 'allowed' us to release a lot of pain, and as the whole is always more than the sum of its parts, the potency of the universal heart enabled many of us to go much more deeply into the world of heart-grief than we might ordinarily have done on our own. Many people found that they began to release sorrow that didn't only 'belong' to them and was not solely centred around the factor of Diana's death.

Like many others at the time, my own grieving began at a personal level with mourning over the actual death of the princess. As the Heart field grew in intensity, however, my heart began to open more widely, and I observed my grief start to move into other areas of my life which I found had not been sufficiently mourned. I realised that there was still a lot of sadness over the death of a particular relationship that had just ended. I also saw that I had not completed my mourning over my mother who, when young, resembled the princess and who had died a few months earlier. So my heart began to move into these other areas, and I let it remain there until I felt the work was complete. It felt so good to release this pain. The tears I wept felt like good tears! A heart full of grief can never be a healthy heart.

As my heart began opening wider, and as its universality began to emerge, I found that it was starting to access realms that had nothing to do with me personally. Interestingly, I found myself grieving for all women who had been abused in one way or another, especially those who had been sold into slavery or prostitution, and for some days I became a kind of weeping heart for wounded womankind. It was a curious experience but very cathartic and it made my heart feel very light afterwards, as if a huge stone had been released from it. I had the distinct feeling that the grief I was feeling was not mine, but belonged to some aspect of humanity's wounded heart that was especially my remit to work with (after all, in my therapy practice, I work mainly with women), and that a lot of healing was taking place as a result.

This kind of work can be challenging, as few of us are good at handling grief. We tend to fear it and believe it is bad to feel it, and so we often tighten around it in the mistaken belief that then it won't affect us. Of course, this approach never works. Our grief simply turns rancid and lodges deeper inside our hearts, poisoning us slowly from inside and further blocking our ability to experience life in a positive way. So many psychiatric disorders and cancers are connected with painful experiences which we have had, but which we have bottled away because we are afraid of feeling our pain. At any rate, for me and for many others whom I discussed this with, the 'Diana effect', which lasted a few weeks, gave us all the opportunity to do healing work in areas that otherwise we might never have known about or bothered with.

The great tsunami as a universal heart trigger

The great tsunami of 2004 was another example of a 'wave' sweeping the planet that had deeply awakening effects and profoundly wrenched open millions of people's hearts the world over. As we all know, in one fell swoop, thousands of people in many countries lost their families, their houses, their livelihoods and, a lot of them, their sanity. A friend of mine, not otherwise known for his softness, put into words how many of us felt as we watched yet another news report on that terrible wave. 'It feels as if my own family have been destroyed,' he told me. 'I feel such kinship with those people at the other end of the world who have lost everything. And even though I do not know them personally, I feel connected to them. I feel I want to go out there and help them, and do something for them.' This was the universal heart speaking at its most eloquent. My friend kept his word. He was wealthy, and not only did he donate a large cheque to the relief effort, but he also put himself in the firing line and went over in person to help in the mop-up operation. He told me afterwards that he felt this was the most important thing he had ever done and that it had changed his life.

I am sure it did. We cannot connect with the universal heart and still remain selfish! Whenever we do something from the goodness of that heart, not only do we make a difference out in the world, but we also make a difference to ourselves. This is one of the great gifts that terrible tragedies can sometimes give us. What had opened up in my friend's heart and in millions of individual people's hearts all over the world at that time was the awareness of a shared brotherhood and sisterhood with people whom one will never ever personally know, but whom one starts to hold preciously inside one's heart. Many of us are doing the same thing today as we observe the death toll rise as a result of the terrible civil war going on inside Syria.

The catalytic effect of crises

One of the effects of these kinds of crisis, then, is that they help jerk millions of us out of our habitual complacency and selfishness. In doing so, they may enable the best of us to emerge. In the case of the tsunami, millions of pounds of relief aid flowed towards the stricken areas. Even people who lived on the streets and who didn't have a penny became touched and gave of what little they had. Suddenly, there was something much bigger, much more real to confront, in comparison to which our own petty storm-in-a-teacup grievances, which generally occupy so much of our time, utterly paled into insignificance. Within a short time, the spirit of generosity, locked inside humanity's collective treasure chest, had been unleashed and began flowing towards that part of the planet where help was needed.

Alas, the opening was only temporary. As with the death of Diana, after the shock effect and after the media discovered that this catastrophe was no longer fresh and front-page news, humanity's heart began gradually to clench shut again and many of us returned to our old, selfish ways and it became 'business as usual' once more. Yes, the universal or species heart had opened; yes, many of us had savoured it; but we were unable to hold the momentum. The backlash of our old heartlessness proved too potent. I think if we wish to be effective activists, we are not only challenged to activate our altruistic and universal 'heart muscles' on our own, but we must also learn to keep up the momentum without requiring any external catalysts.

Jesus as healer

I cannot write a chapter on the healing heart without saying a few words about Jesus, who embodied it in its most sublime form. By all accounts, he was wise, loving, kind, tender and compassionate, courageous, humble, resourceful and peaceful. It also seems that he knew how to enjoy life, and the fact that modern Christianity likes to put so much emphasis on his suffering on the cross has more to do with our Judeo-Christian predilection for emphasising sin and guilt than the true story of the life of this remarkable, whole-hearted and abundant human being.

Jesus both spoke and lived his truth. He never deviated from being the change he wished to see happen. Because he could see the full-heartedness in everyone, he would delight in spending time with all sorts of people, many of whom less healthy human beings might deem to be 'beneath them'. Never did Jesus waver from standing up for what he believed in, which included not holding back from courageously informing the 'powers that be' that the Kingdom of Heaven (ultimate spiritual heart fulfilment) was not 'out there', but inside all of us and could be accessed by us on our own, without our necessarily needing priests as intermediaries.

Jesus had many gifts. He could perform extraordinary miracles, like raising people from the dead. He also revealed what true abundance really meant when he turned water into wine and made a few loaves and fishes feed thousands. 'Come to me, those of you who feel heavy hearted, and I will help you feel peaceful once more,' he would tell people. These words are important for us to grasp, for Jesus, like many other great teachers, existed to show us what might also be possible, or what we might all possibly become, if we were to devote more time to the process of awakening our hearts.

Becoming a disciple

Central to Jesus's mission was the idea of training a small band of people to become his disciples, who would then go out into the world to help spread his message of love. I mention this, as all the things that were important for Jesus's disciples are equally important for the activist today. Jesus was always concerned about how his disciples might be most effective in their work, and consequently he was often stressing how important it was for them to take good care of their hearts. 'Do not let your hearts be troubled,' he would tell them.

I don't think he was implying that they were to hide themselves away from the troubles in the world, not see what was going on and close themselves off to the injustices around them. On the contrary, I think he was suggesting that in order to be tough enough to embrace life in all its heartlessness and suffering, his disciples needed to be clear hearted and, most importantly, strong minded, which in turn required a heart free of pain. He knew that if they went about their work with grieving hearts, it would weaken them and they would be ineffective. As such, they had a duty to work at healing their hearts – emptying them of pain, and I think exactly the same thing applies for us 21st-century activists. Also, like our forebears, we are asked to be 'as wise as serpents and as harmless as doves', where harmless doesn't mean being ineffective. It means not doing any harm to anyone or anything.

Martin Luther King felt that Jesus wanted his disciples to be tender hearted and tough minded, as opposed to the way many people were, which was soft minded – that is, rigid in their thinking – and hard hearted. King rightly realised that a weak, undeveloped, unhealed heart tended to foster this kind of mind that was utterly lacking in vigour. The problem with people with these kinds of inflexible mind is that they tend to be fearful of change and of asking themselves new and challenging questions. As we will be seeing, most of the evil that occurs in the world today happens through people who are hard hearted and consequently rigid in their thinking.

Among the many reasons why the activist needs an open heart, then, is that it allows us to think through our hearts, which activates a subtler intelligence and naturally toughens up our flabbiness. We need both to have an open heart and to be tough, which means that we need to stand up for our truth. Ram Dass, another Heart teacher, from whom I have learned much over the years, likes to tell a story told him by his guru. It concerned a snake which wanted to become more loving and which sought out a guru to tell it how to do this. 'It is simple,' the guru told the snake. 'Go out into the world and love everyone you meet.' The snake did this but got very battered for its efforts as everyone threw things at it. It returned to its guru in a very dejected state. 'What should I do?' the snake asked in despair. 'I never told you not to hiss,' was the master's reply. Hissing can also have healing qualities.

Chapter 5
The Challenges of Being an Activist

Being on a path of heart is like licking honey off a razor's edge –
CHÖGYAM TRUNGPA RINPOCHE

Initiations of the heart

It is challenging enough being alive at this particular 'in between' time in our history where one millennium (the age of Pisces) is coming to an end and another (that of Aquarius) is starting to emerge. However, it is doubly challenging if we are intending to be an activist, since not only do we have our own personal issues to explore and wrestle with, but we also have to remember that we have pledged ourselves to play a significant role in helping heal our planet. This means that we also need to be concerning ourselves with the enormous amount of chaos and confusion that is around us in the air today. In Richard Tarnas's words, 'ours is an age between worldviews; creative yet disoriented, a transitional era when the old cultural vision no longer holds and the new has not yet been constellated'.

Culturally, then, we are in a kind of 'no man's land'. We are marooned between two different worlds tugging at us. One world is trying to pull us back into the familiarity of our past, and the other is endeavouring to propel us forward into the insecurity of what is as yet unknown. What we may observe is that the old world or *'ancien régime'* is truly scared of dying and is desperately struggling to stay alive, yet it no longer has its former potency, while the new world beckoning to us has not yet come into sufficient focus to enable us to know exactly what we may be in for! One of the best ways to view these challenges is to regard them as particular initiations, which are both inner – about what we need to go through internally in order to 'become the change we wish to see happen' – and outer: what we will need to confront externally as a result of our desire to lay down the building blocks of a new society.

Initiation, in Mircea Eliade's words, is about our 'becoming another'. He describes it as being about 'a basic change in our existential condition, where the novice emerges from his ordeal endowed with a totally different being from that which he possesses before his initiation'. For the Tibetan master Dwaj Khul, initiation meant 'a moving out from under ancient controls, into the control of more spiritual and increasingly higher values'. This is important to understand. We cannot be effective spiritual activists unless we come under new controls, unless our psyches start to operate from a very different place from the one responsible for creating so many of the problems which we face in the world today.

Being tested

The moment we step onto the 'path of Heart', life starts testing us. Generally at the start, our tests tend to be gentle. But later, as the capabilities of our hearts begin to grow, they may become more difficult. We may be tested, for example, to see how well we deal with pain or loss, or how willing we are to make certain sacrifices. Or we may find ourselves in situations which cause us to question our honesty and integrity. Similarly, we may discover ourselves in certain challenging circumstances that require us to demonstrate courage and endurance, or where we are challenged to see how kind we are to those less fortunate than ourselves, or how intelligently we can love another person, or how bravely we can deal with betrayal, or how willing we are to endure discomfort and not give in if the going gets tough.

Just as our emotional and physical wounds can be our blessings, as we saw, so too are the difficult times that we may need to go through, at certain points in our lives, as these constitute the lifeblood of our initiations. How effectively, as activists, we manage to deal with our difficulties is intimately connected with how quickly our hearts open and how adept we are at discovering the many human qualities which reside within them.

Awakening into the age of Aquarius

The key thing to remember is that right now we are all moving into the age of Aquarius. Some see this in terms of our going through a new renaissance or a second 'Copernican revolution'. I like this concept. However, while our first renaissance was primarily centred in Italy and began as a rebirth in art, our new renaissance is occurring everywhere on the planet and encompasses a rebirth in all spheres of human endeavour. Richard Tarnas writes:

The twentieth century's massive and radical breakdown of so many structures — cultural, philosophical, scientific, religious, moral, artistic, social, economic, political, atomic, ecological — all this suggests the necessary deconstruction prior to a new birth. And why is there evident now such a widespread and constantly growing collective impetus in the western mind to articulate a holistic and participatory worldview, visible in virtually every field? The collective psyche seems to be in the grip of a powerful archetypal dynamic in which the long-alienated modern mind is breaking through ... out of what Blake called its 'mind-forg'd manacles', to rediscover its intimate relationship with nature and the larger cosmos.

If these times are in no way easy, they certainly offer us ample opportunity to stretch ourselves into whole new areas, to expand our hearts, to be creatively adventurous beyond the scope of talking to someone sitting next to us in a train! In days gone by, initiates would remove themselves from the 'real world' in order to face their 'personal' tests. They would go into caves, pyramids and deserts and be subjected to certain ordeals. They would face their dragons and endure trials by fire, wind and water, alone and far from the madding crowd, far away from civilisation and its discontents.

Those days have passed. Today, we are called to do our initiatory work right in the middle of these discontents. Our tests have become increasingly *universal* — as a species, we are going through a collective initiation which is not only taking place in the highways and byways and boardrooms of the everyday 'heartless worlds' of London, New York, Jerusalem and Moscow, but also in those areas of the Middle East where the Arab Spring is unfurling. Our tests today are occurring in all the areas Tarnas mentions, and our initiatory tools are iPhones and social networking sites and all the many new technologies designed to affirm the emerging reality of our interconnectedness.

Each of us, according to where we are on our journey and what our hearts require for their growth, combined with the particular kind of 'difference-making' work our hearts will have chosen, will find ourselves having to face, in different ways, at different times and at different levels, our own unique ordeals. What is required is that we learn to welcome these ordeals into our hearts, and that we ask our hearts how we may best process the material they provide us with, in order that we may learn and grow from our experiences.

Living in times of crisis

Since newness always carries its shadow in front of it, being on the cusp of a new order means that we are having to face many different kinds of crisis. What we are increasingly finding out is that nothing is certain any more. So many of those structures which, in our past, seemed secure, especially our large institutions, are now being revealed to have been built on shifting sands. While our planet will undoubtedly continue to exist, many entertain doubts as to whether we human beings will. Have we transgressed so much – travelled so far along the path of non-sustainability, polluted our planet so excessively, overpopulated ourselves so prodigiously, created our world to heat up so much, designed so many different types of weapon of mass destruction for ourselves – that now there is no turning back? And what about our financial system? Has it been abused so much that it will go into free fall and totally collapse? All these questions may make us feel very insecure.

Zbigniew Brzezinski, a former US National Security Advisor and now a member of the Center for Strategic and International Studies, also recognises that the world is faced with many challenges. In particular, he senses a new kind of political zeitgeist in the air. In a recent article he wrote:

For the first time in human history almost all of humanity is politically activated, politically conscious and politically interactive ... The resulting global political activism is generating a surge in the quest for personal dignity, cultural respect and economic opportunity in a world painfully scarred by memories of centuries-long alien colonial or imperial domination ... The worldwide yearning for human dignity is the central challenge inherent in the phenomenon of global political awakening ... That awakening is socially massive and politically radicalising ... The nearly universal access to radio, television, and increasingly the internet, is creating a community of shared perceptions and envy that can be galvanised and channelled by demagogic or religious passions. These energies transcend sovereign borders and pose a challenge both to existing states as well as to the existing global hierarchy.

The youth of the Third World are particularly restless and resentful ... And the major world powers, new and old, also face a novel reality: while the lethality of their military might is greater than ever, their capacity to impose control over the politically awakened masses of the world is at a historic low. To put it bluntly: in earlier times, it was easier to control one million people than to physically kill one million people. Today, it is infinitely easier to kill one million people than to control one million people.[1]

The quest for freedom

Another way of looking at what is occurring in the world is to say that at a global level, we are witnessing a vast longing – especially strong among the young – to be free, to cast off the many different kinds of manacle that have for so long been enchaining our hearts at psychological, political, social, sexual, racial, religious and economic levels. In most instances, these chains are both internal and external. We want to be not only *free from* restricting influences, but also *free to* be more fully ourselves – to have more outer opportunities to advance ourselves in the world.

Young people especially are increasingly coming to realise that those forces which repressed them in the past are not nearly as strong as they once believed them to be, while at the same time, they are seeing that they are also much stronger and potentially wield more power than they had formerly believed. We see this in action particularly in the Arab Spring: the world's young are no longer content to be manipulated and hoodwinked by tyrannical leaders and are instead demanding authenticity and accountability from them. Less and less are autocrats feared, increasingly being seen for the brutal, weak and corrupt narcissists and psychopaths which many of them are.

In his play *A Sleep of Prisoners*, Christopher Fry suggested that what is happening in the world today is that:

> *The frozen misery of centuries*
> *Breaks, cracks, begins to move.*
> *The thunder is the thunder of the floes …*
> *Thank God our time is now when wrong*
> *Comes up to face us*
> *Never to leave us till we take*
> *The longest stride of soul men ever took.*

The melting of the suffering species heart

The rigidified and long-suffering heart of species man is at last beginning to melt. (Is what is currently happening to our glaciers perhaps a symbolic outward expression of this?) Certainly the consequences are that a lot of 'ancient misery' is being released. *Essentially what is happening is that our world is becoming increasingly transparent.* We can see much more clearly than in the past what is *really* going on. This means that we are less and less able to 'get away' with remaining in the dark, either as regards our own, or as regards our society's wounded face. The secrets are coming out. A new clarity is shining out of the confusion. Our old patterns of hatred, corruption, violence, abuse of power – everything about us that in the past used to keep our heartless culture alive and which, even a decade ago, used to be hidden – are now surfacing, coming out into the open, so that we can look them in the face. This is so important, for only if we can see and name our various dragons are we going to be able to *do something* about them.

In the same way that the irritation caused by the piece of grit caught inside the oyster shell has the potential of creating a reaction that may turn it into a pearl, so the irritation and suffering caused by the sheer amount of disorder spilling out all around us is similarly propelling many of us powerfully in the direction of wanting to open up the treasure chest inside our hearts so we may embrace the role of change agent more forcefully. Once we say a strong 'yes' to the path of Heart, we find that everything that we encounter in our lives, be it beautiful and loving or ugly and painful, becomes grist to the mill in our journey into our deeper humanity. 'Watch out,' Sant Keshavadas tells us, 'because God will come and He will put you on His anvil and fire up His forge and beat you and beat you until He turns brass into pure gold.' The Sufi poet Kabir understood this and therefore exhorted us to be grateful to 'those who make us return' (who challenge us to be more fully human). He told us to 'worry about the others who give you delicious comfort that keeps you from prayer', that is, who distract us from our path by creating situations that lull us to sleep once more! In his great classic *The Way of Transformation*, Karlfried von Dürckheim confirms this point when he suggests:

> *The man who, being really on the Way, falls upon hard times in the world, will not, as a consequence, turn to that friend who offers him*

comfort and refuge and so encourages his old self to survive. Rather, he will seek out someone who will faithfully and inexorably help him to risk himself, so that he may endure the suffering and pass courageously through it, thus making of it a 'raft that leads to the far shore'. Only to the extent that man exposes himself over and over again to annihilation, can that which is indestructible arise within him. In this lies the dignity of daring ... Only if we venture repeatedly through zones of annihilation can our contact with Divine Being, which is beyond annihilation, become firm and stable. The more a man learns wholeheartedly to confront the world that threatens him with isolation, the more are the depths of the ground of being revealed and the possibilities of new life and new becoming opened up.

If we substitute 'deeper heart' for 'Divine Being', we see that in these few words, the main challenge facing the activist is spelled out. Once we are on the initiatory path of Heart and the capabilities of our hearts begin to shine through, our relationship with the 'opposing forces' starts to shift radically. Whereas in the past, opposition may have felt like an enemy, now it begins to serve a deeper purpose, which is to help evolve our hearts' healing or reconciliatory capabilities. How can we become wise if there are no conflicts challenging us to deal with them in the right way, or how can we grow our courage if we never encounter anything that scares us? From a perspective of Heart, then, difficult encounters no longer take us away from ourselves, but rather help lead us more powerfully towards our core.

The two 'worlds' and the emergence of spiritual Heart fire

In *Shambhala: The Sacred Path of the Warrior*, Chögyam Trungpa Rinpoche talked of two states of consciousness: one which he called the consciousness of the Setting Sun, and the other the consciousness of the Great Eastern Sun. The consciousness of the Setting Sun is equivalent to the world of 'normal' (hard-hearted and flabby-minded) man who is not interested in change. It encapsulates everything about our world that no longer works and that needs to die, everything that is heartless, violent, shallow, plastic, insincere and destructive. The consciousness of the Great Eastern Sun, on the other hand, looks to a new, global culture where Heart will play a central role in determining things, a culture that celebrates justice and peace, and where we share and care for one another and honour those who are different to us, a world where there are no longer vast gaps between the haves and have-nots, and where, most importantly, we take care to 'launder our messes and respect our planet'. The Bulgarian spiritual master Peter Deunov put it like this:

> *We find ourselves at the end of the decline of one culture and the dawn of another which is rising, developing and rapidly imposing itself. From now on a radical transformation is progressively occurring in human consciousness – in our thoughts, feelings and actions as well as in the organisation of human society ... All earthly beings will be subjected to the great purification of the Divine Fire in order to become worthy of the new epoch. And the only thing to know now, is how to put oneself in harmony with this wave of new life which is descending on earth.*[2]

What Deunov was referring to is the awakening of the intelligent, alchemical fire that resides within our own hearts and within the heart of our society, its mission being to incinerate and then transmute everything inside us and inside our society that resists new life and which is embodied in the world of the Setting Sun. Deunov stresses the importance of our aligning ourselves with this 'new epoch', or the world of the Great Eastern Sun, because if we fail to do so – if we insist on remaining identified with our old selfish, separatist and heartless selves – it may mean that the 'whole of us', metaphorically speaking of course, eventually gets roasted! However, to the person wanting to evolve – wanting to work at opening their heart and aligning themselves to the emerging new life – this divine fire is a great asset, *as it only burns up their old emotional dross, which needs incinerating anyway.*

This sacred Heart fire does not behave like ordinary fire, which consumes everything in its path. On the contrary, it is eminently discerning and its aim is only to burn up or transmute the remnants of old life that *need* to die, because they have become anachronistic and thus their continued existence serves to threaten our capacity to move forward and survive as a species. Therefore, the more we choose to open our hearts to this divine fire by choosing to be an activist for change, the more we are aligning ourselves with the values of the world of the Great Eastern Sun, and the stronger and brighter our hearts will become.

As our hearts begin to awaken into their deeper universal nature, our humanity will correspondingly grow and deepen, and increasing numbers of us will be able to hold more and more of the external world inside our hearts. In this context, the philosopher David Spangler's perspective on the instability and confusion and general 'burning' going on around us is interesting:

> *Underneath the patterns of instability in the world, a profound spirit of love and goodwill is at work and is using the instability and the individuals that emerge from it as the farmer uses a plough, to turn the soil and prepare it for new seeds and new harvest.*

So, basically, in order for a new society to emerge, our old one needs to be ploughed up. In other words, all the confusion and chaos in the world today – all the 'ploughing up' that is occurring – is happening for an important purpose. Shortly before he died, one of my precious friends and mentors, Sir George Trevelyan, wrote something not dissimilar in a letter to me:

> *I have come to the conviction that the really major phenomenon in our time is not the violence and breakdown, but a* rising tide of love, *as a living force, released from God's source, to seep into and flood the planet.*

A stupendous thought. The metaphor is different but the meaning is the same. Underneath all the confusion and chaos and uncertainty, lies the spirit of Heart or the spiritual heart ('the rising tide of love' being another way of describing the universal heart). I find this both a comforting and an inspiring proposition. Deunov, Spangler and Trevelyan are all suggesting in their different ways that the chaos and craziness and violence we find everywhere is not because there isn't enough Heart around but because there is so much of it in the world today. Like the hot poultice that causes the poison inside the boil to erupt, so the abundance of Heart in the world is bringing to the surface all that is most heartless, so that we can see it and get to work with it. No matter how dark it gets, therefore, we must know that dawn is always near. *Our challenge is never to lose heart, never to forget the presence of the universal heart or this rising tide of love.*

From 'me' to 'we'

The scientist and futurist Elisabet Sartouris once suggested that these times are analogous to an era long ago, when life on our planet was just starting out, and when all that existed were very simple life forms: unicellular organisms.

Then along came a common enemy called oxygen, which began to threaten these life forms. The result was that the unicellular organisms, in order to survive, were forced to adapt, and what they did was to combine together and morph into a higher-order organism, a multi-cellular one. This new life form was not only able to resist oxygen but actually learned to thrive on it and, as a result, gave birth to a higher-order organism still, namely man. Thus, the so-called 'enemy to evolution' turned out to be its good friend.

Her hypothesis is that something not dissimilar is occurring on our planet today. She believes that the crises which we are all facing are not only having the effect of accelerating our evolution, but are also activating something new inside us and are driving us to team up more closely with each other, as increasingly we come to see that the problem with our world is our 'unicellularism' or our individualistic, selfish, nationalistic identities, which Einstein also saw as a disease and described as 'the measles of humanity'. Sartouris suggests that we are coming to recognise that as a species, we have remained incarcerated in this limited mindset for too long. Unless we make a shift of consciousness and learn to unite with each other in a new way, and come to realise our *'multividuality'* (my term) and recognise that we are all *world citizens* and that the consciousness we need to hold must be *universal*, we will not survive.

If we succeed in making this shift from a 'me' perception of the world to a 'we' one, then we not only succeed in 'becoming another' (the true purpose of initiation), but we also become what Michael White in *An Imaginal Journey of Peace* describes as an 'imaginal cell'.

From caterpillar to butterfly

White explains that when a caterpillar first begins its transformation, an entirely new kind of cell starts growing inside it, which scientists call an imaginal cell, and these new cells contain the blueprint for a new being that will start to emerge. Initially, as these new cells appear, they are attacked and resisted by the caterpillar ones. However, gradually, as they grow in strength, they begin to cluster together to form the first organs of the butterfly, a new entity, which then slowly comes into manifestation. Eventually, the old form dies and a new one is born from within the old.

White believes that this is what is happening on the planet today, and that *a new kind of human being is emerging in the world that is as different from the old kind as a butterfly is from a caterpillar.* Everything that I observe and feel inside my heart leads me to agree and to realise that if we wish to be effective activists, then we will need to work at becoming that new kind of human being. Only if sufficient numbers of us make this transition are we going to weather the many crises which our world faces at this moment.

What distinguishes butterfly or universal-hearted people from their caterpillar or 'normal' counterparts is the way they see the world and consequently operate in it. Essentially, their value systems are completely different. Butterfly man is concerned with becoming qualitatively richer as a human being and having his or her life make a difference, the aim being to work towards the creation of a more workable world for all. Caterpillar man, on the other hand, is more concerned with material wealth for himself and is largely uninterested in what happens out in the larger world, so long as he is unaffected. In a nutshell, butterfly man seeks to empower his fellow men, caterpillar man wants power over his fellow men; butterfly man is concerned with change and renewal, caterpillar man wants to maintain the status quo.

What excites me as I look around the world today is that I see butterflies springing up everywhere and that these new 'clusters', each centring around particular transformational initiatives, are growing in strength and significance. Some evolve around peace, others around love; some address the situation of our rainforests, others look at the problems around education, women's rights and so on. Later, we will be looking in detail at many of these new clusters.

Confronting resistance

The activist needs to understand that not every caterpillar is motivated to transform into a butterfly. As White points out, many caterpillar cells resist and may even attack the emerging new cells. This is not 'bad' but a fact of evolution. I observe two main forms of resistance: one takes the shape of a bland kind of indifference towards change, but doesn't particularly make any concerted effort to thwart it. The other is much more virulent, and as White suggests, will vigorously fight anyone or anything which in any way appears to stand for butterfly characteristics, viewing them as a huge threat.

We see this battle manifesting in many areas of life. In the domain of science, for example, the resistant or Setting Sun forces are evident in those educated in the old paradigm of scientific materialism, who believe we live in a 'dead universe'. These scientists often feel hugely threatened by their colleagues who believe we live in living and conscious one, and may sometimes go out of their way to discredit them. This led one Nobel Prize winner wryly to suggest that 'science only advances through the death of those who oppose new theories'!

Over the years, I have also had my fair share of 'run-ins' with caterpillar-like colleagues who believe that our profession ought to be solely about fixing personalities and that all spirituality is escapist, while the idea of parapsychology or our possibly having had past lives is simply a load of nonsense! In religion, the caterpillar forces may be encountered in all forms of fundamentalism, where people tend to be extremely resistant to anything other than their extremely rigid and narrow interpretation of their god. Sometimes these forces, which can often be self-righteous and, at worst, paranoid and brutal, may, if threatened, respond with violence. In Iran, those who dare to speak up against the authority of the 'Supreme Leader' are raped, imprisoned, tortured or murdered. This represents the resistant forces at their most fanatically evil.

What the activist always needs to bear in mind is that the essential ingredient behind all virulent resistance is fear – fear of change, fear of the unknown, fear of giving up power. While those who are more evolved can understand the mindset of those less evolved (butterflies remember what it was like to have been a caterpillar), the converse is not the case. There is a beautiful Hindu aphorism that illustrates this point: 'When the pickpocket meets the saint, all he sees are his pockets.'

Therefore, to the closed-hearted person, those with big, open hearts are often regarded as a threat and this lies behind why there can be a need to try to suppress them in some way. This is also why greater openness and freedom are so terrifying to regimes habituated to governing repressively. In China, for example, the ruling elite are terrified of democracy, as not only would they not know how to control it (they are habituated to a mindset of control), but it would also see the demise of their affluent and comfortable lifestyles, which they are loath to give up. As activists, then, we need to proceed out of the recognition that many areas of 'Setting Sun-hood' find the emergence of Great Eastern Sun values very threatening and may regard us, quite rightly, as representing the death knell of everything that they hold most dear and are most attached to.

TWO

Heart Work

Chapter 6

Eastern and Western Perspectives on Self-healing

If as a species we are to survive, a radical change of consciousness is required. Mankind has to wake up. Humanity needs to become more mature. This is not going to happen as a result of our adhering to the business-as-usual approach. It is going to take place as a result of a lot of work and effort being put in. If we wish for completeness, we must set the full force of our heart, mind and spirit in this direction –
A NOBEL LAUREATE

Working with the emotional heart

As we have just seen, we cannot be effective activists if we have flabby minds and small, troubled, calcified hearts, or, for that matter, hearts that are forever bleeding. In order to become most receptive to the rising tide of love and in order that we may begin making the transition out of our old caterpillar identities, we will need hearts that are physically, emotionally and mentally strong. Having the emotional component of our hearts in good working order is particularly important as so much of our fear of change may be put down to psychological wounds of one kind or another.

Having an integrated and solid heart requires, among other things, that we know what is going on inside it, and for this we need to be able to stand back and observe our thoughts and our feelings. This not only helps us to become aware of what some of the inner agendas are that drive us, but it also helps us become more honest. Many of us are ordinarily so habituated to repressing, suppressing or splitting off from our own innerness that we are wholly unaware of the many manipulative games which we can play. Carl Jung understood how detrimental this was to our emotional health:

If we understand anything of the unconscious, we know that it cannot be swallowed. We also know that it is dangerous to repress it because the unconscious is life, and this life turns against us if repressed ...

> as is the case in neurosis ... Consciousness and unconsciousness do not make a whole when either is repressed or damaged by the other. If they must contend, let it be a fair fight with equal rights on both sides. Both are aspects of life. Let consciousness defend its reason and its self-protective ways, and let the chaotic life of the unconscious be given a fair chance to have its own way.[1]

Another Jungian, Robert Johnson, put it this way:

> The unconscious is the real source of human creativity ... It is the place where the gods live, where our divinity dwells and where, if we are to be a full human being, we need to learn how to build the right kind of bridges linking it to our conscious realities.[2]

No matter what field we choose to operate in as activists, we will not be properly effective until we learn to build these bridges.

Finding the right kind of therapeutic support

In the interest of becoming a more aware and integrated person, some of us activists may need some external assistance in order to bring more of our Heart life out of the twilight zones which we have often condemned it to, especially if we are not familiar with the process of 'working on ourselves'. And yes, I admit I am prejudiced. I believe one of the best ways to receive this assistance is to see a psychotherapist. However – and this is a big however – not just any old psychotherapist. If we go to the wrong kind of person for help, that is, if we see a 'caterpillar', a fully fledged citizen of the world of the Setting Sun who may have little Heart themselves, we may find that their agenda is to try to help us become more normal – that is, to fit more effectively into a dysfunctional and heartless culture which, as activists, we are doing our best to transit out of. As this would totally defeat our ends, we need to be careful whom we see. Trying to elicit support from people who tend to view life through a reductive lens and who like putting people into boxes and labelling them as being their neuroses, instead of seeing us first and foremost as abundant human beings who may possess certain irregularities in need of some ironing out, is not going to help us heal or strengthen our enheartening muscles. On the contrary, it may do us a lot of harm.

If we wish to become more effective activists, we may need to go to a psychotherapist who works along the more holistic, transpersonal and 'heart-centred' lines that I and those of my colleagues who come from the same place as me try to operate from, where our aim is not simply to fix parts of people that we feel don't work properly, so much as to help them function more holistically and grow more fully into their humanity. The vast proportion of people who come to see me don't do so necessarily because their lives don't work. They come for assistance because they want their lives to function at a *higher* level – they want to live much more honestly and sustainably and Heart-fully, so that they can *be* more as a human being, as well as *feel* better.

This is important, because if, as activists, we wish to succeed in our work, we need to be as pure of heart as possible and crystal clear about our motives, otherwise, often with the very best of intentions, we can project our own internal contaminations, which we may be unaware of, into what we are trying to do, and thus totally thwart the goals that we are trying to accomplish. This is why it is important that we find someone to work with who values the world of Heart and who recognises that our emotional issues always need to be seen and worked with in the light of our spiritual awakening.

I was lucky in that, when I was young and starting out on my journey, one of the first people I worked with was a man who 'came from' this higher-Heart agenda and who therefore always saw me in the light of my 'core magnificence', which I believe is everyone's true core. As a result, I never felt small or put down in his presence. Of course, he saw where I had problems and recognised that, as a young man, I was immature, had a wounded heart, generally lacked confidence, was neurotic, self-centred and basically rather narcissistic, but he never saw me as just being all these things. He never held me fixated in a box labelled 'Serge's problems'. This was a huge gift as it freed me up to see that while I had many wounds – some pretty deep – *my wounds were not who I was*. Which, of course, is the truth for all of us.

Because this man's heart was big and bright, and mine in those days pretty small and dim, at the start of our work, he would, as it were, 'lend' me some of his Heart light to shine upon my particular issues. He continued to do this until my own heart's alchemical capabilities had sufficiently developed to 'kick in', thus enabling me to take over the work myself and bring my issues into my *own* transmuting furnace. I mention this point as many activists may work in areas where we need to do the same thing, and lend those we are trying to help some of our inner strengths, to assist them onto their feet.

In this context, it is important that we try to work with someone who we feel is at the right level for us. Just as it can be disastrous to work with someone who reduces us and won't allow us to move beyond the level that they are at, so it can also be detrimental if we work with a person who is too advanced and not able to come down to our level, and so may not understand where we are coming from. When I work with people, I like to operate from a place which embraces two very different, but in my view, highly complementary approaches to the psyche. One is the viewpoint offered by Buddhism, the other is from Western psychology. I believe that, depending upon what our hearts require for their healing or growth at any time, they will respond to whatever approach seems more relevant at the time. These two approaches may be used together or separately, depending upon a person's requirements.

Western perspectives on healing

Viewed from a Western perspective, there is always something 'wrong' with us and we are not 'OK' the way we are. This is because we are wounded and carry all sorts of scars inside our hearts, emanating, as we have just seen, from many different sources and conspiring to distort how we feel and see and function in the world. Just as in our garden we need to pull out the weeds from their very roots if they are not to grow again, so if we are to be healed, we will need to *investigate* what happened to damage us and try to work down through the various levels until we can connect to the very core of what it was that originally wounded us. If we are able to experience our core wound and so release it, then we are free.

However, this process takes time and most of us need to do this uncovering work gradually, as we may not be ready or able to reach our core wounds without a lot of prior digging. If we go about our investigation thoroughly, we may gradually reach further and further back into our past and may even start accessing our human collective origins and discover that we may also be carrying wounds relating to the universal heart.

A Buddhist perspective on healing

From a Buddhist perspective, the scenario is very different. It recognises that we are the way we are, and there is an 'OK-ness' about it. We don't need fixing; rather, we need to realise that one of the main reasons we suffer is that our attitudes are wrong. Because we don't live in a balanced way and because many of us have lost our organic connection to our planet, we operate out of the illusion that we are separate from it as we feel distanced from ourselves.

Another reason why we are unhappy is because we are always trying to engineer positive outcomes and avoid negative ones, and consequently we find it hard to be content with what we have. Either we desire what we do not have, or we believe that if only we had more, then we would be happy, an attitude that has created a very imbalanced world for ourselves. We also suffer because there is always an inherent clenchedness or contraction going on inside us which makes us loath to let go and trust life. This is not helped by our tending either to live in the past and so be looking back all the time, or always be thinking about the future. As a result, we find it hard to exist in present time, which in fact is the only place where we can feel present, powerful and real. All these things help keep our hearts small and contracted.

What we learn from the East is that in order to be healed (and so have a space open up inside us for our butterfly nature to unfurl), we must learn to unclench and become more accepting of the way we are and the way life is unfolding for us at any time. We also need to extricate ourselves from the many tight conceptual boxes into which our beliefs about who we think we are and what we think will make us happy may have locked us into, and realise that who we truly are has very little to do with the ideas we may have about ourselves. If we can do this work, our hearts will come more and more to the fore and our minds will lose a lot of their flab or rigidity.

We also need to learn that change is the only constant and to let go our attachment to wanting things to remain the way that they were, instead being prepared to go much more with the flow. The aim is to focus less on goals and more on smelling the roses along the way. What from a Buddhist perspective most derails us is not so much the wounds in our hearts as the 'us' that is behind how we see everything and therefore determines how we operate. In other words, *it is our minds that are the problem* and that are out of kilter, and it is because of their imbalance that our hearts close down. Because our minds are always restless, we do not know how to feel calm and so are continually projecting our restlessness outside ourselves. Thus, we are forever creating a disturbed world for ourselves.

If only we could learn to quieten ourselves, our minds would become less frenzied and a space would open up inside us that would enable us to live much more from our hearts, which in turn would allow us to feel much more peaceful and contented. This would make it much easier to access the many treasures inside our hearts. From a Buddhist perspective, then, we heal ourselves and start awakening our butterfly selves by learning to live in a more detached, balanced and whole way, which emerges, among other things, out of our not making ourselves wrong for not being as perfect as we might like to be. The more we learn to be 'in the now' – which enables us to go more deeply into the core 'what-is-ness' of each moment – the more we will be able to savour the magic of life and connect to our truth. If, in addition, we can also learn to speak, think and act according to Buddha's Noble Middle Way, we will be a force for enlightenment in the world and this will bring deep satisfaction.

Here, therefore, our aim is not so much to dig deep but to become more *insightful*. As our minds grow more still, this capacity gradually develops. So while the Western way puts more emphasis on having goals and achieving things, and is therefore more activity related, the Eastern way is more focused on being and is more contemplatively oriented.

What approaches do people need?

What I have found in working with people is that many of us are lacking from both perspectives and may need assistance from both healing arenas. If certain heart wounds are very deep – and we may not realise this until we start exploring – it is unlikely that they are going to be accessed by a Buddhist approach alone, and will probably need to be reached via a digging Western therapeutic approach. Sometimes a person may be in too much pain to be open to any of the many gems that the Buddha has on offer and so the release of their pain needs to be the initial prime objective.

However, one can also overdo the investigative work, with the result that our hearts are continually being aroused and stimulated when what is actually required for their healing is that they find greater equanimity. My experience is that some of us have hearts that will heal better if initially worked with from an Eastern perspective, while others of us will initially benefit more from a Western approach. If we are a workaholic, there is much we can learn from the Buddha. If we are a dozy kind of person, we will probably benefit from Western psychology.

Integration around a higher-order Heart centre

As I hope is by now becoming clear, the name of the 'awakening-the-heart' game for the spiritual activist is the very opposite of our trying to become more normal. On the contrary, our normality, our caterpillar-ness, is the problem; it is what has conspired to get us into all the messes which we are in today. Most of our wars, most of our social, economic and political imbalances may be laid at the hands of normal people engaging in life in their normal unconscious ways. What is needed is for the activist to learn to operate from a very different reference point, one that has more Heart in it and that is more conscious.

Let me explain exactly what I mean. Whether or not we know it, all our lives centre around a particular core set of values, assumptions and beliefs which determine how we see ourselves and the world and how we generally operate in it. Depending upon where we are coming from, we believe certain things to be important and other things peripheral. For example, for 'normal, Western, caterpillar-inclined man', status, wealth, personal success and power are high up on his agenda of what he considers significant. What he is primarily concerned with – and what he organises most of his life around – is his personal life and how it can be arranged most conveniently for him. As a result, most of his energies tend to be 'invested' in different ways of enhancing it. Therefore, helping his fellow human beings (unless there is something in it for him) generally tends not to be very high up on his priority list.

It is not that, as activists, we should not be concerned with advancing our personal lives. On the contrary, our personal lives are very important. However, if there is no input in how we do this from what I will call a 'higher source' or from Heart, that is, if there is not a single flutter of butterfly-ness wafting into the way we go about organising ourselves, then often we can end up arranging our personal lives at the expense of other people's. Indeed, if we look at what is most 'wrong' with our society, we see that it is full of people and institutions and governments organising their affairs in ways that take little account of what is in the best interest of the whole and, in many instances, in ways that prove quite detrimental to it.

Why moving into a place of becoming Heart centred, which occurs as our hearts start opening wider and begin assuming a more significant role in our lives, is so important is because it radically alters our priorities. It expands them. As I just said, it is not that we cease being concerned with our personal lives; it is simply that we don't do so at the expense of other people's personal lives. Indeed, the more our hearts open, and the more receptive we become to the universal heart, the more we start inclining our personal activities to what we also deem to be of benefit to our neighbours and to society as a whole, and the less relevant it becomes whether or not we 'look good' in other people's eyes or whether we are well known or regarded as being successful. What now becomes central is the desire to feel we are making a concrete positive difference to our society in some way. This is why, as activists, it is so important that we make this level shift and have our values constellated around the agendas of our hearts as opposed to those of our egos.

The ego issue

That said, I need to say a few words in defence of the ego, as in many 'spiritual circles', it has a very bad press and is regarded – wrongly, I believe – very much as the big bad wolf. Many Eastern masters, for example, only regard the impersonal aspect of ourselves as being of significance, and consequently, place little importance on our personal lives. All the ills of the world, they tell us, are down to our putting energy into our personal lives, which are equated with 'evil ego'. If we want to be a spiritual person – someone with Heart and substance – they tell us, then ego either has to be killed off or transcended. Only then, when we are 'totally egoless' and 'impersonal', may we be a full human being and create a better world!

I disagree with this theory. I believe each of us has both an impersonal self which wishes to serve and be altruistic, and a personal self that also needs to be fulfilled, and that both dimensions need acknowledging and integrating in the light of each other. And the successful activist is the one who manages to do this. If we try, in the name of some pseudo-idea of spirituality, to suppress or sacrifice our personal self, we will inevitably be unhappy, and this unhappiness will impinge upon our capacity to evolve our Heart life and thus upon our ability to be effective in the work we are trying to do. *The truth is that all of us serve best when our hearts feel full.* Thus, I do not believe we should vilify ego, but rather, come to understand more about it. The problem with trying to kill it off, as some believe we should do, is that it is an impossible task, and we simply make it into an enemy and end up being constantly at war with a part of ourselves that is extremely canny and can be a formidable opponent, able to worm its way into almost anything – even into our most sincere endeavours.

Similarly, the idea that if we just ignore our egos and focus on 'higher thoughts', this will make ego go away, is also an illusion. The spiritual teacher A. H. Almaas made this very clear:

> *My perception of what happens with people who claim to have lost their personality totally and spontaneously is that there often remains a split-off or repressed part which will manifest as a distortion or a lack of integration ... If the personality is abandoned rather than integrated, the totality of life cannot be lived.*[3]

The need for ego integration

This is the key point. *Our egos or our personalities need to be integrated*, not attacked, ignored or transcended, and our hearts are very good at this integrative work if we only allow them to do it. If integration occurs, our ego can then take its orders from the *real* boss or master, which is our heart, and stop believing it should 'run the show', as it lacks the wisdom to do so properly. Having ego dictate our lives is like putting the firm's janitor into the CEO's seat and expecting him to run the business. He is not qualified. His job is to ensure that the doors are all locked up at night, not to know how the firm should be run, and the problem with our world today is that there are far too many 'janitors' in top positions running the show – in business, in government, in the armed forces, in the media and so on. This is why so many bad mistakes continue to be made.

Why this is so – and this is my key point – is because many of us have not yet evolved the parts of ourselves that exist beyond the ego, that is, we have not even started to shift from being a caterpillar (ego centred) to a butterfly (heart centred). The problem is that caterpillar-ness predominates in our Setting Sun culture, which is primarily organised around these values. And *this* is what is most threatening our planet; *this* is what lies behind the state of emergency that it is in – why we consume too much energy, fight wars, don't help each other enough, why we make so many key mistakes all the time. The truth is that ego-centred man lacks the right kind of intelligence. He may be clever, yes (egos are sharp), but he is not wise or compassionate and he does not have a sufficiently expanded vision of the direction which the world needs to go in. This is why we are in crisis and why a radical transformation is called for and called for quickly.

The problem of the unhealthy ego

But the answer is not to hate ego or fight it. *The answer is to work with it to make it healthier*, as the real problem is not ego per se. *The real problem is the wounded ego.* Many of us have unhealthy, wounded or insubstantial egos, and *this is where the danger lies*. Our Setting Sun society is so structured that having a wounded or damaged ego can often work in our favour and, as is well known, many people in positions of authority in business and government have big wounded egos. A recent report, for example, showed that a significant number of CEOs of large public companies possess psychopathic tendencies. A few years ago, I came across an advertisement for a position in a large Swiss bank. It specifically asked for 'a young wolf'! Is it any wonder, with all these predatory young people in positions of power, that our financial institutions are in disarray?

What I am suggesting is that if our personality 'us' or our 'egoic us' can be respected and worked with and effectively integrated into our lives, then this part of us can start to heal and so begin to evolve and become healthier. And a healthy ego behaves very, very differently from an unhealthy one. A healthy ego is not insecure. It is much more likely to surrender the reins of power as it has no need to want to control the show, as it is starting to become infused with the fire inside our hearts that is transforming and refining it. Our inner alchemical machine is beginning to work its magic.

Bridge-building and developing a healthy ego

If we wish to become an effective spiritual activist, we will need to work towards evolving a healthy ego that is content to be our servant – that is, one that 'knows its place' as opposed to being our 'master' and trying to dominate and control our lives. When this starts to come about, it is the *totality* of who we are – soul, heart, mind and ego all working together – that makes key business decisions, decides the most appropriate course of action at any time and knows how best we can be of service to society. This healthy, subservient ego, increasingly becoming aligned with and eager to do the bidding of our hearts, is a completely different creature from the wounded ego, which views the heart as its enemy, always feels insecure, believes it always knows best, and tries to control everything all the time. The wounded ego is terrified of change because, being devoid of vision, it knows it will be pushed out of the driving seat and it has no sense of anything beyond this. This is also why so many ego-damaged people experience such resistance to the idea of a 'culture of Heart'.

Creating a healthy society with ego in the right place

At one level, the struggle out in the world between those trying to work towards a freer, more heart-centred society and those wishing to stay rooted in the old conservative norms and resist change is yet another version of the conflict between the heart and the wounded ego. I must make it clear, however, that just because, as activists, we stand for change does not mean we are trying to eliminate or wage war on our old world. We don't want to destroy our past, or our old culture, just as we don't want to destroy our ego. *Rather, our challenge is to find ways and means of building bridges that will link our old, ego-centred society to a more heart-centred one, so that Heart energy or Great Eastern Sun energy has a means of flowing into our societal wounds and start healing them.* All change agents who, in their different ways, are doing their best to represent the next step of our human and global evolution therefore serve as bridges allowing the new consciousness to flow into the old patterns and thus enable them to transform. Creating a better and healthier world is not about hating or trying to kill off the old order; *it is about allowing the old order to be 'raised up into 'the light' by a new and more heart-centred reality.*

We may see our egos as akin to a kind of scaffolding that we initially erect around ourselves in order to give us some solidity or structure which will enable us later on to build 'higher storeys' to our being – that is, evolve new dimensions of ourselves, grow into our butterfly-ness. If we try to kick away the scaffolding prematurely, it may be disastrous, as we may not be strong enough or have enough structure to support our newly emerging butterfly-self as it tries to emerge. In Ram Dass's words, 'we need to become a somebody [have a strong, healthy ego self] before we can be a nobody [let our egos go and make them subservient]'. When our old structure is ready to dissolve, it will do so in its own way and in its own time, and the same thing holds true for our society. What we see taking place out in the world around us today is also occurring inside us. There is an old Hindu saying: 'When the fruit is ripe, it will fall from the tree.'

Spiritual people are not egoless

My experience of most good, wholesome, heart-centred people who bring solid Heart qualities into the world is that they in no way lack ego or personality. Even a fully enlightened human being is not devoid of ego. Rather, they are someone whose ego is completely and utterly subservient and so totally aligned to the divine purpose flowing through them that it seems as if it is not there, in the way that a good servant has been described as someone who is totally present, yet utterly invisible.

Becoming a good activist is all about our having an ego that is healthy and therefore content to do its 'janitorial work' without any need to try to run the show. The biblical story where Jesus was tempted by Satan (his ego) to climb to the top of the mountain and show off his great powers, so that everyone could then bow down in awe of him, is a beautiful analogy of how to deal with ego. Jesus's reply to Satan was not to tell him to 'get lost' but to 'get thee behind me', that is, be in the subservient place where our egos need to be. Jung understood this. 'The creative urge', he told us, 'comes from sources both light and muddy.' Put simply, the process of creativity is one which involves both our hearts and our egos and if we are to be successful, they need to work in collaboration just like our conscious and our unconscious selves.

For instance, in the writing of this book, both my personal and my impersonal self are involved. If, without judgement, I can recognise my ego, and if, seeing it attempt to raise itself 'beyond its station', I can intervene to clip its wings, then I can ensure that it doesn't get in the way of how and what I write, and that this book doesn't turn out to be some horrendous glorification of myself! Nonetheless, I need to watch out. We all need to watch out. All too often, we think our egos have gone to sleep and hey presto, they suddenly emerge strongly again and in the unlikeliest of places. The gift they offer us is that they demand that we be watchful at all times.

Chapter 7

Investigating Ego Wounds

The cure for the pain is in the pain. Good and bad are mixed. If you don't have both, you don't belong with us – RAINER MARIA RILKE

Going on is going back! – LAO TZU

If we are to move forward with our lives, we will need to address those areas of our personalities or our ego identities which, for the reasons we have already explored, have been damaged.

If we have particular phobias or illogical fears, if authority figures fill us with dread, or if we are extremely suspicious all the time, or self-centred and narcissistic and believe the whole world should revolve around us, or conversely, if we are a 'borderline personality' or are so lacking in confidence that we are forever trying to please people and give away our power, it follows that however desirous we may be to do good in the world, our psychological wounds will seriously handicap us. There is great truth in that old cliché about the road to hell being paved with good intentions, and many of the problems in the world are often made considerably worse by their being addressed by people who in no way have become the change they would like to see happen and therefore are incapable of bringing about appropriate resolutions. What keeps many of us fixated in our caterpillar-ness is our wounded egos. In this chapter, therefore, we will look at a few ways that we can start addressing them.

The listening heart

One good way to embark on our healing journey is to tell our story – talk about how we are feeling and what may be disturbing us. The efficacy of this is beautifully revealed in Coleridge's ballad *The Rime of the Ancient Mariner*, which is about a sailor who one day shot an albatross and felt cursed as a result. Terrible things happened to everyone on board his ship and everyone but that sailor died. He felt the huge burden of what he had done; it was as if the dead bird was hanging around his neck. In the poem, what eventually liberated him was not merely the act of telling his story – which he needed to do over and over again – but most importantly, pouring it out to someone who *listened* to it with their heart, which meant that they took his words deep into that place inside themselves that is able to heal. It is important to remember this. If we want to heal ourselves, we may need to find someone who is adept at listening to us, and if we are concerned with trying to heal other people's hearts, we may be called on to develop our own listening skills.

There is a difference between hearing and listening. When we listen, we go beyond simply registering the words being spoken. Instead, we try to intuit the subtler messages being conveyed to us – that is, the deeper meaning behind the words – as well as offering our own transmuting skills, openness and compassion. If we listen to someone in this way, it is always healing for them, since it is their entire being that we are embracing.

Therefore the quality of the person we are telling our story to, or the degree of their wakefulness, is as important a factor in our healing as the process of our telling it. This is again why it can be so counterproductive if we try to 'pour our heart out' to someone who cannot receive it because they are only hearing us with their clever and generally critical ego-mind. Not only may they possibly not understand our message at the necessary depths, but we probably won't receive any healing, since ego, even if not wounded, is inherently limited in what it can give. Being listened to by someone with an open heart, however, can dissolve all sorts of unpleasant energies that we might be carrying. Even curses. And many of us carry them, often quite unbeknownst to us.

Being cursed

The Ancient Mariner, therefore, was not unique. Even if we have never done anything vicious or nasty ourselves, we can still carry curses, which often limpet themselves directly to our hearts. Generally, they reveal their presence through our feeling blocked or heavy. Curses come in all shapes and sizes and can be shallow or deep, unintentional or intentional. At their worst, they can severely handicap us emotionally and spiritually and make us feel great shame, humiliation and terror, often without our having the slightest understanding why we are feeling this way.

To give a simple example of an unintentional curse, I once worked with a woman who had had to grow up in the toxic and mean-spirited environment of parents who had never really wanted a child. They therefore subtly resented her presence and were never a true listening or loving space for her. Of course, they never voiced this as such, and she never realised this consciously. But unconsciously, as she was growing up, she picked up the feeling of being unwanted, of being a burden, and that her parents were angry at her existence. This woman therefore grew up internalising all these thoughts, always feeling that there must be something deeply wrong with *her* for not being wanted, and believing that the whole world must see her as her parents did. She was a lovely person, basically with a good heart, but it was never able to have the confidence to open and shine as it was coated over with so much shame about being alive.

This curse infected every area of her life, especially her work and her relationships, as wherever she went, she carried a kind of invisible placard around her neck constantly broadcasting her sense of insufficiency out to the world. And of course people picked up on it, even if very subtly, and treated her accordingly. As a result, she would find herself overcompensating all the time, always doing things for others – never allowing herself to feel she deserved to receive anything in return. 'I cannot carry on,' she once confessed to me. 'I am always giving out. My heart feels so desperately sad and unnourished' – which of course it was. She needed to recognise the mean side of her parents, which out of loyalty she had never let herself do, and as she did so, she had to release a lot of indignation and rage, which she had been carrying all her life. Gradually, she began to see things much more clearly and recognised that it was her parents who were deficient and not her. The more this insight dawned, the more she was able to let go of the curse, which finally culminated in her feeling moved to work at forgiving them.

A new space then began opening up inside her that allowed a lot of fresh Heart energy to start flowing through her and fill up those old empty places. As this occurred, she felt warmer and happier and many things in her life which had previously felt burdensome now became easier. Because she was now allowing herself to receive, she was able to give of her many gifts much more to life. She also felt free enough to take up certain Buddhist practices, which further helped her heart to continue to loosen up and her ego to continue to heal.

Some curses take the form of negative thoughts being intentionally directed towards us by people who bear us malice. As at one level, thoughts are very tangible 'things', and this can often cause much damage. How badly we will be affected has to do both with the power of the person sending the negative thoughts and our own susceptibilities. There are two main ways to let go of intentional curses. We can either work our issues through with a heart-centred psychotherapist, or we can get a shaman or healer to help us who specialises in cutting the ties that bind us to the one cursing us. This is important work. If we wish to be a successful activist, it is vital that we be able to operate out of a curse-free zone.

Psychic mines

There are people who carry powerful memory patterns connected with pain, loss and violence. These are different from curses as they haven't been 'put' into us per se; rather, they will have crystallised inside us as a result of our having been exposed to painful experiences or unpleasant environments. I call them 'psychic mines', because the memories remain buried and unseen for a long time and 'explode' into our field of awareness only when we happen to 'tread on them', that is, when we encounter a situation in our lives reminiscent of our original painful experience and which therefore serves to trigger it.

Psychic mines make us vulnerable for two main reasons: firstly because we often find ourselves trying to avoid situations which might activate them, leading us to limit the scope of our activities, and secondly because, when activated, all hell can break loose. Not only do we experience the force of the current upsetting situation, but the original trauma or traumas also get evoked and so we may be confronted with multi-levelled 'whammies'. If we are trying to be effective activists, which demands that our hearts be free and clear, unexploded psychic mines can be extremely burdensome.

I once worked with a woman whom I had promised some information, but when we next met, I had inadvertently left the necessary information behind. When I innocently explained this to her, this ordinarily placid person exploded at me with a ferocity that I felt was totally over the top. Her reaction became explicable when I discovered that old memories around her relationship with her father had been triggered. When she had been a little child, he was continually promising her things and then reneging on his commitments. This had happened to her countless times, and as there had been no place for her to voice her anger and disappointment, she had buried it. I therefore temporarily became her 'bad daddy'. My forgetfulness had reignited the old memory. As it turned out, what had occurred was positive because once the mine had exploded, we could both see it and it gave us the opportunity to work at repairing the damage.

Many of us carry several psychic mines inside our hearts, some with a lot of explosive material in them, others with less. They can often make us feel very vulnerable because they colour our perception of the world. In my own case, because I had a mother who was emotionally distant, and who was also always having to leave me to accompany my father on his business trips, I would often overreact around women I was involved with, if I felt they were not paying me sufficient attention. I would feel they were deserting me, when in fact they were simply attending to other tasks. Of course, my rage was not against them, but against my dear mama. This psychic mine has hugely diminished in intensity over the years as a result of my doing a lot of work around it. Now, if it does ever explode, it only has the force of a very damp squib.

Awareness of the wounded inner child

Another obstacle often preventing us from connecting to our hearts is the existence of the child inside us (known as our 'inner child') who has been wounded in some way. A large number of our damaged-ego issues relate to the wounded inner child. One of its manifestations is that it makes us emotionally child*ish* and may prevent us from ever being child*like* – from experiencing joy and spontaneity – thus making it much harder to connect to the core abundance of life. Generally speaking, the earlier in our lives the damage was done, the more seriously our inner child will be scarred.

Often, we remain frozen into perceiving the world as we did when the original wounding took place. So while mentally we may have evolved and moved on, emotionally we continue to remain immature, and one of the big problems today is that many people in key positions of power are wounded in this way, resulting in colossal mistakes sometimes being made. Many psycho-historians who analyse the speeches of many war leaders and generals often find their language to indicate that they experienced extremely traumatic births, thus programming them to believe that the world 'out there' is a hostile place full of enemies. This stunting to our emotional development tends to keep us fixated in our caterpillar selves and plays a key role in holding our old Setting Sun culture in place.

If the wounding is very severe and if it occurred when we were very young, the heart of our inner child may close down completely, resulting in our being totally cut off from our core, which in turn may debar us from having any feelings at all. Many tyrants have hearts frozen in this way, which is why they often subconsciously try to engineer it that their subjects undergo traumatic experiences similar to those that befell them.

Working with the wounded inner child

I try to work with people's wounded inner child as tenderly and as gently as I am able. Very often a situation in a person's current life will come up that upsets them, and I may ask them if the way they feel has any echoes or holds any memories of how they used to feel as a child. Sometimes a specific traumatic incident may emerge. If so, I request that the person connects to their feelings around the incident and brings them up into their heart so that they may experience them as deeply as possible. I then ask people to do things such as visualise themselves walking hand in hand along a beach with their inner child or taking it into their arms and telling them they love it. All these things assist in its reintegration.

Generally this kind of work takes time. Many people carry a lot of shame in their hearts and this never goes away overnight. If, however, we persevere and begin to accept and love and include our inner child in more and more of our everyday activities, we will soon begin to reap huge benefits, such as a greater ability to enjoy life, to feel lighter and be more spontaneous. I cannot stress enough the therapeutic importance of allowing ourselves time to play and do things which we find fun. If we are lucky enough to have children of our own, we can allow ourselves to learn from them. I acknowledge that the presence of my daughter has done much to heal my own inner child.

Working with negative belief systems

How the world appears to us, and how we operate in it, is greatly determined by how we believe it to be. If we have inherited limited or negative beliefs about life, they may be deeply etched into our psyches and will therefore exert a big influence upon the way we live. Because normal man tends to be so 'unconscious', many of his core beliefs are also unconscious and many of us, therefore, are continually being propelled along by agendas whose existence we have very little inkling of. Our beliefs, however, even if unconscious, nonetheless determine the kind of world and therefore the kind of culture that we create for ourselves.

If millions of us have a pessimistic view of life and, for example, believe that it is 'nasty, brutish and short' or that war is inevitable or starvation unavoidable, or that we don't need Heart to live a fulfilled life, or that having a lot of money is the most important ideal to work towards, then these will be the realities that we will value and create for ourselves and therefore create around us. What also happens is that we become attached to our beliefs and will identify ourselves with them. This is why in extreme cases, we will even die for them, which is what happens, of course, in religious wars.

An integral part of my work with activists in training is to help them become increasingly aware of what they believe and to support them to explore the possibility of changing those beliefs which are not aligned to the vision of their hearts. This work may be seen as a process of 'raising' our ego personalities up into the light so that they may become more radiant and refined – more transparent – in the process of which, our 'rough edges' gradually get hewn away or melted down by the alchemical fiery furnace inside our hearts.

Chapter 8

Healing the Universal Heart

Overcome any bitterness because you were not up to the magnitude of the pain entrusted to you. Like the mother of the world, you are carrying the pain of the world in your heart – SUFI TEXT

It is as though each of us is born with a portion of the unfinished business of humanity at large, which it is our personal and karmic responsibility to complete in one way or another – ROGER WOOLGER

Carrying species wounds

If, despite having done investigative work along the lines we have just seen, certain blockages in our hearts *still* do not seem to resolve themselves, and certain issues *still* continue to be problematic, it may be indicative that unexorcised ghosts are still lurking inside the deeper echelons of our hearts and are continuing to haunt and trouble us. This may mean that the direction of our inner work calls us to journey more deeply into our wounded hearts and that we consider moving beyond our old autobiographical realities. It may well be that our own individual heart scars flow into where humanity's heart is wounded, and that we are now being called to address a particular area of the wounded side of the universal heart that we happen to be carrying. The Vietnamese Buddhist monk Thích Nhat Hanh put the issue very clearly:

> *The kind of suffering you carry in your heart, that is society itself. You bring that with you; you bring all of us with you. You seek solutions to your problems not only for yourself but for all of us.*[1]

His words echo what Chris Bache says:

> *Each of us carries within us the collective diseases of our time. If our society is ill, each of us has a share in its illness, some more than*

others, perhaps, but we are all implicated in varying degrees ... Thus if our society is racist, sexist, violent, consumed by greed, these diseases live in the collective soul. Just as a disease that lives in a physical body may manifest itself by attaching to one particular organ, so a disease of our collective soul may manifest itself disproportionately in the lives of specific individuals.[2]

Implications of species wounding

These words resonate with me. I have always had a sense that there are certain areas of my life which give me pain and where I always seem to struggle, and yet they do not seem to relate to any particular wounding that I have ever experienced in this life. Rather, it feels as if these problematic areas have been purposely 'assigned' to me, as if my deeper heart is saying to me: 'Serge, there are particular portions of the collective human wounding which are your bequests, which are uniquely assigned to you in this life to work through and to try to heal and transform. If you can make some headway, you will be playing your little part in taking some of the charge out of the larger collective wound that you are working with, and as a result, everyone also troubled by those issues will be assisted.'

For just as each of our individual hearts is connected into the species or universal heart, and therefore the more we are able to resolve certain issues in our personal lives, the more we help heal the scarring inside that larger heart, it equally follows that the more we take on and work with issues relating to the species heart (as, for example, happened to me at Princess Diana's death), the more we also bring relief to ourselves personally. One of humanity's big problems is that we continue to act out particular destructive patterns over and over and over again. I do not believe this is because we do not learn from our past, so much as that we will always have a compulsion to repeat it until we heal it or lay it to rest. Just as this holds true for us as individuals, so it also applies at a species level. I think a lot of healing of the deep wounds inside our species heart is being called for today, and that this is the task facing certain activists. I recently came across the following poem by Thích Nhat Hanh:

*I am the child in Uganda, all skin and bones,
my legs as thin as bamboo sticks.
And I am the arms merchant, selling*

deadly weapons to Uganda.
I am the twelve-year-old girl, refugee …
who throws herself into the ocean after
being raped by a sea pirate,
and I am the pirate, my heart not yet capable
of seeing and loving.[3]

The question to ask ourselves is this: does he understand what it is to be these different people because he is connected to the universal heart, which therefore enables him to feel all aspects of world man and world woman existing inside him? Or is it because these are actual characters or are close to actual characters from actual past lives of his and so he holds the specific memories of having actually been a violator and someone who has been violated? Perhaps there may be truth to both perspectives.

Opening to past lives

My very dear, recently deceased friend, Roger Woolger, believed that many of our unusual memories as well as many of our personal troubles come from issues unresolved in our past lives, and that at certain moments, particular memories 'bleed through' into our current existence. He felt that each of us have had many, many prior incarnations, 'coming back' as both men and women. On examining the source of his own depression, he concluded that it had nothing to do with his early childhood or birth. Rather, he sensed that it was 'something I came in with'. He believed that many of our current phobias, such as eating disorders or neurotic fears relating to our material survival, are due to our carrying memories of lives lived as a beggar or an orphan, or that many people's underlying greed and the feeling that however much money they have is not enough relates to their having lived through periods of famine and depression in other lives, often dying with a deep feeling of misery and anger.[4] Could this, I ask myself, be one of the problems afflicting some of our greedy bankers today?

Roger's belief was that unless these old memories are regurgitated and relived, with the core traumas being fully experienced and worked through, they will simply continue to be enacted out. In other words, so long as these memories still reside in a frozen state inside us, they will continue to predispose us towards particular behaviours and inclinations. He believed that what underlies a lot of reckless teenage behaviour – drunken driving, drug-taking, playing with weapons etc. – is memories of dying young and ingloriously on battlefields and never completing the initiation into true adulthood, and that trying to help such people simply by exploring with them what happened in their childhood will, for the most part, be ineffective. In his words: 'They are either unconsciously rerunning old battlefield deaths with a deep residual devil-may-care attitude born of despair and defiance, or else they are trying to prove themselves unconsciously to elders they failed in past lives.'

Roger cites the case of a woman who 'remembered being a tribal chieftain who had failed to find food for his people during a famine and died feeling intensely sad and guilty'. In this life the woman finds herself almost obsessively concerned with the marketing of food and with questions of economics. Seen from this perspective, it may be that no matter what is done at a conscious level to introduce more Heart-ful and soulful patterns into our culture, so long as this 'ancient pain' is not worked through, there will always be limits to how much some of us can stop ourselves being materialistic or greedy.

Having trained with Roger and having myself become a past-life psychotherapist, a large part of me finds this thesis compelling. Like Roger, I have uncovered certain patterns inside me that have seemed to have nothing whatsoever to do with anything that ever happened to me in this life, and like him, I found that they did not respond to conventional biographically oriented psychotherapy, yet they *did* respond very powerfully to past-life psychotherapy.

Personal deep memory

While by nature I have always been a bit of a maverick, for years I was afraid of revealing my true colours – showing what I really thought about things. There was always a lingering fear that I must be a 'good boy' and not upset anyone, and as a result, for many years, I felt predisposed to be something of a 'people pleaser'. I learned not to say certain things if I felt there might be disagreement and people might not like me for it. Being in the presence of powerful establishment figures especially used to scare me, and often I would hypocritically pretend that I shared their values so that they would not find me odd!

This conflict, needless to say, prevented me from getting a lot of my work out, and so creatively I often felt frustrated. Once asked to give a keynote lecture at an important conference, and longing to cover certain controversial ideas I was working with, I exhibited many of the stammering symptoms that plagued George VI in the film *The King's Speech*. Initially, I put my fears down to having been bullied by my father, together with a fear of displeasing my mother. Certainly, some progress was made as I addressed these issues via biographically oriented psychotherapy. But still something didn't shift: whenever situations emerged that required me to proclaim myself in some way – to speak my truth – I always seemed to back down. When I took this issue into my work with Roger, the following scenario unfurled for me:

> *It was some time in the Middle Ages. I was some kind of unconventional preacher. I saw the lies of the existing Church and how priests told everyone that the only way to God was through them, and how they did this in order to receive money. I felt this was evil. I also saw the hypocrisy of the Church and how its leaders lived extravagant lives, while the masses starved, and I was always speaking up against this. I used to rally large crowds around me. Then one night, soldiers surrounded my house, rushed into my room, grabbed me and took me away. I knew something terrible was going to happen, and I remember the sorrow I felt as I looked at the despairing and terrified expressions on the faces of my family, as I was violently dragged away from them, never to see them again.*

As we worked on this issue, what began unfolding was a scenario in which I experienced myself actually being hanged, drawn and quartered. Previously, I had heard that this was some medieval torture, but I did not know what it actually entailed. In the course of our work, however, I actually *experienced* my body being torn apart, as I was tied to horses which then were whipped and ran off in different directions. I screamed and screamed. Just as I came close to my death, I vowed always to be a 'good boy, and toe the line and never to speak out again'. Roger worked very subtly with me to help me release the memory, and it was as if a heavy stone that had always resided inside my heart suddenly fell away. While change did not happen overnight, as it took some time for me to consent to give up my old timidity, I gradually began to experience more ease of being and felt increasingly able to speak my truth without worrying about displeasing people.

A case history of a client

Several years ago, a young woman came to see me. The first thing she told me was that she had been raped on two occasions as a teenager. Naturally, she had huge issues around men, whom she saw as being little else but rapacious beasts. While she longed to be married and have children, the idea of emotional and sexual intimacy absolutely terrified her. When she first came to me, her heart was tightly boarded up. It was as if there was a sign there saying: 'No entry whoever you are, and most especially if you are a man.' She looked at me with great suspicion and resentment, as if I was yet another of those who would try to take advantage of her.

For a long time, we needed to stay with quite superficial issues until some degree of trust had built up. I knew that if I tried to initiate any deeper exploration it would frighten her off, so we worked very slowly, and for a long time our main focus was on her non-relationship with her cold and distant father. Gradually, she felt safe to bring more of herself out of the closet, and we began to look at her many biographical issues in greater depth. She was able to scream out a lot of the rage against the men who had taken advantage of her. A lot of shame and guilt and a sense of worthlessness got released, but she still couldn't seem to move forward. When she encountered men, there still remained an emotional charge, even if it was a trifle less strong. Something still seemed very unresolved, and she began accusing me of raping her financially – taking her money, yet not helping her feel any freer.

She was about to terminate our work when, in a particular session, quite spontaneously, and with no intent to go for any deeper memory, she unearthed a story of having been carried away as a spoil of war and then being gang-raped by Viking marauders, who, after they had finished with her, threw her into the sea. She had had to experience not only trauma but also death, and discovered she carried a memory connecting sex with death. No wonder it had been such an issue for her. Something very powerful inside her seemed to have been loosened, and in subsequent sessions several more stories along similar barbaric themes emerged in quick succession.

At last a chink of light appeared and it gradually grew brighter. In one session she turned up looking quite radiant, and told me that she felt happy for the first time in her life. Then a few months later she announced that she felt ready for a relationship, and within a few weeks of that pronouncement, she met the man whom she was to marry and have a child with. This story again demonstrates that big problems have deep roots and that they will only truly be solved when the root memories are surfaced, experienced and gradually detoxified and transformed as a result of being taken into the alchemical furnace inside our hearts.

Past life or species memories

Whether or not these traumatic events *really* occurred to a past life 'us' that today has been reborn as the 'us' we are now, or whether they are species memories which we 'just happen' to be carrying, or whether they are merely 'good yarns' invented by our psyches in order to facilitate a healing (for example, at night our psyches produce particular dreams for just this reason) is a question I continue to ask myself. Perhaps we will never know the answer. Perhaps, too, it doesn't matter. As regards my own particular experiences, I am not overly concerned if it really was a 'past life me' who had been hanged, drawn and quartered. What is more important is that my psyche knew what was needed for its healing.

So when I work with people around very deep issues, I never ask myself whether their experiences are true or false, whether they are 'made up', a past life or a species memory. Rather, I always trust that their hearts know how best they need to work and that whatever material is surfacing is doing so for a good reason.

Touching into world suffering

Sometimes, powerful memories which most definitely belong to our universal heart may erupt into our awareness out of nowhere, often in a non-therapeutic context. Earlier, I shared my experience of having tapped into deep female grief during the time of the Diana effect. I did not go looking for this. It just happened. Jack Kornfield, a Buddhist meditation teacher, has described how a student of his recognised that choosing to be of service constituted his need to take on world suffering:

> *As an environmentalist, I had struggled for years with the suffering of the world, and all these images of sorrows would come flooding past as I sat in my meditation. It was as if I was in the midst of rainforests being burned and bulldozed. I saw warfare and pollutions, all the images of what we were doing to the earth. I sat and wept, but I stuck with it even when it got intense.*[5]

He then describes how, by taking this pain into his heart, it began transforming, as a result of which he was able to experience a very deep peace. Kornfield also chronicles the experiences of a nun whom who was meditating on compassion and on the mystery of Christ on the cross. She described how she experienced her whole body beginning to ache and suddenly she too, found herself flipping into the collective realm:

> *I was all the mothers who have lost their beloved children in war, accident or disease, who even today cannot feed their hungry children. I was the mother trapped in the earthquake in Armenia ... I was the young men, all the soldiers in the senseless battles, I was the cows and pigs on the way to the slaughterhouse. I was the modern generals and the Roman soldiers, the welfare mothers and the slumlords, the victims and the perpetrators, all who would die, all who are in pain. I lay there, watched over by the pain in the world – so much pain. I couldn't bear it. My heart simply wept.*

Then a shift came. The universal heart accessed its deeper, or higher, spiritual dimension.

> *Then Jesus was there in my body, and we were holding it together, the suffering of the world. And I could see that to hold it in mercy was divine. It broke open my heart; it became the holy pain that opened it. This is God's purpose for our sorrows, to connect all our hearts. There is so much mercy.*

The importance of working with species suffering

I believe that working with particular areas of humanity's pain, enabling it to surface into awareness inside our hearts and thereby become transformed by the alchemical fire that exists there, is a very important aspect of certain activists' work. Those of us who feel drawn to this may be doing more to heal the species-wounded heart than we could ever realise. However, this kind of healing work cannot be embarked upon lightly, and it cannot occur without our going through some suffering ourselves, born of our needing personally to take on and burn away inside our own hearts certain elements of suffering lodged inside the universal heart. Therefore, this work can often be challenging. It demands that our hearts be big and clear and that we have the strength and inner resources with which to engage in it.

Interestingly, what we discover if we partake in this work in the *correct* way – that is, if we do it *consciously* and *lovingly* – is that many indirect benefits may also accrue for us. We saw this in terms of the ecstatic way the nun described the experience of Jesus coming alive inside her heart. In my own experience, I always find that after I have done work around some area of species grief – that is, after having 'gone down into it' and experienced it fully – I always 'come back up again into the light'. I may not, like the nun, have the experience of Jesus inside my heart, but there is very often the sense of a new order emerging or a new plane of consciousness awakening inside me, where instead of the emotions being dark and heavy, they transform and become light and joyful. So if you ever feel moved to engage in this kind of healing work, then do it and do it in a good spirit. Don't fear it. You will get back more than you give out.

One way to train yourself for this is to watch the world news on the television, and when painful information is given, say, of a particular massacre or an earthquake or something tragic, then try to open your heart to the people involved. Tune in to your heart centre, which is located right in the middle of your chest, and imagine yourself reaching out to embrace those who have been devastated. Open yourself to their suffering. Imagine either them dwelling inside your heart or your heart reaching out and enveloping them with its fire. If you do this work properly, I guarantee you will feel very enlivened afterwards.

A personal revelation

I learned about this kind of work quite by chance many years ago. I was feeling particularly unhappy at an egoic level. (The world out there was not giving me the goodies my wounded ego was demanding!) I happened to turn on the television where there was a programme about the starving children in Biafra. The images on the screen gripped me very powerfully and I found myself spontaneously opening my heart to their suffering. I felt these little children crying inside my heart. This process may have lasted an hour, but at the end of it, I felt more content and full and joyful than I had felt for years. It was extraordinary. All my ego angst had evaporated.

At the time, I couldn't understand why this was so, or what had happened. Later, I realised that I had initially been full of my egoic, 'self-pitying' misery and that the act of 'taking on' world pain or real pain enabled me to open my heart and move into a much deeper part of myself, where I could begin accessing my true humanity. As healing energy streamed out of my heart, I also received a healing. The effect was also to wash away my own superficial discontents, which I realised will always have a tendency to raise their heads so long as we are not doing something genuine or are not connected to a place inside ourselves that is genuine.

If only more of us realised that one of the best ways to deal with the pain of our self-pitying egos is not to offer them more placating titbits, but rather to journey into a place inside ourselves that is much more real and from that place to open our hearts to some aspect of life that we recognise requires healing. Whenever we can manage this, we will experience a sense of deep well-being stealing over us which is in no way predicated upon what is going on in our external lives. What we learn is that consciously choosing to open to and to 'take on' world pain also has the effect of opening our hearts. Conversely, if we just let ourselves see the pain and try to block off from it or close off to it, it may well blob into us anyway and remain stuck inside us. This is the condition of far too many people today, and is why so many of us go around in a continuous state of blockage where we are also closed off to the happy and abundant things of life.

So I recommend that if ever you experience yourself blocked in your heart and feeling all the unease that this brings about, you consider sending love to someone worse off than yourself. Think of a friend who is ill or of little children who are starving, or people who are terribly depressed, or families dispossessed by war or natural disaster, and choose to open your heart to them. Your heart will teach you how to do this. If you do this work properly and with sincerity, you will find your heart start to unclench and its alchemical properties grind into operation. It will start to generate a light that will first circulate through you and wash out your own suffering, before flowing out of you towards the object or objects of your intentionality. Please note: this is only possible for those who are already on an awakening path. Those whose hearts are still clamped tightly shut may neither have the desire nor the capacity to engage in this work.

Guidelines for engaging in intentional suffering

- When we encounter suffering, we don't try to run away from it. Rather, we thank it for honouring us with its visit, as we know it has come from very deep levels of spiritual Heart and that it is part of the initiatory process which we realise we need to go through if we are to grow stronger and become more fully human. We know we have a choice: we can confront our suffering with courage and consciously allow it to burn inside our hearts – or we can wimp out and become a victim of it. We choose the former approach.

- We make the choice to open fully to the pain, so we may experience it in as conscious a way as possible. As we do this, we ask it to enlighten and transform us and burn away all the impure parts of ourselves and of species man, which serve to prevent either us as an individual, or humanity as a whole, transforming into our butterfly selves.
- We pray for help and guidance to do the above effectively. We can also meditate for help to enable us to face our pain with greater calmness and equanimity. In addition, we ask for help from our spiritual guides and teachers.
- We create a strong support group of our good friends to be with us in these challenging times, and we must not be afraid to ask for their assistance when we feel we really need it.
- We take special care to look after ourselves and nourish ourselves physically and emotionally. Thus, we need to eat healthily and exercise regularly and generally take care of our hearts, which have so much alchemical work to do.
- We need to be prepared to wait and trust that a resolution will come in its own time and happen in its own way, and never forget that it is always when night is at its blackest that dawn begins to appear.
- We make sure that we do not close down our mental facilities, so we can see with our minds working together with our hearts what the wisest course of action to take is at any time.

My old friend William Bloom, a teacher and educator, advises us that

all this work around suffering must be done from a personal space that is completely centred, confident and relaxed. We must be fully connected to the love, compassion and benevolence of the universe. It is only when we are anchored securely in that benevolence that we can manage, without being overwhelmed or triggered, the suffering that happens on earth and in humanity.

Chapter 9

Understanding the Shadow

Everyone carries a Shadow, and the less it is embodied in the individual's conscious life, the blacker and denser it is. At all counts, it forms an unconscious snag, thwarting our most well-meant intentions –
CARL JUNG

What is the Shadow?

If we are to become effective activists, and develop strong, brave and loving hearts and healthy subservient egos, it is of great importance that we acquaint ourselves, and know how to work, with something that is well understood by those in the therapeutic professions but often little known elsewhere: the 'Shadow'. 'Shadow issues' constitute a large part of what is 'wrong' with our society and play out in a great many areas of our lives – especially in our relationships, our religions, our families, our institutions and our politics.

So what is the Shadow? The term was first coined by Carl Jung. A good definition is given us by the Jungian analyst Dr Ann Belford Ulanov:

> *It is that which is darkness to our light, unknown to what we call familiar; that which comes from the other side of our motives, from the other side of our virtue and from the other side of our vices.*

Our Shadow, then, is what we *don't* know about ourselves, what we are still in the dark about or are unconscious of in ourselves, and so don't identify with. For example, my Shadow side is *not* my laziness or my tendency to be untidy or disorganised, as these are aspects of myself that I am well acquainted with. Therefore, while none of these traits are especially endearing, they are not my Shadow, as I am aware of them and so, if I remain awake and mindful, I can potentially stay on top of them.

While we cannot see or recognise our Shadow, it nonetheless finds expression in our daily lives. It comprises all those aspects of ourselves which, unbeknownst to us, we have learned to split off from, or, conversely, whose existence we have repressed or suppressed or not yet uncovered. This includes our virtuous sides as much as facets of ourselves which may be unkind, cruel and destructive. Later on, we will look at the virtuous or 'light' side of our Shadow. As we are currently exploring the area of healing ourselves, we will here only explore those aspects of our Shadow that cover our less desirable traits.

Shadow projection

One of the problems with the Shadow is that we may often find it repulsive, as it is never pleasant to discover that we have parts of ourselves that may be mean, manipulative and destructive. Therefore, in order to ignore them, we tend to project them out onto other people or onto particular aspects of society. So if, let us say, I am fat, greedy, self-centred and destructive, and I don't want to confront these aspects of myself, I can relieve myself of the anxiety by finding people who are appropriate 'hooks' to hang these attributes onto. Therefore, instead of having to recognise these traits as belonging to myself, I will see those people as embodying them.

The word I will use to describe this 'Shadow projection' is 'enshadow', and caterpillar man is an arch-enshadower, often without having the faintest idea that this is the case, or how destructive it can be. Enshadowing is the direct opposite of enheartening. When we see another person through an enheartening lens, we see them in terms of who they really are – our hearts reach out into theirs and we seek to touch their humanity with our own. The consciousness of both of us is raised in the process. When we see another person through a lens that enshadows, the very opposite occurs. We turn them into whatever we are 'dumping' onto them, and in so doing, we reduce them, and of course, ourselves, to being less than who we both are. Often, so keen are we to remain unaware of the 'mote in our own eye', we enshadow people with negative traits which they simply do not possess. In this way, a huge amount of destructive energy is continually being hurled out into our world, which is damaging both to our personal and to the universal heart. What we may call the universal or collective human Shadow is the sum total of all our enshadowings.

One of the consequences of our society currently being overlighted by the rising tide of love is that this Heart light is constantly shining into our dark sides, propelling them strongly into visibility. They are therefore no longer so hidden, so obscured, and it consequently becomes much easier to be aware of the many different ways that our Shadow sides manifest. This new visibility is very important, for unless we can see our enshadowings for what they are, unless we can see the price that we and those we are projecting upon are paying, and so become aware of just how much our activities hold the world of the Setting Sun in place, we are not going to be sufficiently motivated to do anything about it.

Playing the 'blame game'

Blaming others for our own shortcomings is another typical Shadow trait. We like to see what is wrong with our society as being everyone else's fault. Thus, it is 'they' who start wars, 'they' who overconsume, 'they' who are greedy, 'they' who have destroyed our relationship, 'they' who pollute the planet. Our financial system has collapsed because of our dishonest bankers… *They* are the bad ones; we are the innocents. If only 'they' would change, our world would improve.

This is the typical 'game' that the caterpillar side of ourselves likes to play, as our insecure egos, with their proclivity for self-denial, refuse to acknowledge that we may also be part of all those things that we accuse others of, and that our world might be in the condition that it is in not only because of 'them', but also because of us! I believe that unless change occurs around this issue and that unless you and I look deeply into the darkness inside our own hearts and see where we too constitute an integral part of the problems of our world – and in seeing this, *do something* about it – our world will remain as it is. This is precisely why the presence of Heart is so important, for when we bring it into the equation, it helps us see things more clearly and be more honest, which in turn makes it easier for us to take back our projections and assume greater responsibility for our lives. What Heart endows us with is the courage, love and determination to confront the less acceptable sides of ourselves without condemning ourselves in the process. Without the ingredient of Heart, then, we are much more likely to relegate unacceptable aspects of ourselves to the basement of our being – that is, deny them. With Heart, we are much more willing – and capable – of casting light on the many skeletons adorning our closets.

Personal Shadow explorations

So how do we become aware of our Shadow side? One of the best ways is to recognise the kinds of people who carry a 'charge' for us, as in most cases, they will embody something that we don't wish to acknowledge as existing in ourselves. When I first started doing Shadow work in my late twenties, I observed that I felt extremely critical towards predatory men who went around seducing women. Why? Because that was exactly what I was doing myself at that time in my life. As I worked on this issue, I got to see that like so many of us men, I had basically split myself into two segments: one side that I presented to the world as light and sunny (the 'good guy'), the other that I tried to hide from the world (or thought I did!) and from myself. This 'hidden' me was narcissistic, predatory and pretty macho piggish.

Gradually, the truth began to sink in that if I wished to be remotely human, I needed to do something about these splits of mine. I saw that they manifested in other areas of my life as well, and that the answer was not to detest my dark side, as to do so would only turn it into an enemy, make me even more distant from it, and consequently give it no opportunity to transform. Rather, I saw that I needed to understand it better and in so doing, learn to embrace it more. I repeat the quote from Jung that 'any part of ourselves we do not own becomes our enemy'. And what do enemies do? They fight back, of course. They give us what we give them. And our Shadow side is no exception. Huge chunks of our wounded ego lie embedded in our Shadow. I therefore realised I had to confront my predator without judgement and find out more about him, discover how and why this particular identity emerged, and, as we have seen with all of our wounded egoic traits, keep a good eye on him!

The importance of Shadow work in opening our hearts

Interestingly, the way into the treasure trove residing inside our hearts often lies through our dark side. We saw this demonstrated in the last chapter, where going into world pain would often lead us into feelings of joy. I therefore began to realise that if I wished to grow my heart, I simply had to learn to recognise and work with those dark parts of myself which, in addition to being predatory, I came to see were also vain (this was hard to swallow as I was very critical of vain men), aggressive (oh no, not peace-loving me!), greedy (yuk) and manipulative (ugh!) While I sensed I had a 'good heart' inside me (somewhere), it was not going to be able to emerge so long as these traits were still operating powerfully and so long as so much of my energy was being invested in trying to cover them up. Keeping our Shadow side locked up in the basement of our being to ensure that these dark aspects of ourselves never get out, I realised, is an exhausting process and uses up a huge amount of energy.

My own liberation began when I realised I needed to give up the illusion that I was just this 'nice guy' who only meant well and just liked to help old ladies across the road! I saw that I must not hide from the fact that there was another Serge inside me who couldn't be more contrary, and that I needed to get to know him, my wounded ego, and discover why he was as he was. The interesting thing was that doing this uncovering work also proved key to discovering my real power as a man, and generally becoming more authentic and less artificial. I began to recognise two things: firstly, that so long as our dragons remain in their lair inside us, unseen by us, they have power over us, and secondly, that once we become aware of them and see them for what they are, not only do we begin to have power over them, but, most significantly, they cease being dragons.

The Shadow in society

Our Shadow sides, needless to say, are reflected out into our society. Many of us are inducted into the politics of repression and suppression from an early age, where the no-go areas for our parents become similar taboos for us. For example, if showing emotion was suppressed in our childhood, in all likelihood, we will grow up also stuffing away our feelings, and with them, much of the inner world of our hearts. Conversely, if the world of sex or having fun was embarrassing to our parents and got squashed down, we will probably grow up learning to do the same thing ourselves. Since what we tend to repress is often what we obsess about, the more sexually repressed we are, the more we may tend to become obsessed with it.

One of the things that is so wrong with our current Western culture is that, as ardent Shadow deniers, we are always trying to make everything 'nice' while denying what is unpleasant. This niceness is often reflected in the way that we like to decorate our houses. Not a whiff of Shadow! I remember when I first visited Bali, I was struck by how authentic many of the people were, and I saw how this was reflected in their art. I have a large Balinese painting hanging in my consulting rooms, painted by a community of artists, and it depicts a totally holistic scene. There, people are praying, working and playing. Nature is all about them. However, the dark side of life is also included, and the picture also shows characters wearing fiendish masks to remind us that death and destruction are part of the great scheme of things. As activists working in the midst of one culture trying to die and another seeking to be born, it is especially important that we make space to work through our issues around death.

The shadow of death

Death is one of the biggest bogeys in our Western culture. One way we try to ward off our anxieties around it is by being constantly busy, which is why many of us have turned ourselves more into human 'doings' than human beings. This enshadowing of death not only shuts our hearts down but has all sorts of dire consequences, one being that the more we try to push it away, the closer we seem to draw it to ourselves, which accounts for why so many of us today live very rigid, 'death-like' existences and find it hard to let go of being in control all the time. Our fears around death also explain why we so often find it difficult to 'die to' our old identities, to make the shift from caterpillar to butterfly and celebrate the emergence of a new culture on our planet.

I like the way that medieval alchemists liked to keep a skull on their desks. This was not to be macabre, but rather to remind themselves that death is always a part of life, that it is forever stalking us, and that life is dying all the time, just as it is always giving birth to new shoots of itself. We see this played out beautifully in our gardens when new seeds begin sprouting. I began to realise that if I wanted to live in a full-hearted way, it was very important that I should not run away from death but try to embrace it in all its many manifestations.

The gifts offered us by our dark side

I stress once more how much easier it is to start uncovering and thus relating to our Shadow and working creatively with it once we learn to view it through the lens of our heart. As we do so, we come to see that it is not so much 'bad' (although it can become bad if we continue to hate it and cut ourselves off from it) but rather it is our inferior side – a part of ourselves that we have not allowed to grow because we haven't given it enough attention. I saw that at one level, we needed to learn to view our dark side as our friend – as a part of ourselves that needs to be helped to evolve; if this is done, it may have much to offer us if we wish to become more whole as human beings.

An example of this may be seen in Shakespeare's play *King Lear*. Lear's Shadow side was represented by the Fool, who always spoke the greatest wisdom. Had the king listened to his fool and taken his advice rather than succumbing to the flattery of his two elder daughters, he might have avoided the fate which ultimately befell him. The story of Don Quixote echoes a similar theme. His 'other half' or Shadow side, Sancho Panza, was endowed with streetwise intelligence in contrast to his master's tendency to be somewhat disconnected from the real world. In order to be more whole as a person, Don Quixote needed to remain in touch with his Sancho Panza. Whole, loving, substantial human beings never deny their dark sides, for they have recognised the importance of working creatively to integrate them.

Frankenstein

The evil that can result from our denial and splitting off from our Shadow is beautifully illustrated in *Frankenstein* by Mary Shelley. The 'monster' was not born with a monstrous nature. On the contrary: he started off by being tender hearted and wanting to help people. But because he was not externally beautiful, which reflected badly on the vanity of his creator, the latter disowned him and refused to have anything to do with him, or to give him the companion that he yearned for.

People who saw the creature feared and shunned him too, and ran away from him, and in his sorrow and loneliness, his heart began to harden and he took on the mantle of monster that people projected onto him. As a result, he began to behave in a monstrous and murderous fashion, stalking his creator, making his life a misery and eventually killing him. This story warns us that if we do not own our dark side and the dark side of our society, we may be destroyed by it.

The Shadow in families

A lot of enshadowing goes on in families. My father, for example, refused to own his vulnerable side, so he projected it strongly onto me, and then attacked me for being weak and having insufficient willpower, as in this way he could maintain the illusion of his own potency. I reacted by trying to sabotage many of the things he stood for, which was a pity as he stood for many very fine things and had many excellent qualities.

This is typical of what happens in many families and is why it can be so damaging if we are raised by parents who are not conscious of what they are projecting onto us. If we receive our enshadowing early on in our development, it can take a strong hold inside us. Remember what I said earlier about curses! In some families, one person takes on everyone's Shadow projections and becomes the 'black sheep'. So long as they exist as a kind of 'dump truck' to receive everyone else's disowned vulnerabilities and faults and can be blamed for everything that goes wrong, all the other family members can bask in the illusion of their virtue. Needless to say, the consequences for the black sheep can be absolutely devastating.

Favourite Shadow hooks

The point about caterpillar man is that he is not very conscious, not very self-aware, and as a result has a tendency to scout around for appropriate hooks upon which to hang his dark side. Current favourites include dark-skinned people, Muslims, gay people and overweight people. He likes to project his Shadow onto black people because he is afraid of the wilder, more primeval side of ourselves which their skin colour symbolises for him. When we project terrorism onto Muslims, we isolate them and in so doing increase the likelihood of them becoming terrorists. In a similar way, fat people become repositories for our own disowned sloth and gluttony. Indeed, many of the less acceptable features of our society – racism, sexism, homophobia and Islamophobia, indeed all forms of scapegoating and fanaticism – are Shadow issues.

Much of our enshadowing is unconscious, that is, we do not know we are doing it, which is why, if we wish to be effective activists, it is so important to be aware of the existence of our unhealthy inner agendas. There are instances, of course, where the object onto which we are projecting does actually embody our dark side, as when we project, say, our evil onto our Hitlers and Saddam Husseins. Here, however, another problem can emerge. If these tyrants are made to carry our own evil, we can create the illusion for ourselves that we are snow-white innocents. So long as we 'need' evil people 'out there' in order to get ourselves 'off the hook', we will continually need to create villains and monsters out in the world.

Dr Jekyll and Mr Hyde

The perils of what can occur if we deny our other half are also what concern Robert Louis Stevenson's classic novella. It is about 'the good Dr Jekyll', the respectable, normal, churchgoing, caterpillar-like doctor, who was in complete denial of his wild, primitive and sensual side. However, he was fascinated by it (as we always tend to be obsessed by what we repress), so much so, in fact, that he created a drug to bring this other side of himself to life, and when it eventually appeared, it was shrunken, villainous and ugly. This is because Mr Hyde had always lived in Jekyll's Shadow, had never been allowed to evolve, had always remained 'unfed' in the basement of Jekyll's being.

The tragedy is that the twain never met. Dr Jekyll and Mr Hyde continued to live in their own separate domains, where they soon came to loathe each other. Good and evil were locked in mortal combat, and after a time Mr Hyde increasingly began to gain the upper hand, as Jekyll eventually began to metamorphose into Hyde spontaneously without his taking the drug, and his anxieties grew when Hyde's activities extended to murder. Eventually Hyde took Jekyll over completely. This story shows us how important it is for us not to hate but rather to work at integrating our polarities and how potentially devastating it can be if this does not occur.

The truth is that each part needed the other. Jekyll needed his Hyde to connect him to the earthier, juicier things of life from which, in his dry, conventional 'good doctor' identity, he was largely cut off. Similarly, Hyde also needed the intelligence, moral restraint and decorum of Jekyll in order to not go off the rails. Had such an integration occurred earlier on in Jekyll's life, and had he been able to 'lend' his attributes to Hyde and to receive what Hyde had to offer him, a state of harmony and wholeness could have prevailed. I think this story tells us a great deal about what is so wrong with our society. Ask yourself: might you be a 'good Dr Jekyll' living in denial of your Mr Hyde? If so, I invite you to speculate what may have become of him.

Untangling world dramas through owning the Shadow

If we do not work at becoming more aware of our own and our society's 'other side', and if we do not see how our own personal issues serve to entangle us in the larger world Shadow, then we risk being caught up in the many Shadow dramas which proliferate out in the world. The most devastating of these is war, which not only allows free rein to our Mr Hydes, but may even award them medals for their murderousness. However much our world leaders may try, outwardly, to work for peace, so long as we, the people, fail to address the darkness inside our hearts, their endeavours will never meet with ongoing success.

I remind you again: opposites are not bad; they are part of life and we need them. Each of us has a Shadow side that needs recognising and coming to terms with and even, in many instances, 'embracing'. In the Gnostic gospel according to St Thomas, Jesus tells us: 'We must bring forth that which we are and if we fail to do so, it will destroy us.' These wise words need to be heeded.

Chapter 10

Integrating the Shadow

The tall mountain casts a long shadow – CARL JUNG

We don't become enlightened by sitting in the light but by going into our darkness – CARL JUNG

Identifying and working with our personal Shadow

'We don't become enlightened by sitting in the light but by going into our darkness.' I repeat Jung's statement as it is so important. Put another way, the road leading towards our butterfly-hood lies in our needing to confront and work with the dark side of our caterpillar-ness, and for many of us activists, a large part of our work concerns our need to address and work with the Shadow sides of our society. And if we possess a great capacity for Heart, the chances are that we will probably have a lot of Shadow material come up for us to work with, for Jung also stressed that 'the tall mountain casts a long shadow'. A good way to start out is to ask ourselves three simple questions:

- What images of ourselves are we most identified with, and what do we think is the opposite of these images?
- Who of our own sex do we experience a 'charge' with? Do they perhaps possess certain characteristics that we may not want to accept as also belonging to us?
- What are our prejudices and is there anything that we are fanatical about?

I first began working with my Shadow some forty years ago, and I will share how I became aware of certain issues and how I worked with them.

In addition to my problems with predatory men, I also observed in my late twenties that I never really liked small men, and I noticed I would often be demeaning towards them. I realised that this was probably because my mother had a critical attitude towards small men, and that my father, tall like myself, had constantly impressed upon me the notion that I should beware of short men, 'as they will always do you over'. (No doubt this had been his own experience.) I saw clearly that this contributed to why I carried a suspicion of them and why I had virtually no male friends who were not also well built and over six feet tall.

In working with this issue, I came to the realisation that there was also a deeper reason why I felt uncomfortable with small men. It was because they reflected an inner part of myself that felt diminutive and that I didn't want to face. At that time, a lot of my energy was being invested in developing a macho 'tough guy' image, both to enhance my predatory behaviours, as well as to hide from myself – and of course, from others – the fact that much of the time I felt small and insecure. (Most macho guys are like this.) I saw that I enshadowed small men because this allowed me to get off my own hook. My therapist at the time pointed out that I needed to get to know my own 'small, scared inner man' and find out where he came from. As I began doing this, I realised that 'he' was part of my 'wounded child' that I had grown distant from, that he needed to be taken into my heart and loved, and that all my macho posturing was all about me trying to cover my wound.

As I gradually worked at coming to know and own this part of myself and began taking him into my heart and 'feeding' him – which included doing all sorts of playful things with him – my diminutive inner child slowly began to mature inside me and become more integrated into the rest of me. As this occurred, I gradually began to feel more whole as a person and thus experienced less need for all my old armouring. My projections onto small men began to fade, and my circle of male buddies became richer as it could now include men shorter in stature than myself.

I also realised that over the years, I had done much damage to small men in the ways that I had enshadowed them, and that this needed healing. I therefore designed a process for myself whereby I would imagine all the small men I had ever inadvertently hurt residing in my heart and I would send them healing energy, one by one. I visualised myself talking to the hearts of specific men and apologising to them, and if they were the kind of person who I felt could understand, I met with them and apologised and explained what had occurred. In this way, that part of my wounded ego became healed. I recommend that you, the reader, consider using a similar process around your Shadow issues.

Personal Shadow conflicts

We can enshadow ourselves in the same way that we enshadow other people. At that stage in my life (my early thirties), I was dividing my time between England and California, and it reflected a deep split inside me. I had two distinct identities, one that was quite conservative and the other that was, as certain friends at the time described it, 'somewhat way out'! The problem was that both identities were suspicious of and somewhat hostile to each other. Depending upon which role I was playing at the time, I would often enshadow the other and in particular, those people out in the world who seemed to embody it.

A big shift came about as I started to visualise myself holding *both* aspects of me sitting together inside my heart and having a dialogue. As I worked with this, a gradual convergence began to occur, whereby I could start bringing more groundedness into my 'way out' self, while the old stiff, conservative me could be loosened up with doses of 'California consciousness'. The more my heart entered the equation, the more I could see that these parts of me were actually not opposed to each other, but actually existed within each other and, most significantly, *needed* each other and complemented and gave balance to each other. Slowly, a bridge began to be built between them, the result being that a much more integrated me began to emerge, being a synthesis of both polarities, only *at a higher level of consciousness.* I became more than just a hipper version of a stiff Englishman. Something new emerged that was softer and gentler and humbler and more fun and no longer had anything snooty about it.

I suggest that you inquire into what inner conflicts of identity you might have and see if you can take them into your heart and work with them in a similar way. I like the word 'inquire'. If, as activists, we wish to grow, we need to spend more time engaged in inquiry, as it is the only way truly to discover who we *really* are, underneath all the various images and identities that we construct and which we think are us. Another of the main differences between caterpillar and butterfly people is that the former seldom ask deep questions of themselves, which is one reason why they always remain caterpillars.

Working with prejudice issues

There was one particular man at that time in my life whom I observed I had a particularly strong charge with. Not only was he very unattractive, but he was gay and working class and as such, he pressed three of my then big buttons. I saw that I had inherited my father's homophobia as well as my mother's snobbery and her tendency to judge people very much on appearances. It was very painful to confront how small minded and prejudiced I was, but I realised I absolutely had to own and work with these aspects of myself if I was to become remotely more human. Not only did I have to confront fears that I might be gay, but I also had to see that despite my best attempts to pretend otherwise, I really was extremely class conscious and had a side that was a real twittish kind of toff! This brought up a lot of shame, which I also needed to take up into my heart.

I also came to see that another reason why ugliness in people disturbed me so much was because there were some pretty ugly aspects to my own character, to say nothing of the fact that I was certainly no Brad Pitt! No wonder I would get so pulled in by superficial prettiness and always had to be 'seen' with glamorous-looking women. It was all a great cover-up. I realised I needed to work on all three fronts simultaneously, and that this included learning to appreciate and love myself more (which I will discuss in Chapter 14). I also observed, interestingly, that when I managed to do this, it served to open my heart, and that when this occurred, all these projections, including how I saw myself, began to fade in intensity. I came to see that all our enshadowing projections reflect the fact that we are overly identified with our wounded egos and we don't make enough room for Heart to arise in our lives.

I saw that when I remembered to connect to my heart, that I was linking into a me at a much deeper level and that this me was a much more genuine aspect of myself. It was not prejudiced and did not enshadow; it embraced homosexuality and delighted in holding all people inside its heart. What characterised this me was that he didn't see life through the lens of my wounded ego and therefore he didn't put people into narrow boxes. Therefore, whether or not people were gay or what class they belonged to or how they looked became utterly irrelevant. As I began to make progress on this Heart front, I gradually got to know this particular man very well. I discovered that he was deep, sincere, funny and wise, that he had many admirable traits which my old (Heartless) projections had never allowed me to see, that he was much more developed than myself, and that I needed to learn a lot from him. He became a good friend and is still a good friend to this day.

The 'Tongan encounter'

A couple of years ago, I was in Auckland visiting my daughter for her school holidays, and found myself being included in a game of throwing a rugby ball with a gang of tough Tongan youths, none of whom was under six and a half feet tall. Here is how this came about.

I had been jogging on the beach, saw these guys playing together, and suddenly experienced my heart reaching out strongly towards them and decided to follow up that impulse by risking engaging their leader in conversation, whereby, to my joy, I received a positive response. To cut a long story short, I was invited to join in their game, later had a Coca-Cola and hamburger bought for me, and for the entire afternoon, I was honoured by very generously being invited to 'hang out' in their world and, as it were, be part of their gang.

I have to say those four or five hours spent in their company were an absolute delight and revelation. As my heart opened to them more and more, I realised that though they were all nearly half a century younger than me and came from a totally different culture, in actuality, our worlds were not so different and we shared many common interests. They were totally beautiful-hearted young men and I became strongly aware of a shared common ground of human being-ness which linked us all together. I truly felt that these guys were my soul brothers.

I realised from this experience that we only feel things are alien because our hearts are afraid to reach forward and embrace what is unfamiliar and so we retreat when we perceive apparent differences. But the beauty of Heart is that it knows no boundaries. Heart doesn't care about age or skin colour or nationality or culture. It is not interested in how big our houses are or how many books we have read or what ridiculous social position we may hold. It takes us directly into our core humanity. So for the space of about four hours, this was the place that I related to my new friends from. Whenever I return to Auckland, I always make contact with my new brothers.

Embracing different environments

I mention this little story to stress that what so often limits us and lies behind so much of our enshadowing is our desire only to want to engage with those whom we deem to be 'our kind' – that is, who are of the same nationality, who see the world as we do, who look and think and dress like us, and who share the same political opinions and income bracket. I think this is partly out of laziness and a fear of the unknown, and partly out of an inability (born of an insufficient heart) to discover new surfaces of ourselves. So what we tend to do is view those 'outside our small circle' with suspicion, *which is actually a covert form of enshadowing*. It is this disconnection from our humanity that underlies so many misunderstandings in the world and ensures that so many of our wounds can never heal.

I therefore like to encourage many of my clients to consider entering into unfamiliar worlds as this can be so therapeutic. Several years ago, I was working with a wealthy man who, in the course of a session, casually remarked that he wanted to help poor people more, and that it was difficult as he felt very trapped in the rich set that he always mixed with. He told me that he was outraged by what was going on in Darfur at that time. 'Then go to Darfur,' I told him. 'Go and see the place for yourself. Immerse yourself in it. Do something about it. Don't just talk about it.' The words spewed out of my mouth. 'Use this as an opportunity to embrace this other side of yourself.'

He did this. He went to Darfur and set up an educational programme there and a charity, and he discovered a whole new side of himself in the process. 'I think I have found myself, and', he looked pointedly at me, 'I have got more out of being in Darfur and working there than I have ever got out of therapy sessions with you!' I agreed with him. 'Good. I think the main way that we discover ourselves is through action in the world and trying to be of help to others. A lot of people go into therapy because they don't bother enough to do this and you have bothered. Well done.'

I once worked with a woman whose prime identification had always been with the underdog. She always felt vulnerable, as she could only seem to empathise with people who were going through difficulties, or, like her, felt they were society's underdogs. She came to see me primarily because she felt she was always operating out of an empty tank, confessing that secretly she felt envious of those who were on the other side of the fence, and where good things would seem to happen without their seeming to do anything to deserve it. I suggested that she make a huge effort to connect with the other, more abundant side of her nature that lived in her Shadow, and that at the same time, she also tried cultivating the company of happy, healthy, wealthy and successful people. 'Give yourself the space to find that joyful, wealthy you, as opposed to the you that equates virtue with crucifixion.'

There was a lot of resistance to this idea. (It is so interesting how much we all fear being whole!) But once we had worked a lot of it through, things really began to open up for her. She made some new friends who then invited her to stay in their opulent home in the Bahamas, and this gave her a wonderful experience of how her 'other half' lived. Gradually, more and more good things began to open up for her and she realised that to be a good person she didn't have to be poor and suffer, and that she could actually be more effective if she gave herself permission to live out the other, abundant side of her nature, which up until then, she realised she had mainly kept in the Shadow.

Giving back Shadow projections

Sometimes we are challenged not only to take back the shadow projections which we have hoisted onto others, but also to release projections which others may have pinned onto us. African Americans have shown us very poignantly how this can be effectively done. A hundred or so years ago, they were mainly slaves and the chains around their hearts took actual physical form as they worked in the chain gangs. Just over half a century ago, they were forced by law to sit in the rear of buses, far away from the white folk. Today, America has a black President, who, I am happy to say, has just been re-elected.

This advance of black liberation owes a great deal to courageous and visionary activists such as Martin Luther King, who dreamed his great dream of all African Americans being free. He helped them come to see that they didn't have to collude with what white people were projecting onto them, and that they had the capacity to stand up for their rights and claim back their power and their humanity. The movement began with a few African Americans saying 'I am a human being. I have my rights and I refuse to be put down. Black is beautiful.' Gradually, more and more people took up the cry, and as this new empowered thinking began to grow in strength, the old label of 'second-class citizen' began to flow away like water off a duck's back.

There is still a long way to go, but enormous strides towards freedom have been made and this is to be celebrated.

The issue of the haves and the have-nots

All the big splits existing out in the world reflect splits inside ourselves, both at a personal and at a collective level. The huge schism existing between the haves and the have-nots – between the very rich and the very poor – is very much a Shadow issue and is one of the things that I see as being *most wrong* with our world. Basically, rich and poor people tend to live in two 'opposing worlds', often with each side fearing and mistrusting the other. Many of the world's rich are terrified of looking at their 'other face', preferring only to mix with their own kind, and do their best to keep any whiff of potential impoverishment well at bay by ensuring that they live in super-elite communities. On the one side, then, we have our multi-million-pound estates and private yachts, and on the other side our ghettos.

Needless to say, the poor have a lot of anger towards the rich and exhibit a strong desire to 'bring them down'. Many view them (often unfairly, as a lot of wealthy people do a large amount of good) as 'evil' and exploitative and as being the sole reason for their own difficult circumstances. I see this split becoming worse and feel that unless something changes radically, unless more of the world's haves share more of their resources with the have-nots, the biggest problem we are going to have to face in the coming years is not terrorism, global warming or water shortages, but the rising tide of anger felt by the world's dispossessed.

What needs to be understood here is that whenever we enshadow our 'other half', both sides lose out. The more the poor hate and blame the rich, the more they will be at loggerheads with their own inner potential for wealth and abundance, and thus the more likely they are to remain in poverty. Similarly, the more that those who 'have' close down their hearts to how their 'other half' live, the more isolated from their own humanity they become and the more impoverished they will be at an inner level.

I am acquainted with a fair amount of wealthy people and without exception, the happy ones are those who don't hide away in their big houses, but are willing to embrace the larger world and are not afraid to acknowledge their 'other half' and to share their resources. Such people are aware of their advantages and they do their best to ensure that those who don't have can partake in some way of their good fortune. These people are very blessed. What did Jesus tell us? He said that if we were to throw our bread upon the waters, that is, to share what we have, much more would come back to us. It is so true.

So if you are wealthy, perhaps you can ask yourself the following questions: how do I view poverty out in the world? When I walk down the street and see people lying about in sleeping bags, or when, in the news, I hear about some new crisis hitting very poor people, or if I go to India and see hundreds of beggars all around me, what does all this bring up for me? Do I ignore it and step away, or do I allow this information into my heart? How much do I really care? How much do I try to help those less fortunate than myself? Just observe your replies to these questions with no judgement whatsoever.

Revelation of the world Shadow

As we have been seeing, the rising tide of Heart is continuing to illuminate for us the many different skeletons which in the past used to be securely hidden away in all kinds of dark closets. In today's increasingly transparent world, and equipped as we are with Facebook, WikiLeaks, Twitter and other internet resources, it is now much harder to cover things up, and therefore, those who still persist in engaging in nefarious Mr Hyde-ish activities are finding it much harder to keep them a secret. The dark side of life is coming more and more into the open and I view this as very positive.

For example: no longer are certain Catholic priests able to continue to get away with covering up their crimes against young children. No longer can large banks and other multi-national companies keep their dubious machinations secret, nor certain wealthy individuals get away with evading taxes. No longer are war criminals being allowed to remain on the run. Less and less are we in the dark about the dishonesty of certain politicians or public figures, as the truth of their private lives comes increasingly into the light of day. By the same token, it is not by chance that Osama bin Laden's hiding place was discovered, or that Al Gore's film *An Inconvenient Truth*, about how badly we have damaged our environment, came out at this time.

In fact, information which perhaps even a decade or so ago could be discovered only through some 'underground press' (if at all), is now readily available 'above ground' via many of our daily newspapers and news channels. Similarly, the records of the atrocities perpetrated by the British on the Mau Mau in Kenya in our colonial past, long kept hidden, are also now out in the open, just as the horrendous way that the Australians originally treated the Aborigines, or the Russians the Chechens, is no secret any more. The list could go on forever. And this is to be celebrated. But first we need to face our personal Shadow sides. The more effectively we work with our personal issues, the greater our capacity to be effective when confronting Shadow issues out in the world.

Making the choice to confront or 'take on' the Shadow side of our planet, wherever or whenever we encounter it in our daily lives, is always an act of great love. The more Heart we have, the greater our capabilities in this area. Just as it is often through our personal pain that we learn to connect to, and hopefully work at transmuting, world pain, so it is primarily through our personal Shadow challenges that we are led to connect with larger issues of world Shadow.

Initially, confronting such vast and dark shadows may seem a daunting task. Where do we start? What do we do? Are we up to it? Once we realise that our hearts will guide us to what kinds of issue we may need to address and, if we listen to them, instruct us how best to approach our task, we will feel more comfortable. Just as there is no 'one way' to deal with our personal Shadow issues, so the same applies to Shadow issues out in the world. Different scenarios require handling in very different ways. I will return to this theme in more detail later, when we examine the topic of evil.

THREE

Cultivating the Garden of the Heart

Be energetic in the work that takes you to God – SANAI

The work of love is to open that window in the chest and to look incessantly at the beloved – RUMI

Don't hide your heart but reveal it, so that mine might be revealed and I might accept what I am capable of – RUMI

Chapter 11

Opening to the Spiritual Heart

*To imagine we can open the heart without preparation
is like expecting to buy an elephant for two pence! –*
THE SHIVAPURI BABA

*Know the mirror of the heart is infinite ...
because the heart is with God, or indeed the heart is he –*
RUMI

The need to surrender 'substitute transcendent' activities

Thus far, we have focused primarily on addressing the darkness and the blockages inside our hearts. In this section, we will continue to explore our healing or 'whole-making' process, only we will now do so from the perspective of how we may consciously expand our hearts and begin to activate their butterfly dimensions with the specific aim of our actually beginning to embody the changes we wish to see take place. This work is of crucial importance. While refining our egos, embracing our dark sides and addressing our heart wounds is vital, and if done effectively will certainly open up a space for us to start moving in this new direction, it is only part of the process. If a further blossoming is to occur, if our butterfly self is to start to emerge, if qualities of the kind required to be an effective activist in whatever field we choose to commit to working in are to unfurl, a whole other dimension of Heart work is also required.

In a word, as activists, we are called upon to play a 'new game', to engage with life at a new, more abundant level, where, as we have seen, ego will start to play an increasingly subservient and minor role. We need to know that deep down, our true self or our genuine heart always wants *real* abundance, always desires to experience union with the world around us, but so long as we are still bound into our separate self/ego-identification and thus are not properly connected to this deeper part of ourselves, the best we can achieve is an 'approximation of the real thing' or what Ken Wilber in *Up from Eden* calls 'substitute transcendence'.

How the ego-focussed us is accustomed to live, then, is often in ways that may actually prevent genuine Heart from emerging. For example, instead of being able to value our quality of life and knowing we are wealthy if we have good health and good friends and are surrounded by the beauty of nature, we may instead devote our lives primarily to accumulating material wealth (where however much we possess is never sufficient). Similarly, instead of being able to fuse with the ones we love, we may try to possess them, or instead of realising we are one with our environment, we endeavour to buy it. Since being disconnected from our hearts in this way results in a kind of yearning and a subtle kind of emptiness (which we often don't recognise as it is so widespread), we may also use food, possessions, fame, our social life, knowledge and power, alcohol or drugs or whatever else we can lay our hands on to try to 'fill us up'. Not only does this not work, but it is counter-productive and has many negative effects upon our society. For example, those who are attached to having to be in control all the time or who radically abuse the capitalist system inevitably experience a degree of spiritual emptiness. All these kinds of activities, Wilber maintains, are 'substitutes for true release in wholeness … so instead of being one with the cosmos, we try to possess it, instead of being one with God, we try to play God'. For example, the addict's desire to get high is an attempt to replicate artificially the natural sense of elevation we experience as our hearts open in joy.

As activists, it is crucially important that we understand this and are clear that a new and better world cannot be built out of such substitute activities, which only serve to perpetuate the dying world of the Setting Sun. Therefore, if our attention is not consciously directed towards expanding our hearts into more spiritual domains, there is no guarantee that we will be able to do more than touch into the universal heart occasionally, and as a result we may not make too much headway in graduating out of our caterpillar identities. We will still remain a caterpillar, albeit perhaps a healthier and stronger one with a more solid ego, but with the ego still in control, as *our egos don't consent to giving up the reins of power unless we have also begun evolving a more open and awake Heart self that they may be assured of safely surrendering into.* The following section of the book explores how, as activists, we may start leaving our old 'substitute activities' behind and begin moving in the direction of our butterfly-hood. Here, the name of the game is consciously to align ourselves with the rising tide of love in order that we may increasingly come under the embrace of the world of the Great Eastern Sun.

Cultivating the garden of the Heart

Many spiritual teachers see our hearts as being akin to a garden of beautiful flowers. I like this analogy, as all our many Heart virtues really are like magnificent flowers, each with its own delicious scent and exquisite colour. Also, if we want a fine-looking and well-kept garden, we need to take great care of it – mow it, weed it, water it and so on – and exactly the same is true of the garden inside our hearts. If we are truly to move into our *deeper* humanity, we must be willing to do this extra piece of work that will not simply make us *feel* better (the aim of therapy), but also *be* better (the aim of spiritual work). And nobody other than ourselves can ensure that we commit to it. As the spiritual teacher Graf Karlfried von Dürckheim put it:

> *The destiny of everything that lives is that it should unfold its own nature to its maximum possibility. Man is no exception. But he cannot – as a tree or a flower does – fulfil this destiny automatically. He is only permitted to become what he is intended to be when he takes himself in hand, works on himself and practises ceaselessly to reach perfection.*[1]

Holding an image of higher human possibilities

One thing that can be very helpful for those of us starting out in this new phase of Heart work is to seek out the company of big-hearted or universally hearted people whom we can look up to and who can inspire us, people who already hold the next stage of our evolution in their hearts and who no longer engage in substitute activities, but rather whose lives are committed to 'becoming what we are intended to be'. The gift which such people can offer us is that they can mirror butterfly states of consciousness for us and can help us come to understand that life beyond caterpillar-ness is truly rich and worth aspiring towards.

In a word, we need a new kind of hero in our lives; we need people who are not just committed to the glorification of their ego, but who are genuine and humble and committed to doing good for the planet and are happy, if necessary, to work behind the scenes. Such people may reveal to us that many things may be possible which ordinarily we might not believe. The philosopher Jean Huston put her finger on the problem of caterpillar man when she wrote that 'we are all born Stradivariuses, but raised to believe we are plastic fiddles'. Once we start evolving and understanding the fallacy of this mindset, like the hero in that magnificent film *Avatar* (an absolute must for all aspiring activists), we begin realising that 'most of what we have been taught to believe was real is false, and most of what we had learned to believe was illusory is what is most real'.

Our challenge is to expand our consciousness, to shift from being an enshadower to an enheartener, and in the process to start bringing Great Eastern Sun values and ideas 'down' into our existing 'normal world'. I say 'down' because it is about bringing a higher level into a lower one. But first, we have to reach up to that higher level. For the great Indian sage Sri Aurobindo, becoming a genuine human being meant achieving

> *a conversion of our whole nature into a soul instrumentation where we may experience the divine in every cell of our body … where we experience a spontaneous sympathy with all of the universe … where there is no bondage to interior forces, no defection from our highest truth, thus enabling us to enter into contact with the Greater Reality beyond and pervading the universe and be in communion and union with it.*

To do this, as I just said, it is very helpful to have the company of people who will understand these words and not laugh at them, and who will encourage us to regard the 'Greater Reality' as a beautiful ideal to aspire towards. Even if we do not manage to enter into 'full contact' with it, and only get a little of the way there, this is nonetheless a considerable achievement and will enable us to do an enormous amount of good for our planet.

Four basic requirements for success in heart-awakening work

There are four requirements which are absolutely necessary, if as activists we are to be successful in our mission of growing our spiritual heart (out of which our universal heart will emerge).

- Firstly, we must truly want to wake up and be a real person (find our butterfly self); that is, we must genuinely desire to know with all our heart who we truly are and to allow this realisation to shine through everything we do. We also need to be thoroughly fed up with our old plastic-fiddle 'normal' identities, lifestyles and behaviours, and be fully aware of the damage which our substitute unitive activities can cause.

- Secondly, we need to acquire a regular spiritual practice or regular spiritual practices. This is of the utmost importance as it enables our Heart life to evolve. As Chris Bache put it:

Without the grounding of a regular spiritual practice, the centre too often fails to hold and the rising unconscious too easily falls apart into distracting triviality or washes through one, causing exuberant excitement that does not really change the fundamental structures of the psyche.[2]

Essentially what spiritual practices do – provided we use ones that are right for us, and we do them conscientiously and do not superficially jump from one practice to another – is that they enable us to make this shift.

- Thirdly, we require discipline. This is so important. Another great Indian sage, the Shivapuri Baba, once said: 'Without discipline, the spiritual life is impossible.' By discipline I mean being ordered and organised, which, among other things, means that we persist in our practices and don't just do them haphazardly or only when we feel like it.
- Fourthly, we need to recognise that we must always be seeking to realise the treasure inside our hearts. 'Seek', Jesus told us, 'and ye shall find.' Here our seeking has a different focus to what it had initially, when we were trying to heal ourselves and where our focus had been on investigating where and how we were wounded. Now, we are trying to open up to what will illuminate us; we are endeavouring to discover that, as some teachers express it, we are truly all pearls beyond price. In Sri Ramakrishna's words, 'there are pearls in the sea; but you must dive again and again until you find them. God is in the world, but you will have to persevere to find him.' Thus, we need to be good and persistent divers…

There are two further points to remind ourselves about. The first is that the more we advance, the tougher our tests or our initiations may become, and the second is to understand that, as the Dalai Lama put it, 'our seeking … is not only for ourselves. It is for all of humanity, and each of us is always a little evolving cell in the awakening heart of species man!' In other words, we are never alone. We are all on a journey together, and one of the best ways to succeed or to 'find God' is to help each other to do so.

Working with the re-re-emerging feminine principle

It is important to understand that at different times in our history, our spirituality has been subject to different influences. What is currently giving a particular potency to the fire inside the universal heart is the fact that it is being overlighted by a presence which we can simply call the 'feminine principle', embodying everything that we understand as constituting the female spirit. This is extremely important because for eons, this presence remained underground, existing in the Shadow, and consequently the patriarchal mindset was allowed to reign supreme, which has been one of the main factors responsible for so many of the imbalances on our planet. The negative consequences of this are especially prominent in the domains of business, politics and religion.

The dominance of the patriarchal mindset explains why there has been so much extremism and rigidity, why humanity has been so warlike, why the domain of Heart has been so excluded from mainstream life, and why hardness has triumphed over softness, pragmatism over mysticism, doing over being, reason over feeling and initiating over surrendering. It also explains why women the world over have for centuries had such a hard time of it – why they have so often been objectified, why their enormous contributions to the world have received such little recognition, why their rights have often not been acknowledged, and why, in many cultures today, they are still enormously repressed and regarded as second-class citizens.

Things are now slowly beginning to change. The feminine principle is resulting in a new empowerment for everything that is feminine and it bodes very well for the future. In particular, we can see its influence in terms of women coming increasingly into positions of power. It also lies behind the whole women's movement, which continues to grow in stature and strength. It also means that there is more space for greatly needed Heart qualities such as gentleness, kindness and love to come more fully into their own. Last but not least, its presence is making it much easier for men to begin 'outing' their female, receptive sides in the recognition that the more we do so, the more whole we become, and the more likely we are to make significant advances in the direction of our own butterfly-ness.

Different levels of Heart

The activist needs to understand that there are many different stages of Heart to embrace, many different levels of becoming a butterfly, and just as at school we needed to progress through different forms or grades, so the same thing applies in our spiritual life. There are four big mistakes we can make which can interfere with this:

- We can be lazy and not make any effort.
- We can choose the wrong path for ourselves by taking on a practice or finding a teacher that is not right for us or by trying to be of service in a way that is not appropriate.
- We can overstay our time in the beginners' class and not move on when we are ready.
- We can engage in what my old friend John Welwood calls 'spiritual bypassing' and try and go into too high a class too soon, before we are ready.

If we trust our hearts and allow them to be our guide, we will know exactly what we need at every step along the way, and we will draw to ourselves those teachers and teachings and activities that are most relevant for us at any time.

Early stages of spiritual seeking

When we first embark on our activist path of Heart, we are not particularly intent on discovering 'greater realities'. Here, our aim is more to try and develop a healthier and happier ego. Here, our spiritual work links in with our therapeutic explorations. Here, we hope that becoming more spiritual or having a more open heart will make us feel better, be more effective or be more successful. Therefore, a lot of our efforts are geared towards using spirituality to boost our self-esteem, which we hope will give us more confidence and increase our capacities. This is absolutely appropriate and it enables us to begin to open ourselves up to the first rudimentary flutterings of our butterfly-ness. Ken Wilber refers to this spirituality as translative. For him what happens is that

> *our old separate ego-self is simply given a new way to think or feel about reality. In other words, the self is given a new belief – perhaps holistic instead of atomistic, forgiveness instead of blame. The self then learns*

to translate its world and its being in the terms of this new language or new paradigm, and this new and enchanting translation acts, at least temporarily, to alleviate the terror in the heart of the separate self.[3]

Deeper stages of spirituality

After we have been in this phase for a long time, doing our spiritual practices and going through our various initiations, some of us may suddenly begin to sense a new stage gradually starting to reveal itself to us. We observe our whole orientation subtly shifting. We are no longer as concerned with trying to align ourselves with the universal heart, refining our sense of self and trying to bring greater Heart into our lives. Instead, we find ourselves increasingly moved to play an entirely different kind of 'game', which is much more about surrendering and letting go of everything and anything about ourselves that experiences any kind of separation from the world around us. Our aim now is to evolve a surrendered Heart self, to merge with the 'Greater Reality', to become one with the greater Heart of God. Describing this new phase, Wilber suggests:

The very process of translation itself is challenged, undermined and eventually dismantled. With typical translation, the self ... is given a new way to think about the world; but with radical transformation, the self is enquired into, looked into, grabbed by the throat and literally throttled to death ... The self is not made content; the (old) self is made toast![4]

This 'toast stage' is very important for those activists whose service work is particularly focused on helping the species heart awaken to higher states of consciousness and whose lives therefore evolve around bringing greater enlightenment into the world. We must know that the more awake our hearts are, the more spiritual force we carry and therefore the greater our capacity to help our fellow human beings and be instrumental in helping birth a new society. However, a huge amount of good can be done without our ever reaching such elevated heights of butterfly-ness. The vast majority of the wonderful activists around the world, doing extraordinary things to help heal the planet, are not yet operating out of this unitive or non-dual level, but it does not stop them being very successful and influential in their various fields.

Being stalked by enlightenment

That said, I believe that these very elevated states of heart are nonetheless stalking all of us, forever beckoning to us and looking for opportunities to 'drop down' into us and remind us to devote even more energy to our inner development by giving us brief 'sneak previews' of who we truly are or of what it truly means to be *fully* human. Even if we are not yet resident in this greater 'surrendered reality'– that is, if we do not live all our days in a non-dual space and are still primarily focused on translative spirituality – we may nonetheless be touched by very elevated states of heart and to remain in very beautiful spaces of consciousness for considerable periods of time. What will happen is that we will have certain 'visitations' from the land of grace; we will experience a temporary 'descent' into us of states of consciousness that ordinarily reside in much more elevated or refined realities.

This descent can occur in many different ways. Sometimes, a 'higher heart' experience just 'drops' into us out of the blue when we are least expecting it. Sometimes, it comes as a result of our spiritual practice or our being in the presence of a spiritual master. (I will discuss this later.) Sometimes it comes because particular activities of ours will have evoked it, for instance, if we have done something that takes us to the edge in some way. It has occurred for me in many different situations. To give an example of a most bizarre one, as a young man, I used to do a lot of ski racing, which quite often took me to the edge (especially in downhill races), and in one particular race, I experienced myself entering a blissfully transcendent state of heart where I experienced everything occurring in slow motion; for many days afterwards, I remained in a beautifully heightened space of love. The same thing sometimes happens when I am teaching on my spiritual retreats, and it happened once during the writing of this book, where for four extraordinary days, in a space of extreme calm and clarity, I wrote three chapters that hardly required any changes and where my condition of severe attention deficit disorder, which ordinarily handicaps me quite considerably, completely vanished. I mention these things to remind you that very ordinary, flawed people like myself can also be touched by states of grace and that the moment we embark on a spiritual journey, we need always to be open to visitations of the unexpected.

I would like to leave the last word with the Shivapuri Baba, who was replying to a question asking him for advice as to how we can best help our world. (He happened to be 112 years old when he gave this reply.) For me, it beautifully answers the question in a most grounded and practical way of what the spiritual life is really all about.

> *We can best help our world by living the right life and practising charity. Mentally to wish everyone well, even our enemies. Serve other people physically. Give ten per cent of your income to deserving people and poor people. We are unhappy because we do not live the right life, which is a life with a definite aim, a planned and discriminative life. A right life is one where we think only good thoughts of others, speak only good words of others, do only good deeds to others, and give of our substance to help others.*[5]

We all need to meditate deeply on these words.

Chapter 12

Opening to the Meditative Heart

Free from desire, you realise the mystery. Caught in desire, you see only the manifestations – LAO TZU

When the mind is at peace, the world too is at peace – LAYMAN P'ANG

So long as the mind is unsteady and fickle, it availeth nothing, even though a man has got a good guru and the company of holy men – RAMA KRISHNA

The importance of meditation

To be an effective activist, no matter in what areas we work, we need to have presence, we need to be able to see and think clearly, and we need to operate out of an intelligent and open heart. There is no better technique to facilitate all these things than meditation. One of the reasons for all the disquiet, stupidity, drama and chaos out in the world is that there is so much disquiet, stupidity, drama and chaos inside us, and what lies behind this is an undisciplined mind, which always aligns itself with our egos.

Meditation, if practised properly, both disciplines and tames our mind. By calming the mind's restlessness, it allows a deeper and quieter dimension – which Buddhists refer to as 'no mind' or as 'the mind behind mind' – to arise, and when it does, it puts a powerful damper on the possibility of ego running the show. The mind behind mind is also full of respect for Heart, and is fully aware that Heart is the boss.

The beauty of meditation is that it also opens up a space for our hearts to grow, as well as making it easier for us gradually to let go our identification with our clever, ever-restless egos. If we are to be an effective activist, it is so important that we start moving in this direction, as whenever our egos start grappling with a problem, all too often the solutions we come up with only augment it or, conversely, move it elsewhere for others to fret over. Meditation also enables us to experience what in Zen is known as 'beginner's mind'. This is the capacity to experience the intrinsic freshness of life in each moment, as opposed to our 'normal' way of viewing 'what is', which, as we have seen, is primarily through the lens of our remembrances about what was.

The problem with caterpillar man

I recently watched an interview on television with a 'clever' financial analyst talking about hedge funds and derivatives. As I watched his staccato replies to some of the questions being put to him, I thought to myself: this man absolutely encapsulates all that is problematic about caterpillar man. He lives entirely out of his head. He has no self-awareness at all, he is utterly disconnected from his body and his heart is totally hidden away. He is insecure, restless and defensive, and our world is in the mess it is in partly because we have a system that enables thousands of people exactly like him to occupy positions of responsibility. As I continued observing the interview, where he began pronouncing upon the world economic situation, trotting out clichés utterly devoid of depth or wisdom, I saw that he certainly was not a 'bad' person and was not even a greedy person. Rather, something about him was utterly hollow and inauthentic. His Stradivarius self was deeply hidden away.

The problem about people like him – and so many of us today are like him – is that our genuineness lies in Shadow and so our actions never really contribute to life. Often, we are restless and anxious not necessarily because our minds are burdened by big problems or because we are carrying deep species wounds, but because we have spent most of our time acquiring external know-how and have never considered it worthwhile to look inside ourselves or work at quietening or deepening ourselves. Everything we do is reactive, our minds become overloaded with information that has never been properly digested and so we are always too full of 'stuff' ever to allow anything new to enter us.

The best antidote to our restlessness and clutter is meditation, which is why it is so important. As we begin meditating, a natural emptying process is activated; a door begins opening inside our hearts to allow many of our fears and anxieties – all the emotional grit or psychic debris that we have been accumulating over the years – to flow out of us. This kind of release is key, as one of the reasons behind much of our lack of integration is emotional bunged-up-ness or psychological constipation. Our derivatives expert couldn't let anything new in because he was already too 'full'. The more we can let go of what no longer serves us, the lighter we will feel, emotionally, intellectually and spiritually. Our physical health also improves. Meditation has also been shown to alter the hard wiring inside our brains. Research published by the American Academy of Sciences has revealed that within three or four months of meditation, we can switch off 500 genes that increase the likelihood of cancer, cardiovascular illness, auto-immune deficiency and certain types of infection.

'Fasting of the heart'

Chuang Tzu was a Chinese Taoist sage who lived many years before Christ, and who understood all about the science of emptying. He realised that one of the most important things required if one were to become a whole human being was to engage in a process which he called 'the fasting of the heart'. Asked to explain what this meant, he replied:

> *The goal of fasting is inner unity. This means hearing, but not with the ear; hearing, but not with the understanding; hearing with the spirit, with your whole being … This hearing is not limited to any one faculty … Hence it demands the emptiness of all the faculties. And when the faculties are empty, then the whole being listens.*
>
> *Only then can there be a direct grasp of what is right there before you, which is nothing that can be heard with the ear or understood with the mind. Fasting of the heart empties the faculties; it frees you from limitation and from preoccupation. Fasting of the heart begets unity and freedom … If you can do this, you will be able to go among men in the world without upsetting them. You will not enter into conflict with their ideal image of themselves. If they will listen, sing them a song. If not, keep silent. Do not try to break down the door. Do not try out new medicines on them. Just be there among them, because there is nothing else for you to be but one of them. And then you may have success. If you follow human methods, you can deceive. In this way, no deception is possible.*
>
> *Look at this window. It is nothing but a hole in the wall, but because of it the whole room is full of light. So when the faculties are empty, the heart is full of light. Being full of light, it becomes an influence by which others are secretly transformed.*

In these few sentences, we have an entire treatise on effective Heart activism! While explorative psychology helps empty us at a psychological level – we gain insights into our problematic issues and the sting gradually goes out of their tail – meditation empties us in a much subtler way. As we learn to quieten down, it becomes easier to see ourselves more objectively, and consequently not only to become more aware that there may be a deeper purpose to our lives, but also to be more mindful of the many 'ego games' we play which obscure it for us. As our sensitivity starts to deepen, our capacity to see clearly into the true heart of whatever it is we are focused on at any time increases.

Meditation's gift to me

Given meditation has been a huge gift to me in my life. It hasn't solved any of my emotional issues (it is not intended to), but it has quietened me down and given me more space to understand and to work with them more effectively. It has also made me more connected to myself and more content with my life. To use Buckminster Fuller's well-known phrase, it has given me the necessary equipment to derive 'more out of less'. I find I use less energy to get more done and I also consume less. I am no longer restless and so don't need to use a lot of petrol to travel all over the place to be stimulated by new landscapes. Because my heart is more abundant, I also don't need to own lots of things in order to feel rich.

Meditation has helped make my heart stronger and clearer, and my life has, over the years, become much simpler. I have gradually found myself naturally inclined to downsize – only to focus on what is essential –and far from this being a sacrifice, I have found it to be a gift, as I have given up certain activities which never really added any quality to my life anyway. Because meditation has helped me to live so much more through my heart, my appreciation of life has expanded, and little things which in the past I wouldn't even have noticed I now find give me a lot of pleasure. This is especially so with people, whom I can now see with greater clarity and savour more fully.

what is going on in the world economically, it may well be necessary for all of us to consider downsizing in the years ahead. However, unless there is a significant shift in our value systems, it may be difficult for us to do so without the feeling that we have somehow failed or 'lost out'. I think meditation helps counteract this. I also think that the more we allow ourselves to quieten and let go, the more our old identities, predicated upon and held in place by our tension, start dropping away. As they do so, our natural Stradivarius-ness is given space inside us to begin blossoming and to draw the warm rays of the world of the Great Eastern Sun closer to us.

As a result of meditation, I find that it takes much less to make me content, and much more to disturb me, and I am much more able to accept 'what is' and handle difficulties in a calm way, as and when they arise. When crises hit, they still biff me, but I am more resilient, and so less likely to be knocked flat and more able to stay on my feet and derive meaning from them. I find I am also more forgiving of myself and others, more able to see my Shadow issues clearly and so work calmly with them without needing to judge myself. I put much of this down to meditation.

It is not that I have no ego left – I would never be so pretentious as to assert that this part of me is now reduced to toast – but it is not as wont as it used to be to run the show. If it starts to try to do so, I have more space available to rein it in. I therefore perceive meditation to be not just a, but *the*, prime tool in our awakening process. For the Tibetan master Tarthang Tulku, meditation is

> *a way of opening our lives to the richness of experience … allowing us to embrace and learn from whatever we experience … As we learn from our experience, our appreciation of life increases; our senses grow keener; our minds grow more clear and more perceptive, so that eventually our entire frame of reference becomes transformed … Once we are aware, we can then function properly even amid the confusions of the world.*[1]

Presence

Meditation also assists us to be more present. And when we are more present, we have greater presence, which is something inherently spiritual and has nothing to do with having a charming or compelling personality. It is enormously important in all areas of activist work, and it cannot be faked. A person with true presence can achieve extraordinary things.

Recently, I attended a lecture given by an elderly South Korean peace activist. Although she was minute in stature, her aura was immense; she bestrode the stage like a colossus and her words inspired and touched the hearts of all of us who had come to hear her. People with this kind of aura radiate a powerful spiritual light. One just *knew* that she embodied the changes she was talking to us about and that she walked her talk exquisitely and came from a deep place of love and wisdom. A vast calmness and steely determination pervaded her and all of us were transfixed and inspired by her humility and humanity. Her presence was vast. I don't believe she can have arrived at this place without meditating.

Practising meditation

It is now time to look at practising meditation, and I will give you a very simple 'Heart practice' that I often do. Sit down in a comfortable position, either on a chair with your feet firmly on the ground, or on the floor cross legged, whichever is the more comfortable. Do not sit too rigidly or too floppily. One meditation teacher told me to 'sit as if you were holding a little bird in your hand. If it is too tight, you will crush it, and if it is too loose, it will fly away!' Then focus on your inner heart or your heart chakra, which, as you know, is in the middle of your chest, and consciously imagine yourself connecting to your 'best friend' there. Ask your heart to help you in your meditation.

Spend a few moments imagining that you have lungs inside your heart, and breathe in and out of them. Let your connection with your heart begin to expand. Allow it to talk to you and tell you about itself – what it can do for you, what it wishes of you. Continue breathing in and out of your heart.

As you do this, your restless mind (which is linked in to your ego) will begin to play up. All sorts of thoughts will start surfacing and will distract you, and resistances will emerge, as ego doesn't like being subdued; it wants us to stay agitated and feels threatened by our being calmed. Here, you need to remember not to give these restless thoughts energy. You need to observe them, but not to fight them, all the time going back to focusing on your breath going in and out of your heart. This process of being distracted and then returning to observe your breath may happen many times during a sitting. Also, there are many external sounds that might distract you, such as traffic, phones ringing or birds twittering. Again, you are not to give them energy, but rather include them in your meditation.

Often, as our practice begins to deepen, we start observing just *how* restless our minds are, just how *much* they resist being still. Here our aim is not to be judgemental or hard on ourselves. Rather, we need to be patient and practise the art of detached self-observation in the realisation that if we have spent most of our lives with an undisciplined mind, it is hardly likely to give up its position overnight.

This is why a disciplined practice is so important, as the more we impose this new habit on ourselves, the more strongly it will become entrenched inside us. The more we practise, the more our mind begins to feel emptier and quieter, and we may start to gain the sense that it is not us doing the breathing, but rather that the breathing is happening through us, or that we are being breathed.

Begin with twenty minutes a day. The first thing in the morning is a good time. If you can do this, it will set a strong tone for the rest of the day. If you can do the same thing at night as well, that will be fantastic. When you feel ready, you might want to extend twenty minutes to thirty minutes.

Never think in meditation, 'Now I have made it – I am quiet, so I need to stop practising.' In actuality you haven't 'made' anything. You have simply touched a particular kind of inner space, which, if it is to persist, needs continually working at to be maintained. An analogy is with an athlete, who, in order to remain in shape, needs to keep up his training. What you will find is that the more you meditate, the easier it gets, and soon you will reach a place where it may become a delight.

The late spiritual master Osho certainly believed this. For him, meditation needed to be seen as a play, something to be enjoyed as an art in itself. In his words: 'The festive dimension is the most important thing to be understood, namely the capacity to enjoy, moment to moment, all that comes to you.' My experience is that when we first embark on a meditative path, we need to make a strong personal effort and use our own personal will. Eventually we will find that something else – we may call it 'higher will' – begins to operate through us and guides us. When this happens, we need to think much more about totally surrendering to this higher will.

Stages of meditation

There are many different stages of meditation that we will go through. Here, I will quote from scholar activist Ken Wilber once more:

> *Resting in the formal witness [Wilber tells us that this is what meditation induces in us] brings both a radical liberation and a*

compelling duty. Liberation in that you are free from the bondage to the world of objects, and duty in that ... you feel compelled to help others find the same salvation, which is their own truest self and deepest condition ...

When people first start meditating, normal life becomes more dreamlike and loses its power to overwhelm us. Life looks like a big movie, and one is the unmoved witness watching the show. Happiness, joy, pain and crisis come up and one just witnesses them. One cannot manufacture turmoil with the same conviction

He goes on to suggest that

Enlightenment is to snap out of the movie of life ... to wake up and shake it off. When you take life seriously – when you think the movie is real – you forget you are the pure and free witness and you identify with the little self, the ego, as if you were part of the movie you were making.[3]

The deeper aim of meditation (here he is talking about transformational spirituality) is to 'find a deeper identity. You are still conscious when there are no objects, no subjects, no hope, no fear; there is nothing at all and yet you are; you exist but only as pure consciousness.' Indeed,

if we want to realise our supreme identity with spirit, we will have to plug ourselves into this current of constant consciousness ... which will (i) strip us of an exclusive identification with mind or ego, and (ii) allow us to recognise and identify with that which is constant or timeless.[4]

Imagine for a moment if our world leaders and our top industrialists and scientists and generals and entrepreneurs and bankers were to do deep meditation work. Imagine if our university professors and our educators and our social workers, our artists and our environmentalists, began to do the same thing. Imagine if all of us all over the world were to do this, how much the universal heart would sing and how quickly the world of the Great Eastern Sun would come into being.

Different kinds of meditation

I have shown you only one very simple kind of meditation. There are many different kinds, and the activist must select that kind which he or she feels most drawn to. Some meditations we do sitting down with our eyes open; others we need to do standing up with our eyes closed. For some meditations we need a mantra, while with other kinds we need nothing. Some are silent, others require that we use our voices; some request us to be still, others that we move. Some meditations enable us to follow our inner heart guidance; others call us to respond to guided meditations which we are given.

In my week-long retreats, I usually get my students to do several different kinds of meditation practice. One which I am particularly fond of is to guide people into an imaginary world of Heart and get them to sense how it would feel if they were to live in a world where everyone operated out of their butterfly selves and treated each other with love and respect. The importance of such a meditation is that it helps us plant new tracks in our mind.

It is also powerful to meditate on particular symbols. I especially like working with symbols of the heart, and one of my favourites is a red rose. I ask people to imagine a red rose growing bigger and bigger in the middle of their chests and radiating its scent out to all corners of their being.

If we have a particular spiritual master who is important to us, then it can be useful to meditate with him, or if he is not present, to meditate on him and imagine him residing inside our hearts, guiding and awakening us. It is also very powerful to meditate directly on God and to imagine God dwelling inside our hearts, or even to contemplate our dwelling within the heart of God. As with other forms of Heart work, if we are starting out, it can be helpful to find a teacher to give us some rudimentary instruction. Conversely, we can do our practice in places where plenty of people will have meditated in the past and therefore where a powerful 'meditational field' will have built up, as that will enormously help us.

Meditation, however, is not a panacea; we can't just meditate our problems away, and it certainly is not a substitute for investigative work. By endowing us with more energy and insight, however, it enables us to uncover unconscious material more effectively and understand it more comprehensively. But not all of us can meditate, or are ready to do so. For instance, if we are deeply traumatised or suffering from shock or are very emotionally disturbed, meditation might be the very last thing we need.

In certain instances, it is unwise to meditate as it can often cloak over our problems and so give us the illusion that they do not exist and so don't need working on. Here is where we are challenged to connect to our hearts, which, if listened to, will instruct us accordingly. I will leave the last word with Ken Wilber. Again, in *Up from Eden*, he reminds us:

> *If we are to further the evolution of mankind, and not just reap the benefit of humanity's last struggles, if we are to contribute to evolution and not merely siphon it off ... then meditation – or a similar and truly contemplative practice – becomes an absolute ethical imperative ... If we do less than that, our life becomes ... a case of merely enjoying the level of consciousness [that is, caterpillar consciousness] which past heroes achieved for us. We contribute nothing; we pass on our mediocrity.*

Chapter 13

Awakening the Heart of Prayer

> *Despite anything anyone can say to the contrary, never forget the importance, the absolute necessity of prayer, of union with God. Neither knowledge, nor love, nor wisdom on earth are in any way compatible with what prayer brings about: union with the Primordial Principle –*
> PETER DEUNOV
>
> *More things are wrought by prayer than this world dreams of –*
> ALFRED, LORD TENNYSON

The significance of prayer

Prayer is another very important practice which serves to 'polish' our heart and thus assists the blossoming of the flowers inside its beautiful garden. While meditation helps connect us to our source, prayer is a means of engaging with it more actively and intentionally, whereby dialogue also enters the equation. With prayer we try to communicate directly with our source, and then allow it to communicate back. Thus, it is a kind of 'heart-to-heart' with the deepest part of ourselves. Thomas Merton described it as 'freedom and affirmation growing out of nothingness into love. Prayer is not only dialogue with God: it is the communion of our freedom with His ultimate freedom, His infinite spirit.'[1]

Jesus was always telling his disciples that they needed consciously to invoke the sacred domains and that if they wanted to receive certain things from life, they needed to ask. In St Matthew's Gospel, Jesus's instruction was specifically to 'knock, and it shall be opened unto you', and prayer may be seen as a precise means of knocking on the specific door that opens to the higher worlds. Perhaps one of the reasons many of us don't always receive what we need in our lives is that we don't pray enough – we don't engage sufficiently in this kind of 'knocking'. In times of trouble we may obtain relief by having a good friend to pour our hearts out to; prayer is a not dissimilar activity, only here we are pouring ourselves out to, and hopefully being listened to by, a 'friend' at a whole other level.

Prayer, therefore, is a means of developing a deeper intimacy with the transcendent realms. It permits us to connect that aspect of ourselves that lives in the three-dimensional worlds of space and time with the multi-dimensional or subtler realms that exist beyond space and time. It enables us to have greater access to, or to draw into our hearts, what I will call a 'higher-grade spiritual fuel' that is only to be found in these timeless realms. Today, given the complexity and deep roots of so many of the problems we face, we as activists are all greatly in need of this spiritual sustenance.

Connecting to a 'higher power'

There have been occasions in my own life where I felt truly stuck and where, as a result of praying, doors opened up for me in ways that I would never have dreamed possible. I will give you one small example. Many years ago, I was devastated when a woman whom I had been living with, and whom I loved very much, suddenly chose to leave me and go off with a close friend. No amount of psychological work seemed able to make any difference to my grief or to address the shock that this caused me, and my own personal efforts to empty my heart of this particular person, whom I had allowed in so deeply, were of no use. Two years later my heart still felt as bruised and battered as ever. So I decided to pray and ask for help. 'Please, higher power, help me. I am in so much pain and I don't know what to do.'

A few days later, I felt moved to attend a particular conference, and there I happened to encounter a woman who suggested to me that she would like to go and visit a spiritual teacher in Germany, called Mother Meera, and would I accompany her? Thinking it a nice idea, and in no way being open to any 'romantic possibility', I agreed.

Something extraordinary happened during those four days I spent in silence in Mother Meera's powerful energy field. Not only did my pain miraculously start melting away, but my body also began to unlock and I found myself able to open my heart once more, allowing me to appreciate that certain kinds of wounds often require a good deal more than psychotherapy if they are to heal, and that there are times in our lives when the assistance we require has to come from much higher levels of consciousness. Something in the powerful Heart field generated by Mother Meera (a beautiful embodiment of the feminine principle) enabled a certain kind of release to occur for me that seemingly could not happen in any other way. As a result, I found myself able to allow in, and respond to, the love and kindness of the woman who had invited me to come with her on this particular healing journey, and thus to feel free again.

One might say: 'How do you know that this healing happened as a result of prayer? How do you know that what occurred for you might not have happened anyway?' Answer: I don't. But in looking back, I think it extraordinary that as soon as I began to pray for help, I was put in touch with two very remarkable women, one who was extremely kind to me and the other who was revered as a saint, and that the combination of their different kinds of Heart magic enabled the release of something inside me that had been stuck fast. So many other little miracles have happened for me in my life, all of them connected to my praying, that I have learned over the years to trust in this process deeply.

I believe that the way we pray is of huge importance. In this particular instance, I think that the sincerity of my asking – my passion having been fuelled by my pain – gave a certain genuine imperative to my invocation and, as it were, drew to me the attention of what I will later be referring to as the 'higher helping forces'.

The healing power of prayer

I will give you another example of the healing power of prayer. Fifteen years ago, I was diagnosed with a serious disease and I decided I would try and address it in a non-conventional way. I took off on a kind of magical mystery healing tour, which eventually led me to a particular cave monastery in the middle of Russia, where I encountered monks who lived in silence and who did nothing all day but pray. I remember being immensely struck by the sanctity of their environment and the immense purity of their being – their beautiful faces looking exactly like those depicted on old Russian icons.

These monks saw I had come a long way to meet them, and they agreed to pray for me – even asking to be informed when I died, so that they might continue to pray for me in the afterlife. Again, there is no way of proving this, but I feel sure that the fact that there has never been any worsening of my symptoms, but only an acceleration of my awakening process, is due, in part, to the potency of the monks' intercessions for me.

If we look around the world, we realise that there are many examples of people who spontaneously recover from serious diseases without 'doing anything' other than giving thanks, which is a very potent form of prayer, and engaging in inner work. Perhaps 'not doing anything' is at times the significant catalyst that enables a healing to take place. Certainly, if we are very ill, while I am in no way suggesting that we should discount orthodox medical treatment, we should also never dismiss the complementary efficacy of prayer. Dr Larry Dossey is an American physician who has done a great deal of research into this subject, and always prays for his patients three times a day. He suggests that in the medicine of the future, there will come a time whereby if a doctor does not practise prayer as part of the prescription for his patients, he will be found guilty of medical malpractice. I welcome this approach.

As over the years I have come to see prayer as a natural expression of our hearts' own will to be, I too always pray for my clients, and regard this as very important. I have found that the more our hearts open, the more they delight in prayer and the more they seem to instruct us in the art of how best to pray. This has led me to believe that if we were more fully to utilise the power of prayer, many of the things in our lives that we currently find difficult would become much easier. Some years ago, someone quite close to me did something that at the time I considered quite reprehensible. I saw my heart fill with resentment towards them and I also saw how ill this resentment made me feel. I prayed for strength to try to deal with this situation with love and without 'filling' either of us with negative energy, and again I received a great deal of help. I found I was able to begin seeing this person through the lens of my heart once more, and as this occurred, my anger and sorrow began to dissipate and today, most of the time, I feel affection and goodwill towards them. They did something bad but they are not a bad person. As we will be seeing later, when we explore the theme of evil, so much of it comes out of a deeply wounded heart, and very often prayer is one of the best strategies to deal with it.

Why prayer does not always seem to work

In my retreats, I often discuss the power of prayer with my students. Many have come up to me and have said, 'I have prayed and nothing has changed. I do not think that prayer works.' Discounting the fact that certain things which we pray for may take many years to materialise, or may not even be possible, I believe there are several reasons for this. One is that we do not always believe in the power of prayer. We are too attached to our 'normal thinking', believing that only things that are visible and concrete – 'scientifically proven' – have any value. It may also be that we do not engage in prayer with a quiet enough mind, and so are unable to connect deeply enough to our source. Perhaps, too, we do not pray with our full hearts, with enough sincerity and passion, as it is these qualities that serve to give wings to our supplications and so allow them to be heard by those helping forces in the higher worlds. This is why so often our best praying comes about when things are really desperate.

When a close friend of mine was dying, I did a lot of prayer on her behalf and also instructed a lot of other prayer groups to intercede for her. When she still died some months later, I felt rather a failure. In the middle of my praying a few weeks later, I realised that nothing could have prevented her demise, and that in actuality her time had come. I felt my heart telling me that I needed to pray for the highest good to take place, rather than requesting a specific outcome, and that being sick and dying may be a very significant part of a person's own transformational journey. 'Those in the higher worlds have a much wider perspective of what wholeness means than you, so don't always be so quick to impose your limited judgement on how you believe things ought to turn out,' was what my heart said to me.

Our hearts know how to pray

I never go along with those who say 'But I don't know how to pray'. Actually, prayer is easier than meditation. An old university friend of mine, who always professed to be an agnostic and who was always critical of what he called my 'unworldly lovey-doveyness', once suffered a severe tragedy. His young daughter was killed in an accident. Despite being fit, healthy, wealthy and in some respects, not unwise, nothing offered him any solace. So he decided to try and pray in his own way. He told me that the more he practised it, the better he became at it, and that gradually he received the inner strength to carry on with his life, when he had wanted to give up.

'My heart will always bear the scar of this tragedy,' he told me, 'but I now feel motivated to get on with my life – indeed, to change many aspects of it, and in particular, to have more compassion towards other people who have suffered similar losses. At the start I did not know how to pray but, in trying, something inside me showed me how. While what has happened was terrible, I feel that in rising to this challenge, I have somehow become a slightly better human being, and that surely is the purpose of all our lives.'

Something undeniably 'spiritual' or 'Heart-ful' had opened up in him whereby he was able to see his personal tragedy from a much wider perspective and gradually shift away from being a 'broken man' to someone afire with a new vision and purpose. In Thomas Merton's words again:

> *We have to face the existential reality of our wretchedness, nothingness and abjection, because it is there that our prayer begins. It is out of this nothingness that we are called into freedom ... out of this darkness that we are called into light. And we need to recognise this as our true starting point. Otherwise our prayer is not authentic.*[2]

I believe that our world at this time deeply needs our prayers, and that *praying is a powerful form of activism.* When we say to someone 'My thoughts are with you', we are in effect implying that we are sending prayerful thoughts out to them. It is a very potent way to be of assistance, and as we have seen, the more we are connected to our source and the greater the intensity of our passion, the more prayerfully effective our thoughts can be. Praying for another is akin to sending them a blessing, whereby we wish them to be touched by that which can enlighten, heal and inspire them. There are four main ways that we can pray: personal prayer, interpersonal prayer, impersonal prayer and prayer in action.

Personal prayer

Here we simply pray for ourselves. How we do this and what we pray for will be determined by what level we are at, how open our hearts are and what we may require at any time. I agree with Thomas Merton when he suggests that prayer is 'servile' if we use it solely to try 'to draw to ourselves gifts which we then incorporate into our own limited, selfish life', whereas 'authentic prayer enables us to emerge from our servility into freedom in God'. I would therefore seriously question whether it ought to be used to ask God to give us a Mercedes-Benz, as in that famous song by Janis Joplin.

However, at another level, if our attempts to develop a genuine spiritual life are continually being thwarted by a real lack in our personal lives – if, say, we cannot afford a car to drive our kids to school – then I feel there is nothing wrong with asking for a car (if not necessarily a Merc!). After all, significant financial or social deficiencies of any kind can severely handicap us emotionally and so compromise our endeavours to awaken into higher-order Heart states. (In Janis's case, perhaps her prayer might have been 'Please help me to be content with my old jalopy and so feel grateful for what I have and therefore not feel so deprived or envious that all my friends have Porsches'!)

Some 'prayer specialists' suggest that our personal prayers should only ever be general and never specific, and that we should only ask that what happens for us be for our highest good. While there is certainly much truth to this advice, I think there are certain instances where being specific is necessary, for when we request something in particular, it helps focus our attention in a particular direction, and that may be exactly what is required.

When we pray, we also need to accept that our prayers may not always be 'answered' in the way that we might wish for, and similarly, they may not always materialise within the time frame that we request. One childless couple came to see me once who had gone through all the various IVF treatments, to no avail. I suggested that they pray for a child. They did so. Only it took four more years for their desires to be fulfilled.

Interpersonal prayer

Here we pray specifically for another person – perhaps that they be blessed with health and well-being or that they be protected or healed of something. In my personal prayers, I always ask these things for my daughter, for those close to me, and for my clients. If any friends are going through difficult times, I will also pray for them. Although my parents have long been dead, I still sometimes send out prayerful thoughts to them, thanking them for all the good things they did for me, and apologising to them for all those years where I had made them so wrong for not having been, in my estimation, 'good enough'.

Often, if we are very stuck in our relationship with someone and cannot manage to work things through, praying for them or praying for a resolution can be very useful, as the sending out of 'good thoughts' always helps to bring someone closer to their own hearts and therefore indirectly closer to ours. I remember once sending out prayerful thoughts to an old friend who I had heard had fallen on hard times and whom I had not seen for several years. A few days later he called me to say that he had suddenly been thinking about me, and was sorry that we had lost touch, and might we perhaps meet up again?

Impersonal prayer

Here we pray for something general to happen: for example, that in areas of the planet where there are droughts, it may rain, or that help may be given to the victims of some natural disaster, or that assistance find its way to the Syrian people. We might also pray for peace in the world or that our world leaders make the right decisions, or that terrorists wake up and open their hearts and see how misguided their actions are, or that humanity as a whole be less greedy. Here, we will tend to pray for things that exist in our particular sphere of concern. Much of my praying focuses on asking that humanity's heart may open up more.

Prayer in action

As activists, one of the most important forms of prayer lies in our consciously seeking to involve ourselves in the situations we are praying for. For example, in my own case, I do not feel it enough that I simply pray for the human heart to open. I also regard it as part of my prayer that I do concrete things to help advance this vision. Writing this book, working with clients, teaching my retreats, working with business leaders, starting a school to train activists are all expressions of my prayer in action. When disasters like tsunamis hit the world, prayer in action could take the form of our actually going out to the disaster zones and physically involving ourselves in the relief efforts, like the man I mentioned earlier who went to Darfur. All human rights activists are experts in this area of prayer. These active interventions play a very important part in the 'heart-polishing' process, as the more we actually demonstrate our courage or express our love or our compassion in terms of concrete action, the more these qualities bloom and the more luxuriant the garden inside our hearts becomes.

Set prayers versus spontaneous praying

We can either use set prayers that have been designed for specific occasions, or we can make up our prayers on the spur of the moment. There exist many set prayers to protect us, prayers that can be said for the dead, prayers for night-time and early morning, and so on. They can beautifully focus our hearts in a particular direction and may be especially useful when we are first learning to pray. For example, when my mother died, as she had never wanted a memorial service, I used the set prayers designed by the Bulgarian spiritual master Peter Deunov to create a ritual that enabled all members of our family to say a proper farewell.

The disadvantage of set prayers is that if repeated over and over, they can lose their meaning and become stale. The phrase 'to know something by heart' is therefore misleading, as simply remembering particular word formations is more of a mental process and is no indication that their meaning has actually taken root inside our hearts. For some of us, it may be preferable either to select set prayers from other traditions – and there are some excellent prayers in the Native American traditions or in Celtic mysticism – or to design our own prayers out of the moment, as in this way they can have a certain freshness and sincerity. I particularly like doing this. If we belong to a specific religion, we may feel more comfortable doing our praying in those places of worship specifically designated for this purpose. But if not, we can pray anywhere. I find I do my best praying when I am out in nature, where I can hear birdsong and feel the wind in my face, as then I always feel closely connected to my heart.

My prayer this morning, for example, took the form of my giving thanks for the beauty of the countryside around me, for the gift of having some wonderful friends in my life, for my health and for the many blessings I have. I gave thanks for the privilege of being able to do my work. Then I prayed for my clients, my daughter and her mother, and for another very, very special person in my life, as well as for a couple of friends going through hard times. I ended with a prayer that relief somehow come to the people of Syria.

Peter Deunov's views on prayer

Peter Deunov has some beautiful observations on prayer. The following selection is taken from a delightful little book entitled *Gems of Love*, compiled by my dear friend David Lorimer:

> *Without prayer, a person cannot make progress ... People must pray if they wish to learn ... Pray to be liberated from all impurities which tarnish you ... Prayer should express the gratitude for all the good things and blessings which God is giving us ... Prayer is a conversation*

of the soul with God; it is the greatest and most powerful means of linking with God. In the life of a loving person, everything is prayer. When a person thinks about God, they are protected. You should pray both when you are well and when you are unwell.[3]

Deunov suggests that we need to choose a particular time for prayer work, and informs us that the most favourable hours are just after midnight, no doubt because many people are asleep, and therefore there is less restless energy around. Also, whenever we feel an inclination to pray, he recommends that we should follow that impulse and that if we do not, it may not visit us again so urgently. 'If breathing is so essential to human beings,' he tells us, 'thinking of God is a thousand times more indispensable. The power of prayer is that when a person prays, they activate all their virtues. Prayer must simultaneously contain the qualities of

love, wisdom, truth, justice, compassion and many other virtues. If you go to God with a prayer of this kind, you will resemble a tree laden with ripe fruit. When God sees you adorned in this way, He will be glad to have an intelligent child near him. It is thanks to prayer that we become conductors of higher powers and beneficial means by which the whole human race is sustained. Thus prayer is the most important work in life.'[4]

Opening to contemplative awareness

As we begin conscientiously to engage with prayer and meditation, a new state of being may gradually start to reveal itself which is a mixture of both and which I will call 'contemplative awareness'. It is very definitely a 'Heart state' and it is very important that we learn to access it. Many people wrongly associate it with 'churchy-ness' and believe that in order to be 'contemplative', we need to remove ourselves in a nun- or monk-like way from society. Nothing could be further from the truth. Our problem is that in our speedy-Gonzalez culture and with our obsession with rationality, we often forget how important it is to give ourselves time to mull certain ideas over inside our hearts and allow ourselves space for them quietly to marinate.

The contemplative state is therefore one where we allow ourselves time and space to ponder on particular issues and where we quietly invite the intelligence inside our hearts to help draw us closer to understanding some of life's great mysteries. These could include why we are here on earth, why evil exists, and whether we have free will. None of these questions can be answered if we try to approach them quickly or rationally. Rather, we need quietly to feel ourselves gently into them. This is so important, as many of us don't ponder over things nearly enough and consequently allow ourselves to trot out the agreed-upon opinions on particular subjects without having given genuine thought as to whether or not we really agree. This is especially true in the field of politics. To be a contemplative person is particularly important if we are to be an effective activist, as how we view any particular situation will have a significant effect upon any course of action which we may choose to take.

It can also be helpful to carry an interesting book around to dip into from time to time, as this can greatly help strengthen our contemplative muscles. My current favourite 'contemplative bible' is Sri Nisargadatta Maharaj's great classic, *I Am That*. I have just opened it, and here is an example of a passage that requires a lot of contemplation:

> *A student asks: 'How can I find the way to my own being?'*
> *The Master replies: 'Give up all questions except one: "Who am I?" After all, the only fact you are sure of is that you* are: *the "I am" is certain. The "I am this" is not. Struggle to find out what you are in reality.'*
> *Student: 'I have been doing nothing else for the last sixty years!'*
> *NM: 'What is wrong with striving? Why look for results? Striving itself is your real nature.'*
> *Student: 'Striving is painful.'*
> *NM: 'You make it so by seeking results. Strive without seeking, struggle without greed.'*

If we really take these words into our hearts and mull over them, it can take us very deep. And it is in the depths, we remember, that the answers to so many key questions may arise. A few months ago, I conducted a week-long retreat in Majorca. One evening, I suggested that my students sit outside under the night sky after dinner and, looking up at the stars (with a glass of wine in their hand, very important) silently contemplate the immensity of the cosmos. Such activities are so important, as they serve to stretch our awareness and help pull us away from the arrogance of our own self-importance – especially from the belief that mankind is the only intelligent life in the universe.

Contemplation also enables us to see ourselves objectively, to dwell upon what our real needs are, as well as what is really required out in the world. Such activities help awaken and develop the 'higher intelligence' inside our hearts, which in turn makes it far less likely that we are going to be as open to being seduced by what Thomas Merton referred to as 'the contagion that emanates from things like advertisements and from all the spurious fantasies that are thrown at us by our commercial society'. For Merton,

> *the contemplative life isn't something objective that is 'there' and to which, after fumbling around, you finally gain access. The contemplative life is a dimension of our subjective existence … One might say it is a flowering of a deeper identity on an entirely different plane from near-psychological discovery, a paradoxical new identity that is found only in loss of [ego] self. To find oneself by loss of self: that is part of contemplation.*[5]

The wisdom of *wu wei*

As our contemplative capabilities start to grow, we may come to appreciate, for instance, that doing more of something is not necessarily always doing what is preferable. Indeed, the more we open to the contemplative life, the more we start realising a virtue which the Taoists of old always acknowledged, and which they referred to as *wu wei* or 'not doing'. Many years ago, I received a profound teaching on this particular topic. I had been quite ill and I went to visit a master acupuncturist. He took my pulses, and then just sat quietly beside me for what seemed an eternity, saying nothing. Eventually, he stuck just one needle into me.

I felt quite cheated. Firstly, I felt he had wasted my time just sitting there doing nothing, and on top of that, he only had given me one needle. After all that money I'd given him! Surely, if I were to get better, I needed a lot of needles. I voiced my concerns to the maestro. He looked at me as if I were mad and told me that he had spent a long time preparing himself and contemplating my condition and realised that one needle, in the right place and at the right time and applied with the right spirit, was the appropriate treatment for me. Of course he was correct, and about two days later I found myself not only fully restored to my old zip but endowed with a lot more of it. There is a beautiful verse in the Tao Te Ching that tells us:

A person not connected with the Tao may do many things and nothing really gets done, while a person connected to the Tao does nothing and yet there is nothing that does not get done.

If we wish to be effective activists, we need to contemplate the wisdom of the Tao as it will probably increase the likelihood of the force being with us.

Chapter 14

Cultivating the Heart of Love

Love is the finest and most powerful educational force for the ennoblement of humanity – PITIRIM A. SOROKIN

Love is a force which nothing can resist – PETER DEUNOV

Defining love

As the quality which we most associate with the heart is love, it is important that we have a chapter looking at it in greater depth in order to explore how, as activists, we may draw more of it into our lives. I will set the tone by quoting at length from an extraordinary book, *The Ways and Power of Love* by the great Russian philosopher Pitirim A. Sorokin.

> *Love keeps the world going and living ... Love is the experience that annuls our individual loneliness, fills the emptiness of our isolation with the richest value, breaks and transcends the narrow walls of our little egos, makes us co-participants in the highest life of humanity and expands our true individuality to the immeasurable boundaries of the universe.*
>
> *Love is literally a life-giving force. It beautifies our life because the love experience is beautiful by its very nature and beautifies the whole universe. To love anything or anybody means literally to immortalise the mortal, to ennoble the ignoble, to uplift the low, to beautify the ugly. Anything that one looks at through loving eyes becomes 'lovely', that is, beautiful.*
>
> *By its very nature love is goodness itself; therefore it makes our life noble and good. Finally, the love experience means freedom at its loftiest ... In this sense love and freedom are synonymous ... Where there is love, there is no coercion; where there is coercion, there is no love. And the greater the love, the greater the freedom. A person who loves all humanity is free in this human universe. The love experience*

is marked by a 'feeling' of fearlessness and power. It cuts off the very roots of fear. Where there is fear, there is no love. Where there is love, there is no fear. Finally, the love experience is the equivalent of the highest peace of mind and happiness.

Unselfish love has enormous creative and therapeutic potentialities, far greater than most people think. Love is a life-giving force, necessary for physical, mental and moral health. It is the most powerful antidote against criminal, morbid and suicidal tendencies, against hate, fear and psychoneurosis.[1]

Beautiful and inspiring words, which encapsulate the heart of love in the most poetic way. The kind of love Sorokin was referring to is a very 'high' love or a very deep spiritual love. It is the kind of love that no doubt Krishnamurti had in mind when he told us that 'without love, all our plans for a perfect social order in which there is no exploitation, no regimentation, will have no meaning at all'. It is crystal clear that if only there was more of this quality of love in the world, it would be the answer to many of our problems. Our world would radically change. We wouldn't play all our manipulative ego games and be so greedy, because we would no longer feel so insecure and empty. The rich would be only too eager to help the poor more. People would feel happier. Terrorism would fade away. And so on. As activists, therefore, we are challenged to try to embody this kind of love, or at least get close to doing so. Just imagine the kind of transforming power we would possess if, wherever we went and whoever we encountered and whatever kind of difficult situation we were up against, our hearts were to operate from this place.

The 'love problem'

This, however, is easier said than done. As with all human virtues, and as we saw earlier on in this book, love exists at many different levels, and the kind of love Sorokin was describing is sadly, rather rare. It is the kind of elevated love that only becomes accessible to us after a great deal of 'heart-polishing' and only once we have started graduating more deeply into our butterfly selves. Yes, caterpillar man may occasionally tap into this level of love, but it is not a world which he is ordinarily much acquainted with. While this love certainly exists as a possibility inside all of us, and at one level, hovers very close and is eminently reachable, if our egos have anything other than a subservient role in our lives, we are going to find it hard to get very near it for any length of time.

Sorokin's love is a divine love; it is a love imbued with sacredness, and is a long way off from the 'reduced' or eminently mundane kind of love that many of us see as love and which we ordinarily encounter in our Setting Sun culture. Indeed, in our caterpillar identities, love is primarily emotional and unpredictable, tends to be somewhat selective and sexual, and only gets bestowed upon certain people if we believe they are 'deserving' of it, that is, if they fulfil certain conditions for us. Also, unless someone professes to love us, we feel we have no way of accessing it.

Setting Sun love, then, is light years or, more accurately, light worlds away from Sorokin's love. It possesses few enheartening characteristics and has little or no transformational capability. Often, it revolves around shadowy and manipulative egoic agendas concerning a need to control or possess. At worst, we can even kill in its name, as is demonstrated in crimes of passion. As activists, therefore, we need to be asking ourselves what is necessary or what we need to do in order to draw closer to divine love.

Activities designed to access spiritual love

Indirectly, we have already begun answering this question, as working to clear out the debris inside our hearts and strengthening our egos is certainly a good beginning. However, as I have just stressed, unless we make a serious commitment to try to deepen our spiritual life and be of genuine service to our planet, this 'higher love' and ourselves will always remain in two distinct camps. Remember the four basic requirements which I stressed in Chapter 11? If we want our hearts to open to a 'higher' love, we need to be prepared to work for it and be very committed and diligent and disciplined. I finished that chapter with a quote from the Shivapuri Baba in answer to the question of how we might live. We need to write his words down and be continually thinking how we can incorporate them more fully into our daily lives. If we can do so, we will be embodying Sorokin's love. *That* is our work.

We may also draw closer to this higher love through committed meditation and prayer and especially prayer in action. So I recommend that every morning when you get up, you do a short meditation on 'higher love', and you imagine your heart being full of this quality. You need to visualise it entering into everything you think and everything you do as you go through your day. You may also want to consolidate this with an affirmation along the following lines:

> *Who I am is love. It is my true nature. A higher love fills my heart at all times and is being continually expressed by me and entering all my actions. Every moment of the day, I am radiating this love out to the world.*

If we seriously commit to doing this, eventually this new 'love habit' will begin overtaking all our other less-than-loving habits and they will slowly begin evaporating. It can also help if we spend time in the company of some great Heart master who naturally vibrates with this higher love, as this can enormously speed up our process. We also need to observe ourselves carefully and see where in our lives we are not embodying this love. Where are we still being critical and selfish? And why? In what areas of our lives are our old ego patterns still trying to hold on? As we see where we are deficient, this does not mean that we make ourselves wrong and invalidate ourselves. We simply say to ourselves: 'No more. I choose to let go all behaviours that are not aligned to this new direction that I am choosing to go in my life.'

Loving ourselves

To best attune to this higher love, it is important that we include ourselves in our hearts. Thus we need to examine ourselves and see if we are still carrying 'old negative programmes' which prevent it, such as the thought that focusing on loving ourselves is self-indulgent.

Actually, it is not. Not loving ourselves is. We don't become more loving by hating ourselves for not being loving enough. Often, our old self-hate patterns are a product of our Judeo-Christian fall/redemption theology informing us that we are miserable sinners, deserving of nothing good. If we discover this to be the case, then we need to drop these beliefs very quickly, as holding onto them keeps us locked into our small-/hard-heartedness. Just as damage is done if we turn other people into hooks for our negative projections, so it is equally harmful if we hold ourselves to ransom in the same way.

Process to help us love ourselves

There is a process I use in many of my retreats designed to help people take themselves more fully into their hearts. I get them to start off by centring themselves in their hearts and to begin tuning in to the quality of love. Then

I put on some gentle 'heart music' (the Pachelbel canon is a good example), and ask them to begin slowly moving to its rhythms. I then ask them to visualise their heart centre becoming more and more alive and radiant and generating more and more love, and to imagine this love starting to radiate a light that totally fills their hearts, which consequently grows bigger and brighter, with the light then flowing down their arms and into their hands.

I then instruct them to stroke every part of their physical body – starting with their hair, eyes, ears, neck, chest and then gradually moving down to their stomach and legs etc. – and to imagine the love from their heart being directed through their hands. As they do this, I suggest that they let themselves be touched by their own beauty, and that they thank all the many parts of their body for the loving service which they have given. 'Thank you, eyes, for giving me the gift of sight. Thank you, ears, for allowing me to hear sounds. Thank you, legs, for giving me the gift of walking. Thank you, stomach,' and so on.

I then ask them to do the same thing with their internal organs, that is, to imagine the love from their hearts flowing to their lungs, their kidneys and livers, their adrenal glands and such like, and then flowing through their blood and purifying all the toxins that might be there. After they have done this, I ask them to lie on the ground and, still listening to gentle music, to then visualise their hearts expanding even more so that they become as big as they are.

> *Just feel all of you being radiated in the higher love inside your heart. Feel its light penetrating every atom and cell of your body. Let yourself become more and more open to being touched by the beauty of your true nature as you ask it to reveal itself more and more to you. Experience yourself falling in love with you.*

As they do these things, I also get them to imagine their hearts growing bigger and bigger until eventually they are as big as the world and to then imagine themselves living within the love of the universal heart. If appropriate, I might then suggest they imagine themselves radiating out that universal love to the various trouble spots on the planet.

This is a powerful process if people do it properly. Because there is a strong link between love and gratitude, I may also suggest that they imagine all the many things which they are grateful for, and allow those things to fill their hearts. As this progresses, a strong 'field of gratitude' also starts building up, which eventually becomes immense. Often, this process brings up tears as our Stradivarius or butterfly self is strongly evoked. People have often reported back to me that during this process some disease state has improved or they have evolved a whole new image of themselves, which has not gone away. Such is the power of higher love.

I may also suggest that people write down all the things they love about themselves and affirm them and give them energy. This is not boasting; it is being real. All too often we are only knowledgeable about the things we see as being 'wrong with us', which is sad and reflects the topsy-turviness of our culture. We may also need to engage in forgiveness work if we feel that we may have done something 'unforgivable', as this may subtly stand in the way of our ability to love ourselves. I may also suggest to some people that they change their cultural diet and disengage from all situations that take them away from love. For example, they should not watch films that are violent, but only those that model positive emotions, or not listen to music that agitates, but only to what uplifts and is composed by people residing in spaces of higher love. It is also helpful to read books written by people of genuine Heart, as their words also carry the vibrations of a higher love.

The importance of romantic love

Love not only exists at many different levels but also has many different faces, and we cannot talk about a higher or a divine love without also mentioning romantic love. If, as activists, we are ever fortunate enough to be hit by Cupid's little arrow, and if we can understand what is happening and manage to work with this energy wisely, then we also have a golden opportunity to connect powerfully with higher love. How so? It is because romantic love is a reflection of higher love and has a powerful transcendent and divine component to it. It also possesses an emotional intensity that enables it to 'sneak' past our habitual defences.

Romantic love is also a very total kind of love. It encompasses all areas of ourselves and sees no separation between eros and agape. By this I mean that we not only experience a strong sexual desire for our beloved, but we are also graced with the capacity to recognise their heavenly face, as before our very eyes, they become transformed into a god or goddess, whom we would willingly give our lives for. Psychologists call this a projection, which of course it is, but it is also a projection of truth, for when under the 'romantic spell', we are in fact experiencing the world much more fully the way it really is.

While operative, romantic love also has a beautiful unconditionality about it, in that our partner doesn't have to be or behave in a particular way in order for us to embrace them in our hearts. When we fall romantically in love, we may be capable of acts of great selflessness and generosity that come straight from the deepest parts of ourselves. Often, all that is most noble about us as human beings is awakened. I like the term 'falling in love' here, for we are, quite literally, falling out of our egoisms and surrendering to the depths of our own humanity. Also, the degree of Heart fire that romantic love sometimes ignites inside us can be so powerful that it can temporarily burn through many of our fears and resistances to our being the truly beautiful Stradivarius self that each of us naturally is. When we love in this way, it is much easier for us to experience that this is who we really are and that the real pretence is to believe we are plastic fiddles.

The challenges of romantic love

Having fallen in love and having been elevated in this way, however, is no guarantee that this love will continue. Here is where, as activists, we are most challenged. Unless we are aware of what is going on inside our hearts, our egos may well resurrect themselves, grab onto this new energy coursing through us and use it to satisfy their less than noble agendas. If this occurs, our feelings of joy, power and ecstasy may be used to gratify selfish as opposed to selfless agendas. Especially around sex!

If our sexual energy is abused or overused – and our hearts will always tell us if this is the case – it may well unbalance us, and in so doing prematurely snuff out our connection with the divine, whereby we can tumble out of love with the same rapidity with which we earlier fell into it. We must not forget that any excess of light also serves to activate the dark side, which is why the history of romance is strewn with the corpses of those who fail to deal effectively with their Shadow. The tragic consequences of romantic love are excellently portrayed in Tolstoy's great novel *Anna Karenina*.

With romantic love, it is important to remember that our beloved is not the source of how we feel. We are, and they are merely the catalyst helping connect us to a deep part of our hearts. If we can use this love wisely and consciously, it will mean that when our romantic feelings start to fade (as they always will, for romantic love is just a stage of loving and will not be with us for ever), we will then have residues of goodness stored inside our hearts to help us through any rainy days that may lie ahead. If we can use the ecstasy that is bequeathed to us, to remind us more deeply of our inherent spiritual abundance, and that to be joyful – to give and receive love with joy – is our inherent birthright, we will truly remain rich.

Love as initiation

The more we ascend into love, or the more we start accessing a higher love, the more this quality begins to test us and the darker may be the Shadow material that we may need to confront. Kahlil Gibran describes this in a very moving passage:

> *When love beckons you, follow him, though his ways are hard and steep…*
> *And when he speaks to you, believe in him, though his voice may shatter your dreams*
> *As the north wind lays waste the garden.*
> *For even as love crowns you, so shall he crucify you.*
> *Even as he is for your growth, so is he for your pruning.*
> *Even as he ascends to your height and caresses your tenderest branches that quiver in the sun,*
> *So shall he descend to your roots and shake them in their clinging to the earth.*
> *Like sheaves of corn, he gathers you unto himself.*
> *He threshes you to make you naked.*
> *He sifts you to free you from your husks.*
> *He grinds you to whiteness.*
> *He kneads you until you are pliant;*
> *And then he assigns you to his sacred fire,*
> *That you may become sacred bread for God's sacred feast.*[2]

Many years ago, when I lived in California, I taught my first ever weekend workshop on love. I remember that by the Saturday night, I felt full of joy. It felt as if a big 'love field' had been generated in our group, as if somehow we had all created a magically blissful new world for ourselves – a little microcosm of a culture of Heart. The sweetness and goodness of everyone in the group felt immense. I went to bed that night with a heart that felt light and happy.

What I was not prepared for was the enormous aggression and even hatred that filled the room the next morning. Conflicts spewed out everywhere, either between individuals in the group or primarily against me. In the eyes of some female group members, I had transmogrified into the great Satan, with two women in the group explicitly telling me how much they resented my manipulative tendencies and how dark they considered me to be. Were they simply picking up my own Shadow side? Perhaps. Certainly, at that stage in my life, my narcissism and predatory tendencies were still unhealed. But this did not seem to be the whole picture. I was then very naïve about how Shadow scenarios operated and did not understand that what had transpired was that the collective Shadow of the group had been powerfully evoked. After the workshop ended, and after I had managed to dust myself down, I took this issue to a wise teacher of mine, and this is the gist of what he told me. It serves as a good teaching to the would-be activist as regards how to deal with the dark side:

You must understand that while people all want love, they are also afraid of it. Love is a big problem in our society. Many people are simply not used to having it in their lives or feeling good about themselves. If someone has had an unhappy childhood, with parents disconnected from their hearts, for example, this will make them yearn for love, yet also they will fear it and experience it to be very threatening, as it will be so unfamiliar.

I suspect you had a lot of very emotionally wounded people in your group, who unconsciously found the loving energy that had been generated to be very threatening. Probably they were unknowingly rekindling old childhood dramas that had never been worked through. While the women who personally attacked you may well have been picking up something of the dark side of your own nature, they were probably also projecting a lot of their cold, unloving and uncaring fathers onto you as well.

Remember that the more closed hearted a person is, the scarier love will be for them. Indeed, the scarier all Heart qualities will be. If people never got to experience joy and kindness as a child, they will fear it. If the culture of their childhood had been cold and turbulent, they will hugely desire peace and compassion, yet may also resist it if it comes along. It is important when you work with people who are wounded in this way, that you never try to deluge them with love, which is perhaps where you may have gone a little astray. Those people whose hearts have become very arid are limited as to how much love, or indeed any other aspect of Heart, they can take in at any time. They need to start off by being fed very small doses.

Conscious love

Another of the challenges the activist faces in aspiring to a higher love is that it doesn't always flow out of us as spontaneously as when we are under Cupid's spell. Sometimes, we find it difficult to love. Or we feel upset or we don't feel like being loving, especially if we find ourselves in the company of people whom we may not especially like!

On such occasions, we may need to *choose* to love, that is, make a conscious effort to do so – and it is possible to open our hearts to someone even if we don't like them. Yesterday morning, for example, I was doing some shopping and for several reasons I was feeling a bit hassled, when I bumped into someone whom I realised I had never felt much affection for, as I had always felt this person was rather inauthentic. Luckily, I observed what was going on in time (was it my own inauthenticity I was confronting?) and just managed to stop sending out a negative projectile. Phew!

I then said to myself: 'Why should I judge this person? She needs loving. Yes, she may have traits that annoy me and probably annoy a lot of others as well. But why should I not hold her warmly inside my heart, for I know she is lonely and insecure? Why should I react to her personality difficulties and on the strength of that, withhold my humanity?' My heart told me that there was no reason. So at that instant, I chose to bring her into my heart; I chose to see the best in her and to send her enheartening energy. I observed as I did so that almost at once, she seemed to change and become more genuine, and I noticed myself feeling much warmer towards her. Was this because she actually *had* shifted or was it because I was choosing to perceive her through a more loving lens, or were both these factors connected? What I observed, after we had chatted for a few minutes and then went our respective ways, was that my heart felt happy and I realised that its true nature is to want to love, and that the more we choose to honour this requirement, even if we sometimes need to remind ourselves to do so, the more it will consent to open.

Appropriate love

Sometimes, the act of choosing to love may not, of itself, be sufficient, as there are many ways that we can love, and we need to make sure that how we are expressing it at any time is appropriate. In other words, if we are trying to love someone from a higher or more spiritual perspective, we need to do so in an intelligent way – in a way that is most conducive to what their hearts require at any time, what we sense may best assist them in their evolutionary journey. So, for example, if we feel someone needs compassion, then we must give them compassion. If we feel they need comforting or advising, then our love must take the form of giving comfort or proffering advice. If we sense they need space, then we give them space. If we listen carefully to our hearts, they will always guide us appropriately.

Sometimes what a person's heart requires is 'tough love'. I have some experience of this. Some years ago, a teacher came into my life who decided that I got away with too much and that I needed more 'calling on my stuff', and that what would most benefit me at this stage of my journey was to be tough with me in those areas of my life where he considered I was still flabby. He knew I was strong enough to take it, and while it was often difficult for me, I have to say that in hindsight, I was very grateful, as his approach enabled me to be much more honest with myself.

We also need to remember that it is as important to be able to receive love as to give it. If we do not allow others to love us, if we put up barriers, we are also doing them a disservice, and if we find ourselves doing this, we may need to do more inner work on ourselves to discover why we are resistant to being loved and what it is that we fear.

I will conclude this chapter by looking at what a higher or a Sorokin-type love might look like in action, through two examples: firstly, how, as a parent, we might love our children, and secondly, how we might bring love into our work.

Loving our children

Nowhere in our lives are we more challenged to see that our loving is both appropriate and comes from a deep and conscious place than in the area of parenting. If we are tough with our children when gentleness is called for, or are boundary-less when what is required is that they learn about boundaries, they are going to suffer. Being a loving parent, therefore, is a big challenge and often it demands a degree of sacrifice of our own comforts. Also, it requires that our hearts be big enough so they can fuse with the hearts of our children, thus enabling us to sense from *within* them what they may need of us at any moment. It is also important that we stay mindful of the many developmental changes that they are continually going through, so we may continue to love them in the right way.

We must never forget that our children are not there for us (although, of course, their presence gives us huge joy), but we need always to be there for them and find the best way to be as selfless as possible. As Kahlil Gibran put it, our children 'are the result of life's longing for itself … They come from us, but they do not belong to us.'[3] We must, therefore, always be asking ourselves what will best support their health, freedom and well-being and never try to hang on when we deem it time that they fly the nest.

The kinds of question which we, as parents, need to put to our hearts include: how can I protect my children without imprisoning them; how may I love them without smothering them; how may I help them to develop in the way that their hearts intend, as opposed to forcing them to be or do what I would like them to do? We are also challenged to find that middle ground of being firm without being controlling. We need to learn to say no without sounding rejecting, to be unconditional without spoiling, gentle without being weak and spontaneous without being undisciplined. The more balanced and self-aware we are as parents – the more adept we are at facing our own issues and working through our own conflicts – the less we will project onto our children, and the better equipped for life they are going to be.

Our children also need to develop a strong moral sense, so that they realise from an early age that certain behaviours and attitudes are worthy, while others are not. Here, they will learn not so much by our words but through our actions – how they observe us conduct our daily lives. So rather than lay down the law about how we think they ought to be, we need to create a sufficiently enheartened environment for them that will enable them to come to their own conclusions. When I am with my daughter, I don't always get it right, but I try to conduct myself in such a way that she knows that she is always hugely and unconditionally loved and always lives inside my heart, as I know that this will give her confidence and allow her own heart to feel strong and capable.

Loving our work

As going to work occupies a major portion of most of our lives, it is important that we choose to bring love into the workplace and do not leave our hearts at home when we set out for the office. If we do so, not only will we and also our work colleagues pay a price, but in all likelihood, we will never access the true soul of our work. The Buddhist master Tarthang Tulku suggested we see our work as an opportunity to grow and deepen our humanity:

> *Caring about work, liking it or even loving it, seems strange when we see work only as a way to make a living. But when we see work as the way to deepen and enrich all experience, each one of us can find this caring in our hearts and waken it in those around us, using every aspect of work to learn and grow.*[4]

If we relate to our work via our hearts, if we see it as another opportunity to express our activism, then bringing in money is only one part of the equation. I know people who bring no love at all into highly paid jobs, thereby demeaning the nobility of their profession. Similarly, I know people who bring a huge amount of love into so-called 'lowly jobs', thus hugely elevating them. I once knew an Indian woman who used to work as a cashier in my local supermarket. Her loving presence would radiate throughout the store and I would always try to pick her till, as I enjoyed being bathed in her big, radiant heart and warm smile, which she would freely offer to every customer she served. There was something about her nobility of being that elevated everyone and everything around her. If we remember that whenever enheartening energy emerges, it has a positive effect on the environment around us, then we understand how the unconditional loving presence of people like Devi contributes so enormously to making our world a better place. I always feel it is people like her who are our real heroes and the true aristocrats of life.

Yes, if we are able, it is preferable to work at something that is 'close to our heart', as then it is certainly easier to bring love into what we do. But if we don't have such a job, it certainly need not preclude this act, for, as we have seen, if we make a conscious choice to love, we can bring our hearts into almost anything (except perhaps being a drug dealer or selling armaments!). So in these tough economic times, I counsel you against quitting your existing job. Perhaps your challenge is to re-envision what you are already doing, choose to see your work in a new light. As David Spangler once put it, 'we need to sprout where we are planted'.

When I lived in California, I had a friend who worked for a big merchant bank who told me that he wanted to quit and 'do something more spiritual'. 'I just can't bring love into what I do,' he told me. 'Don't give up yet,' I said. 'If all the lovely, honourable people like you leave the banking industry and go and sit on mountain tops in the Himalayas, it'll just leave your world inhabited by the sharks. You have many gifts in this area. Why don't you take a long sabbatical and see what you feel like on your return? Perhaps, if you can learn to open your heart more in your office, you will see things from a new perspective.'

He did this. He spent six months in a Zen monastery. On his return, his heart was much more open and he saw that it was not appropriate to leave banking. He realised that he needed to bring his loving intelligence into the corporate world, as this was the area that he felt he could best make a contribution. He managed to get his bank to invest millions in a project to help irrigate deserts in a very arid part of Africa, as well as offer lower rates of interests in loans to certain Third World peoples. This was pretty radical as it took place in the mid-1980s.

Our world is changing very radically, and symptomatic of the many economic upheavals facing our planet is that in many countries, less work is available and many people are unemployed. This can be a bane, as not having work is not good for the spirit. It can make us feel isolated and downhearted and even very frightened if not enough money is coming in to pay the bills. At another level, it may be a gift, as many new jobs more relevant to the needs of the twenty-first century may come into being with the result that increasing numbers of us may find a job that directly benefits the planet. Dag Hammarskjöld, who many years ago was Secretary-General of the United Nations, once wrote:

> *We give to our daily work what is in our power to give, when we meet the demands facing us to the full extent of our ability. This will ultimately lead us to greater justice and goodwill, even if nothing would seem to give us hope of success or even of visible progress in the right direction.*[5]

This is a statement of great love.

Chapter 15

Embracing the Virtues of the Heart

For as he thinketh in his heart, so is he – PROVERBS 23:7

Whatsoever things are true, whatsoever things are honest, whatsoever things are just, whatsoever things are pure, whatsoever things are lovely, whatsoever things are of good report; if there be any virtue, and if there be any praise, think on these things – PHILIPPIANS 4:8

Love is not all we need

The Beatles didn't quite get it right when they sang 'All you need is love'. Yes, love is the central human quality; yes, it constitutes the core of our heart; and yes, we can say that all other qualities emanate from it. On its own, however, it may not be wholly sufficient to address all of our problems. For example, I don't believe that evil will be defeated solely by love. Many other Heart qualities are also required. Similarly, unless we spend time considering the vital role that courage may have to play in helping our world move on, or unless we remember the significance of peace or truth or wisdom, we are not going to be able to endow our newly emerging culture with the breadth and depth which I believe is merited, if it is to come fully into its own.

Through a combination of processes, it is possible to accelerate the development of other virtues inside us which can serve as 'antidotes' to help us heal our personal and our societal wounds more effectively. The more a particular virtue starts to grow inside us, the more a particular deficiency that primarily existed because that virtue was absent begins to fade. For example, as our ability to appreciate beauty emerges, less and less will we be moved to engage in activities that uglify life. Similarly, as our courage grows, our fear diminishes. While psychotherapy can certainly help us address the source of our anxiety, we must also not forget to work on stretching our 'kindness muscles', as this particular quality helps anxiety melt away and transform into compassionate concern. As all our inner treasures (or garden flowers) are interconnected, often what occurs is that the development of one particular quality will result in the unexpected emergence of another.

In this chapter, we will explore how we can help facilitate the development of eight particular Heart virtues, eight beautiful flowers inside the garden of our hearts. There are, of course, many more, but I have just chosen some that I feel are most relevant. Don't worry if not all eight mentioned here feel applicable to you personally. As activists, each of us has a different path to follow and what is very appropriate for one person may be quite irrelevant for another. For instance, beauty may not be as important as courage to someone whose work is primarily in the field of conflict resolution, while courage may be less significant to someone whose path primarily consists in meditating for world peace.

Cultivating wisdom

If there is one core quality required by all activist enhearteners, it is the ability to be wise. In Proverbs we read: 'Wisdom is the principal thing; therefore get wisdom: and with all thy getting, get understanding.' Why wisdom is so important is that all too often, our understanding of things is too shallow; we become too fixated in our concepts and in our cleverness, and so we make serious mistakes. If we cultivate wisdom, it will enable us to enter more fully into the heart of any particular issue we may be grappling with, and thus be more able to intuit the best way to proceed.

If we are to start 'growing' the 'wisdom eye' inside our hearts, we are challenged both to try to move beyond our being so identified with our egos, and to learn to be less reliant on factual information. As the flower of wisdom starts blossoming inside us, we become increasingly aware of the relation between the part and the whole and from this context, we will intuitively know whether or not to take that new job, or how best to deal with a difficult person, or whether it is appropriate to make a particular business decision. Often, our blossoming occurs most effectively in an atmosphere of silence and contemplation, when our ever-restless mind has been laid to rest. Thus, the more we meditate on peace and allow ourselves space to ponder, the wiser we will become.

Just as if we want love, it is good to be around loving people, so with wisdom the same is true. Wise people treat us wisely and may often ask us important questions, which in turn helps evoke our wisdom. We can also read books written by wise people and make sure we spend time digesting their ideas, so that they don't simply enter our minds, but are allowed to marinate quietly inside our hearts and thus penetrate us deeply. If we really want wisdom, we can also pray for it and meditate on it and choose to have it be our guide. We need to know that the wiser we become, the more we will be able to give the world what it needs and receive from it what we require.

Cultivating vision

I believe each of us has a 'visionary side' (it lives inside our hearts), and if we wish for a better world, it is important that we uncover this aspect of ourselves so we may look to the future and decide how best we can serve the emergence of a healthier society. Therefore, the more fully we uncover our vision, the more we will be endowed with the passion to persevere in our work and be given the strength to endure any difficulties or obstacles that may stand in the way of our attempts to move forward.

The chart that inspired Columbus and which gave him the strength to carry on and discover America lay inside his heart, as did Martin Luther King's vision of a world where all African Americans would be free. However, we don't need to be famous to be a visionary. Rather, we need to give ourselves time to contemplate life more deeply. What can be very helpful here is to do something invented by the Native Americans which they called a vision quest. The aim is to go out into nature, perhaps for a week, and engage in an intensive 'fasting of the heart'. We take only a blanket, a supply of water and perhaps a journal to write some notes. Nothing else. We converse with no one but with our own heart, the aim being, in shamanic language, to 'dance our dream awake', which means to uncover our soul's purpose or our deeper reason for existing. I have done many vision quests in my life and have found them invaluable as they help us let go the surplus 'dross' obscuring our hearts and in so doing enable us to come much closer to what is truly essential.

Cultivating beauty

All the great contemplative traditions have recognised the cultural significance of beauty and have striven to bring beauty into the world. We can think of the great cathedrals, the Russian icons, the simplicity of the great Zen gardens, the exquisite illumined manuscripts of medieval mysticism. If our new culture of Heart is to be characterised by anything, it will surely be by beauty. One of our great tragedies today is that many of us have lost the ability to recognise genuine beauty and have become obsessed with deifying ersatz aspects of it.

As with wisdom and vision, if we wish to embrace the heart of beauty, we will need to quieten down and go deep into the sacred echelons of our heart, as it will enable us to see into the deeper nature of what is. From this place, very simple things, such as a baby's smile, the generous act of a friend, a particular sunset, a song or an interesting idea, may reveal themselves to us as being beautiful. This reminds us that beauty is always there, but ordinarily, we are either too 'full' or too busy with all our doing and striving and obsessing to recognise it and allow it in. If we wish to tune into beauty, we may need to slow down and quieten ourselves.

This can be enhanced if we also meditate on beauty or pray for an enhanced ability to see beauty in all things – and this includes inside ourselves – as well as to be released from the pull of all the uglinesses of our world that may have seduced and contaminated us. We can also bring beauty into our everyday lives by intentionally choosing to do things beautifully – perhaps the way we cook or serve a meal. Here I think particularly of the Japanese tea ceremony. It is also important to make our homes beautiful, so that the vibration of beauty may be all around us. This may involve simplifying things. We don't need to have expensive artefacts around us to have beauty in our lives. A vase of freshly picked flowers rightly placed in a room can work miracles.

Each of us needs to discover what we particularly find beautiful and 'go for it', as this will feed our hearts. I have a friend who finds beauty in certain mathematical formulae, another who delights in philosophy and another who finds great beauty in climbing mountains. Then, of course there are the beautiful worlds of literature, art and music, and it naturally follows that the more we immerse our hearts in beautiful thoughts and spend time in the company of friends with beautiful hearts, the more the beauty eye inside our own hearts will be fed and nourished.

Cultivating joy

If we can discover the joy inside our hearts, it too can serve as a wonderful antidote against all forms of negativity and evil. Joy and love are also closely connected, so if we connect to a higher love in any way, it will always be accompanied by joy.

Many people say that they derive joy from helping others, and I agree, as this activity takes us beyond the boundaries of our ego, which is always the great joy stopper. We also derive joy from doing things that our hearts naturally love doing, as well as engaging in activities that are fun or inspiring, and so it is very important that we allow ourselves time to do these things. I find that the more I allow myself to live in the now, the more joy I feel, as there is always a connection between this state and a heightened awareness. Whenever I find myself able to taste more subtly, smell more sensitively, see more clearly or touch more delicately, I always feel joy. In contrast to happiness, which tends to be dependent upon externals going our way, joy emerges from inside our hearts and is not necessarily connected to what is going on in the outside world.

The more open our hearts are, the more we will feel joy, while the more numb we are, the less able we will be to experience it, so it is very important that we continue to work at unpicking those locks on our hearts that may still incline us to experience fear, guilt and sadness. Sometimes joy may descend on us quite unexpectedly, and if and when it knocks on our door, it is very important that we recognise that we are being graced by the visit of a beautiful friend and that we gladly invite it in, as it is the most delightful and healing of companions.

Cultivating peace

Wars are not going to end unless there is a greater desire for peace, and this in turn is not going to happen until sufficient numbers of us work at cultivating this quality inside our hearts. This is so important, for however hard some of our world leaders work at promoting peace, so long as our hearts are still full of aggression, hostility, hatred, anxiety, fear, greed and many other such dis-equilibrating attributes, peace will continue to elude us.

Being peaceful is not, as some believe, being passive. On the contrary. Peaceful people are generally extremely active (think of Gandhi). Therefore, to cultivate this very important quality, we need to continue working at transforming everything about ourselves that is still warlike. Generally, a lot of Shadow work may be required. If, for example, stress is a factor in our lives, we may need to find ways of addressing it, for we cannot be at peace if we are always feeling anxious.

We also need to work at directly 'building up' our peace muscles. Here, we again come back to meditation. No genuine peacefulness can be gained without meditating regularly. Again, it is useful to choose the company of peaceful people and to try to spend as much time as possible in restful environments – or at least visit such environments from time to time. Being at peace is not about an absence of conflict – for conflict, we have already seen, is built into life. Rather, it is an ability to deal with it in a more 'Heart-centred' or reconciliatory way. In an article entitled 'What Is Peace?' David Spangler sheds additional light on this very important theme:

> *Peace is the resolution of conflict in ways that are mutually empowering to all concerned ... It is the ability to accept and embrace conflict and not be threatened by it, and thereby to use it in the interests of life ... Implicit in this image of peace is the role of communication and communion: the recognition of an identity we share that transcends our differences even as it is enriched by them, and an ability to touch each other lovingly within the context of that identity.*
>
> *When embraced in a peaceful spirit, conflict becomes a source of teaching, a light upon the way. When our spirit is not peaceful and is unaccepting of the diversity about us, we kick the lantern of conflict and its spilling oil becomes a conflagration about us. The way of peace must take us inward to train ourselves in serenity and the cherishing of the other, that we may grasp that lantern and make it an illumination and not an instrument of arson.*[1]

Sometimes finding peace comes from changing our perceptions. I remember someone once coming to see me who said: 'I can never earn more than £100,000 a year, so I can never be at peace with myself.' I whistled. '£100,000 is quite a lot of money! Why don't you own how well you've done to be able to earn that, instead of berating yourself for not earning more? Is feeling you should earn more the agenda of your own heart, or is it the voice of your banking family speaking through you? If it is the latter, see if there might be some way that you might silence that voice, and be grateful for what you have, and then you will find peace.'

Cultivating courage

To be a force for truth, beauty, integrity, peace and love in a world so full of deceit, ugliness and closed-heartedness – which, as activists, we are seeking to do – demands courage. This can be challenging, for not everyone likes the courageous person, as they can often be a notorious disturber of our 'comfort zones', their presence conspiring to remind us of where this quality may be lacking inside ourselves.

I remember being very touched by the courage of that lone Chinese student in Tiananmen Square who single-handedly stood up to the full force of those advancing tanks. I often think about the bravery of those thousands of young 'Green' Iranians who every day risked their lives by taking to the streets, peacefully protesting against a fraudulent regime full of violence, hatred, repression, fanaticism and corruption. How extraordinarily courageous Aung San Suu Kyi has been all these years in her continued refusal to bow down to the evil and corrupt Burmese generals destroying her country. By such extraordinary feats of bravery, huge differences in the world have been made and we need to allow ourselves to be inspired by these people, as they again constitute the real 'great and good' on our planet.

If more of us gave up our tendencies to take the easy way out or to toe the line, and if instead, like these great spiritual warriors, we were to stand up and not only speak our truth, but also be prepared to act on it, our courage muscles would grow and our world would change very quickly. Why we don't do so is often because we fear being different, which, put another way, means we lack courage. This is sad, as to possess this quality has never been more important than at this crucial time in our world history where, as the spiritual light grows brighter, the forces of darkness also grow darker.

Courage, like all Heart qualities, evolves gradually inside us. One way that we may start 'growing' our courage muscles is simply by choosing to live every day in as honest a way as we can. We can start by doing small things that scare us and then slowly build up our capabilities in the realisation that being courageous is not about our not having fears or doubts, but rather is about our willingness to move forward despite our feelings, because we believe in the integrity of what we are standing for. This also means that we don't adjust our ideas to suit those around us because we think that people may like us better. Similarly, if we happen to encounter evil in any form, we confront it with a strong and resilient heart; we don't ignore it and walk away or pass it over to others to deal with.

Cultivating kindness

The Dalai Lama always puts kindness at the very top of his priority list of qualities required in order for our world to work more effectively. I could not agree more. Kindness heals. Kindness inspires. Kindness integrates and reveals. Kindness enables us to reconnect to ourselves when we feel lost, and it ennobles those who practise it. If I think about what I am most grateful for, it is probably all those people who, at different times in my life, have shown kindness to me and who have helped and guided me and been there for me when I have felt despondent and confused, and needed love and support. These people will always live inside my heart.

I remember a particular time when I was quite young and in a great crisis over something and poured my heart out to an old friend. He listened to me, was tender with me, cancelled his schedule for the day to be with me, and generally 'held me'. The effect of this was that it reconnected me to my own heart, which, in my crisis, I had somehow lost touch with. Enabling us to reconnect to what is best about ourselves is the precious gift which genuinely kind people offer us. They never go out of their way to help people in need; rather, they realise that being there to support others *is* their way.

There are basically two sorts of kindness; one is general, the other is specific. General kindness is where we make the choice to live out of a space of unconditional goodwill towards the world as a whole. Specific kindness is where we choose to share a particular commodity that we may possess in abundance – be it love, money, information, wisdom, etc. – with those whom we experience to have a need of it. To be kind actually costs us nothing, but to be unkind costs us a fortune, as there will always be a residue of heaviness inside our hearts, as their deeper yearning is always to want to share what is precious.

We cultivate kindness by recognising its importance and by thinking about it and choosing to bring it into more and more areas of our daily lives in such a way that it starts to constitute an increasingly core part of who we are. The more we make the practice of kindness an integral part of our daily Heart work, the more it will radiate out from us into the world, and the kinder our world will become.

Cultivating truth

To be effective activists, we need to love truth and be prepared to stand up for truth and desire to have it infuse as much of our lives as possible. The deeper we journey into our hearts, the more this will happen naturally and the more we will feel saddened and disturbed by falsehood, whenever or wherever we may happen to encounter it.

Like all Heart qualities, truth tends to reveal itself slowly and seldom shows its full face to us all at once, as it needs assimilating gradually. However, if we consciously cultivate truth by meditating on it, by deeply desiring it and by refusing to participate in anything that is in any way duplicitous, its deeper face may appear more quickly than we believe it can. We need to know that our hearts naturally desire truth and want to live by the laws of truth, so the more we listen to our hearts and allow ourselves to be guided by them, the more effective we will be as agents of liberation in the world.

Chapter 16

Entering into the Heart of Relationship

In all things we learn best from those we love –
JOHANN WOLFGANG VON GOETHE

For one human being to love another: that is perhaps the most difficult task of all, the work for which all other work is but preparation. It is a high inducement to the individual to ripen ... It is something that chooses us out and calls us to vast things – RAINER MARIA RILKE

If enough of us can rise to the current challenges of the man/woman relationship, using them as opportunities to peel away illusions, tap our deepest powers and expand our sense of who we are, we can begin to develop the wisdom our age is lacking – JOHN WELWOOD

The importance of intimate relationships

Since one of the most important ways where, as activists, we are called to 'be the change we wish to see happen' is in the area of relationship, and since being in a committed relationship is one of the most potent of all heart-arousing adventures, I have decided to dedicate a full chapter to this very important topic.

Relationship is so important because life is relationship. Simply by being alive we cannot help but be in relationship: with ourselves, with those around us, with our immediate environment and with our planet. Choosing to be in an intimate relationship with another human being, which involves our daring to open up, bare our hearts and souls, and incur all the many risks and challenges which this entails, is, in my experience, one of the best ways to deepen our hearts, as it demands of us that we explore the full range of the many treasures that reside within it.

This is not only because being in a relationship offers us the opportunity to realise and practise what is best about us, but also because it helps us come to recognise what is worst. Indeed, if we allow ourselves to go deep with another person, we cannot help facing many of the shadowy parts of ourselves that we prefer to keep hidden. Relationships, then, are essentially about revelation. The more awareness and commitment we bring to them, the more deeply we will journey into the garden inside our hearts, where we will not only encounter the many beautiful flowers growing there, but we will inevitably also have to come face to face with our many weeds and brambles.

If I look back over my life, I can truly say that my relationships with women have been a core part of my own unfolding journey. Every woman I have been close to has been an important teacher for me in one way or another. Through them, I have discovered very sublime dimensions of my heart, as well as having had to weather the pain of betrayal and rejection and come face to face with selfish and manipulative parts of myself that I would have liked to pretend did not exist.

The healing power of relationship

To demonstrate the healing power of a loving relationship, and to show just how profound a 'weapon of transformation' the heart can be, I want to tell you briefly about a very important relationship I had when I first arrived to live and work in California, when I was in my mid-twenties. At that time, my heart was very closed and I primarily lived in my head. I knew very little about 'higher love', my ego self was still pretty wounded and I was very disconnected from myself and, of course, from others. Needless to say, I was not especially happy.

I then met a woman who, Heart-wise, was quite advanced. For many years she had been a student of a particular guru and as a result, had learned a great deal about love and spirituality. This fine human being not only 'saw' me – that is, saw beyond the many limitations of my outer persona and recognised depths in me that I was then wholly unaware of – but she was willing to do me the honour of taking me into her own huge and tender heart to hold me there and love me. In so doing, she taught me the rudiments of love.

No matter how difficult I could be, her love never wavered. She never made me wrong, although quite rightly she challenged me and would not let me get away with my old ego games. Even though there were times when my behaviour certainly upset her, at no time did her heart ever close down to me, as a result of which, I was at all times given a consistent point of reference to allow my own heart to begin opening and a lot of the iron inside it to start to melt. In choosing always to see the best in me, she was able to help me recognise that I had value, which in turn allowed me to begin believing in myself.

I learned how being in a relationship with someone who is much more developed than us, and who is merry, open to life, optimistic and loving, can really open our hearts if we will only allow these qualities to sink into us. In the time we spent together, my happy heart was coaxed more and more out of hiding and a lot of sadness got released, and I think I learned more from her about what it meant to be a genuine human being than I have ever learned through any books, seminars or gurus. I also learned that we cannot give to others what we do not yet possess inside ourselves and that the more we believe in the myth of our unworthiness, the harder it is to allow in the appreciation of those who do not collude with our self-perceptions.

This woman's Heart genius was that she never flooded me with too much warmth at a time when I was not ready for it. She seemed able to intuit what kind of 'heart food' I required at any time. Of course, she also had her own vulnerabilities, insecurities and fears (who doesn't?), which she had the courage to share with me, and never tried to pretend they did not exist. As such, she also gave me a beautiful teaching in the art of being vulnerable, which enabled me to see how powerful this is. We cannot work at opening our hearts if we are not prepared to risk vulnerability.

Our relationship only lasted a few years. There were certain cultural differences that came up and I realised that, although I may have been living in California, my true home was back in England, while my friend realised that being in my social milieu there was not her scene and that her spiritual roots lay in California. When eventually we did split up and go our own ways – I won't use the word 'separate' as her deep goodness and kindness will always stay inside my heart – because she taught me to be honest and open and to work through any difficulties if they came up, there was very little 'stuff' left over that needed resolving. My friend John Welwood had this kind of relationship in mind (or rather, in his heart) when he wrote:

> *If we can recognise that relationships, by their very nature, continually call on us to develop greater consciousness, then their difficulties are no longer a nuisance: instead they can be seen as an integral part of love's path. For they compel us to bring the light of awareness to the dark, unconscious parts of ourselves and mobilise inner resources*

– such as patience, generosity, kindness and bravery – that give us a larger, deeper sense of who we are. So instead of trying to ward off the challenging questions that relationships pose, we need to let them work on us, like an inoculation. Though our questions may be irritating at first, as they work on us they stimulate our creative intelligence, triggering larger healing, transformative powers within us. This is what will provide the strength and courage to keep moving forward on love's path, regardless of the difficulties we encounter.[1]

Relationship problems as allies

Relationships, then, have purposes other than the more conventional ones of producing children and providing sex and companionship. They can help heal our emotional hearts and open us up to the higher reaches of spiritual Heart. This is also true when we draw to ourselves a 'difficult partner' – someone to whom we may feel particularly attracted, yet have a lot of clashes and conflicts with – as often we discover that they have wounds which are similar to our own and that what enrages us about them is often some facet of ourselves that we have not yet properly examined.

I have had several partners in my life, who have pressed every button I have ever had (as I did for them), and for this I am also grateful. So many times we discover that what we cannot tolerate about the other – believing everything would be OK if only *they* would change – is in fact a reflection of some aspect of our own wounded heart where we need to shift. It is therefore through relationship that we may often learn that the way we choose to see and therefore to relate to our partner generally plays a significant part in how they behave towards us. If we belittle someone, they may well do the same thing back to us. If we respect a person, they are much more likely to treat us honourably in return.

If we manage to bring butterfly capabilities into our relationships, we may discover that in fact our conflicts and differences, rather than being seen as the enemy, are welcomed as contributing to the relationship's potential aliveness. Love's many rough edges become a powerful resource, as they actually help connect us much more fully with our heart. In Welwood's words again, 'through cultivating a taste for our rawness – which has a sweetness all of its own – we invite our heart to show us the way'.

The problem with many modern-day relationships

Not enough of our relationships today are entered into from a deep Heart perspective. All too often they are engaged in from a place of the 'reduced, conditional egoic love' which we explored earlier. In other words, we 'do' our relationships much more from our caterpillar than from our butterfly selves. While, as we have seen, some degree of genuine Heart will inevitably arise in the initial romantic phase, when both parties are still under Cupid's little spell, all too often we allow our love to peter out when the romance fades because we fail to make the necessary efforts to shift it to a new level. In part this is because we do not know how (we cannot yet conceive of a 'higher love'), and in part because we mistakenly believe that relationships do not need working at and that they primarily exist for us to have a comfortable little corner to go unconscious into!

If this is what we believe, much of our initial passion and aliveness will soon evaporate and our relationship will quickly be drained of energy. People who get trapped in this kind of liaison often get bored with their partners very quickly and always believe that the problem is the other person's. We feel that things will be solved if only '*they* would change' or if we can find someone 'better' – 'more loving' or 'more exciting'. When our reason for being in a relationship does not come from our heart's deeper knowing or yearning, but is primarily dictated by ego or status or security or convenience or financial needs, it is unlikely that much growth and development is going to take place. In such liaisons, when difficulties arise, as they inevitably will, there is generally insufficient awareness to work them through creatively.

Do not get me wrong. I have nothing against comfort and predictability, and in no way am I suggesting that all relationships, to be 'deep', have to be uncomfortable and continually challenging. Far from it. Rather, I am suggesting that without real Heart and soul being intentionally put into them, they risk remaining superficial and can easily degenerate into both parties either consuming the other or, conversely, demanding that the other behave differently. Couples can get entangled in the 'let's play the hide-everything-under-the-carpet game, called "Don't call me on my stuff and I won't call you on yours"'. If this occurs, the likelihood is that when challenges come up, they are not properly dealt with, until eventually things get so bad that the relationship falls apart.

Modern relationships in crisis

Our economic and political systems are collapsing because our old ways of engaging with them are no longer working, and the same holds true for relationships. To have them work, we need to learn how to inject genuine Heart into them. Change, however, is difficult, and as we have seen, we often resist it. A few months ago, a middle-aged couple who had been together for nearly twenty years came to consult with me, telling me that they both felt they wanted more out of their marriage; yet the first thing the man said to me upon entering my consulting room, was that he hoped they would not 'get into anything too deep', as he felt it might be upsetting for his wife. She then told me that her parents had always said to her that it was impolite to talk about feelings, so she hadn't. He had colluded with her as the world of emotions had also been a no-go area in his family. As a result, neither partner had ever said what they really felt about anything – ever! It was little wonder that their relationship had completely ground to a halt.

This closing-off to our emotional heart – this position of our being scared to 'reveal our true feelings' – can sometimes also come about because we are so disconnected from ourselves that we do not know what they are. Over the years, I have worked with so many couples where emotional numbness has reigned and where it has not been OK to cry or shout or get angry or reveal that one may feel fear, uncertainty and sadness, and even, God forbid, have sexual urges! One woman admitted to me that she had never, ever told her husband that she loved him, in case, in her words, 'he might get too full of himself'!

That zeitgeist or 'spirit of change', however, which is making itself known in all other areas of our world is also blowing into the world of relationship. I see this as very positive, as it is challenging many of us to seek to engage in our relationships much more with the love, passion, wisdom, creativity and imagination of our hearts. For this to occur, of course, we have to feel connected to our hearts and to hold inside them an image of how we would like our relationship to unfurl. We also need to recognise how limited many of our old egoic models are. Certainly, I see the many kinds of dishonesty that characterise so many of our international relationships as mirroring the dishonesties we exhibit in our personal ones. I believe that if more of us make a conscious effort to 'do' our personal relationships in a new way – move them to a higher level, put them on a deeper footing, make them more authentic – that we may start seeing a corresponding shift in the way different countries start relating to one another.

Confronting our relationship wounds from a place of Heart

Remembering what I said earlier about our heart's reconciling capacity, we see that choosing to confront our difficulties from a place of Heart opens up many new possibilities for healing. When a relationship becomes less about rivalling ego agendas – with both parties struggling to see who holds the power – and more about the desire to have something new and more qualitative emerge, a space opens up for virtues such as tenderness, respect, kindness and compassion. As these Heart qualities start emerging, the 'war between the sexes' begins to diminish, and both parties may feel increasingly less moved to 'want to be right' and increasingly more inclined to think of the most appropriate and loving ways of relating to one another.

When we begin addressing our wounds from these new perspectives, and when we also recognise that perhaps one of the more important ingredients of a loving relationship is for both parties to be there to support the other in their evolutionary development, a whole new context comes into play. Instead of seeing what we can get out of our relationship, it becomes more important to discover what we can put into it, to find out who our partner really is, and how we may both grow in love and truth and wisdom together, and in so doing become the fullest human beings that we can be. When I lived in California, I had the good fortune to become a friend of a wonderfully wise woman called Virginia Satir, who was a formidable relationship guru. This poem of hers beautifully characterises the essence of a genuine heart-centred relationship:

> *I want to love you without clutching,*
> *appreciate you without judging,*
> *join you without invading,*
> *leave you without guilt,*
> *criticise you without blaming,*
> *and help you without insulting.*
> *If I can have the same from you,*
> *then we can truly meet and enrich each other.*

Re-envisioning sexuality

When the domain of Heart starts being invoked, a relationship increasingly becomes an instrument to help us look at our lives from a new vantage point. This can have a liberating effect on our sex lives, which, in our old model, is all too often engaged in quite separately from our hearts, as a result of which neither partner may feel adequately nourished by the experience. Some of us, therefore, may need to confront our sexual wounding, which with women can often take the form of feeling guilty about allowing oneself to experience pleasure, and with men tends to lie much more in an attachment to our old patriarchal attitudes, resulting in a refusal or an inability to bring sufficient tenderness or subtlety into our love-making.

Since a full life needs to be about our learning increasingly to embrace the totality of who we are, and since much suffering can occur if our sexuality is either repressed or, conversely, indulged in heartlessly, it follows that for many of us, our sexuality may also require working on so that it too may be 'taken up' and integrated into the centrality of our hearts. This can help an ongoing convergence between eros and agape, which in the romantic phase takes place so effortlessly.

Many of my clients have remarked at the difference it makes to their sex lives if they devote time and energy into first recognising, and then releasing, their negative beliefs about sex. If, in addition, and prior to love-making, they are also willing to meditate together, visualising themselves blending at all levels, while at the same time praying that a higher spiritual force may enter their sexuality, couples often report a spontaneous shifting away from the idea of the man 'doing it' to the woman, to the experience of both parties surrendering to a higher power delighting in 'dancing through' both of them and filling them with joy. (A word of caution. If either party suffers from a particularly deep sexual wound, such as may be caused by abuse, such abundant experiences may not be possible until such a time as the emotional traumas have been more fully worked through and healed.)

Ending a relationship

In our traditional model, the idea of a relationship coming to an end is often associated with guilt and failure. Why is this, I ask myself? Who says that all relationships need to last for ever? The truth is that some relationships play out their natural course and come to an end quite organically, often through the fault of neither party, and the appropriate thing is for both to recognise when this occurs, and then choose to move on. While I admit that this is easier said than done, especially if children or money are involved, or if particular attachments are strong, the mistake many of us can make is to abandon a relationship prematurely because we are unwilling to look at ourselves and work through the issues it is bringing up for us – instead preferring to make all our difficulties the other person's fault. Conversely, mainly out of fear or guilt, we may also try artificially to prolong something which, if we were only to listen to our hearts, we would realise was well and truly over.

Of course, breaking up can be difficult and sometimes very traumatic, especially if we have been close, as something of our partner's essence will still reside within us, and it can take time to release what is no longer ours and reclaim what is. Nonetheless, it is important that we do this work. As with all endings, we need to complete them properly and for many couples, forgiveness work and inwardly 'thanking' their partner for all that they meant to us and did for us is very important. Simply because something has now lost its allure does not mean that we have to drown out the fact that in the past many magical moments may have been shared.

Let love always remain in our hearts

If we do our completion work properly, many of the ties that bind us can gradually be cut. This may require some prayer and ritual (see what I say about this later), perhaps a lot of giving thanks and letting go of our attachments and generally working through whatever psychological entanglements may still remain. The more effort we put in to clear out all our resentments and regrets and projections and whatever other kinds of debris may have accumulated over the years, the clearer a space we will have inside our hearts to appreciate all that the other represented for us and, most importantly, to move on. Simply because a relationship has come to an end need not imply that we have to banish our old lover from our hearts. If we are aspiring to embrace a Sorokin-type love, we need to take special care to ensure that the currency of love is never devalued. There is a little poem by Rumi that reminds us of this:

> *The minute I heard my first love story,*
> *I started looking for you,*
> *not knowing how blind that was.*
> *Lovers don't finally meet somewhere;*
> *they are in each other all along.*

The couple's journey

My old friend Susan Campbell is a great pioneer in the field of conscious relationship. In her book *The Couple's Journey*, she outlined five stages in the evolution of a relationship.[2] The first is the romance stage, which we have already explored. When this phase comes to an end, a second stage emerges which she calls the *power struggle*. Here, the image of the 'perfect other' gets shaken, and the many qualities that we once adored them for may become a source of annoyance. We either try to reform our partner or punish them for not living up to our ideal. The obstacle here is the belief that by manipulation or domination we can get what we want.

If we manage to work through this stage – and many couples do not – we reach a place that Campbell calls the *stability* stage. Here, both parties accept their differences and have the sense to recognise that the relationship is never going to fulfil all their needs. There is a much greater sense of security at this stage: the main obstacle is the attachment to peace and stability at the expense of change. The downside is that we may refuse to 'move on'.

The next level is what Campbell refers to as the *commitment* stage, where each party in the couple experiences great joy and harmony and a sense of unity in the other's presence, and where a 'we' starts to emerge that both of them will have created and may draw upon, yet which is more than the sum of their individual parts. The obstacle here again is that the couple can become too self-contained and feel they don't need to be concerned with the wider world beyond themselves. The great antidote to this is the emergence of the universal heart.

The final stage, which Campbell calls the *co-creation* stage, is reached when the surplus of energy created by the couple's synergy impels them to feel moved to give something back to the world, to become increasingly conscious and creative participants in furthering human and planetary evolution. In other words, *a couple grow a joint activist self* as they come into the realisation that the *deeper purpose* of their coming together is to work together as a powerful difference-making unit, and they are there to support each other to work for causes which touch and inspire them. Here, to feel one has a loving partner sharing one's challenges with one can be a source of immense comfort and support.

Of course, not all these stages are linear, and often intimations of the higher levels may reveal themselves early on as 'sneak previews' to inspire us to move on towards what lies ahead. The abundant worlds of Heart are always signalling their presence to us, are always hinting at our own enlightened self to us, and it is always a question of how open we are to hearing the call. With a couple working together towards a similar goal, the emergent Heart field is much bigger and more powerful than for an individual simply working on their own. It may be possible, therefore, if we have the right partner, to make very significant strides into the 'higher worlds' of Heart and my experience is that today, more and more couples are beginning to realise this. Without the ingredient of conscious Heart, we may reach the *stability* stage, but it is unlikely that we will advance any further, as the final two stages require a lot of emotional and spiritual intelligence in order to be effectively navigated.

Eleven brief guidelines for successful relationships

- While the one who is more evolved can help the other take a step up, we must not overly rely on our partner, as it is abnegating our own responsibility and may prove too much of a burden on them.
- At all times, we need to recognise the importance of listening to and sensing into our partner in as open-hearted a way as we can, as it enables us to be aware of the most appropriate way to relate with them at any moment.
- To have a successful relationship, we must have shared values. If one of us has an agenda of wishing to grow spiritually and the other only wants to be a social success, the kind of conflicts that would result may prove too challenging to reconcile.
- We must work at retaining our own sense of personhood while also being part of a couple, and therefore work at not losing ourselves within a relationship (a trait more common with women). If this occurs, we may come to resent our partner and feel we can only thrive on our own.
- We must always guard against 'unconsciousness' or taking our partner for granted, and realise that the fresher and more full hearted we are, the more alive and vibrant our relationship will be.
- Good communication is one of the most essential ingredients in keeping a relationship healthy, so ensure these lines are open at all times. Always say what you feel and need.
- Never blame your partner for any difficulties that may arise in the relationship, but remember that both parties play a role in what happens.

- If difficulties come up, we need to be aware of them and deal with them at once. We must not allow them to fester by pushing them under the carpet. If we feel we have not got the capacity to handle them, then we may bring in outside assistance.
- As much as possible, we need to pray and meditate together with our partner and find ways of linking our spiritual practices, as this helps to strengthen and deepen the Heart field growing between us.
- We need to be imaginative and try to do things with our partner that bring a spirit of play, laughter and humour into the relationship. Such qualities not only bring depth and lightness but are able to break up negative patterns should they arise.
- If a couple can find a noble project or task to commit to participating in together, it will help unify them at a much deeper level.

Chapter 17

Working with the Sacred 'Help Forces'

If force is to be pulled down upon us from above ... it must come down through intermediate levels and by various routes – CHARLES LEADBEATER

The more profound the struggle for spiritual mastery, the greater the exposure to unusual obstacles and opposing forces, and the deeper the mobilisation of helping forces – MICHAEL GROSSO

Living in a supportive cosmos

I believe we live in a supportive and intelligent universe, one that is very much 'on our side', so long as we understand that this means the side of soul and Heart and evolution and not the side connected with the placating of ego. I think the great heart of the cosmos is there to assist us – it wants us to draw ever closer to it, wants to open up to us, wants to support our growth and evolution and assist us in the building of a new society. Earlier I used the analogy of the higher worlds of Heart choosing to 'stalk' us.

I think the reason deeper Heart or enlightened Heart is currently drawing so close to us is that, since we are living in times of great crisis and are therefore in need of a lot of help, we are unconsciously invoking it. This is so important as many believe that the whole process of our 'becoming another' and making the shift from caterpillar to butterfly, in addition to working at trying to usher in a whole new society, is anyway so challenging that we are simply not capable of achieving it on our own. Certainly John G. Bennett was vehement about the difficulties:

> *My own belief is that the transformation of man is by nature such a slow and difficult process that scarcely one person in a hundred million could accomplish it in a lifetime. However, help is available which makes it possible for quite ordinary people to achieve it. What is needed is what is called in chemistry a catalyst, which acts in a marvellous way to make an almost impossible process go quickly and easily.*[1]

In *The Doors of Perception*, Aldous Huxley touched on the same point. He suggested that the reason we often have such difficulty sustaining higher states of awareness is that we 'know only what comes through the reducing valve and is consecrated as generally real by the local language'. For Huxley, only 'certain persons seem to be born with a kind of bypass that circumvents the reducing valve'. Here we think of people who are spiritual virtuosos like, for example, Ramana Maharshi, who became enlightened at the age of sixteen with no direct outside assistance. As most of us are not born with this 'bypass valve', if we are to evolve into becoming more fully awake spiritual activists, we may need to make contact with certain Heart-opening catalysts, in order to give ourselves a kind of evolutionary 'leg up'.

Help may take unusual forms

A lot of the time we don't recognise the assistance being offered us by the cosmos, often because the way it is presented to us is somewhat bizarre. This is because this help comes to us from 'worlds of being' existing beyond what we understand as constituting the normal workings of our three-dimensional space/time reality, which caterpillar man believes is the only reality there is. What we need to understand about these higher-order, more multi-dimensional worlds is that miracles and apparitions and all matter of strange phenomena which we like to bracket under the heading of 'weird' or 'supernatural' are as natural a part of their landscape as, say, cars, banks, computers and televisions are a part of our normal society.

Because we don't ordinarily live in these higher worlds and consequently are ignorant as to their scenery, and as many of us have learned to conceive that only what we can smell, touch, see, hear and feel has any existence, it may be hard to believe that these other dimensions of life are real, let alone that they may have something important to offer us. Because we have a tendency to split off from what doesn't fit into our limited belief system of how we conceive the world to be, in order get its assistance through to us, the cosmos may at times have to employ singularly dramatic or, at times, even 'shocking' means to attract our attention. Sometimes these 'help forces' impress themselves spontaneously upon us without our consciously going looking for them. On other occasions, they may only be accessed if we intentionally search for them and position ourselves in environments conducive to encountering them.

Synchronistic 'help forces'

I have always been aware of a certain 'supportive presence' throughout my life that has seemed willing to instruct, guide and protect me. On so many occasions, I have found exactly the right kind of support that I needed. Sometimes, the right person has come into my orbit at exactly at the right moment. In the writing of this book, for example, often exactly the information which I required at the time has seemed to wing its way to me from a variety of obscure sources, without my having intentionally called for it. Staying once in a hotel in a remote part of the world, I contracted a rare and potentially fatal disease and quickly became very ill. Luckily, one of the hotel guests, whom I had met only the night before, happened to be not only a doctor, but an expert in my particular illness, resulting in me getting the right diagnosis and as a result, the right treatment. I do not believe this was just by chance.

A close friend told me of an encounter with a mysterious and curiously dressed and extremely 'angelic-looking' woman, who appeared on four occasions in her hospital room in Indonesia, where, putting her hands on her leg, completely healed her of a gangrenous condition, where there had been no alternative but to amputate her leg. The hospital doctor could not understand how she had recovered so quickly and, as no one in the hospital had ever heard of or laid eyes on this 'mysterious woman', refused to believe that she existed. In the space of four days, however, my friend shifted from being in the dangerous position of being about to lose her leg, to being well enough to get up and leave the hospital. I know her well enough to know she was speaking the truth. Extraordinary things like this can sometimes occur when we are truly up against a wall.

Several times in my life I have also been in difficult, and at times hazardous, situations, and something has always seemed to intervene to rescue me. Not only has my life been saved on two specific occasions, but there have been other times when I received a very special empowerment that enabled me to deal calmly and wisely with extremely problematic situations which I would otherwise have been wholly unable to handle. Just recently, I read of a woman driving her car who suddenly saw an apparition of her dead mother telling her to put on the brakes and drive slowly, which she did. A few seconds later, a lorry pulled out from a side turning and she narrowly missed it. We all probably know of similar stories.

Sometimes these 'help forces' manifest in our dreams. I once had a client dream that a wise person told him to sell up and move his business to another country. He took the advice and as a result saved himself vast losses. All these incidents again confirm for me that a very loving and supportive presence permeates our cosmos. I suspect that the more open our hearts are, the more easily this presence is able to communicate with us.

Apparitions, UFOs, corn circles, and near-death and out-of-body experiences

Sometimes 'help forces' come to us as apparitions. For example, Christ appeared to his disciples after death. Today, visions of the Virgin Mary, perhaps symbolising the return of the repressed feminine heart, are appearing in many places. A recent appearance was on the roof of a bank in Brazil, which is very symbolic if we think of the transformations that are today required in this area. I have worked with people who have had near-death experiences and out-of-body experiences. In all instances, these 'close encounters' with unusual or what we may call 'non-ordinary' realities (so named because they occur outside our definition of what is normal) triggered significant awakenings. Two people who had near-death experiences afterwards reported a complete absence of the fear of death.

Although UFO sightings are not as common today as they were in the latter part of the last century, I think they still have an important message for us. Some regard them as symbols of wholeness or of transformation. Whether or not they are 'real', come from 'inner' or 'outer' space, or are simply projections of our own unconscious is not as important as the fact that their presence serves to remind us of the need to surrender our cosmic provinciality whereby, in our arrogance, we believe that we are the only significant intelligent life forms in the universe.

Corn circles connect us into the inherent mystery of life in a different way, and each year they seem to manifest in increasingly complex geometric forms. While some are undoubtedly man made (although I cannot think of anything more tedious than spending hours in a field bending back sheaves of corn), I believe that the vast majority are genuine and may well represent the 'voice' of our planet reminding us that we need to start thinking in new ways and move beyond our old destructive modes of living. What for John Bennett all these 'help substances' have in common is that they are 'like knowledge, inasmuch as they have to enter our present moment from outside or beyond. They are unlike knowledge inasmuch as they do not enter through the mind.'[3]

In their different ways, then, they help wake us up. They stretch us. They remind us that the world we live in may be more all-encompassing and miraculous than we believe it to be, and that there may be much more to life than meets the eye. To be an effective activist, it is very important that we begin thinking along these lines. I would now like to focus on four particular areas where especially important help substances are to be found in concentrated form:

- In the presence of a highly evolved human being – someone who has fully awakened to their 'deeper humanity'; they may also be found in an environment of study with an awake spiritual teacher who offers a particular spiritual development programme to his or her students.
- In places where intensive transformations have occurred. These are holy places or sanctuaries. They include tombs where great saints have been buried.
- In certain rituals.
- In the ingestion of certain sacred substances.

The role of the guru

One of the most important and powerful help substances is that offered us by the genuine Heart-awakened spiritual master. Such a master is known in Christianity as the spiritual director, in Sufism as the sheikh, in Zen Buddhism as the roshi, and in Tibetan Buddhism as the lama. Simply being in the physical presence of someone whose heart is fully open cannot but have a profoundly awakening effect upon our own heart, regardless of what tradition the teacher belongs to, as their higher vibration rate has the effect of amplifying our own. The genuine guru or adept doesn't work at all like a psychotherapist and isn't remotely interested in the life of our egos. Rather, they have a function analogous to that of a power station, in that in being connected themselves to the source – to the deeper heart of the cosmos – they are able to bring 'source energy' to us, only 'stepped down' in such a way that it may expand us without electrocuting us.

In his spiritual autobiography, John Bennett described how, while studying with Gurdjieff, who was his teacher at the time, he was struggling to accomplish a particular task that he had been given and which he was wholly unable to do. He was feeling utterly stupid and depleted. Gurdjieff walked towards him and gave him one 'catalytic' look which not only filled him with huge energy and joy, but empowered him to complete the task very quickly. Immediately, all his tiredness vanished and he found he had all the energy in the world.

This is a classic example of how a spiritual master can 'bring down' higher energies from the sacred worlds and make them available to us. Given the huge danger that so many situations in the world present us with today, we see how important it could be if more of us activists were to learn to avail ourselves of this 'higher level' assistance or even, perhaps, contemplate graduating into becoming enlightened activists ourselves so we might offer it to others.

While it may appear as if the master or adept is the same as us, because they look and speak and eat like us, we should never be under any illusion that this is the case. As divine representatives or as embodiments of many of the highest and noblest of Heart qualities, they live out of very rarefied and evolved worlds. Their role is to reflect our own truth back to us, to remind us of our Stradivarius nature and that who we *really* are is eternal and timeless. In this way, they may induct us into the mystery of realising that our true Heart self is always there and has never been born and has never died! As the great mystic poet Hafiz put it:

When you sit before a master like me,
Even if you are a drooling mess,
My eyes sing with excitement.
They see your divine worth.[5]

The fact of our 'being seen' by someone who is a citizen of a higher, sacred heart world is so important, and the experience always elevates us. The great Indian saint Ramakrishna understood this and suggested that we all should

seek spiritual advancement from one who is advanced. One should take some trouble to live in the company of the good. The society of pious men is like water in which rice has been washed. Just as the intoxication caused by wine is dissipated by rice-water, similarly the only way to dissipate the intoxication caused by the wine of desire is the society of the pious.[6]

Masters teach in different ways

A genuine master, needless to say, is immensely threatening to our normal ego-infused reality and simply cannot be understood from within the de-sacralised and rational world of scientific materialism. This is why they are so often described in disparaging terms. Of course, there are bogus spiritual masters around – one can find fakes in every field – but the integrity of the vast majority should not be prejudiced by the rascality of the few. Different teachers also teach in different ways. For example, Ramana Maharshi helped awaken his students in silence, while the late Heart master Adi Da, who embodied a tradition known as Crazy Wisdom, saw his role as needing to be absurd. 'A spiritual master is absurd like everyone else,' he would tell his students. 'He is a function that seeks to awaken human beings from this condition that is absurd.'

These approaches could not be more different to the approach taken by 'Papaji' (now, sadly, no more with us in body), who had been a teacher of mine and whom I would go to visit in India from time to time. His approach was always gentle, humorous and loving. In his autobiography he wrote:

The real master looks into your heart and sees what state you are in, and gives out advice which is always appropriate and relevant.

He gave me good advice when, many years ago, I first went to India to meet him at his ashram, loaded up as I was with all the spiritual books I had taken with me to try to 'improve myself'. He told me:

Stop struggling so much to get better. Give your heart a chance to breathe, and realise that real knowledge does not come through the mind. You are someone who talks a lot about peace, but you are always anxious. You bring too many of your neuroses into your quest, which is why you never seem to get very far. When you spend time with me, allow yourself to rest quietly into your deeper being.

Gurus 'zapping' us with spiritual Heart

His words were painful to hear, but I knew that they were true. Indeed, it was on the wings of the 'help substances' that came to me as a result of being in Papaji's presence that I was given a direct experience of what it truly was to feel awake, free, quiet, surrendered, without anxiety and released of the need to impress others or prove myself. I felt very simple and ordinary.

My ego was (temporarily) reduced to toast.

Basically, I had been 'zapped' by Papaji's powerful, loving and awake Heart. The whole experience was both hugely awesome yet terribly simple. It felt like the final liberation out of my old narcissistic contractions. I no longer needed to be more special than others and, released of this burden, everything around me became impregnated with quiet meaning and beauty that just was – with no need for analysis. The gift he gave me was to strip me of much of my bogus self-importance that I had erected around myself for so many years, in order to compensate for feelings of inadequacy. Without it, a much more genuine 'me' was able to come into expression, one that was full of quiet joy and love. I felt so connected to the universal heart. Life was very precious.

I would love to tell you that this deeper Heart state remained indefinitely and that my ego remained toast-like forever after. Sadly, I would be telling a lie. Slowly, my old contracted self began to claw its way back. But not as powerfully as before. Something indefinable had shifted, and the help substances (or the 'spiritual seeds') planted in me so delicately by Papaji all those years ago have continued to work in my system. I had been given a sneak preview into a higher-order Heart world, and this experience has continued ever since to inspire me in everything I do. I never became Papaji's disciple, nor did I ever want to live at his ashram, but by dipping into his sacred world from time to time, I could continue to be reminded of who I truly was and what the real purpose of my life was about.

An example of a very different kind of help substance was offered me during my five-day visit to another teacher, known as Mother Meera, whom I mentioned earlier. Her gift to me was quite different from Papaji's, and more specific. During my daily sittings with her (called 'darshans'), it felt as if all my pain was being gently sucked out of my heart, rendering it easy for me at last to forgive and therefore release from my heart the particular woman who had hurt me so and who had consequently become lodged so tightly there.

Spiritual surrender
To best receive a master's help, we are challenged to surrender to them. In Papaji's words: 'If the devotee truly surrenders, then he is finished. No more karma will be accumulated. From then on the divine will look after him.' However, it is important we remember that we are not surrendering to a

person but to what they represent. Thus, it is not the same thing as giving ourselves up to the control of some charismatic individual. Here, what we are surrendering into is the embrace of the spiritual heart. We are letting go our need to control things – the sense that 'we have to do it all ourselves', or that 'it is all up to us'. We are also seeking to give up our attachment to seeing ourselves according to the images given us by our ego personalities. *A spiritual master, therefore, may be seen as an activist of self-realisation.* By helping shift us out of our attachments to a limited view of ourselves, they make it easier for us to understand what our true purpose for being alive really is.

Yes, of course we can all do important activist work without ever accessing the higher reaches of our human nature and without ever eliciting the services of a master. But if we ever do feel inclined to work with someone to help accelerate our deeper entry into butterfly-hood, our capacity as activists will be much enhanced. However, we should only try to find a master if we believe we are ready for what they have to offer us and if we encounter someone whom we feel a genuine resonance with. If we still have strong unresolved personal issues which give us pain, probably the last person we should seek out is a spiritual master, as helping us feel better is not their true remit. It would be the equivalent of a GCSE student eliciting the services of a university professor to help them with their work.

The significance of ritual

Ritual is another important help substance which, if engaged in wisely, can also enable us to connect more deeply to our core Heart self. In particular, it can accelerate our awareness of the larger environment of which we are a part, and make us more effective in serving it. Sadly, ritual has almost disappeared from our Western society, apart from weddings, funerals, the haka performed by the New Zealand rugby team before a match, and families gathering to watch TV!

Lorna St Aubyn explains the importance of ritual:

Rituals can help us see that we are part of something larger, a part of a living, breathing earth. They can give us a feeling of unity and a sense of security and support in an increasingly difficult world. We can again begin to sense the sacredness in the ordinary, which can add the depth and meaning so often missing from our lives ... At this time of crisis, we need rituals as never before. They are as important to us as they were to our ancestors.[7]

Over the years, I have participated in many sacred medicine wheel rituals, which have an extraordinary beauty and poignancy and evoke the power of what in shamanism is known as the Four Directions. By drawing to us those life presences that live to the north, south, east and west, such a ritual helps deepen in us the realisation that we are all part of the great web of creation and are connected to the animal, vegetable and mineral 'subhuman kingdoms', as well as to all our fellow human beings and those beings who exist at higher levels of consciousness.

Rituals serve many different purposes. If done intentionally and consciously, they help link us very powerfully to the unseen helping forces of life which our prayers call into existence. For instance, if we wish to 'bring in' sacred energy that may be utilised not only for our own development and well-being, but also for the well-being of other people or for our world, then consciously participating in spiritual festivals which happen on particular dates and which are designed to honour certain important occasions can be very important. As Charles Leadbeater explains, 'as the stars move through their courses, there are certain times when certain energies are more readily available than at others – when the bridges are clear, the channels are open'.[8] He stresses how important Christmas and Easter are for Christians. The Tibetan master Dwaj Khul recognises the significance of the full moon and how much we can benefit by doing ritualised meditations on those occasions. 'No price', he tells us, 'is too high in order to gain the spiritual illumination which can be possible at that time.'

Practical rituals
I always use ritual in my retreats. Over New Year, I teach a specific course to help people let go the old year and usher in the new one. I like to build a big fire and tell my students to go out into nature, decide what parts of themselves they no longer want to hold onto, and then gather up stones, leaves and branches and other aspects of nature to symbolise those parts, and tie them together in a bundle. For example, a stone could symbolise some hard-heartedness that we want to release, dead wood could stand for an old job we want to give up, while clinging ivy might represent a co-dependent relationship which we are trying to exit from. People then throw their bundles onto the fire,

imagining these old patterns burning away as they watch the fire taking hold of them. This is a powerful process and yields very positive results.

We may wish to design our own rituals to serve specific purposes. Recently, some good friends created their own ritual to celebrate their marriage. The ceremony was not only very meaningful for them, but also for everyone present, as what transpired drew a great deal of spiritual help to the whole gathering. (It occurred to me at the time that perhaps so many marriages break up today because an insufficient amount of spiritual substance is invoked during the conventional marriage ceremony, so that when difficult times come along, as they inevitably will, couples have less stored-up help resources upon which to draw.)

If we truly wish to be free of a particular encumbrance, and if we have personally worked on the issue to help loosen it up inside our psyches, then using ritual to complete the release can be very helpful, as it both serves to anchor our intention in the physical world as well as to 'call in' the assisting forces. For example, someone who is wanting to let go an old relationship could burn photos of their old lover. If I have done some spirit-release work with someone in a session, I might suggest that when they get home, they have a shower and imagine the water flowing through them and washing away whatever remnants may still linger.

In my Majorca retreats, I like to design rituals on the spur of the moment, and if I feel it appropriate, on arriving at a particular part of the countryside, I might suggest to my group that they spend time praying and thanking the spirit of that place. (If we are sensitive to nature, we become aware that different areas possess different presences.) When we arrive at a beach, I might ask my students to thank it for its beauty and its healing capabilities, and when they get into the water, to imagine themselves being purified and nourished accordingly. As I stressed earlier, if we hold a sacred space inside our hearts, then we bring that particular presence into our environment. We sacralise it. At one level, then, ritual is prayer in action; it is simply another way to 'knock on the doors of the higher worlds', asking that they open for us and reveal their contents to us. In St Aubyn's words again:

> *All major life stages need to be clearly marked: puberty, marriage, menopause, death and so on. In addition, many situations such as retirement ... now need to be acknowledged. Events particular to our own life story may also need to be externalised.*[9]

Healing rituals

Rituals are often used as strategies for healing. If a particular disaster has occurred, a ritual can be extremely important as it can help break up thought forms of anguish, terror or perhaps of violence and hatred (depending on the nature of the catastrophe). Often, until dissolved, a negative thought form will continue to hover over the place where the tragic event happened, serving as a kind of toxic mist and creating a polluting influence for everyone in the vicinity.

Just as addressing the dark side of the species heart is not for everyone, the same thing applies to this kind of work. We can engage in a ritual like the one I am about to suggest only if we feel in our hearts that we are strong enough to do so and if our role as an activist particularly calls us in this direction. If we do participate, I suggest it be done in conjunction with other people who feel similarly inspired, so that the load may be shared.

A ritual to perform in the face of a great catastrophe

Firstly, we need to prepare the room where the ritual will take place, by cleansing it with incense or a 'smudge-stick', used by shamans specifically for the purposes of purification. We may put three chairs at different ends of the room. In the centre will be a table representing an altar, onto which we will place certain sacred items, such as, perhaps, a Buddha or an icon or a vase of fresh flowers. One chair will stand for the tragedy itself, another for all those traumatised as a result of it, and the third for all those killed as a result.

It is helpful to find something symbolic for each chair. If our ritual is to cleanse the effects of a tsunami, for example, a bowl overfull of water with stones inside it or a drawing of a tidal wave would be appropriate. If we were thinking of a ritual to heal the 9/11 tragedy, a drawing of planes flying into the Twin Towers would be an apt representation. Those engaging in the ritual will sit on other chairs in the middle of the room and take time to centre and quieten themselves, and ask that their hearts be ready to partake in an important piece of healing work. In all rituals it is very important that we prepare ourselves appropriately beforehand, as this sets up the whole tone and intention of what we are about to embark upon.

Then we begin to pray and ask that those unseen healing forces that work with terrible tragedies be present with us in the room and help us in our work. If we are Christian, we may like to call in the presence of particular angels that work in this arena. If we are more shamanically inclined, we may call on the four elements to help us: the earth to transmute the tragedy, the air to dissolve it, water to wash it away and fire to burn off whatever elements still remain.

We might also invoke the presence of particular spiritual teachers, dead or alive, whom we feel would be useful in such situations. For example, if I were partaking in such a ritual, I would call on Papaji, and on Jesus and the Buddha. I would also ask for the qualities of light, love and peace to be present strongly in the room. We need to know that the full force of the spiritual elements which we have called into being will be directed to the particular disaster.

When we have called in all the helping forces, the ritual can begin. We start by asking with our hearts that whatever is needed to heal this scenario will take place. We may have the sense that a healing current is moving through us, and we will generally know when a ritual is over and the work is complete, as we will stop experiencing this energy .

Having done this, we then spend a few minutes clearing ourselves, either with the smudge-stick or with the incense. This is very important, as to stay filled with the pain would be counterproductive. We now need to address the issue of the badly traumatised survivors. Here, we imagine ourselves talking with our hearts to the deeper domain of their hearts – to that part of them that is eternal and so has not been scarred by the tragedy. Here, we ask that people receive the healing which they require. Again, we go through the process of cleansing ourselves afterwards.

In the last section of the ritual, we imagine ourselves talking to the souls of those who have been killed and who have not yet 'moved on' and so are still 'hanging around'. We need to tell them that they have been part of a collective event, that they have died, and that help will be forthcoming to assist them to pass over into the next realm. Here again, we ask that those spiritual forces that deal with such incidents be directed towards helping these people. If there are people whom we personally know who have been killed, we might inject a special prayer or a particular message of love.

If difficult things have occurred in your life or if your work involves you in problematic situations, you might feel drawn to devise your own rituals along the lines suggested here.

Plants as sacred help substances: the power of ayahuasca

The healing power of natural herbs and plants is well known to all naturopaths and herbalists. What is less well known is that there have always existed particular plants which, when prepared and mixed together in a certain way, have the effect of opening up the doors of our perception in a most radical fashion, making us more aware of the existence of other dimensional worlds, or of higher-order realities. All these sacred 'catalytic substances' have their own unique properties and gifts to offer us. I want to confine myself here to talking about one specific sacred help substance which I have worked with extensively, which has been known to man since 2500 bc, and which today continues to be used by many shamans in their healing work. It is known as ayahuasca.

Ayahuasca is a Quechua term meaning 'vine of the soul'. The substance is prepared by soaking the bark and stems of a particular tree with various other admixture plants. Not only may it enable us temporarily to by-pass our 'reducing valve' and open us up to the profoundest domains of our butterfly-hood – it has certainly done this for me – but it also has great healing capabilities and can help people overcome serious addictions. For example, since one particular session of ayahuasca (not taken for that purpose), I have never wanted another cigarette.

For me, ayahuasca is the most healing and the most transformational of all sacred substances. If taken in the correct setting and with the correct spiritual intention (I have always done these rituals in the presence of a shaman, and would never dream of taking it alone or in a non-sacralised setting), it can do much to prepare us to face the many challenges of evolving ourselves and building a new culture in the twenty-first century.

Whenever I have partaken in an ayahuasca ritual, I am always reminded of this fact. Indeed, as a result of my work with this sacred substance, together with my meditation work and the time I have spent with spiritual masters, I can unequivocally say that I *know* that I am a divine being, I *know* that God lives inside my heart and I *know* that this is true of *all* of us, and that our greatest pretence is to think that we are just plastic fiddles!

One little reminder, though: we must never be under the illusion that the *temporary* experiencing of very high states of consciousness is in any way indicative of our necessarily embodying this knowing and so being able to live out of this state twenty-four hours of each day. In other words, temporarily accessing very elevated states of Heart and living out of these states all the time in an embodied way are two very different things. Unless we can embody this divinity from the tips of our fingers right down to the soles of our feet, we are not yet there and should never believe anything to the contrary!

We also remind ourselves that being spiritual is not about being high; it is about being real and free, and, most important, treating our fellow human beings and our planet with reverence and kindness. Certainly, this is what ayahuasca has told me over and over again. I say this as I have met far too many people who have been hijacked by their egos and who think that because they have had one or two very transcendent experiences, they are therefore some highly evolved super-being, and superior to the rest of us. The reason I also know this is because I have also been that inflated person (see Chapter 19). In actuality, the moment we find ourselves thinking that we are 'very spiritual' or 'more spiritual than others', it is merely an indication that our egos need a lot more work doing on them, and that they are still running too much of the show.

'The professor'
But back to ayahuasca. Sometimes it has been referred to as 'the professor' because it often talks to us from inside our hearts and may give us important information about our lives, suggesting things that we might or might not do, or where we might go for help with some particular issue that may be bothering us. Thus, it is rather like an inner guru or oracle inside us. In certain instances, it can even instruct us what we need to eat. I remember the first time that I drank this brew, it introduced itself quite formally to me and told me that, as a plant intelligence, it was closely allied with humanity and was helping us with our spiritual evolution and that it would answer any questions which I put to it. I put many, and always received the profoundest of answers. After my first weekend of working with ayahuasca, I woke up early the next morning feeling very strong and vigorous and took myself for a five-mile run, imbued with all the grace and strength that I used to possess when I was in my twenties.

Revealing the Shadow
Another of ayahuasca's special properties is that it does not hold back from revealing to us the contents of our Shadow side together with the limitations of the egoic games which we may be playing. Thus, it beautifully integrates the worlds of psychology and spirituality. Often, when I drank it, I would

find that it not only introduced me to great visions of beauty and filled my heart with great love, but it also endowed me with extra courage to enable me to confront deeper, darker aspects of the collective Shadow side of humanity, which on my own I might try to avoid. Much of my species Shadow healing work has been done with the aid of this brew.

In a recent session, my journey took me deeply into the heart of the totalitarian or fascistic mindset. I felt the huge pain that this particular energy causes for those millions of people the world over whose freedoms have been brutalised and who live horrendously reduced lives as a result. The experience was extremely unpleasant, but I felt so empowered by the brew that I put up no resistance. Afterwards, my heart seemed strengthened by the experience, and it also felt as if a very old, hard and encrusted pattern inside it had begun to dissolve. The fascistic me? In the ensuing days, I experienced a renewed desire inside myself to stand up to oppression in all its many forms.

'The professor' also seems at times to endow our heart with extra fire, enabling us to burn through our negative patterns more effectively. 'All you need to do', it would tell me over and over again, 'is to remain awake; stay centred in the light and fire of your heart and be the observer of all the debris that is brought up into it, and then the transformational work will be done.' This was similar to the message given me by Papaji. As with all other help substances, however, ayahuasca is not a shortcut to the divine. It is not, nor indeed should it be, a substitute for meditation or prayer or for our engaging in all the many other forms of Heart work that we have been exploring thus far.

Ayahuasca as psychotherapy
For me, ayahuasca is a highly useful tool that may be used to assist us in many different areas of Heart work. In different sessions, I have worked on everything from curses to painful past lives, negative spiritual infestations, ancestral karma and even issues belonging to current family members. Here is what Dr Ralph Metzner has to say about it:

> *It is recognised that psychotherapy with hallucinogens invariably involves an experience of a profoundly expanded state of consciousness in which the individual can not only gain therapeutic insight into neurotic or addictive emotional dynamics and behaviour patterns, but may come to question and transcend fundamental self-concepts and views of the nature of reality.*[10]

He suggests that psychedelics could play the same role in psychology as the microscope does in biology – opening up realms and processes inside us to direct and verifiable observations that have up until now been largely hidden or inaccessible. He also reminds us that people who take ayahuasca

> *who do not have any appreciable toxicity in their system may find themselves releasing the toxic residues of past emotional entanglements, the guilt and shame of traumatic abuse, or the self-defeating thought-patterns of addictions, compulsions and other neurotic behaviours. Some people might even find that what they are discharging is not so much their personal 'stuff' but some portion of the collective-bands of humanity.*[11]

Working with a guru may not be everyone's cup of tea, and the same holds true as regards the ingestion of sacred substances. If you are someone who feels strongly averse to taking anything that will change your consciousness, I wholly respect your decision and ask that you honour it at all times and have nothing whatsoever to do with the world of sacred substances. All I ask, however, is that you do not endarken those of us for whom ayahuasca has been of great benefit, or place us in the category of druggies! There could not be a greater difference between people who take recreational, so-called 'hard' drugs solely for kicks and those who, in particularly ritualised and sacred settings, from time to time elect to work with certain sacred help substances in order to deepen themselves and to attempt to draw the universal heart ever closer to them.

The 'help force' of sacred sites

There exist particular physical locations on the planet where sacred help is to be found in a densely concentrated form. Either making a particular pilgrimage to such places, or engaging in prayer or performing certain rituals in those areas, can, if done in the right spirit, be of enormous assistance. Often these places exist or are built in locations known as 'power points', where strong earth energy streams converge. Spiritual help is also to be found in those areas where powerful sacred rituals have been performed over many years. I have found it especially concentrated inside great mosques or cathedrals constructed in the days before man had lost his sense of the sacred.

When I visited Chartres Cathedral (built on a very strong power point), and did prayer work in front of the great rose window, I was aware of a huge spiritual presence filling me. I found a not dissimilar kind of presence when I was doing my shamanic training in the Mexican jungle, as our teacher made us do much of our work in a particular area that had been used for this purpose for centuries. At night, we would be instructed to sleep in the caves in that area, and it was especially in our dreams that we trainees would become aware that we were dwelling in a field of consciousness impregnated with powerful sacred memories. As I was a complete novice, envelopment in this field made it much easier for me to understand the essence of shamanism.

The locations where great spiritual masters currently live and teach or where, when alive, they used to live and teach, are also areas endowed with particular grace. The old ashram at the foot of the sacred mountain where Ramana Maharshi lived and taught is still a place that many people venerate and continue to flock to for spiritual inspiration. For a Muslim, journeying to Mecca, the birthplace of the great Prophet Mohammed, holds enormous significance. The same is true of Lourdes if one is a Catholic. About 150 years ago, the Madonna appeared in a vision to a young peasant girl and guided her to find a spring of water there, which she did. People began to drink from it and were cured of all sorts of ailments. Every year, thousands of Catholics flock to Lourdes, to be healed and to receive spiritual sustenance. There is a definite miraculous presence in that area.

Florence, which was the birthplace of the first Renaissance, has always been a very special city for me, and in 1975 a group of us decided to put on a conference there to celebrate the birth of what we saw as the 'second spiritual renaissance' that was now occurring. We felt that the success of our venture was enormously assisted by the particular location that we had chosen. When I made the journey across Russia to the cave monastery at Pskov to encounter those monks who, I mentioned earlier, had prayed for my healing, I discovered that inside their monastery were deep caves, built into the hillside, where lay the relics of many great Russian holy figures. Upon venturing into these caves, I found my heart opening very powerfully. Apparently, so great had been the purity of those saints buried there, that their physical bodies had never decayed. Being granted permission to remain in this vast Heart space inside those caves for a full two days, I felt as if I were being given a huge spiritual gift. Not only did the monks heal me physically, but my Heart life seemed to accelerate as well.

Many years later, I wondered if this 'close encounter' with such a sacred presence had had anything to do with a lot of the good luck that has seemed to come my way, where, in times of difficulty, something beneficial has always seemed to intervene on my behalf. We will never know the answers as we can never 'scientifically prove' the effects of any of the help substances that we either encounter by chance or specifically go searching for.

There is a beautiful monastery called Lluc, situated close to where I teach my retreats in Majorca, where I always take my students to spend a day in prayer and meditation. It is a profoundly sacred location and houses a statue of the Black Madonna that is supposedly endowed with miracle capabilities. This monastery was used in the past by the Knights Templar and is a place of pilgrimage. Just outside its entrance is a 'spiritual walk' which takes one up through different levels of consciousness. I always suggest that our group do this walk in silence, imagining as they ascend the steps that they are also ascending towards or being drawn ever closer to their deeper Heart self. Engaging in Heart work in such environments is always a powerful and transforming experience.

Concluding comments

When I teach my retreats, I like to start off the day with readings from poets that have a particular spiritual message relevant to the theme we will be exploring. In addition, I will always play music that activates the heart chakra. I also remind my students that the more they read sacred literature – the Upanishads, the Bhagavad Gita, the Bible, the Qur'an etc. – as well as books written by the great masters, and the more they learn to wean themselves away from literature that appeals to those parts of themselves that need to fall away, the more they will also be assisted in their spiritual journeying.

Whatever form the help substances take, or wherever they come from, what they all have in common is that they do not discriminate. They don't take into consideration what culture a person belongs to or what religion we abide by. While many of us may feel more predisposed to avail ourselves of support couched in sources and traditions that we are familiar with, we can certainly receive assistance from avenues that may be alien to us. The key ingredient is the fact of our needing help, our asking for it and our being willing and open to receiving it.

I believe in miracles because I see that what we define as miraculous is merely a manifestation of what is natural in a higher order of reality, stepped down into our ordinary world. Over the years, I have been privy to many extraordinary healings, but none more miraculous than what I once saw being performed by a great Heart master in Cyprus called Daskalos, whom, unbeknownst to him, I had flown out that day to visit out of the blue. To my utter astonishment, I saw an old lady, who, half an hour ago, had been all bent over in agony and hardly able to walk, have her spine straightened by him and canter out of his little house with a huge smile of gratitude on her face. While conventional medical science would say that a healing such as this is not possible, and that obviously some kind of chicanery must have been at work, I do not believe this. Why would he and the lady have colluded to put on this pantomime especially for me, when neither of them knew me or had any knowledge that I was coming that day to visit?

Daskalos, who is now dead, was yet another Heart master, who, like many other extraordinary human beings, lived out of the higher laws of love. He operated – or one could say that he performed his healing operations – out of a wholly different reality from that in which most of us ordinarily function. In these higher worlds, more dimensions of life come into play, and this in turn radically alters the laws of physics as we understand them. Perhaps Daskalos's world was not too dissimilar from that 'higher Heart reality' that Jesus operated out of, where it was utterly natural to walk on water, calm storms, raise the dead and feed five thousand people from a few loaves and fishes. Jesus could do what for us seems miraculous because his heart had opened and He had become one with the Heart of all life. He and 'His Father' had become one. He had ascended into being one with the cosmic force of life and so was able to bring down to us what comes from realms of spirit existing beyond space and time.

Just imagine the kind of power for good that an activist could wield if he or she were also to tap into these self-same higher-energy sources. What if we learned to use this spiritual power to address our many social, political and economic problems? We will return to this theme in the last section of the book, where we will explore what we can do to build a more just and holistic society.

I have just moved a pile of books beside my computer, and a little card popped out and fell on the floor. On it was a quotation from *A Course in Miracles*. It said: 'No miracle can ever be denied to those who know that they are one with God.'[12]

Chapter 18

Exploring the Heart of Forgiveness

The weak can never forgive. Forgiveness is an attitude of the strong –
MAHATMA GANDHI

We must develop and maintain the capacity to forgive. He who is devoid of the power to forgive is devoid of the power to love –
MARTIN LUTHER KING

The importance of forgiveness

To open that dimension of our hearts which is able to forgive is of huge importance both psychologically and spiritually. Not only does forgiveness liberate and bring a sense of peace, but it is also an integral component in the resolution of many different kinds of conflict. Whether it is ourselves we feel we need to forgive, whether it is another person, or whether we are challenged to forgive in a more general sense – whenever we embark on this mission, we open up whole new possibilities for peace and harmony emerging in the world. Certainly I cannot see any new culture of Heart taking root *effectively* on our planet unless huge dollops of forgiveness are doled out by many people in many different areas.

Whether, as activists, it is we who need to do the forgiving, or whether it is others whom we need to help to do so, there are several things we need to understand about it. The first is that genuine forgiveness is often difficult and may need some perseverance. The second is that it is essentially a spiritual process and cannot be done effectively without the involvement of our hearts, as it is only our hearts that truly know how to forgive. Certainly our minds might recognise the necessity for doing so, and yes, we can say to someone 'I forgive you'. However, unless, in so doing, we touch into the heart of what forgiveness is all about, and unless those words therefore come from this place inside us, they will have little power.

The challenges around forgiveness

Forgiving is especially challenging if our hearts are very wounded. For example, there may be a situation where we want to forgive someone as we recognise the benefits it could bring. However, we may find it extremely hard to do so because the very circumstances that we need to forgive them for have so embittered us that they have caused our hearts to shut down. Also, so long as our egos are still prominent and unhealed – and wounded ego, we remind ourselves, always 'knows best' and 'likes to be right', and thrives on revenge and retribution – we may not feel predisposed to forgive, which is again why it is so important that we move into states where it is less prominent. If we can start doing this, we may gradually begin to see that forgiveness is actually not something that we do, so much as something that we are – or rather, a space that we enter into gradually, as we increasingly learn to open to those dimensions of our hearts that naturally desire bygones to be bygones.

Forgiving usually happens gradually. Most of us don't suddenly forgive. Often, when we start out in this direction, our capacity may initially be small, but as our hearts slowly begin to grow (and the process of wanting to forgive actually helps this growth), we may become more adept at it. Why it is so liberating for all concerned and why it is so strongly emphasised in all the world religions is because it is a process of letting both the forgiver and the one being forgiven off the heavy hooks that both have become pinioned onto. (Resentment can, in many instances, bind us as close to someone as love.) As a result, a potential space may open up for a higher love to peek through and show its face. Indeed, forgiveness and love are intimate bedfellows. In many instances, the one or the ones we are needing to forgive are also people whom we once used to love.

Another problem we can face is that if we have been badly hurt, while we may see the advantages of forgiving and letting go, we may not want the other to feel liberated. We may feel so hurt that we have no desire to take them into our hearts (which is part and parcel of the forgiveness process). We may prefer to remain filled with our hatreds or resentments (or whatever other emotions are uppermost) in the sure knowledge that those whom we are resenting are continuing to pay the price of what we feel they did to us, by remaining skewered in the turbulence of our negative projections upon them. In other words, we may feel loath to release our hatred as it seems to be the only thing we have left.

I once made the acquaintance of a Palestinian doctor, who told me that on top of what he saw as the humiliations continually being imposed upon his people by the Israelis, three members of his family had been killed by Israeli soldiers, and this made him hate the Jewish people very vehemently. When I asked him if he could ever consider forgiving them, he replied: 'Never. I would rather die than forgive, as all I have left is my resentment. If I give that up, then I give up a lot of what gives my life meaning, and then I truly would have nothing. How can I forgive such evil? How can I let go my deep desire to see those people suffer who have deprived me of all that was good and beautiful in my life and caused me such total devastation?' I understood how he felt. His words reveal for us how difficult forgiveness can often be in certain circumstances. I have no doubt that were I to talk to an Israeli whose family had just been wiped out by a Hamas rocket attack, that they would share not dissimilar sentiments.

Another difficulty is that if we have suffered serious sexual or emotional abuse or endured ethnic cleansing or years of warfare, the result may be that we strongly internalise the negativity or violence that has been thrown at us, identify strongly with it and even believe we deserved what we got, and so there is nothing to forgive. And we can do strange things when filled with pain.

I often come across this in my couples work. I worked with one couple where the wife discovered that her husband had slept once with a call girl when away on a business trip – this being his sole indiscretion in twenty years of marriage. He apologised profusely and let his wife know he loved her very much – which was the truth – but his wife, whose insecure ego was anyway very vulnerable, simply wouldn't let her hurt go. Rather than forgive, she plotted her revenge and did her utmost to destroy the entire relationship and everything that they had built up together as a family. Years later, I met her again by chance, and she told me what a fool she had been, and that out of her desire for vengeance, she had also destroyed her own life, to say nothing of the damage inflicted on their children, by getting rid of a good man whom she deeply loved. This is an example of what the wounded ego is sometimes capable of doing, and why *not* forgiving can be so destructive.

The issue of 'victim consciousness'

Our incapacity to forgive and our feeling of victimhood, therefore, are often closely enmeshed, and in many instances, the choice to forgive is also a choice to give up our attachment to victimisation, which I always feel is defined by the position we take around painful events that have happened to us, rather than by the nature of the events themselves. I say this as I know people for whom the slightest cold wind blowing in their face has been the excuse to go into 'poor me' mode, and I have also been privileged to have met people who have had truly atrocious things happen to them but who have never allowed themselves to feel a victim.

At a conference once, I met an extraordinary young Indian woman who told me that she had been sold by her very poor family into prostitution at a very early age. Despite her suffering, she never blamed or stopped loving her family, telling me that 'such things were done in my culture'. She never felt a passive victim, and told me that when an opportunity presented itself for her to escape her servitude, she felt very fortunate and took it. Today, she works as an activist, dedicating her time and energy to helping other young girls also caught up in the same tragic business. I thought to myself: this woman is an extraordinary human being! They ought to award BBB medals to such individuals, standing for 'Brave Beyond Belief'.

This young woman was able to be so naturally magnanimous and courageous because she naturally had a lot of heart. Because of this, her painful experiences had somehow not disconnected her from her own innate 'heart of forgiveness'. Thus, *there was no need for her to forgive those who had caused her to suffer, because she never resented them in the first place.* Although she had not had much of an education, her heart was big and wise and loving, and she understood, as she explained it to me, that her parents were desperately poor and needed the money, and that all concerned were caught up in an unjust system.

Requirements for forgiveness

What, then, is required of us, if, as activists, we are called to forgive, and if our hearts may not be as exceptionally big as that young woman's? To start with, we need to be sufficiently connected to our feelings to know that we are most probably carrying resentful or, in certain cases, murderous or revengeful thoughts inside us towards those whom we believe are responsible for our grief. Secondly, we must realise that these thoughts are poisoning us and restricting our lives and also poisoning the larger collective heart, and that if we were to forgive and let go, not only would we feel a lot better, but the planetary heart as a whole would also be that little bit less toxic. Thirdly, we need to remember at all times to take our rage or our grief up into our hearts and experience it fully and not suppress it. We cannot forgive unless we are also willing to work with our suffering at the same time, along the lines that we have already explored.

If the issue or issues we are dealing with are complex and need greater clarification, it may be that we will need to enlist outside counselling support to assist us. Sometimes, in doing so, we may uncover an egoically self-righteous part of ourselves that has placed us up on some moral high horse, whereby we think that this 'bad thing' done to us couldn't possibly, given different circumstances, have been ever done by us. Perhaps we are right. Perhaps it couldn't. But if in any way it could, and we can recognise it, it can help us get off our superior stance and enable us to be more understanding. It may also be, if we choose to work with our issue, that we uncover some ancient, long-hidden memory, locked into a past life or inside our species heart, of actually having perpetrated onto others the very atrocity that we are suffering from right now, thus allowing us to see that we may possibly be suffering some kind of 'karmic retribution'.

As with other facets of the heart, meditation, prayer and contemplation are also key ingredients of the forgiveness process, as they serve to soften and open our hearts and reveal for us where that special part that we may call 'the heart of forgiveness' resides.

If we make progress along these lines, and are beginning to open up to the possibility of forgiving someone or some group or tribe or race (or whomever), we will find that this needs to be accompanied by one of the most difficult aspects of the whole process: we need to start to consider taking into our hearts those who were responsible for damaging them in the first place, for, as I stressed earlier, forgiveness is much more than simply saying 'I forgive you'. There are also other factors to consider. In the Lord's Prayer, we are not only to ask for help to forgive those 'who have trespassed against us', but also, equally important, we need to ask for forgiveness for where we also might have trespassed – that is, where wittingly or unwittingly, we may have hurt or injured others. This is also important. Sometimes, we cannot forgive others because there may be things about ourselves that we also find it hard to forgive.

Forgiving ourselves

Before we can love another person, we need to open our hearts and first love ourselves, and the same thing holds true in the area of forgiveness. Even if we haven't ourselves committed some terrible atrocity, often unconsciously we may still have pinioned ourselves on all sorts of mysterious hooks for not being perfect enough. If we can work through our Judeo-Christian guilt around feeling a 'sinner' because we are not as 'perfect as our Father in Heaven is perfect' and start accepting and honouring ourselves for being the way we are, then the forgiving dimension of our hearts has a better chance to start surfacing and working in our favour.

That said, there may be certain instances where we may genuinely feel we have done something unforgivable. For example, the parents of Madeleine McCann, the little girl who was abducted when they went out to dinner one evening while on holiday in Portugal, leaving her insufficiently supervised, may initially have felt like that. In such very difficult circumstances, it is so important that we do not live the rest of our lives strung up on the crucifix of our own creation. I am sure Madeleine's parents eventually realised that continuing to hate and berate themselves for their 'sin of omission' would not only do nothing to bring their daughter back, but would render them less capable of being good parents for their remaining children. What they did as an act of atonement/self-forgiveness – and I recommend it to anyone in similar situations – was, in addition to doing all they could to find their daughter, to commit their lives to helping other parents who had also lost their children in similar ways. They started a foundation and became activists for their cause and raised a lot of money. In doing so, I am sure they were able to convert much of their grief and self-recrimination into something useful, especially if, as a result of their work, other lost children have been returned to their parents. Being willing to surrender our suffering by choosing to devote our lives to trying to make a difference in the very area where we made our 'unforgivable' mistake may do a lot to remedy it. It is another expression of 'active prayer' that we explored earlier on.

An old friend of mine, when young, had been very greedy and became very rich as a drug smuggler. Later in his life, as his heart began to open, he felt ashamed of what he had done and made a 180-degree shift. Today, he lives very humbly and has used most of his ill-gotten gains to start schools in India to help and educate children from the back streets. This has enabled the heart of forgiveness to blossom inside him.

If we are trying to forgive someone or to ask them if they might forgive us, it can often be very helpful, if at all possible, to arrange a face-to-face meeting. The advantage is that it enables both sides to share thoughts and feelings, talk things out and, very importantly, hear each other's side of the story. I remember once meeting someone who had cheated me financially, and on telling him how hurt and angry I felt, and then hearing him apologise with great sincerity, and informing me about the desperation that lay behind what he did, I found my heart being touched and filling up with warmth towards him (a sure sign that the forgiveness process is underway).

An example of a forgiveness process

A man once came to see me who had just lost his only son, who had been run over by a drunk driver. Although the culprit went to prison, my client could not and would not forgive him, and continually felt possessed by thoughts of revenge. 'All I ever think about is doing the same thing to his son, so that his family can suffer as mine have done,' he confided in me, 'and these thoughts are killing me.' I could see that this man was closing his heart down more and more and that he could not, on his own, move out of that deadening and vengeful world that he had sunk into. He was also starting to drink a lot, and once or twice had driven dead drunk himself. I feared he too might run over someone. I saw that he needed extra help to move into a domain of being where forgiveness might be a possibility, so I suggested he come on one of my Majorcan retreats. 'Let us see if, with the help of the group and the healing power of this wonderful island, you can move into a new place that I know at some level you want to move to.'

Somewhat reluctantly, he agreed. The island soon began to work its magic and after a few days, and with a lot of support from others in the group (very important), things began to shift for him, and a new viewpoint began to open up. He started to accept more fully what had happened – he had up until then been primarily in denial – and found himself starting to walk in this other man's moccasins and to realise that the person who had killed his son was not a bad person, that he had not meant to do so, and that he felt huge remorse. As my client's heart slowly began to open, he was also able to recognise that sometimes tragic and terrible things happen in life and, if it transpires that they have to happen to us, that 'being a man' (his words) means that we need to accept them. Up until then, he had not fully accepted and thus let into his heart the full realisation of what had taken place.

His heart now began to open to another level that was much wiser and softer, and consequently, through tears, he was able to start releasing a lot of his grief, which he had kept bottled up. I did a guided visualisation with him, asking him to imagine his son sitting inside his heart. This moved him very deeply. 'It feels as if my son is telling me that he is fine, and that I need to let him go and give up my thoughts of revenge and get on with my life,' he told me. As he touched into these realisations, the presence of the 'forgiving heart' inside him began to reveal itself very strongly. 'Let go into these tender feelings,' I told him. 'Don't harden up again. If you stay soft and connected to yourself, something very profound will increasingly open up for you.'

It did. Many, many more tears flowed. As he allowed himself properly to mourn, he began the long process of forgiving and therefore taking his son's killer more deeply into his heart. 'Build on this process every day,' I said to him. 'Every morning when you get up, choose to forgive a little bit more. And do it your way; your heart will show you how.' Six months later, he told me that he had twice visited in prison the man who had killed his son.

Forgiving God

Sometimes the 'one' we need to forgive is the same one we pray to, to ask for help in this process. Sometimes we can get very angry with God, not only for not always giving us those goodies from life that we would desire, but on occasion, for seeming to deal us very hard blows. This can apply in particular in situations where people are hit by so-called 'natural disasters' and everything precious is engulfed in an earthquake or washed away by a tidal wave. The kind of argument people tend to use to justify their anger towards God generally goes along the lines of 'If God is good, if God is love, then why did God bring this suffering into my life?' I can imagine many people in Japan, having recently been pulverised by a catastrophe quite on a level with what hit them in 1945, feeling this way.

This is an important issue, and I believe that if God is to be properly or whole-heartedly forgiven, some thought needs to be put into it, as I have certainly encountered people whose refusal to 'let God off their anger hook' has resulted in their hearts clanging tightly shut to everything, for just as we will separate ourselves from people whom we cannot forgive, so exactly the same thing holds true with God. If we feel resentment towards God, it means that we are not going to allow our hearts to open to God's 'other face' – the one of joy, love and tenderness.

If we are to move towards the possibility of forgiving God, we also need to contemplate the issue a little and move beyond the naïve idea that 'God's goodness' is predicated upon God seeing to it that everything in our lives always goes the way that we would wish. This is an egoic and childish view of the divine. We need to 'get it' not only that God moves in mysterious ways that we may never ever understand logically, but also that death, devastation, tragedy and evil all seem to be included in them. (We will touch further on this theme in Chapter 23.)

Forgiving God therefore requires that we give up our juvenile images of the divine and instead be willing to open to the realisation that purposes exist in the cosmos that are deeper and subtler than we will ever understand, and that what from our egoic viewpoint may appear retrogressive may, from a much broader perspective, be progressive. We can even pray to God to help enlighten us and to help us forgive God.

The need for international forgiveness

The hurt caused by wounds perpetrated upon ourselves personally is also mirrored out in the wider world. Tribes are angry with other tribes, nations with other nations, religions with other religions. We see this rage and hatred manifesting itself very strongly in the enormous amount of bitterness that many Palestinians hold towards Israelis, and in how an unwillingness and inability on the part of both sides to forgive ensures that the particular conflicts between them grow increasingly difficult to resolve. Similarly, so long as many Muslims continue to despise Christians, so long as people in Iraq continue to find it hard to forgive Iran for having invaded them, peace will continue to be elusive in that part of the world.

Of course we need peace initiatives instigated by our politicians and it is good that they take place. But if no initiatives around forgiveness are ever initiated from the bottom up – if there is never any impetus to work at letting go resentments at a grass-roots level – then whatever politicians manage to achieve will always have limitations. Sometimes our resentments are not even conscious and only surface on particular occasions which evoke them. I remember talking to an elderly African-American man at the time of Barack Obama's first inauguration as President, and he told me that the joy he felt at the huge strides that his race had taken over the last half-century had also brought up deep anger, which he didn't even realise until then that he still carried, and which, he explained to me, related to the way his parents and grandparents had been treated at the hands of white people. 'I discovered a huge amount of antipathy towards your people,' he said, pointing at me, 'and I know I have probably got a whole lot of forgiving to do!'

I could talk about the lingering resentment between Serbs, Croats and Bosnians or how certain Irish people must feel towards the IRA, how the Chechens feel towards the Russians or how many Syrian people feel towards Assad. The truth is that we human beings have treated each other quite abominably over the centuries. We have raped and tortured and pillaged and betrayed and destroyed and ethnically cleansed, and as a result very powerful hate memories have grown up inside our species heart. If this particular dimension of world Shadow is to be more fully transformed, a great deal of forgiving is called for. For this to occur, the universal heart of forgiveness *also* needs to be brought into expression.

Evoking the universal heart of forgiveness

Spiritual activists from all over the planet and belonging to different tribes, races, religions, nationalities and ideologies therefore need to come together and participate in intelligently designed forgiveness rituals. I do not see this as being wholly impossible. What would happen is that large numbers of people, instead of going on an outer demonstration, would congregate for an inner demonstration. They would examine the contents of their hearts, see where their hatreds lie and against whom they are directed, and then would engage in a ritual of forgiveness with the aim of bringing about a greater sense of peace and reconciliation.

After all, large numbers of people gather together to celebrate sporting or artistic events or to attend music festivals. So why can't this powerful group energy be channelled creatively to help heal our planet? Why can't those performing artists or musicians who particularly care about the 'state of our world' – and there are many today who claim to do so –include healing prayers and specific rituals of forgiveness as an integral part of their show? If this could happen, I think it would be very powerful. I think the person in the street dearly wants to do good for the world and that a lot of our sadness today is that many of us feel powerless to change anything. This could shift those feelings.

Those attending concerts or events of one kind or another could have the satisfaction that they are not just being passive listeners or onlookers, but are also lending their energy to do something concrete to 'help the planet'. It would make them feel good as well. I say this because I feel we are rapidly approaching a time where we cannot any longer just leave it to our politicians to get us out of our messes (to say nothing of the fact that all too often, they are the ones who initially got us into them), and that if we wish for real change, then we, the people, need to take our world more and more into our own hands. Creating forgiveness rituals is one very concrete way of doing this.

Palestinians and Israelis engaging in forgiveness rituals

Let us for a moment focus on the situation existing between the Israelis and the Palestinians, which is such a thorn in the heart of allowing any goodwill initiatives to succeed in that part of the world. The iron-heartedness, hatred and refusal to 'budge an inch' that both sides always seem to show whenever the prospect of peace is discussed somehow has to melt. But it is not going to do so unless some kind of genuine forgiveness starts to take place, unless a new viewpoint emerges on both sides, unless something occurs whereby both sides stop seeing the other solely through the lens of occupier or terrorist, and instead start relating to each other as fellow human beings whose grief over the loss of a child through a bullet or a bomb is equally great.

Palestinians have to open their hearts and come to see that Israel feels very insecure. She is a tiny country hemmed in on all fronts by enemies and she has to act strongly in order to protect herself, especially in the light of Hamas's continued refusal to acknowledge her right to exist. This is utterly insane and absurd, and emerges from a totally 'low life' mindset, to say nothing of the negative consequences for Hamas, who some months ago had to endure a fearful onslaught and see most of their structures destroyed by Israeli war planes. (It is the doctrine of 'what you throw out on the waters comes back to you'. If you give out love, you get love back. If you give out violence, violence gets returned.)

The Israelis also need to make a huge attitudinal shift. They need to acknowledge that they are regarded as 'occupiers', and that so long as they never do anything to respect the hearts and minds of the Palestinians, and instead do everything to keep them weak and boxed in, and, in particular in Gaza, keep people living in the most deplorable of conditions, nothing is ever going to change as regards the way they are viewed. Both sides, therefore, need to recognise that holding onto their hatreds and resentments is killing them both. The Palestinians need to give up their obsession for revenge, while the Israelis need to see that an 'eye for an eye and a tooth for a tooth' mindset is totally counterproductive in the long run.

There are many activists on both sides who are already working for peace. What if, having designed a ritual to release their enmity towards the Palestinians, a thousand Israeli spiritual activists were to gather together in the spirit of that ritual, which would address the Palestinian heart and apologise to that heart and ask it for its forgiveness? Just think how healing this might be if a thousand Palestinians also gathered together and did the same thing. Could this not result in a new way in which the Israel–Palestine dilemma might be approached? Could this not help both sides start to move beyond all the same old stalemates and politics of viciousness and revenge which continues to determine how both sides still see and relate to one another? It could even be that particular forgiveness rituals would be designed by both sides together and embarked upon collectively, which in turn might include both sides also congregating to mourn the death of their loved ones who have perished along the way. Mourning is so important: we cannot forgive properly unless we will have allowed ourselves fully to mourn.

I know this idea may sound totally wacky to those who are attached to the way politics has always been conducted and who believe there is nothing beyond the grim formalities of realpolitik. The point is that this Heartless approach doesn't work and never has done. I think that there will be a new way in which we will start conducting our politics in the future, and that it will incorporate our humanity. I believe that if the universal heart can somehow be invoked, that miracles can and will start happening – that goalposts can and will start changing. What if in every nation gripped with old hatreds and resentments, big-hearted activists or celebrity activists who understand the potency of forgiveness and its capacity to nullify the vicious cycle of repetitive violence, were to take certain initiatives?

Operation Forgiveness

There is nothing as powerful as an idea whose time has come, and the above idea just might be one of them. The idea of forgiveness could be made fashionable! T-shirts could be designed with the words 'Reaching for Forgiveness' or 'Have You Forgiven' imprinted on them. The initiative, or call to Heart, can be labelled 'Operation Forgiveness', and it would take place in many countries. Naturally, such initiatives would be harder to organise in non-democratic regimes. But if only a small percentage of the population of a country participated, it would still be enough to empower the forgiveness thought-form and thus gradually have it take effect.

Certain nations could have their own 'forgiveness committees'. (I heard that after South Africa cast off apartheid, that there was talk that a 'Ministry of Forgiveness' would be formed. What a pity this idea never actually materialised.) It is so interesting that despite a huge amount of brutality having occurred under the apartheid regime, no revenge killings took place afterwards. Why was this? You may laugh, but I put a great deal of it down to President Mandela's huge healing heart which was able to hold all of his people inside it in one vast integrative embrace.

These forgiveness committees could be composed of people from many different walks of life and disciplines, who would decide both what needed to be on the agenda and how the initiatives designed to promote forgiveness would be carried out in practice. There could also exist particular 'forgiveness days', where people could turn out in city squares (there would always be a holiday on these days) and where a particular message would be broadcast. This same message would also be available on all the news channels, which would enable people to participate in these rituals without needing to leave their homes.

People could be helped to let go their old hates, fears and resentments, while at the same time, they would be guided to imagine that the old holes or wounds in their hearts were being filled up with healing energy or love. They would then be encouraged to visualise this healing energy travelling directly into the hearts of those people whom previously they had resented or seen as their enemy. Prayers might be said along the following lines:

If people hurt me or tortured or abused me or members of my family or tribe or race, then I recognise that this enchains all our hearts. In the interest of the spirit of peace and reconciliation, I herewith declare that I choose to let go my attachment to my hatred and my desire for revenge. As I do so, I forgive my persecutors and I pray for their well-being and request that they also be liberated. I also pray that whatever pain exists inside their hearts may also be cleared out, and that all of us be united in the recognition that, as human beings, despite our national, religious and ideological diversities, we increasingly come to recognise our shared common ground as members of one human family.

This idea needs a lot more thinking through.

Chapter 19

Understanding the Crises of the Heart

Crises draw upon the resources of the heart – DWAJ KHUL

When a true spiritual awakening and transformation is underway, one often encounters images of death and destruction of the world itself. The psyche does not express itself gently – JOHN PARRY

The significance of crises

As activists seeking to awaken the deeper layers of our hearts, it is highly unlikely that we are going to go through some of the radical shifts required of us without having to weather crises of one sort or another. I therefore would like to explore some of the more common kinds of crisis we may possibly have to face at this time, since it will not only help us to 'survive' and, hopefully, learn from them, should we have to encounter them personally, but it will also prepare us to deal with some of the huge crises currently going on out in the world.

The first thing to understand about crises – which generally come out of the blue and hit us when we are least prepared and least expecting them – is that to our egos, they are always seen as 'bad' and as being indicative of something having 'gone wrong' somewhere. However, when we are in training to be an activist, and are seeking to move away from our old caterpillar selves, we may start viewing them in a new way. Even though a crisis will still cause us pain, we may now start seeing it as having something significant to reveal to us. Indeed, if we listen with our hearts to its message (and all crises have one), it may often be capable of pointing us in an entirely new direction. As Paul Kingsnorth put it, 'a time of crisis is also a time of opening up, when thinking that was consigned to the fringes moves to centre stage. When things fall apart, the appetite for new ways of seeing is palpable.'

A core aspect of all crises is that they revolve around a theme of loss – often of something precious to us or something we may be greatly attached to. Sometimes, as a result of loss, we realise that something that at the time we never properly valued is in fact precious. For example, it is only when our partner leaves us that we realise how special they were, or only when confronted with a serious illness that we realise how valuable our physical health is. What many of our crises today are also helping bring home to us is how inextricably interconnected our planet has become and how, for example, a disaster on one side of the world can have immediate repercussions on the other. This is particularly visible with our financial crises.

The 'shock-gift' of crises

What the terrible tsunami and the death of Princess Diana both showed us is that while ordinarily we may be good at holding back our emotions and living with our egoic blinkers on, when a crisis actually hits, often these blinkers shatter and our heart may get forced open. While different crises work in different ways and affect us in different areas of our lives, the one common denominator they all possess is that they shock us. This shock wakes us up – and if it is severe, we may be woken up in a big way. Because their reverberations always affect us at a deep level, crises will inevitably cause us to ask ourselves new questions about the meaning of our lives and what is important for us.

Thus they test us, and so constitute an integral part of the planetary initiation that we are all undergoing at this time. Sometimes, by shaking us to the core, they make us realise that we have a core and as such, they assist us to 'get real' and consequently enable our old, false identities to start to loosen up. This is why the spiritual teacher Gurdjieff always welcomed crises: 'Given man's tendency to be unconscious, the only way he will wake up is if he experiences a shock greater than the sum of his own inertia.' This is so true. By hitting us in areas where we are vulnerable, crises often make us more aware of new possibilities. As the Tibetan master Dwaj Khul put it:

> *Man has a habit of crises. They serve to test the purpose, purity, motive and intent of the soul. Crises foster compassion and understanding, for the pain and inner conflict they engender is never forgotten, especially, they draw upon the resources of the heart.*[1]

Indeed, the Chinese were right when they defined a crisis as a 'dangerous opportunity', for there can also be times when the crisis can be too big for us, and we just break down without breaking through. How well we handle a crisis often depends either upon how much Heart force we possess at the time of initially confronting it or upon how much is evoked from us as a consequence.

Crises therefore serve as potential gate openers. They can galvanise resources inside us that we never knew we possessed, and in so doing, they can often take us right to the edge of what we feel is possible. Remember what I said about edges earlier on. They are precarious places; they are zones where death and rebirth occur and thus where transformation into new worlds may take place, as the edge of one world is always a doorway into a new one. Sometimes that edge may be financial (we go broke); sometimes emotional (we nearly go mad). 'Are we about to take a huge leap into the unknown?' is often the big question which many crises present us with.

Crises as illuminators of the Shadow

As we have seen, one of the ways that our emerging new culture is coming into expression is by casting its Shadow in front of it. It is throwing up everything that is most inhuman and unworkable about ourselves and about our society, in order that we can see these sides of ourselves and of our world exactly for what they are, so that hopefully we may be inspired to make certain radical changes. I think this is why we are confronting so many crises in so many different areas today. For example, if our environment was not in crisis, would we think twice about our polluting tendencies and question the fact of our heavy carbon footprints? I think not. Similarly, if our financial system was not teetering on the edge of collapse, would we be as concerned with asking ourselves what radical changes need making? Again, my reply is no.

Some crises signal their presence well in advance and seem to have an early warning system built into them. If we are sensitive to it and can pick up the signals in time, we can perhaps make the necessary adjustments and cancel out the need for them to happen at all. However, because of our fear of confronting what is unpleasant, we are often 'crisis blind' and may choose to ignore these signals. We particularly see this attitude manifesting around illness, where we may exhibit particular symptoms but because they don't seem sufficiently severe, we ignore them and only elect to take action if they become much worse, by which time it may be too late. We were certainly blind in the face of our recent financial crises. In truth, the writing had been on the wall for some time, but most of our 'clever experts' chose not to recognise it because they didn't want to.

Personal crises revolving around the theme of death

Many crises revolve around death, which, as we saw earlier, is one of our big taboos. The thought that one day we will be no more, or that the kind of society which we are so familiar with may be on the way out, is terrifying to many of us. Often we deal with these fears by employing various neurotic defences to keep them at bay, such as overworking or continually filling our lives with distractions. Another core defence is to pretend we are special, and that death is something that only happens to other people. About thirty years ago, I was as 'guilty' of these approaches as anyone, so it was perhaps not inappropriate that my soul 'set up' a somewhat big, multi-level crisis for me around death. Since what happened to me is typical of what can occur for people on a path of Heart who have a lot of learning to do, I will go into my particular experiences and how I tried to deal with them in some detail.

I was in my thirties, and suddenly, from one day to another, I was required to confront the spectre of death at three different levels. A great friend was killed in a road accident; I suffered a severe financial loss; and I was rushed to hospital with a life-threatening disease. A few days before, I was fine. Suddenly, my old 'safe world' had imploded.

Many of us first relate to crises by denying them, and this is exactly what I did. 'This cannot be happening to the immortal me,' I thought, 'I don't believe this *is* happening.' Then I became angry with God. 'Why, God, are you doing this to someone as special as me?' These ploys, of course, didn't work. The fact that I was lying in a hospital bed filled with tubes going into me, and was physically very weak, meant that my resistance became harder and harder to maintain. I realised that I had no choice but to surrender. So I let myself go into the space that for so long I had told others in all my courses that they needed to go into, and yet had never quite dared to do myself. I allowed myself to surrender – to go into the heart of my agony.

'OK, death, damn you, I will confront you,' I silently shouted out with my heart. 'I will give in to you. Do with me what you will. If I have to die, so be it. Teach me what you have to teach me.' I let myself fall into a vast desolation, in which I experienced total emptiness – not Buddhist emptiness that is very full, but empty emptiness where, quite literally, there was only dark nothingness. I missed my old friend very much. I felt very insecure without my money. I looked down at my frail, thin little body and mourned the loss of my strength and muscularity. I got to see how attached I had been to my old 'tough guy' image and how I often used it to proclaim a certain kind of superiority over people. Now, everything had fallen away. I saw how scared I was of dying. What was going to happen to me after death?

As I lay there, my Shadow side paraded itself to me in its full colours. I got to see conceited, manipulative and arrogant sides of myself. I recognised how selfish I could be, and how scared I was of really engaging with life and leaving my old comfort zones. It was also painful to see what a poseur I could be, and that I had a cold, unkind side that didn't really know how to love anyone properly or let anyone who tried to love me into my heart. It was horrible. I went deeper and deeper into a dark, dark hole. There was a lot of suffering.

Dark night, early dawn

Very, very slowly, however, I observed tiny, almost imperceptible shifts start to take place. Something that had always been granite-like inside me, I observed, was beginning to soften. I felt it the day that a nurse came in and told me that I was being taken off the drips, as the severe fungal infection in my lungs which nearly killed me was at last responding to a new medication. Despite still being very weak, it felt as if something new was coming alive inside me, the beginning of a whole new phase of my life journey. I observed as I slowly 'came back to life', that I now felt gratitude for the little money I still had, as opposed to resentment for what had been lost. I also felt gratitude for being alive. I also came to accept that my best friend was no longer with me. I began to feel very close to life's intrinsic 'goodness'.

I also observed that I no longer felt so special or so afraid of dying. Somehow a space of 'trusting life' that had never existed before had opened up. As with my experiences with Papaji, I felt much more ordinary, much more part of the human race. I no longer needed to try to be the 'big shot' (a neurosis which had grown up in me largely because my father had always made me feel small). It felt as if a huge abscess that all my life had obscured my heart was being lanced and that for the first time, it was safe to be 'just me' without all the froth that I used to continually create around myself!

I am happy to say that I fully recovered from my illness and found that big changes occurred for me. I had 'burned through' a lot of the debris inside my heart. Suddenly my work began to take off in a big way and almost compensated for my financial loss. I observed that I felt stronger and more purposeful than before. Again, I realised how generous the cosmos was and how it is that as our blockages begin dissolving, a space starts opening up inside our hearts that enables its beneficence to pour through us. I later asked myself: could I have made these kinds of shift without going through what I did? In my case, the answer was, probably, no; I don't think I could have done. I think I needed a shock greater than the sum of my inertia to wake me up. This experience marked the beginning of my realising that I wanted to dedicate my life to the process of awakening my heart and helping others do the same.

Crises relating particularly to spiritual emergence

Many of the crises which we are facing today, both inside ourselves and out in the world, may be seen as relating to the awakening of the universal heart. They are spiritual crises and concern the emergence of our Stradivarius or our butterfly selves and the coming into being of a new and more evolved society. The great Italian psychiatrist and visionary thinker Roberto Assagioli, founder of Psychosynthesis, was an expert at working with people going through such crises, and having been a student of his approach, I owe many of my insights in this area to his wise teachings. In a paper detailing some of the main challenges people face on a spiritual path, he wrote:

> *Spiritual development in a person is a long and arduous adventure, a journey through strange lands, full of wonders, but also beset with difficulties and dangers. It involves deep purification and transformation, the awakening of a number of formerly inactive powers, the raising of consciousness to levels it has never existed at before and its expansion in a new internal dimension. We should not be surprised, therefore, that such major changes pass through various critical stages, and these are often accompanied by neuropsychological and even physical and psychosomatic symptoms.*[2]

I particularly learned from Assagioli that many of our crises are not so much the consequence of a lack of Heart, but are more about the kinds of challenges that seem to accompany its gradual emergence. (Remember the quotation I gave you earlier by David Spangler about the way our society is currently being ploughed up to allow the new seeds, hidden deep underground, to come to the surface?) It is important that we understand this, especially when going through the kinds of crisis where we feel that we have somehow 'got it all wrong' and feel deserted by everything good and spiritual. I will now explore six specific 'crises of the Heart' and show how we may recognise them and how we may work with them. See if any of them are applicable to anything that has ever transpired for you.

The crisis caused by an inappropriate spiritual practice
Earlier, I mentioned the benefits of spiritual practice and how important it is that our practice be one which is both right for us and at the right level for where we are at, and that if this is not the case, there can be serious repercussions. I discovered all this to my cost.

I was in my early twenties and had just left university. I was starting out on my spiritual journey, but had not yet done any psychological work on myself; in fact I had hardly even heard of the word 'psychotherapy'. I had, however, heard about Kriya yoga, and decided to become a student of it. Not yet being aware of what to look for in a spiritual teacher, I apprenticed myself to a third-rate one who failed to inform me that I was far too immature and unready to take on such an advanced practice and that by so doing, I might be biting off more than I could chew.

Nonetheless, I took up my practice diligently, and after a few weeks, I began to experience a great deal of light around me and to feel very euphoric. However, what transpired was that my narcissistic or wounded-ego self (which at the time I was wholly unaware of) began 'grabbing' at this spiritual light and using it for its own devices, that is, to proclaim me as some super-duper, special human being, superior to the rest of humanity. I became vastly inflated and believed I had a unique mission to save the world! I suffered from a kind of Christ complex!

Basically, what had occurred was that the shifts I was starting to make became hijacked by my wounded ego, and instead of my becoming more loving and compassionate, I became full of disdain for 'ordinary people'. Many weird habits came over me (I was then working as a book publisher) which included my insulting a world-famous novelist and telling him that his writing was not spiritual enough!

Something pretty bizarre was going on. In actuality, I was becoming a little mad. Unable to ground or process the high-frequency energy that this practice was generating, at times I felt I would explode. And I eventually did. Like Icarus, I had sailed too close to the sun and, like him, I fell. The fall was simple but dramatic. I awoke one morning and the light had gone out, and I felt enmeshed in total and abject darkness, feeling like the lowest scum that had ever walked the earth. I went into a black, black depression which lasted several weeks. Luckily, I had a few wise friends around me who saw my plight, and insisted that I stop all my practices and start doing ordinary things again. The gift of this crisis was the realisations (a) that our egos are relentless and always need working on if we have any spiritual aspirations, and (b) that it is unwise, unless we have an excellent teacher who knows what he or she is about, to embark on things that we do not properly understand. Had I continued, I could easily have become psychotic. Again, the problem was not with Kriya yoga, which is a valid practice. The problem was with me trying, in my arrogance, to run before I could walk.

A similar kind of damage can happen through an unwise usage of psychedelic substances, taken without supervision or knowledge about what one may be doing. On many occasions over the years, I have had to come to the assistance of people on 'bum trips', and in all instances, the drug had taken them too deeply into the collective Shadow and their level of development was insufficient to enable them to process the surfeit of problematic material that it was bringing to the surface for them.

The Kundalini crisis

Another typical crisis that people on a path of Heart may encounter is a premature rising-up of what is called Kundalini energy, which is an evolutionary energy stored at the base of the spine, dormant in most of us. Again, psychedelic drugs or overly powerful spiritual practices can sometimes prematurely activate its arising. If our system is not yet ready for it – if the locks on our heart and on our other psychic centres or chakras are still too strongly in place – this energy is unable to flow freely through us and becomes blocked. When this happens, all hell can break loose. People have reported terrible burning sensations all over their body, and severe confusion and emotional distress.

If one is undergoing such a crisis, as with the Kriya yoga crisis, it is wise to stop all spiritual practices at once. One needs to do grounding, physical activities such as jogging or chopping wood, and eat plenty of meat. If a spiritual master of substance happens to be close by and if we feel they are someone whom we can trust, we can go to them for assistance.

The existential crisis

Just before a major-level shift, or when we are on the edge of moving into a higher meaning system, our heart may radically contract or coil back into itself in order to prepare for a powerful new leap forward. During this kind of crisis we may become increasingly aware of our deficiencies and realise the limitations of our 'normal state', and as a result we may experience great despair. It may feel as if we are caught in a kind of 'no man's land' between two meaning systems. We see how little our hearts and souls are actually being fed by our old 'caterpillar' life, yet we have not begun fully to access the new, more Heart-centred us, the Great Eastern Sun us, which we can sense, somewhere in the future, beckoning us forward to draw closer to it.

When I work with people going through this kind of crisis, I do my best to give them this overview; yet I never try to comfort them or take them out of their pain, as that would mean they would probably not 'get' the learning required from such a crisis. If a person is mature enough for this kind of work, I may suggest that they imagine bringing their pain up into their heart and letting it 'burn there' for a bit, as in order for their newly emerging awareness to become sufficiently 'cooked', it may need to simmer in 'crisis juice' for a while longer.

I may also remind them that they are feeling bad not because they have done anything wrong, but because they are in a kind of 'hatching' phase, and that when a new awareness does eventually emerge, and I reassure them that it will, it must never be used to attack or deny their past, but rather to try to integrate it. I might remind them, if they really desire a transformation to occur, that states of discomfort may need to be experienced from time to time and that there is often no way around this. If a person feels suicidal (and sometimes this will occur in crises of this nature), I may also remind them that they are right to feel that a death is in the offing, only that they understand that it is most probably of a psychological nature, and is much more likely to be about the demise of their old identity or self-image. I may explain that it is only through a genuine confrontation with our own barrenness that a more genuine kind of richness has a chance of emerging. The Heart master Adi Da put it like this:

> *It is not possible to affirm and realise the existence of God or the Living Spirit Divine until the self-contraction is thoroughly observed, understood and transcended.*

The crisis caused by a surfeit of abundance
This is a curious kind of crisis, as one would have thought that the experience of 'good things coming our way' is always healing in nature. But this is not so. If, metaphorically speaking, the existential crisis is about the tide in our psyches

going out and leaving us exposed to all that is unhealed and barren on our inner shores, this crisis is about our being flooded with too much abundance, which, because of our having experienced impoverishment early on in our lives, we may have difficulty in allowing in. (We saw this crisis emerge at a group level when I told you of that first workshop on love that I taught.) As a result, the experience of joy or of a greater 'fullness of being' can be very disconcerting.

During such a crisis, it can be helpful to take time off, to go on a retreat and actually give ourselves space and time to try to digest our new experiences. Sometimes people coming on my courses may be going through a crisis of this nature, and the advantage of being in a group environment is that it allows one time to process and discuss one's difficulties and so try to assimilate the new Heart space that is seeking emergence. In this kind of crisis, we are trying to move into new spheres of being where our egoic identities are less preponderant.

The 'dark night of the soul' crisis

This crisis is very prominent in the world today for people who are wanting to awaken their hearts and it may well be that in the years ahead, humanity as a whole will have to go through a long dark night of the soul. Its essence lies in these words by Martin Luther:

> *God works by contraries so that a man feels himself to be lost in the very moment when he is on the point of being saved. When God is about to justify a man, he damns him … This is the pain of purgatory … In this disturbance salvation arises, and when a man believes himself utterly lost, light breaks.*[3]

Characteristic of the 'dark night' experience is that we feel alone, damned and totally cast out by anything remotely divine, as if our souls have utterly dried up, and that we have done something deeply sinful for which we are being punished. When in the heart of this crisis, we feel there is no one and nothing in the world that can help us. If there ever is such a thing as God, then that God has totally and utterly abandoned us. I would describe this crisis as one whose prime purpose is to empty and purify us; it is a kind of radical 'fasting of the heart' forced upon us with a particular twist to it. Through our sufferings, we become increasingly aware of our many faults and impurities, together with our capacity for being deluded and artificial. I was going through a 'dark night' when I was lying in hospital.

In the throes of our dark night, we often also feel ugly, unloved and the most unworthy wretch that ever existed. All grace appears removed from us, and all we feel left with is darkness and meaninglessness. We may come to see how co-dependent we are, or how attached we are to particular attitudes or styles of living that in no way serve our well-being. In the transformational literature detailing the experiences of people undergoing dark nights, we learn that they go into barren deserts or wilderness spaces and that from those places they get 'fed' from a new source. For example, the Israelites in the wilderness received 'manna from heaven', while Elijah got fed by the ravens.

This is because so much of our ordinary emotional debris has been burned up that we consequently have a much more direct line to the spiritual 'help forces' and can allow them to draw much closer to us. When I work with people going through a dark night, I try to give them plenty of support and encouragement, and help them to dis-identify with the contents of their experiences, as this allows them to be increasingly receptive to the new value system slowly starting to assemble itself inside their hearts.

The crisis born of a fear of the sublime

Sometimes we can go into crisis solely as a result of having a mystical experience of some kind or other, or accessing some higher state of Heart. This occurs because we are overly attached to our dualistic thinking and, as we have already seen, to believing that the reality filtered through our normal five senses is the only one there is. As a result, it can be scary if we receive 'visitations' of a more unitive or transcendent nature. We are frightened not only because of their innate abundance, but also because they conspire to turn our old beliefs around what we think is possible on their head.

On the surface, it may sometimes appear as if people going through this kind of crisis are having a psychotic break. In most instances, however (unless someone is very damaged and emotionally unstable), if we are intentionally on a path of Heart, this will probably not be the case, and most likely our difficulties are being caused by accessing unfamiliar emotional and spiritual material which we do not yet know how to process. If this is the case, and the activist finds himself or herself in difficulty, the very last thing we need is for someone to tell us we are 'ill' (normal man's traditional response), or have some reductively oriented psychiatrist try to dope us up with suppressant drugs. Rather, we need someone with an open heart and an intelligent, non-flabby mind to explain to us exactly what is going on and encourage us to remain as open as we can, in order that our hearts be as fully engaged in our transformational processes as possible.

Our resistance to the sublime tends to show up in the following three ways. We may repress – that is, both deny and not allow ourselves to experience – what is most abundant or beautiful about ourselves; secondly, we may pretend that everything existing outside our normal three-dimensional space-time reality really does not exist and is a load of nonsense; and lastly, we may even project our Shadow onto higher states of consciousness and thus demonise sacred states trying to do their best to come knocking at the door of our hearts. What our resistance does in effect is to close down the possibility of new doors opening and our allowing in grace. If this is the case, we just go into crisis but fail to break through into the light.

The consequences of demonising the sublime

Whenever we demonise the sublime, we are effectively waging a covert war on more abundant 'Stradivarius states of being' seeking to make themselves known to us, which in turn plays a key role in keeping alive the old status quo that is needing to die. Everything that is most wrong with our planet and that most needs to change is therefore rendered unable to do so. (As I have said so many times: if we ourselves don't change, we can't and we won't be able to change the world outside ourselves.)

Our repression of what is sublime has other, more immediate negative consequences. We place those who are unashamedly dedicated to awakening their hearts – namely, our saints, adepts, mystics and miscellaneous visionaries – in the same bracket as people who suffer from paranoid schizophrenia or other serious psychopathic disorders. In other words, saint and schizophrenic both get shoved into a box labelled 'Abnormal', yet the only thing a saint shares with a psychopath is that both are experiencing 'non-normal' states of consciousness. There the comparisons end. One is the possessor of a deeply awakened heart and the other is a citizen of a very discombobulated and disoriented reality.

I mention this because, as we have already seen, many of us activists, in the course of our Heart journeying, may spontaneously have close encounters with deeply spiritual states, and unless we are aware of what is happening, we too may become victims of self-doubt and start equating our emerging non-normality (our non-caterpillar state) with pathology, in which case we will also find it difficult to welcome in sublime states of awareness, should they choose to come knocking upon the door of our hearts.

The suppressive role of conventional religion and psychology

Sadly, contemporary religion often does not help us much, as our existing church is itself deeply identified with caterpillar-ness/normalcy (a fact perhaps connected to why ever-dwindling numbers are coming through its doors). While the church talks a great deal about Jesus as a healer and teacher, it does not really offer us any programmes designed to assist our own hearts to awaken. (Hearing a sermon about God's love doesn't necessarily make us more loving.) Also, while there are, of course, some notable exceptions, far too many priests, in my opinion, despite the very best of their intentions, are simply not connected to that divine source which they purport to represent, and thus cannot serve as conduits to make higher states of Heart available to us.

I also find it bizarre that although the Bible is peppered with accounts of sublime occurrences – miracles, burning bushes, raisings from the dead, etc. – the Church recoils in terror should anyone actually report a transcendent occurrence. I think that if a new culture of Heart is to be born, many of our religious leaders need to be more spiritually adventurous and try to let go some of their attachments to theological dogma. Knowing a great deal about religious scripture by no means implies that we are the possessor of those many human qualities which exist inside our hearts.

Sadly, many traditionally oriented psychoanalysts and psychiatrists are just as bad, and can be equally dismissive if a patient comes their way reporting anything as heretical as, God forbid, a mystical experience! I remember a woman once coming to see me whose higher Heart self was beginning to open. She told me that she felt angelic presences were communicating with her and that she was having profound intimations about things that were about to happen, and that they would turn out just as she had predicted. She told me that when she had explained this to a psychiatrist whom her doctor had recommended, he threatened to have her admitted to a mental hospital. You can guess who I thought needed the straitjacket!

Yes, of course, there are people who hear voices in their heads telling them to do destructive things. I am not denying that there are many very highly disturbed people around. But the person who receives messages from outer space telling them to kill, and who *is* emotionally ill, must not be put in the same category as someone who is becoming increasingly attuned to their Heart and is becoming increasingly aware of the presence of divine guidance operating in their lives.

If a new culture of Heart is to emerge, we need CEOs and scientists who are also mystics, we need doctors who also possess natural healing abilities and we need visionary economists and compassionate politicians. If we grow up in a world that tells us we are weird and abnormal if we can heal or look into the future or experience ecstatic joy, then we will grow up fearing what may be most genuine and butterfly-like about ourselves and thus ensure we remain fixated in the stagnation of our caterpillar-hood.

Saying 'Yes' to our spiritual gifts

A woman once came to see me with terror in her eyes. I looked closely at her, and everything told me that she was a balanced person. But she was shaking. Here is the essence of what she told me: 'I am going through a big crisis. I feel I am going mad. I'm starting to know the answers to many things. I knew my old job would end in six months, and it did. I knew my brother would become ill and that my sister would have a son and that as a family we would all be going on a long holiday to Russia this year – and all these things happened. And it scares me. I also know what the company I now work for needs to do if it is to expand, but I am afraid to speak up because I think they will think me mad and give me the sack. What do you think I should do? I have been so depressed by all this that my doctor has put me on strong anti-depressants.'

Super-sanity

'What should you do?' I replied. 'Well, I would feel very blessed if I were you. I wish I were the possessor of higher sensibilities like you. It seems that you are beginning to develop a prophetic capability which has a lot of wisdom in it. Perhaps the gift that is coming to you now is one which many more of us may have in a hundred years, so I see you as a kind of "future human". What I would say to you is to find out more about your gifts. See how they operate. Rejoice in them. Do not necessarily talk about them to people who you think might laugh at you for them.'

'So you see this as a gift, then, not an aberration?' she asked.

'Very much so,' I replied. 'It is something deeply to celebrate.'

'So this isn't madness, then?'

'Not at all. But it is naturally scary, because it is new, and our current society is afraid of newness as most people around you are not like you. Because it is new, you need to be very protective of your gift.'

'That sounds exciting,' she said. 'Perhaps I can use this gift to help others.'

'You bet,' I replied, '*and* to help you!'

Her eyes brightened. 'Thanks. I just needed this reassurance that I wasn't going mad.'

'Far from it,' I replied. 'I think you are moving into a state of super-sanity. Oh, and you can throw away all your pills. You don't need them any more.'

In a further session, I read her something that Plato had written about this kind of madness in *Phaedrus*:

The greatest blessings come by way of madness, indeed of madness that is heaven sent. It is when they were mad that the prophetess at Delphi and the priestess at Dodona achieved so much for which states and individuals in Greece are thankful; when sane [that is, when they were in a 'normal state'] they did little or nothing … Madness is a divine gift when due to divine dispensation.

There are, in fact, many people like this woman all over the world who are blessed in this way, and who go through unnecessary torment because they feel that because they are 'different', this means they are abnormal, and that therefore they have to cover up their gifts and pretend to be less than who they are. Our problem today is that too many of us define caterpillar or Setting Sun man as being normal and equate normality with sanity. I would strongly disagree and argue that a great deal of what passes for normal today, together with the damage it does out in the world, is actually pretty *insane*.

Categories of madness

I see madness existing in basically four different categories. The first category is one that most of us are in agreement about and comprises those who suffer from a severe mental impairment, such as paranoid schizophrenia, that may grossly impinge upon their ability to function in the world. As the purpose of this book is not to explore extreme mental instability, I will not go into more detail.

Divine madness

My second category of madness I will call 'ecstatic madness' or Plato's 'divine madness', which was what my client was beginning to 'suffer' from. This I regard as the highest form of sanity. It may 'afflict' us in different ways. Many divinely mad people feel so close to their Heart self and so ecstatic a lot of the time that they often have little interest in playing all the 'conventional substitute games' that normal man is so attached to. My lovely Papaji and the great sage Sri Aurobindo were divine madmen. From a normal viewpoint, Adi Da, with all the tricks he would play on his students to help them wake up, was a totally crazy eccentric, as was Ramana Maharshi, who primarily taught in silence.

Over the years, I have continually sought out such divinely mad people, and I have tried to learn as much from them as I can and to spend as much time as possible in their company, as they are always hugely interesting and can teach us so much about what it means to be authentically human. It is so refreshing to be in the company of people who are not remotely interested in political correctness or in pleasing you or letting you know how wonderful or rich or clever or important they are , but are solely concerned in living a life that is passionately alive. *Such people for me are the true enhearteners, the true future humans, the true builders of the world of the Great Eastern Sun.*

What such people model for us is the kind of graced insanity that can come upon us when we no longer have ego exerting its strong influence in our lives and we are consequently able to see the world through a sacred lens where we just feel overwhelmed with joy and love, and we want to embrace everyone because we recognise the divinity within them, we know how beautiful they are and we know that every raindrop and every leaf on every tree is tinged with holiness. But we must beware, since there are certain consequences to this affliction. If politicians become afflicted, it may cause them to practise humility and to dedicate their lives to working for peace and improving the lot of the have-nots in their countries. If millionaires are struck down, they may feel moved to get rid of their yachts and to share their wealth with the poor. The beautiful thing about this madness is that, just like the common cold, it is catching, in particular if we choose to spend time in the kinds of environment where it is prevalent.

So if you, the reader, ever feel afflicted from time to time with divine madness – and it can touch us in big or in little ways, can stay with us for five minutes, five weeks or forever – then say a big 'yes' to it. Celebrate it. Surrender to it. Give it permission to possess every fibre of your being. Give yourself space every day to sing about it and dance it. And don't forget to expose yourself to others so that they too may catch it from you. But also, most important: don't make anybody wrong for not being a loony like you. The true divine madman or madwoman never makes anyone wrong. Instead, devote your energies to figuring out how you can translate your insanity into doing most good for the greatest numbers of people.

A small footnote. Sometimes one comes across an 'ecstatic crazy' who is also tinged with aspects of my first category of madness as well. I once met a truly wonderful wild man who, although institutionalised, wrote poetry of the very highest calibre and told me he was channelling the spirit of William Blake. As a Blake aficionado myself and having read his poetry, there was nothing in me to disbelieve what he said.

The psychopathology of normality

We now come to the domain that I see as being the most genuinely and perilously insane, namely, that of normal, caterpillar man. The great psychologist Abraham Maslow described normal man with his wounded ego as 'living in a state of mild and chronic psychopathology and crippling immaturity'.

This is an apt description. Why 'normal man's' madness, which is forever hovering on the borderline between stupidity, unconsciousness and downright evil, can be so dangerous is because it lacks the insight to recognise its insanity. On the contrary, it thinks it is eminently sane and regards those not subscribing to its worldview as insane. This is the kind of madness that can take hold of us when we only worship the god of reason and forget the god of Heart or when we believe true happiness resides in owning lots of things. It is the madness that compels us to 'have' because we don't know how to 'be', where we are forever projecting out our Shadow onto all and sundry and playing our many 'substitute games'. It manifests itself in utterly horrendous kinds of worldview like those that advocate 'perpetual war for perpetual peace' or see poverty and war as quite normal (just the way life is!) I will give you one concrete example of this kind of insanity to illustrate my point.

A few years ago, I was watching the inquiry set up to explore the reasons why we went to war against Iraq, and Tony Blair was being interviewed. He did not show a hint of contrition. There was no sense of his being sorry that so many British soldiers died as a result, or that nearly half a million Iraqis lost their lives. Half a million! That's a mighty lot of people. Nor was there any recognition on his part that the world had become a much more dangerous place as a result. Which it had. On the contrary, Blair, in his blinkered self-righteousness, said, 'hand on heart', that he would do the same again – i.e., that he'd be willing to sacrifice another half million people – and that Iraq today without Saddam Hussein was better than before, implying that therefore the ends justified the means. This is how the wounded, inflated ego operates; it always has to be right.

This loony logic (which flows so easily when Heart is excluded from the equation) is like suggesting that the First World War, which secured rights for women and began to crack the class system, justified all the slaughter in the trenches; or that because Europe has been safer and more prosperous since the conclusion of the Second World War, the Axis powers were therefore right to have launched it. I have been around on the planet for quite a few years now and *I have never yet come across any example of anyone afflicted with divine madness ever doing anything harmful to anybody,* yet normal crazies, who are at war with everything (themselves, crime, drugs, illness, you name it), love to lock up people whom they see as being too happy, too unconventional, and who refuse to 'play their normal game'.

The looniness of the pre-personal person

As activists, we also need to be aware of a further level of pathology and know that there are many people on the planet today whose madness relates not simply to the fact that they have a wounded ego, but more to the issue that they have not yet developed *enough ego*. In such people no sense of self has as yet emerged. Put simply, they haven't yet become a person.

The problem with such people, many of whom may also carry deep scars inside their hearts, is that they show little sense of responsibility or morality or have little capacity to think for themselves. They are even more immature and unconscious than 'normal man' and their outlook on life is often extremely primitive and for these reasons they can be highly dangerous. Possessing few inner resources of their own, they tend to need leaders to latch on to and they generally choose people with large wounded egos.

Many terrorists and members of rogue militias fit into this category, as do members of criminal gangs, all of whom might have a high sense of concern for their 'own clan', yet may think nothing of murdering an 'outsider' or making money out of getting people addicted to drugs or trafficking women and children and causing unspeakable suffering in the process.

This is an evolutionary problem and there are currently many people out in the world who operate at this level. This is not an easy issue to deal with, as such people are generally not capable of awakening along the lines we have been discussing (we can't let go ego-identification before we've developed an ego), and consequently they tend to be highly resistant to and extremely fearful of change.

In praise of super-sanity

I stress once more that the best antidotes to these domains of madness that are currently destroying our planet are (a) our full awareness of how truly insane so many of us are, and (b) our intentionally working at evolving an awake, tender, loving, wise, creative and, hopefully, genuinely ecstatic heart ourselves that can help absorb them. As our hearts grow in stature, we start seeding species man with a higher consciousness, which helps speed up the evolution for all human beings. Pre-personal man may be helped to evolve a firmer ego, while egoic man is assisted to come to see that a more expanded self may lie beyond the separate self he has been so accustomed to identifying with and is so fearing letting go of. I will conclude with a little story that beautifully defines sanity.

I read recently of a man, who had worked hard all his life in a job that he enjoyed but that didn't give him a lot of money, who won the lottery. Everybody said to him, 'Now you can live the good life. Buy a big house and big car and stop work.' They were amazed when he continued working, continued to drive his old car and continued to live where he had always done, and gave ninety per cent of his money away to good causes. They called him mad. His reply was: 'I already live a good life. I enjoy my work. It gives me a lot of meaning. I don't want to stop working. I am happy with my family. Given how much need there is in the world, it would have been mad to have spent all this money on myself and not to have given most of it away to support what I believe are worthy causes.' *May all our crises conspire to drive us this super sane!*

FOUR

The Great Heart Work

Inspiration is not garnered from litanies of what is flawed; it resides in humanity's willingness to restore, redress, reform, recover, re-imagine, and reconsider. Healing the wounds of the Earth and its people does not require saintliness or a political party. It is not a literal or conservative activity. It is a sacred act –
PAUL HAWKEN

We have the opportunity to join together to experience what very few generations in history have had the privilege of knowing: a generation mission, a compelling moral purpose, a shared and unifying cause, and an opportunity to work together to choose a future for which our children will thank us instead of cursing our failure to protect them against a clear and present danger with equally clear and devastating future consequences –
AL GORE

We can give to our future glory or gloom. If we are to co-operate with the will of the universe, we must give up egocentric illusions of modern sovereign nations, give up parochial conceptions of society, and develop loyalty to the human community. After all, there is only one race and that is humanity –
SARVEPALLI RADHAKRISHNAN

Chapter 20

Looking to the Future

A critical mass is not only ready and able to elect leaders who stand for change; it's also ready and able to provide active support for enlightened policies – ERVIN LASZLO

Change will not come if we wait for some other person or some other time. We are the ones we've been waiting for. We are the change that we seek – BARACK OBAMA

A new order on earth will not begin ... until we all learn to see the pollution in our own hearts. And that will not happen until many of us, a critical mass, experience with remorse a real change of consciousness – JAMES GEORGE

The freedom challenge

We now come to the most important part of the activist's work. After all the purifying, releasing, forgiving, integrating and transforming work that we have been personally engaged in, after all our many initiations and personal crises, now that we have grown saner and our hearts more expanded, we are now much more ready to *do* what we have been preparing ourselves for, namely, to play an active part in creating a new and better society.

As activists, it is so much easier to address this issue now that we are no longer operating out of a place of 'mild psychopathology and crippling immaturity'. We may not yet be a fully fledged butterfly, or divinely mad, but we are certainly on the way, and perhaps what we now manage to accomplish out in the world will result in those last few butterfly cells coming into place that will give us new colourful wings to enable us to soar. Whether we feel called to champion human rights, campaign for a cleaner environment, design a more efficient solar energy system, or join Greenpeace or Friends of the Earth – whatever kind of work we choose to be engaged in – we are now increasingly starting to operate out of our Stradivarius selves.

An overview of the world situation

To be most effective, however, it is important that we know what we are dealing with and what might lie ahead for us. I will therefore remind you once more that we are all living at a time of massive breakdown of the 'old order'. Less and less are we able to get away with doing things as we have been used to doing them. Today, fewer and fewer of our old approaches are working. Culturally, politically, relationally, economically, philosophically, scientifically, huge shifts are in the air and they call us to be part of them. The world of the Setting Sun or our old ego-created and ego-sustained industrial system is no longer tenable and it is crucially important that, as activists, we are realistic about the fact that we have some huge challenges on our hands. In the last chapter, one way I defined a crisis was as a 'dangerous opportunity'. Today we are being presented with plenty of them.

Firstly, there is the issue of world starvation. Millions of people die of it each year. How are we going to deal with this? How can we change this? Our financial system has also become increasingly unsustainable. We Westerners, in particular, have lived beyond our means for many years (another example of our madness), and world debt continues to grow larger and to become ever more unserviceable, because it was encouraged since it was so profitable to those who issue and control money. At the time of my writing, while the economic situation inside Russia, China and America is hardly healthy, the crisis in the eurozone is severe and could easily escalate, and if certain countries default, the financial spin-offs could have devastating effects worldwide.

There is also huge instability in the Middle East. Just because dictators heading evil and pathological regimes have been unseated by revolutions, this is no guarantee that the problems of those nations are over. On the contrary, the way has merely been cleared for many more deep-seated issues which had previously been obscured to come into the light, and we are now seeing the emergence of the Shadow side or the 'winter' of the Arab Spring. In particular, the situation in Syria continues to be deeply troublesome. Over 70,000 have been killed to date, and there is little reason to see the bloodshed being curtailed. It is also not impossible that terrorists could lay their hands on Syria's chemical weapons of mass destruction and that they could be used against Israel, or that the situation could result in a conflagration involving all the countries in that region and turn into a major war between the Sunnis and Shi'ites. A third world war is also a not wholly impossible scenario, especially if Israel or America were to invade Iran and try to knock out her nuclear facilities or if North Korea persists with its macho posturings. (By the time this book comes out, we may be clearer on some of these matters.)

Meanwhile, climate change continues to create ever more freakish weather conditions. The excesses of growth capitalism with its immense exploitation and impoverishment of people and cultures and the devastation of ecosystems have deeply damaged the environment, and in the years ahead we may expect many more heatwaves, floods and extreme storms. We have given Mother Nature a serious disease and from time to time we shall have to reap the consequences of her high fevers.

Another huge problem is the vast discrepancy that exists between the lot of the haves and the have-nots. In fact, the gap grows wider every year and the latter's disenchantment and outrage at being excluded from the system often spawns conditions that are conducive to crime. If we wish to stop the trade in drugs or the cutting-down of our precious rainforests, then we need to ask ourselves why it is that we, the wealthy nations, have kept people in poor countries so poor that simply in order to survive, they have sometimes had no choice but to plant poppy fields or grow coca or, conversely, cooperate with the greed of certain large multinationals.

Breakdown or breakthrough?

There are therefore some key questions which we need to be asking ourselves about the breakdown of the old world which is currently taking place around us. The first is: is it going to continue and what will it lead to? Will it result in a total collapse of everything, with all hell breaking loose everywhere? Our already vulnerable system, teetering on the edge, pushed over it by one problem too many, resulting in the end of humanity? A pandemic? A nuclear holocaust? A worldwide ecological disaster? No breakthrough to a new civilisation, just the end of the noble experiment of man?

Or will it result in a breakthrough into a higher-order world with increasing numbers of men and women making the transition from caterpillar to butterfly, with a whole new society founded on the values of Heart and the realisation of our interconnectedness coming into being? And if this is to be the case, how is it going to happen? Will the breakdown speed up even more? Also, what is this going to mean for those of us who are resistant to change? How are we going to react?

I am no scholar or historian and everything I have to say on this matter is purely speculative and comes from the intuitive part of my heart, as I try to feel myself into what is really going on around us today. The only thing I can say for sure is that is that things cannot continue in the way that they have been going. Our attempts to apply sticking plaster to a system which is a total construct of the wounded ego and which is inherently unsustainable are becoming increasingly ineffective. At some stage they will no longer work, and the resultant explosions will be even bigger than the ones that are already taking place!

What I find interesting at this time is that we seem to be being fed two contrasting scenarios. In certain quarters, all we hear is that 'the end is nigh', we have gone beyond the point of no return and from now on, everything will be downhill. No hope. Other sources, however, give us a multitude of reasons to be optimistic and suggest that a new and better world is definitely coming into being. Perhaps it is appropriate that we should be fed these contrasting perspectives. If all we ever heard was the doomsday scenario, we might give up in despair and thus see our catastrophic expectations turned into reality. Conversely, if we knew for sure that we would break through to a new and better world, we might just sit back and so not make the effort to work towards it, and so it wouldn't happen! Therefore, it is good that we be kept apprehensive enough to stay on our toes yet hopeful enough to remain encouraged.

The importance of holding a positive image of the future

What is very important, however, is that as activists, we all subscribe to the breakdown-leading-to-positive-breakthrough scenario, as it is vital that we hold a *positive* image of our world in our hearts. In his book *The Image of the Future*, Fred Polak, a Dutch futurist, told us that 'bold visionary thinking is in itself the prerequisite for effective social change'. He found that in every instance of a flowering culture, there had been a positive image of the future at work. When the opposite happened, or when the images of the future were weak, the culture decayed – as was the case with the fall of the Roman Empire. As activists of the Heart, therefore, no matter in what areas our efforts are focused, if we are effectively to work towards concretely *building* the kind of world that we want, then we must devote time, effort and energy into *visualising* the emergence of a fully functional and sustainable society, a world that works, a society run by men and women who are coming into an ever-greater connection with their butterfly-ness.

This is extremely important. There is a huge amount of fear, pessimism and insecurity around at this time as we all move into unknown terrain, and as activists, not only must we never add to it, but we need to be the *antidotes* to it. An integral part of our enheartening presence must be that we carry the next step of our human and global evolution inside our hearts, and the more powerfully we are able to do so, the more we can instil hope in people's hearts and inspire them not to focus on what humanity will be losing from this breakdown, but on what they will be gaining by the breakthrough. We need to be beacons of shining butterfly-ness in a dark forest of frightened caterpillar-ness. Thus, I advocate an approach which is positive yet realistic, and which recognises that there is no avoiding the fact that we are all probably going to be mightily stretched and challenged in the years ahead, and may well need to be prepared for some bumpy rides!

Towards a breakthrough

I am going to be presumptuous enough, then, to suggest that while I think we will continue to see a continued crumbling away of the old world, and that the speed of its decline may well accelerate, for, as W. B. Yeats quite rightly put it, the old 'centre [the egoic one] cannot hold'. I do, however, see a breakthrough; I do see definite light at the end of the tunnel; I do see dawn breaking after a dark night. I don't think we will see sudden collapses – although certain parts of the system may implode more rapidly than others. What I see is that all the time that the breakdown is occurring, the new pillars for a new society are gradually being erected, so that when the final collapse occurs – as I believe it will – humanity will be ready for it. So I don't think the rug will be pulled away from beneath the world of the Setting Sun until a sufficient number of Great Eastern Sun strategies have been put in place.

We need shocks greater than the sum of our own inertia

Bearing in mind what I said earlier about the divine alchemical fire burning up the old structures, it may well be that things will increasingly 'hot up', especially for those who continue identifying with the *'ancien régime'* and who still insist on playing the old games and espousing caterpillar values. I also say this in the light of my earlier quote from Gurdjieff regarding the relationship between shock and inertia. It is therefore not improbable that some or many of us will have to face some quite hefty crises in the coming years. I am not going to try and speculate what these crises might be or if they will come in the form of one big crisis or a series of smaller ones. But as we have already seen, the gift of really big shocks is that they not only force us to confront our dark sides, but they often compel us to *do* something about what we see.

This is again why it is so particularly important that we focus on awakening our hearts at this time, as it so radically affects the way we deal with our difficulties. If we suffer a big shock and we have little heart, we may well go into victim or denial mode and there is a chance we will not survive it. Breakdown but no breakthrough. If, on the other hand, we have evolved big heart, the chances are that we will be able to pull ourselves up by our bootstraps and 'get' the deeper meaning inherent in whatever trials and tribulations we may have to endure. *Just as the mystic often has to undergo a dark-night-of-the-soul crisis in order that their old separate sense of self be 'reduced to toast', the same thing may well have to occur for species man if we are properly to make toast of our attachments to our insane society.* Certainly Kenneth Ring thinks something pretty astounding may happen:

> *For me, the cataclysmic prophecies that are rife in current literature foreshadow a revolution of the most astounding proportions ... I sense the approach of a psychological earthquake the magnitude of which has not been experienced in the human awareness for millennia and may not have been experienced in the human awareness ever before.*

So it probably behoves us all as a species to be prepared for a dark-night-of-the-soul crisis whereby conditions will be forced upon us requiring us collectively to undergo some kind of radical fasting of the heart. Whatever kind of crisis or crises we may face, we need to remind ourselves that they are spiritual in nature and are happening not because there is not enough Heart in the world, but because there is oodles of it, and as with our personal selves, our society needs to be radically ploughed up so as to ensure that its new Heart seeds come increasingly to the fore.

Shocks activate a higher awareness

As we saw when we explored our personal crises, 'something' deeply transformational often occurs for us when we are truly 'up against it', when psychologically we find ourselves right at the edge of a precipice. I recently read an account of a mountaineer whose arm got caught in a rock. He had to cut it off with a penknife in order to survive but somehow he went through this ordeal and made his way back to safety. No mean feat. Ilya Prigogine, in his well-known study of dissipative structures, has also shown that one of the properties of systems when driven into difficulties is that they evolve a capacity for higher self-organisation. They don't just break down. They generate new structures that pull higher forms of order out of the resultant chaos.

Earlier, I discussed Elisabet Sartouris's idea of unicellular organisms linking up and becoming multicellular ones, implying that crises force us to team up or group together and increasingly start thinking and operating from a human collective or from a 'we' perspective. Hopefully, one expression that this will take is a greater pull towards communal living (not least because fewer and fewer of us may be able to afford our individual mortgage payments!).

I think this is very important. Many years ago, I lived at the famous Findhorn community in Scotland and it was a most profoundly empowering and nurturing experience. It forced me right out of the 'I am an island unto myself' thinking that our existing culture indoctrinates in us, and reminded me that I was truly part of the family of humanity and needed to stop thinking only in terms of my own needs and requirements. Given how one of our big problems is the sense of isolation or alienation that so many of us experience (especially if we happen to be single) together with the negative effect this may have on our Heart life, community living is a powerful antidote. Not only does it shift us away from our selfishness, but it is also much cheaper and more life-sustaining than living on our own and may be the way of living for many of us in the future.

But to return to my theme of how being up against a wall can so often evoke or 'invite in' the higher 'help forces', I will tell you a little story of this happening in an interesting way in my own life.

Inviting in the 'help forces'

While I was a young man at Oxford, after a year and a half of reading history, I decided to give it up (I could never remember facts) and change over to studying English literature. I was given permission to do so. However, I was not given any extra time, so basically, I found myself having to do the whole history of English literature in just over a year. My reaction was to freak out. I didn't want to fail and go out into the world without a degree, but I didn't have a high opinion of my academic capabilities and I became so nervous that I simply capitulated. I couldn't study properly and could hardly write an essay. I had a breakdown. The stress and fear of failure utterly collapsed me and as time ticked on I was on a fast train going into a very dark tunnel. I couldn't concentrate, open a book or do anything.

Then, about three or four months before I was to take my final exams, something suddenly shifted. It was not of my volition in that I did not consciously engineer it. It just happened. I woke up one morning to find that a light had suddenly been switched on inside me. I saw what failure would mean, and that I absolutely had to do something drastic. In those last few months, therefore, my fears utterly evaporated and I found myself able to work with an intensity and a purpose that I have never before or after been able to get remotely near to. I was full of energy, working fourteen-hour days without getting tired, reading three or four books a day and taking everything in. Something much 'bigger' inside me had become activated. I felt connected to a whole new world of intelligence and creativity, and the end result was that I passed (just!) my final exams on basically three months' work instead of three years'. It was truly a miracle. Undeniably, I had temporarily tapped into a higher energy source. I had shifted worlds. What this showed me was that given the requisite stimulus, certain things may sometimes become possible which ordinarily are quite impossible. Crises as well as gurus may make higher worlds available to us.

Humanity may need to 'nearly die' in order to be born

My point is this. To be an activist and to feel drawn to create a new culture on the planet based on higher-order values is a calling that I believe is summoning all of us. If we can 'hear the call', if we can manage to tap into a deeper part of ourselves, we may come to see that being a conscious agent to help bring about evolutionary change is in fact our true vocation and is actually what being a human being is all about. Such realisations may well cause us to want to reorient the way in which we live in a very radical fashion.

However, if we do not come to this realisation by natural means, if we insist on remaining fixated by our old value systems, *the required shifts of awareness may need to be brought about in another fashion, from the outside, via the ingredients of crisis and shock.* It may be that in order for many of us to rise up and confront our addictions to our caterpillar-ness or sever our attachments to our Setting Sun selves, we may need to go through some kind of radical experience of 'nearly dying', either emotionally or physically or even both at the same time. As we have seen, severe crisis, born of the rising tide of love, can cause extraordinary shifts of consciousness and potentially have the power to bring people much closer into the embrace of the universal heart.

From a concrete perspective, I therefore suspect that in the immediate future, a lot of things in the world may progressively worsen. Our financial crises may well deepen. Certain nations may go bankrupt; terrorism and cyber-warfare may increase; there may be severe water shortages and more serious ecological disasters. It will be all the scarier as we will be able to see all these things happening on our television screens, so it may appear as if Armageddon is upon us. As activists, however, our role is always to remember, and to help those around us also to remember, that if these things do occur, that they are all happening for a specific purpose and that night is always at its darkest just before dawn.

The power of the millions of change agents worldwide

What leads me to *know* in my heart that we *will* break through to a new and happier world is realising just how many millions of people all over the world are today working tirelessly for change and who, as a result, are drawing huge dollops of 'help energy' not only towards themselves, but towards everyone on the planet. As a result of their efforts, a new and better world is also starting to come into being. The visionary entrepreneur, writer and environmental activist Paul Hawken made us aware that this activism is truly a global phenomenon, in a very moving address which he gave in 2009. Activists, he told us, exist all over the planet and come in every shape and form:

> *They are ordinary people willing to confront despair, power and incalculable odds, in order to restore grace and beauty to this world. The*

> *work is occurring in schoolrooms, farms, jungles, mountains, campuses, boardrooms, deserts, refugee camps and slums. Thousands of groups and organisations all over the world are working on the most salient issues of the day – climate change, poverty, peace, deforestation, hunger, human rights ... Rather than control, this group seeks connection. Rather than dominance, it seeks to disperse concentrations of power. Like the Mercy Corps, it works behind the scenes and gets the job done ... It provides hope, support and meaning to billions of people in the world. Its clout resides in idea, not in force. It is made up of teachers, children, peasants, businessmen, rappers, writers, organic farmers, nuns, artists, government workers ... weeping Muslims, concerned mothers, poets, doctors without borders, grieving Christians and politicians.*

Why we don't hear more about these big-hearted people and all the many extraordinary things which they are doing in the world is because our media is still primarily attached to the old world and prefers to report on tragic occurrences, since wounded egos are in love with drama, and drama sells newspapers. The vast majority of these activists are also not famous or glamorous, and, as Hawken suggested, primarily work behind the scenes.

The Heart-fulness of the young

What particularly excites and fills me with hope is that so many of these big-hearted, 'butterfly people' are young. The spirit that motivates them may be summed up by this statement by a female university undergraduate:

> *When I was twenty-two I was angry. Now that I've been twenty-five for a whole ten minutes, I'm still angry, but I'm also hopeful. All around me, and across the world, young people are organising, educating themselves, building new alternative communities, joining resistance movements, becoming activists on behalf of freedom and starting to talk about the possibilities of a future that our parents never expected. Fed up with waiting for a better future to be delivered, we have realised that we are old enough ... to build one for ourselves.*

I have just watched *The Stream* on Al Jazeera, where the most amazing young Palestinian rapper was being interviewed. I was bowled over by his knowledge, eloquence and brilliance, by his incredibly clear understanding of world affairs. If our world is to change, I thought, we need people like him to be in charge: youthful, humble, wise, honest, devoid of cliché and politically savvy. Indeed, maybe people like him *will* be our leaders in the years ahead and the closer we draw to the turning point, the more such people will be propelled to positions of power. He also talked about how he was working to bring about change through his music. This also touched me. In our rational and pragmatic mindset, it is often forgotten how powerful an instrument of transformation music is. It can open hearts and shift consciousness like nothing else. Its presence is really a sign of civilisation and progress in a society, and there have never been more creative and talented musicians around on the planet than at this time.

The point about people like this young man is not only that are they deeply committed to change, but they are also fully clued up as to how best to bring it about. They are naturally connected to the global heart. They know what they want, they stand up for their rights, and they say 'yes' to the forces of freedom and 'no' to those of repression. They wised up long ago to the fact that there is one law for the rich and another for the poor, and that far too many of our world leaders today are either arrogant and self-important or, conversely, corrupt and more interested in wealth and power than in doing what is best for their people, and they are no longer willing to put up with this. They are taking the world into their own hands as true planetary citizens.

Whether they are the young people making up the Green Revolution in Iran, those currently demonstrating in Russia, those who took to the streets to overthrow their leaders in Libya, Tunisia and Egypt, or those campaigning for a better environment or for greater rights for women or poor people, I feel enormously inspired by their courage and vision. I think many of these young people have come into the world with all their activist credentials fully formed. (Perhaps in past lives, they had already awakened their hearts and so have incarnated already fairly 'awake' in this life!) I think their brave actions today are planting many powerful seeds in their societies which, if not always visible right now, I know will germinate tomorrow. All this makes me feel very positive about our future.

Transformation in autocratic countries

I have a sense that a quiet inner revolution is also going to occur in China and that despite the authorities continuing to clamp down on human rights and its people's use of the internet, the genie has been let out of the bottle, and the masses are going to consent less and less to being ruled by faceless, heartless and often corrupt bureaucrats. (There is never any moral compass in totalitarian regimes.) Though at this stage, the leadership do not want to consider the possibility of democracy, it may well be that in the years ahead, it will be forced upon them.

I feel too, that in Russia, when Putin eventually goes – and hopefully, it will be sooner rather than later, as the opposition movement (again consisting mainly of young people) continues to grow in strength, despite his repression of it – there will be such a reaction against his corruption that the leader who replaces him will once again be a visionary, built of the same stock as Gorbachev, someone who will once more embody all that is most noble about the great Russian soul.

It is because of all these things going on in the world that I can say that I don't just believe, but I know, *deep inside my heart*, that despite the near-death experiences and the suffering that we may possibly be called upon to go through as a species, we are definitely going to break through to a new and better world and experience the light at the end of the tunnel. The question is: when?

The significance of critical mass

To understand breakthrough, we need to understand something about the idea of critical mass, namely that when a certain 'critical' number of people start embracing or taking on a new pattern – start seeing the world in a new way and acting in a new way –a powerful impetus for change is set into motion which then starts affecting our species consciousness as a whole. In other words, once a sufficient number of us have made the shift from ego-centredness to heart-centredness, the resultant new attitudes and behaviours will eventually start 'breaking through' everywhere. Everyone will consequently find it easier to make this dimensional shift.

To give you an example of what I mean, we can remind ourselves of three areas where something new has already 'broken through'. Forty years ago, the idea of complementary medicine (then known as alternative medicine) was seen only as something that eccentric people involved themselves with. Similarly, energy sources such as wind, wave or solar power were far from orthodox. Also, in those days, organic food was only eaten by a tiny minority of people, and when a wholefood vegetarian restaurant was eventually opened in London, it was appropriately named 'Cranks' after the kind of people who were expected to frequent it (of which I was one!)

In the past, all these stood at the edge of society. Today, all have become to some degree mainstream. We therefore need to ask ourselves how many more people are required to embrace how many more new patterns, and at what *depth*, to enable us to come to the point where the values of the world of the Great Eastern Sun become increasingly dominant on our planet.

Approaching the turning point

While we don't know the answers to any of these questions, what I *do* know if I listen to my heart is that I hear it telling me to hurry up with my own personal transformation, so that when the turning point *does* come about – if it does so in my lifetime – that I will be ready for it. This is important. My heart tells me that when this point is reached, as many of us as possible need to have aligned as much of ourselves as possible with the world of the Great Eastern Sun, as life will become much easier for those of us who have managed to make the shift, and increasingly difficult for those who still insist on remaining identified with Setting Sun values. Their suffering may well intensify, since the values which they will be continuing to stand for, and which currently (as I write) are still mainstream in our society, will increasingly be relegated to the sidelines. This means that nothing they do will really work out for them any more. What we will witness is a kind of 'turnaround' whereby those still subscribing to the old value system will become the new marginalised!

So when I hear people talk about 'the end of the world being nigh', it makes me feel hopeful, for while many interpret this as implying the end of everything, I agree with those writers who view it as signifying the approaching demise, not of the world, but of the old world order, thus making more room for the new world of the Great Eastern Sun to start moving towards centre place. I see the turning point, therefore, as being about a gradual yet radical shifting of levels, which will result in an enhanced empowerment for everything pertaining to the world of the Great Eastern Sun and a corresponding disempowerment of everything pertaining to the old world of the Setting Sun. In this context, patriarchy, corporate greed, tax avoidance, not laundering our messes, anti-Semitism, hard (as opposed to soft) power, ego games around fame and glory, dictatorships, political corruption, the 'American dream', Sharia law, imperial ambitions, the 'old boy' network, the rich/poor divide – all concepts which are currently being challenged – will become marginalised.

At this moment (April 2013), the world of the Setting Sun probably still has more adherents. But things are changing very, very rapidly and if we activists continue to do our work properly, I believe that the poles will soon be reversed and that increasing numbers of people will come to recognise the madness of persisting with old lifestyles and attitudes which merely continue to prop up an unsustainable system. They will see the necessity not merely to think about new ways to live, but actually to start living in a new way and so will be increasingly open to allowing into their hearts the new, more holistic guidelines for living that are currently being offered us today by many spiritual teachers.

As the turning point approaches, the distinction between those still trying to hang onto a past doing its best to die, and those desiring to move into a future doing its best to be born, will become increasingly pronounced. I see it becoming much easier for activists of the Heart to have their ideas heard and recognised, while life for caterpillar/plastic fiddle man and for all who still insist on remaining invested in the politics of separation, materialism and control will become increasingly precarious. I believe our suffering will be in proportion to our willingness or resistance to change.

Different laws for different worlds

I need to make it clear that the world of the Great Eastern Sun, as it comes into being, is not simply a more integrated version of our existing society. It is an entirely new society – a more humane one, it exists on a wholly new level, and it will have a wholly new value system and set of laws. And each of us can start bringing this new world into being in our own lives right this moment, by choosing to bring Heart into everything we do – into our work, our relationships, our families and so on – and by practising activism in those problem areas of our world that we feel particularly moved to commit ourselves to.

A new culture, then, is not something mysteriously bestowed upon us, somehow, from 'on high'. It is birthed by millions of individuals choosing to live right now in a more Heart-centred and integrative way, where everything we think and do emerges increasingly from the many qualities that exist inside our hearts. In other words, whenever we choose to operate out of kindness, love, wisdom, intuition, truth, integrity, courage and the like, we are helping usher in the world of the Great Eastern Sun. And what this means is that we are going to be able to achieve things which in our old caterpillar mindset would have been quite impossible. As John. G. Bennett put it:

> *What is impossible in a lower world can be possible in a higher world. What can happen and what cannot happen, depends on which world we are in.*[1]

It is so important that we fully understand this. Earlier, I suggested that an open-hearted person, because they are embracing more dimensions of life, possesses more capacity than someone whose heart is closed. Well, the same holds true of an open-hearted society for exactly the same reasons, and thus, *we will be able to make social, economic, ecological and political progress in ways that were simply not possible before*. Not only will we feel freer (inwardly and outwardly), and so have a greater capacity for self-expression, but this capacity will also empower us to make particular changes which we feel will benefit society, more easily, effectively and quickly. Certain restrictions that will remain in place so long as we subscribe to the rules of ego-centeredness will spontaneously become lifted. The great Indian master Sri Nisargadatta Maharaj understood this need for a higher-order consciousness only too well, when in his great spiritual tome *I Am That*, he reminded us:

> *Only when you are free of the world [of the Setting Sun], can you do something about it. As long as you are a prisoner of it, you are helpless to change it. On the contrary, whatever you do will aggravate the situation.*[2]

Only from a place of Heart will we be able to help all those who feel marginalised and excluded and who constitute the ranks of the have-nots.

The challenge posed by the 'underworlds'

While many of the poorest people on the planet actually enjoy a very high quality of life – far, far higher, probably, than the vast majority of wealthy Wall Street brokers – precisely because they live in loving and supportive communities which are closely connected to the natural environment around them, this, sadly, is not the case for all of them, especially those who live within the system yet who are excluded from it, as they can much more easily see the material advantages which they are being denied. These 'exiles from Main Street' or 'underclasses' tend to live in abject poverty and consequently spend much of their lives at a bare subsistence level with all their energies being devoted to merely trying to survive.

There are two main reasons why the plight of the many millions who fall into this category has never been comprehensively addressed. The first is that caterpillar man has been able to get away with not doing so, as marginalised or impoverished people generally don't possess the clout to stand up for their rights! The second reason is that not addressing their issues has also been to caterpillar man's advantage, as he has been able to grow wealthier as a result. One example of this may be seen in the way that large companies often make their products in poor countries where the workforce can be paid a pittance. A recent report I read concerning all multinational companies with operations in Third World countries has quite staggered me. It shows that in the last year, they have managed, quite legally, to avoid paying £110 billion of tax to those countries, so in need of extra aid. They have been able to get away with this because of certain tax loopholes. In our new world order, loopholes such as these will be plugged, and legality and morality will be much more closely aligned.

Haves need to support have-nots much more

We haves, then, are challenged to open our hearts, our ingenuity and our pockets much more to our have-not brothers and sisters, and remember that one of the symptoms of being dispossessed is a feeling of weakness. If you are very poor and deprived, you are generally not able to pull yourself up by your own bootstraps and in all probability you will inhabit a world that does not greatly empower you to determine the course of your life. As such, you initially need help from the haves, as we possess voices; we inhabit realities that have much more freedom in them.

If we haves wish to continue enjoying this freedom for ourselves, then we need to learn to share it. However, simply throwing money at problems is not necessarily the answer, and all too often it has been done to enable us to avoid facing the real issue of why we have created a world – or, more accurately, an 'underworld' – of outcasts on our planet. We are called, therefore, to offer our services wisely and creatively, and see that deprived people are helped to become strong enough to pull themselves up by their bootstraps, and then are given extra support to ensure that they become self-sufficient and not dependent. Above all, what such people need, after food and shelter and love and acceptance, is education and especially the opportunity to work. So much poverty is held in place as a result of a lack of education. So much shame and helplessness is born out of an inability to earn a living, not because one doesn't want to, but because either there is no work or, if there is, one is too weak to do it. In this context, we also need to focus more attention upon all those billions given away in aid, which all too often either get diverted as a result of corruption or, conversely, are squandered on irrelevant activities like, say, fighting wars and then rebuilding the infrastructures of countries that have been devastated as a result! Such financial transactions can no longer be countenanced.

Creating a culture of Heart

As activists, we particularly need to hold in our hearts the idea that the new culture we will be helping usher in is an integrated one and is increasingly being orchestrated by the universal heart, and so will cater for the needs and requirements of *all* peoples and *all* nations on the planet. No longer will we have one law for the haves and another for the have-nots. Just as at a personal level we cannot effectively evolve without working with our Shadow sides, neither can we at a societal level. And we need to begin this work right now. Unless we do so and start to integrate those many aspects of our world that we have enshadowed – and in the process, create a genuinely holistic society for ourselves – we will be destroyed by our underworld. This is our greatest threat. As I suggested in my invitation at the beginning of this book, all of us who are not ill, destitute or damaged are challenged to take on this responsibility. The more we haves choose to help those who are dispossessed, the more we will facilitate our own shift into Heart as we seek to co-create a rosier future for all concerned.

Chapter 21

Exploring the Path of the Spiritual Activist

*This is the true joy in life, the being used for a purpose
recognised by yourself as a mighty one. I am of the opinion
that my life belongs to the whole community and as long as I live,
it is my privilege to do for it whatever I can* – GEORGE BERNARD SHAW

*A new, spiritually based social activism is beginning to assert itself.
It stems not from hating what is wrong and trying to fight it, but from
loving what could be and making the commitment to bring it forth* –
MARIANNE WILLIAMSON

The activist as world server

One way to describe the activist is to refer to him or her as a 'world server', for whatever specific kind of work we may be engaged in, we are essentially committed to serving the planet. The religious philosopher Andrew Harvey uses the term 'Sacred Activist'. For him, 'Sacred Activism is the fusion of the mystic's passion for God with the activist's passion for justice, creating a third fire, which is the burning sacred heart that longs to help, preserve and nurture every living thing'.[1]

I like this definition. Many activists choose to give some or all of their services for free. Some of us bring activism into our everyday work life simply by slanting it in a particular direction. For example, if we are a lawyer, we may decide to dedicate ourselves to defending people's human rights in countries where they are being abused, or if a doctor, we may choose to work for an organisation like Médecins sans Frontières. Others of us may do something entirely different from our everyday occupations. I read yesterday that a group of British Syrians have raised thousands of pounds and have bought supplies and food and are driving out in ten lorries to help those of their fellow countrymen who have fled the fighting and are living in refugee camps.

As we engage consciously in activist work, we realise that it is actually the most natural way to be, as it enables us to be fully ourselves. (I never feel more 'me' than when I am giving lectures, working with people to help them open their hearts, or teaching my retreats.) While certain aspects of our work may sometimes be tough and stressful, it makes us feel fulfilled because it stretches us into our humanity; it makes us feel that we are contributing, and so we realise that far from our activism being about going out of our way, it actually is our true way and that not being of service is going out of our way. We also come to see that the best way to do our work is to be spontaneously ourselves. I will introduce you more fully to the path of the activist by telling you about four friends of mine, each of whom is actively helping usher in a new culture in a completely different way.

Different examples of activism

There is my dear old university friend, Mike, whom I've known since we were boys of nineteen. He is one of the kindest and biggest-hearted men I will ever be privileged to know. Despite working extremely hard, and having four young daughters to look after, he always has time for everyone and his spirit is always buoyant and cheerful. When I went through a difficult patch a few years ago, he was always there to support me. In addition to practising as an acupuncturist and herbalist, he works tirelessly travelling all around the world, mostly at his own expense, to educate politicians about natural medicines. He believes deeply that complementary medicine makes a difference and he is continually 'taking on' the big drug companies with their many vested interests, who regard it as a huge threat to their supremacy and who often go to enormous lengths to try to discredit what he does. He does this part of his work because he believes with all his heart in it. I would describe Mike as a herbalist activist.

Another friend of mine, Andrew, a psychiatrist, is also a significant difference maker. He has founded an organisation to help encourage psychiatrists to bring greater spirituality into their work. As a result of his efforts, several thousand UK psychiatrists are now starting to recognise the connection between mental illness and a lack of heart and soul in people's lives. Through his organisation, many doctors are gradually coming to see that the answer to many of their patients' difficulties may not necessarily be to dope them up with stronger anti-psychotic medication, so much as to explore with them alternative ways and means to awaken their hearts and souls.

I also think of my elephant warrior mate, Max, founder and CEO of Space for Giants. His life is wholly committed to supporting elephants, and it is tough living out in the wild a lot of the time, just as it is tough raising money for what he does, as most people don't place elephant rights very high up on their scale of priorities. Much of his work involves finding the best ways to deal with poachers who shoot elephants for their tusks. In his mission statement, he tells us that his aim is 'to secure a future for the largest mammals on earth forever, to be enjoyed by humanity forever, by ensuring that they have the space and security to live and move freely in the wild forever'. Good on you, Max.

Wonderful, concerned, compassionate Liz has been an environmental advocate activist for over thirty years. She has worked on getting global treaties established (including the Rio Earth summit), and has devoted many hours building campaigns that take away the social licence to destroy the last great North American wilderness areas. In the early 1990s, she launched a campaign that resulted in the protection of over five million acres of the coastal temperate rainforest, now Canada's Great Bear Rainforest. By working closely with the local people, all the way up to the CEOs of some of the biggest companies in the world, her campaign successfully stopped the industrial logging that had been denuding the land.

Most recently, she has worked on an even tougher issue – the extraction of oil from the tar sands in the heart of Canada's boreal forest. 'Serge, the battles are never over,' she tells me, 'but we have engaged those who care around the world, to help give a voice to local people and to these amazing places, by using our power as consumers and advocates to ask questions about where our wood, our oil and our fish come from, and pressuring companies to adopt procurement policies that protect these vital places. Together, people from disparate parts of the world can come together to work towards a common purpose.'

These are just four examples, but what each of them has in common is that they are very committed and, in their different ways, they stand for the values of Heart. Thus their work has a sacred dimension to it. They each remind us that we can make a difference and that we have the power to make Heart-centred and informed choices as to how we do so, and that the resistant forces always need to be stood up to and challenged.

Working with the world soul

To be most effective in what we do, as I have just pointed out, we need a clear and positive vision of the kind of world we wish to create. This is something that only our souls know, as only they can sense the subtle relationship that exists between the part and the whole. So when, through our hearts, we start connecting to our souls, we are not only linked in to our own individual 'higher purpose' or the 'deeper reason' for why we are here on this planet, but we are also connected to the 'higher purpose' of humanity as a whole. The Tibetan master Dwaj Khul expressed it as follows:

> *Man's self-conscious soul is in rapport with the soul of all things. It is an integral part of the universal soul, and because of this, can become aware of the conscious purpose of deity, and can intelligently cooperate with the will of God and thus work with the plan of evolution.*[2]

Just as within the little acorn, there exists a certain intelligent blueprint enabling it to move through all the many stages it needs to, in order for it to become an oak tree, so there is also a similar blueprint stamped into all of life. The more our hearts open to their universal nature, the more connected we become to that blueprint – in particular in those areas where we work – thus enabling us intuitively to 'know' what is being asked of us.

Being of service or being an activist, for many of us, is very often about our continuing to do what we ordinarily already do, only now from a *new* or a *higher* perspective. The main requirement is that our egos become the servant to our hearts and that we are increasingly operating out of the Great Eastern Sun paradigm. This is what distinguishes us from those who are active in promoting their own egoistical visions for change based on the value system of caterpillar man. Often our work may take the form of trying to right certain wrongs, or bring more justice or health or honesty or integrity into the world in some way or other.

Finding our right sphere of work

Just because we may be zealous to help bring about change in the world doesn't mean we feel we have to do everything. The most important thing is that we identify what we believe are our particular contributions or where our strengths lie, and that we focus on those areas. I recently saw a documentary on one of my heroes, Bob Dylan. Joan Baez, who played a big role in getting Dylan started, was being interviewed. She talked about her sadness that she could never get him to join her on protest marches: 'It took me a long time to realise that this was not his thing,' she said. 'What Bobby did was sing protest songs, and getting up early in the morning and going for long marches was not for him. His activism just took the form of writing and singing.'

We serve best, then, by doing what we feel *most moved* or *most inspired* to do, for *that* is where our souls call out to us, and that is the work we are supposed to be doing. Yes, we may be concerned about many situations, but concern and concrete action are often two very different things. For example, I am concerned about the loss of certain species of animals due to pollution and the cutting-down of rainforests. I am deeply concerned about the trafficking of women and children. However, I don't feel it my remit to go out to the places in question as a campaigner. The best thing I can do is to give a donation to Friends of the Earth and Greenpeace every month. Also, being fond of wild cats, I 'sponsor a jaguar', and I also try to support Max in a small financial way with his elephants. It's not much, but the small contribution feels OK. I will leave the more directly 'activist' side of this work to those who experience these causes to be their direct remit.

We need to be clear, then, that there are *primary areas* of our activism – where most of our energy needs to be employed – and areas of *secondary* concern, where we can help a little. These secondary areas are also important, for if a lot of us help a little, great changes can come about. For example, if all us haves in the world just gave £2 a month to the have-nots, poverty would go a long way towards being eradicated.

Primary activism

However, it is in those areas where we feel specifically concerned, and where we are willing to take strong stands for our beliefs, that we may call ourselves primary activists. Here, the two key questions we need to be asking ourselves are (a) are we going to be whole hearted in our activities and (b) where, specifically, are we best able to make a difference? For example, if our 'cause' is the plight of the rainforests or the erosion of our great coral reefs, are we truly going to be fully committed to fighting for their survival? If so, then what does this require of us? What role should we specifically play? Questions to ask ourselves could include: do we simply raise public awareness of the issues? Or do we give money to our cause? Do we do our 'activism' on our own, or, in order to avoid reinventing the wheel, do we try to join forces and collaborate with fellow activists with similar concerns?

Perhaps, if we are a good writer or public speaker, we can write or lecture about the problems which concern us. Conversely, we may choose to become a protestor, or like my friend Liz, use our connections to campaign behind the scenes to try and get certain laws changed. It may also be in our remit to 'name and shame' those organisations which we feel are specifically responsible for causing destruction. Or if, say, we are concerned about the trafficking of women, we can ally ourselves with, or specifically work for, organisations which also have that on their agenda, or make a documentary film about it (as the actress Demi Moore has recently done). Conversely, we might feel brave enough physically to confront the gangs that kidnap young women, or we could try and rescue them. Conversely, we could leave the rescuing to others and try to do something to assist those women who have been rescued, but who do not now know where to go or how to get on with their lives.

How we address the particular cause or causes we choose to take on depends not only on how deeply we allow our hearts to be touched and by how much time and effort we are willing or able to put in, but also on what assets we bring to the table. For example, are we rich? Do we have good connections or acute intelligence? Are we more of a behind-the-scenes person or do we prefer to be out there as a 'doer' on the front line?

We cannot do everything. Dylan may have preferred to lie in of a morning – good for him – but there was no shortage of Joan Baezes willing to get up early and protest against the Vietnam War as well as sing. Dylan's weapon, as she said, was his poetry and his music. She added the 'going on marches' bit. And that was mighty powerful. Today, I often like to contemplate how much more quickly 'the times are a-changin' *now* than when Dylan originally wrote that immortal protest song, about half a century ago!

Serving women's rights

In the Western world, primarily due to the re-emergence of the feminine principle (which we have already explored) and the hard work of many committed feminist activists over the last half-century, women have increasingly come into positions of power. Sadly, in many other parts of the planet, this has not been the case, and women are still treated as inferiors and possess no rights. Indeed, the patriarchal mindset that still reigns supreme in certain countries ensures that women cannot be educated or allowed out of the house unless accompanied by a man. In some countries, women are subjected to genital mutilation and 'honour killings' and can even be sold off to a husband whom they have never met, often when they are as young as ten or eleven years old. This is all horrendous.

If a culture of Heart is to be implemented, we need to have a society where the female spirit of life is fully respected, and where the enormous contribution that women make at every level – and which very much includes their role as mothers – is fully honoured. In response to this need, therefore, hundreds of extraordinary women activists with huge hearts have emerged in many countries where women are most suppressed, and have been doing extraordinarily brave things. Let me give you just four examples.

In 2004, the Nobel Peace Prize was awarded to Wangari Maathai, the first African woman to be given this award, chiefly for her work creating the Green Belt movement – a grass-roots effort to encourage rural women in Kenya to plant trees and help reverse a catastrophic trend of deforestation in their country. She didn't stop there. Her organisation inspired Kenyan women to stand up for themselves and see the forests as something they had a civic right to preserve. Like many brave female Heart warriors, Maathai paid a price for her activism. She was repeatedly jailed and beaten, as were many of her followers.

More recently, this prize was awarded to three more champions of women's rights in Africa and the Middle East, one of whom was Leymah Gbowee of Liberia. Leymah Gbowee devoted her life to campaigning for the rights of women against rape, as well as organising Christian and Muslim women to challenge the patriarchy of Liberia's warlords. In 2003, she led hundreds of protesters to demand a swift disarmament of fighters who preyed on women during her country's civil war. Another great female warrior is Beatrice Mtetwa, a human rights lawyer who won the Inamori Ethics Prize in 2011, and who has dedicated her career to helping victims of human rights abuses in her home country of Zimbabwe.

In Afghanistan, a schoolgirl, Malala Yousufzai, stood up against the Taliban, whose view of women is utterly medieval and barbarous. They don't believe women should receive an education. Malala said 'I am going to stand up for my rights' and courageously continued going to school. In October 2012 the Taliban shot her in the head at point blank range, but she survived, and her courage has been celebrated worldwide. Despite being the subject of a fatwa, she has vowed to continue her struggle as soon as she is able, and there is talk about her being awarded the Nobel Prize. If so, she would be a worthy recipient. I am totally in awe of her bravery.

What all these remarkable female activists reveal to us is that being of service is one of the best ways to surrender one's servility, to rise above victimhood, empower oneself and create a freer world. These are just a few out of many thousands of 'new women' – brave, literate, focused, big hearted and committed – all emerging in response to the call of the universal heart.

'Heart-centred' politics

This global heart is gradually causing a new kind of politics to emerge, which I will simply call Heart-centred politics. What the 'rebels' in Libya fought for, what the Greens in Iran were demonstrating about, what the Russian young people want – what, deep down, young men and women in every nation the world over yearn for – is a tyrant-free world where a genuine spirit of liberty, equality and fraternity prevails, and where justice is available not only to some, but to everyone. In our new world, people want to be free to elect the leaders they want – and they will want them to be men and women of principle, genuine human beings who don't talk in political clichés and riddles or give themselves airs and graces, and who aren't in the business for status reasons and who won't take our power or use their positions to grow rich. We want leaders who will enable us, the people, to feel powerful, and whom we can trust to stand up for our rights and work to serve our best interests in creating a just and fair society.

Activism and danger

Certain kinds of activism, sadly, are fraught with danger. We need to accept this, which is why the activist needs to be well trained and possess a brave and strong heart, as often the more we 'go for' or stand up for our truths, the more our light will illuminate what is dark and shadowy. The sad truth is that sometimes activists get killed, sometimes in their many thousands.

Therefore, I have nothing but huge admiration for those courageous Greenpeace activists who drive their rubber dinghies right up to those huge Japanese whalers, risking their lives to protest against the illegal slaughtering of whales. I also think it extraordinarily brave when members of local tribes in Latin America also risk their lives to protest against the gun-toting, powerful companies that try to pull down their natural habitats. Liu Xiaobo from China is another wonderful example of an activist who flirts daily with danger. He was recently awarded the Nobel Peace Prize for single-handedly standing up to the violation of human rights that has so long been an integral part of his country's policy. This university professor is constantly reminding China of its dark side and having to submit to being beaten, threatened and imprisoned for his efforts. Currently, he faces trumped-up charges of not paying his taxes. (Dictatorships love inventing this charge.) Despite all these obstacles, his courage to stand firm on behalf of the values of freedom and democracy remains unwavering.

Knowing exactly what will happen to him, this extraordinary man constantly takes on the whole Chinese nation. 'I believe that my work has been just,' he tells us, 'and that someday China will be a free and democratic country … I have long been aware that when an independent intellectual stands up to an autocratic state, step one towards freedom is often a step into prison. Now I am taking that step, and true freedom is that much nearer.' What he is doing is embodying the true soul of China and thus showing us that his noble country is so much more than a worn out, fear-ridden, old-style authoritarian dictatorship. I will talk more about 'the path of the dissident' in the next chapter.

I am particularly moved by the work of a small British charity called War Child. This organisation doesn't attempt to stop wars or reform hopeless governments. It gives help directly to children whose lives have been wrecked by conflict – those who have been left homeless, with no education or prospects of any kind. It works in perilous places where major non-governmental organisations often refuse to go, in order to find the most vulnerable children and try to improve their lives. What a totally awesome service. It is people who run organisations like this who should be awarded medals and given knighthoods.

What is it that moves all these brave and beautiful people to do all the many extraordinary things that they feel committed to do, if it is not the force of our emerging universal heart? This big heart is forever beckoning to us inside our own hearts, asking us to 'go for it', requesting us to find our cause or causes and commit fully to them, even moving us at times to put our lives on the line in the name of our humanity. As Martin Luther King, activist par excellence, put it:

> *The ultimate measure of a man is not where he stands in moments of comfort and convenience, but where he stands at times of challenge and controversy. The true neighbour will risk his position, his prestige, and even his life for the welfare of others.*[3]

Are you also willing to do this?

Chapter 22

The Many Faces of the Activist of Heart

Service is of many kinds, and he who wisely renders it, who seeks to find his particular sphere, and who, finding it, gives effort gladly for the benefit of the whole, is the one whose own development proceeds steadily – DWAJ KHUL

The path of the committed activist is a very heroic one and has many different faces, as there are many different ways that we can work actively at making a difference. In this chapter, we will look at ten of these ways. See if any apply to you.

The Radiator

The Radiator activist serves by radiating healing and uplifting energy into the environment through the power of their light-filled heart. *Being* is their weapon. Their activism is focused through the power of silence, gentleness and love. The great Indian saint Sri Ramana Maharshi, who primarily taught in silence, was a famous Radiator. Many people experienced becoming enlightened – having their egos reduced to toast – through the power of his silent presence. This was his great gift to humanity.

If we think of how noisy, fragmented and speedy our existing culture has become, we realise that people who embody peace and stillness and who are able to emit a sweet and loving presence that embraces everyone and everything have a unique and priceless gift to offer the world. I would like to feel that one of the characteristics of our new culture is that it will be quieter, deeper and less rushed, and will allow more space for the intrinsic soul life within each of us to emerge. This is why I believe that the contribution of the Radiator activist is so immense. As we draw closer to the turning point, I believe that Radiator activists will become increasingly valued for the important work they do.

The Initiator

The Initiator is the activist who recognises that certain things need doing and then initiates the appropriate action. Unlike Radiators, Initiators are movers and shakers. They are 'out there' in the world. Dame Ellen MacArthur, initially famed for her courage in sailing single-handedly around the world and now an eco-warrior, comes into this category. All her activist training, she explains, came as a result of many hours spent alone on the sea, where her very life was dependent on the need to remain awake and alert. As she couldn't consume more than she had brought with her, she learned to live sustainably.

She has talked about how she had 'two options: to continue sailing or to confront the problems of the planet regarding how we use or abuse our energy', and she chose the latter. Instead of continuing what she was good at, which earned her a lot of money but, she realised, did not make a difference to the world, in a true activist spirit, she decided to dedicate her life to helping save the planet by using the skills she had acquired at sea. Over the last few years, she has put her considerable resources towards that end. 'I have spent three years speaking to governments, businesses, local councils and NGOs and the public about our reliance on a finite supply of resources, which is a real issue for us in the developed world,' she tells us.

She has set up a charitable foundation to help people understand more about this issue, and her vision is to find and communicate to people more sustainable ways of living, as well as working as a change agent within business and setting up projects with specific measurable goals. In her words, 'when faced with a storm at sea, I always try to see through to the other side, and I see this challenge no differently. I firmly believe that we can find the solutions – it will not be the first time that the human race has achieved the impossible, through sheer necessity and determination.' This is the strong-willed voice of the Initiator.

What is so encouraging today is to see just how many wealthy and well-known people – sports stars, pop singers and various celebrities – are also making decisions similar to Ellen MacArthur's and are increasingly choosing to use their money and fame to be of service. Whether we are talking about Prince Charles's Prince's Trust to help disadvantaged children, Richard Gere working to help the cause of the Tibetan people and to spread a greater understanding of Tibetan Buddhism in the West, Elton John's AIDS Foundation, George Clooney's work in Darfur, Demi Moore's film about women trafficked for prostitution, or my troubadour buddy Donovan touring the world and giving concerts to raise money to encourage the teaching of transcendental meditation in schools – and I could give a hundred more examples – it is all symptomatic of people in the public eye actively taking important initiatives to make a difference. I totally celebrate this spirit of altruism.

I need to point out, however, that we don't have to be rich, powerful, beautiful or famous to be an Initiator. Little old you and I can also initiate things. Yes, we may not have quite the same clout, but if our heart is strong and we are committed, in an abundantly humble way, we too can move mountains. As Martin Luther King so beautifully put it, 'anybody can serve. You don't have to have a college degree or know about Plato and Aristotle to serve … You only need a heart full of grace and a soul full of love.'

I want to include in this category another important way to be of service and that is engaging in what I will call 'random acts of kindness'. It is akin to the boy scout ideal of doing a good deed every day. It may take the form of our choosing to mow the lawn of our elderly next-door neighbour who cannot do so herself, or giving a few hours of our time to listen with our hearts to a friend in distress, or putting money in the parking meter of the car next to us because we see it is about to run out. Such actions help build up a 'kindness field' that serves as a powerful antidote to all the greed and selfishness that is so prevalent around us today. Whatever our specific service path, each of us can be kindness activists.

The Infiltrator

The Infiltrator is the transformational equivalent of the double agent. We present ourselves outwardly as a caterpillar – as part of the old order – while secretly working on behalf of the consciousness of the world of the Great Eastern Sun. In many instances, we need to do this so that we don't appear threatening to those who might otherwise be resistant to us, which would defeat our objectives.

This approach is very important, as many organisations and institutions today are secretly longing to change, but they also fear doing so and consequently need approaching very delicately. People with visionary ideas working inside such organisations may therefore need to operate as Infiltrators if they wish to make any headway. Certainly, when I work with certain corporations, I dress like them, try to talk like them, find it more appropriate to use words like 'relaxation' rather than 'meditation' or 'right side of the brain' rather than 'heart'. By not appearing 'weird', I can be more effective and can introduce Heart values into an organisation much more subtly. As critical mass operates at a local as well as at a global level, in many companies, if just a small percentage of the personnel can start to make little changes, the whole organisation may gradually become 'infected', and certain positive shifts may start occurring within the corporation as a whole.

The Proclamator

Proclamators work through the power of the spoken word, with which, if they have a well-integrated head and heart and possesses the ability to inspire, they can do much to open their listeners' hearts and minds and make them receptive to new ideas. This was one of Barack Obama's gifts. What helped him win his first election was that when he spoke, he made the American people feel that with him in the White House, a new and better world was possible.

Tennyson told us that 'more things are wrought by prayer than this world dreams of'. I say that more shifts can also potentially come about through the power of the spoken word than anyone would believe. If inspirational public speakers who are in touch with the next step of our human evolution possess open hearts and so are able to have their ideas carried on the wings of love, then they wield a truly powerful weapon. Transformational ideas have the capability both to penetrate and to illuminate closed and endarkened hearts, as well as to bring hope to those lost in fear.

The Innovator

The Innovator brings something entirely new to the table, like a Beethoven, a Carl Jung or an Albert Einstein, a Wilhelm Reich or a Nikola Tesla. What they create is not just a synthesis of what has gone before, but something entirely original that no one had ever thought of until that moment. If a new culture is to emerge on our planet, we need many innovative activists operating in many different fields. For me, Ken Wilber, who writes at great depth on almost every single subject, is a wonderful example of an activist of this ilk. People like him are the trailblazers for us. They inspire us to move into entirely new terrain that no one has ever dared enter before.

We need innovative scientists to take our sciences to the 'next level'; we need visionary politicians to come up with new ways to conduct politics. We need free-thinking economists who are able to delve more fully into the soul of economics, just as we need a new kind of philosopher – one who is able to design multi-dimensional philosophies for us – in contrast to our many 'Setting Sun' philosophers whose insights are solely based on seeing the world through the old, parochial lens of a three-dimensional space–time reality.

The Innovator activist designs new bottles to house the new wine. By laying down distinct new tracks, they make it safer for the rest of us to step out of our old ruts and start taking risks and seeing the world in a new way.

The Investigator

The role of the Investigator activist is very important, for they are the ones committed to having truth emerge as a result of exposing falsehoods. Thus, they bring darkness up into the light and expose evil and dishonesty. They are the whistleblowers and fraud detectives who explore the dark side of our social, economic, ecological and political worlds – often at considerable risk to their own personal safety. Sometimes, in order to get the information they desire, they also may need to shape-shift and pretend to be other than who they are. Some Investigators also don steel helmets, go out to the front lines of battles and risk life and limb to report on what is really happening. The brave warrior Marie Colvin, reporting for *The Times* in Syria, recently lost her life doing exactly that.

This role can be dangerous because the forces of corruption and dishonesty don't like being exposed and will, as we have seen, often fight back. As I write, one of the more prominent bloggers in Russia has just been tortured and thrown into prison. His 'sin' was to have exposed President Putin's corruption. Thanks to the role of him and other Investigator activists, it is no longer 'underground information' that many Russian law enforcement officers are corrupt and that if you try to oppose them, you will probably find that your property will be confiscated, or you will be thrown into jail on trumped-up charges. Those journalists who shine lights into the murky recesses of how certain cosy cartels operate and rogue institutions work, therefore, perform a very valuable service as it is so important that the dark side of the corporate world is also exposed for all to see. Knowledge is power. The more such abhorrences come up into the light of day, the more we can see them and, hopefully, do something about them.

The Educator

What prevents many of us moving forward into the new millennium is that we don't hold any vision of the future. We are too firmly rooted in the 'comforts' of our egoic consciousness, reflected in the way we 'do' everything in our lives, ranging from how we conduct our relationships to the way we work. The role of the Educator activist is to inform people of the existence of the emerging new paradigm, to let them know that a whole new way of seeing and operating in the world exists, that many of the things which they believe to be true may be false, and that many things which they believe to be false are in fact true.

Another gift that Educators may impart is to remind us that we all have access to an 'inner teacher' and that knowledge gained as a result of our learning to listen to our hearts may be as informative as – if not, in many instances, more so than – what we learn from external sources. Today, Educators are required in all spheres of life and those scientists who are able to bring their mystical side into their profession have much to teach their materialist colleagues who believe that nothing can exist that cannot be rationally proved. Certainly, if I look back at my life, I am ever grateful to those Educators who came into it at different times, and who cajoled or shocked me out of my old viewpoints and attachments. I needed a lot of educating to come to see that my old world really was limited, and that a new reality might have far more dimensions to it and be far more mysterious than I would ever have believed possible.

The Protestor

The Protestor activist is the person willing to dedicate their time and energy – often making a big sacrifice of time away from their work – to make a certain statement by going on a protest. This is a very potent method to effect change. (We remind ourselves that it was hundreds of thousands of people taking to the streets that brought down the Iron Curtain.) While there is the satisfaction of being united in a common cause, the Protestor again may risk their life by making their intentions known, especially if they happen to be protesting on the streets in a non-democratic country that does not countenance such activities. Under dictatorships like those that exist in Iran, you may get raped, tortured or gunned down for your efforts.

Protesting, however, is a powerful strategy of service, for when thousands of people gather in the streets to make a particular point, and if the demonstration happens to be captured by the news media, it sends out a powerful message to the rest of the world and is therefore an important way of drawing attention to a cause. When people go on marches to demand better wages, or to call for greater democracy, or for an end to bribery and corruption, or to have peace not war, and if these marches are peaceful and get televised, they often play a significant role in helping set up the conditions in which all these issues can be examined in greater depth.

The Agitator

While the Radiator's job is to fill us with love and greater ease of being, the role of the Agitator is totally the opposite: it is to stir us up and shake us out of our complacency and make us realise that we need to stop being so passive in the face of the many problems in the world and that each of us needs to *do* something concrete – right now!

The gift which Agitators impart to us is to remind us forcibly that it is not enough merely to think or talk about what we feel is wrong with the world or what needs to happen to improve things. Rather, they let us know – often in no uncertain terms – that we all need to take concrete action of one kind or another.

Bob Geldof, famous for having raised large sums of money via his Live Aid concerts, which he put on in the 1980s for the famine in Africa, is a good example of a skilled Agitator. His strategy was to rile and disturb people and make them feel guilty about their complacency. It was successful. He raised a lot of money for his cause. He would snap us out of our comfort zones and compel us to reach into our pockets and put our money where our hearts were.

Given the huge amount of need out in the world and the fact that so many people have so much more than they need and so many millions have so much less, this strategy is vitally necessary. If a new culture of Heart is to gain further expression, we need many Agitators in the mould of a Geldof to galvanise us into action and remind us to stop dreaming about change, but instead do something positive ourselves if we want it to come about.

Agitators do not heal. That is not their mission. They are continually reminding us that we need to be instrumental in bringing healing about, and that there is a whole lot wrong with our world and a whole lot of action required if certain things are to be put right. The Agitators' gift to us is that they light rockets under our backsides to wake us up.

The Dissident

To be a genuine Dissident is an extraordinary act of service and sacrifice, and only truly remarkable people choose this path, which is, in effect, one of challenging the legitimacy of evil and corrupt totalitarian regimes. Of all the service paths, it is the one that can best teach us how great abundance may be discovered in hugely restricting conditions, and many dissidents have reported how they have discovered their true humanity by taking themselves right to the edge of their deepest fears. As dissidence is one of the best strategies to bring down totalitarian regimes, and as so many of these regimes are being challenged today, I want to spend a little time dissecting this particular path in more detail.

Understandably, being a Dissident is not one of the most frequently chosen vocations. However, it is one of the most noble ways to serve one's country, if that country is non-democratic. It requires enormous courage, a vast commitment, a true 'warrior spirit', an ego that is happy to be servile and, most important, a willingness to forsake personal comfort, since the Dissident often needs to spend large periods of time in prison as the most appropriate way of embodying the stand they are taking.

The Burmese human rights activist Aung San Suu Kyi, imprisoned for many years by the generals in charge of her country, explains the kinds of challenge which confront people who live under totalitarian regimes. Her words also help us understand why tyrants have such difficulty relinquishing their power. When she talks of the pathology besetting them and the need to have a 'revolution of the spirit' if they are to be overthrown, she is talking about what in my language I describe as an awakening of Heart.

> *It is not fear of power that corrupts, but fear. Fear of losing power corrupts those who wield it, and fear of the scourge of power corrupts those who are subject to it. The effort to remain uncorrupted in an environment where fear is an integral part of everyday existence is not immediately apparent to those fortunate enough to live in states governed by the rule of law. In societies such as Burma, there will continue to be arenas of struggle where victims of oppression have to*

> *draw on their own inner resources to defend their inalienable rights as members of the human family. The only effective way to confront totalitarian regimes is through having a 'revolution of the spirit'.*
>
> *The quintessential revolution is that of the spirit, born of an intellectual conviction of the need for change in those mental attitudes and values which shape the course of a nation's development. A revolution which aims merely at changing official policies and institutions with a view to an improvement in material conditions has little chance of genuine success. Without a revolution of the spirit, the forces which produced the iniquities of the old order would continue to be operative, posing a constant threat to the process of reform and regeneration.*[2]

The Dissident therefore presents himself or herself as someone who has effected this 'revolution of spirit' (awakening of Heart), as a result of which a certain spiritual power is given to them, which is then able to flow out of them and into their society. Aung San Suu Kyi is therefore reiterating Gandhi's point about our need to embody the changes which we wish to bring forth. I find what she says about fear very interesting, especially when she suggests that 'fear may be a gift'!

> *But perhaps more precious is the courage acquired through endeavour; courage that comes from cultivating the habit of refusing to let fear dictate one's actions; courage that could be described as 'grace under pressure' – grace which is renewed repeatedly in the face of harsh, unremitting pressure.*[3]

Scilla Elworthy, a peace activist and another extraordinarily courageous woman, told me of an incident in Aung San Suu Kyi's life when she and hundreds of her democratically inspired followers were surrounded by the full force of the Burmese military, and the order had been given to shoot.

> *No one moved as this extraordinary woman, small in stature but with a presence as vast as a mountain, calmly walked up towards the barrel of the guns and with her head held high and looking directly into the eyes of the officer in charge, quietly told him to put down his weapon and order his men to do the same thing. He did so and not a shot was fired.*

This is an excellent example of what the power of a big-hearted human being can accomplish. Primarily as a result of Aung San Suu Kyi's efforts, the Burmese generals have relented, and over the last year, extraordinary strides have been made in Burma towards democracy and Aung San Suu Kyi, who for many years had been under house arrest, is now an elected member of parliament. She is free to move wherever she desires and to meet any foreign dignitary who visits her country. I celebrate this.

Natan Sharansky, who in the Cold War years was a prominent human rights activist in the USSR, and was imprisoned in a gulag for his beliefs, sheds more light on the extraordinary experience of freedom that can come to those willing to stand up for those rights:

All totalitarian regimes fear the Dissident and always offer them 'freedom from prison' if they will only recant and sign a forced 'confession of their crimes' ... [One] become[s] a dissident when one first crosses the line from doublethink and fear, and begins to say openly what one believes ...

The transition from hiding one's thoughts to speaking them is a moment of tremendous relief and liberation. You achieve an inner freedom in which there is no discord between what you think, say and do. Being a dissident is not a momentary decision. Once made, it must be tenaciously defended ... As the pressure from the regime grows, you come to understand how terrified it is of your independence and how desperate it is to recapture the space you have conquered from it – your own mind. The regime is right to be scared ... since no Dictator can survive a citizenry that no longer fears them, and non-Democratic regimes must battle constantly, often desperately, to keep one citizen's fearlessness from spreading and making others forget they are afraid. Realising the regime's deep-seated insecurity, you (as Dissident) begin to feel an awesome responsibility not just for your personal independence, but for the wider struggle against the regime's repression. The two causes become one ... Paradoxically, it is in prison that one gains a level of moral clarity and simplicity that is impossible to achieve in any other situation.[4]

Sharansky's words shed much light not only on what is going through the minds of the leadership in Syria and Iran and the degree of paranoia that lies behind the ruthless war they are conducting against their own citizens to try and keep them in states of terror, but also on the extraordinary power that a revolution of spirit or an awakening of Heart can bring about.

If all activist stands demand unwavering consistency and commitment, then in no area is this of greater importance than in that of being a Dissident, for as an individual, one is not only 'taking on' one's nation's deeply wounded ego as it has become embodied in its leadership, but one is doing so from a place of representing one's country's soul and conscience. The great paradox that countries like Syria, China and Iran have to confront is that the more such regimes engage in terror tactics designed to inspire fear and to keep their subjects subdued, the more their regimes are despised and hence the greater the desire of the people to wish to rise up to try to unseat them. If one already has very little life, one has that much less to lose.

Comment on the ten paths

If we examine ourselves closely, we may see that we utilise one, two or even three or more of these ten service approaches. For example, we may be an Agitator and a Proclamator or an Initiator and an Educator. Our focus may be more inward or it may be more external, or it may be both. Some of us may simply have the role of pointing out the wrongs in the world; others of us may have this role but combine it with a remit to address how they may be best righted. It may also be that we find ourselves called to do things that we have not done before and so may not be trained for. If so, we must not allow this to hold us back and we may need to learn what to do through the doing of it. So long as we follow our hearts, we can be sure of receiving assistance from the 'help forces'.

There are certain arguments which some of us may use to justify our not lifting a finger in service. I will list some of the main ones followed by my comments.

Arguments to avoid being of service

The problems of the world are too big and too far gone. What can little me do?

How do we know the problems are too far gone? Are we not just saying this to avoid taking any responsibility ourselves? If each of us begins thinking with Heart and visualising the kind of world we want, and if we realise that we each have our particular job of work to do, a huge amount can be achieved. Lots of 'little mes' working together can make up one big, effective, collective 'we'.

Everything will work out, so there is no need to worry. Besides, it is up to those who have power in the world – our politicians, our economists and captains of industry – to change things. It is not my responsibility.

Again, faulty thinking. If things work out, it is because we, the people, make them work out. We cannot simply rely on those 'at the top' to rescue us, not least because many of them are responsible for getting us into our messes in the first place. Our world is not going to change unless we take responsibility for changing it. In Mikhail Gorbachev's words:

> When I left the United Nations after seven years of designing and coordinating research into the social and economic aspects of what … we used to call the 'world problematique', I became more convinced that fundamental change would not come from 'above', from the elected or appointed leaders of contemporary societies, but must come from below, from the people who live in those societies.

I don't like what is going on in the world, so in order to survive and remain safe, I will hide away in some safe area on the planet.

This is the way of the ostrich, whereby we bury our head in the sand. But it doesn't keep us safe, as the more we try to hide away, the more our hearts shrink and the more vulnerable we become to whatever negative currents may be in the air at any time. As such, our survival may actually become more, not less, precarious. Instead of being ostriches, we need to become giraffes and stick our necks out!

What is important is my personal health, development and spiritual growth. I want to stay pure, so I don't want to sully myself by engaging in all the messy things out in the world.

Again, this is faulty thinking (unless our role is to be a mystic), as one of the best ways to evolve and grow Heart is to engage with life as fully and as deeply as we are able. Our hearts don't become pure by our hiding away. We become pure by doing the work our hearts intend us to do and by going to where they intend us to go.

I am too busy to serve, as my family and personal work engagements take up all my time.

Again, this is a cop-out. It is inappropriate prioritising. Of course, we need to honour our personal life and work, but not at the expense of engaging with the larger whole of life. Here, we need to ask ourselves why we keep ourselves so busy (what are we trying to avoid?), and secondly, given the precarious times we are living in, if all the 'personal things' we are engaged in are really that important.

The world is in a bad place because of our greedy bankers and stupid politicians. It is their fault. I blame them.

When we play the 'blame game' in order to get out of doing anything to address the many evils in the world, we are again avoiding our responsibilities for being a human being. Besides, those who have caused our problems are seldom those who can best get us out of them. Remember: the solution always lies at a level beyond that at which the problem exists. Hence our world problems can best be solved by those who have worked on themselves and as a result are able to see things in a new light and so can 'operate in the world' from a wiser perspective.

I am scared to say what I think and do what I believe is the right thing, as it goes against the grain of the world and I feel I won't be liked or accepted.

Martin Luther King understood this fear:

> *Many people fear nothing more terribly than to take a position which stands out sharply and clearly from the prevailing opinion. The tendency of most is to adopt a view that is so ambiguous that it will include everything and so popular that it will include everybody. Not a few men who cherish lofty and noble ideals hide them under a bushel for fear of being called different.*[5]

If we choose to be an activist, while we may at times need to modulate our light or temporarily conceal our hearts under our kimonos, we must never hide them under a bushel! We need to confront our fears and move through them.

There are other cop-outs as well. For instance, if we don't think we can do something perfectly, we might do nothing. Conversely, if we think that being of service is only about doing something vast and grandiose, we might also not do anything unless we can be sure of saving the entire world single-handedly! We can call these our 'ego obstacles', and if we have these reactions, it may be an indication that we still have a lot more inner work to do.

Ask yourself: do any of these avoidances apply to you? Is there more that you could be doing or would like to be doing? Do you perhaps need to push yourself a bit more or bring more conscious love to the fore? I also remind you that we are of service not only in what we do, but also in who we are and in the way that we choose to live. Remember that beautiful quote I gave you from the Shivapuri Baba in response to how we may best live?

Eight basic guidelines for being an effective activist

- Whatever our line of work, we need to carry our abundance of heart with humility and modesty and seek to be loving, kind, strong and gracious in the way in which we engage with all the many different people and different situations that come our way, never forgetting that the stuff of our daily life, with its many challenges, is our sacred practice.
- With a full and loving heart, we also need to ensure that we live as the stand we are taking at all times, and never give way or compromise our values, no matter how vulnerable we may sometimes feel.
- We must find a lifestyle that works for us and that enables our creativity to flourish. Generally, the more simply we can live, the more effective we can be.
- We must never desist from confronting with a steady heart whatever it is we are called to confront, even if it is difficult or challenging.
- We need to eliminate all negative gossip from our lives and never use language that is in any way enshadowing.
- We must remember that we are an agent of enheartenment and are being of service wherever we go and whatever we do.
- We must choose to be harmless at all times, which does not mean we be ineffective but that we ensure that nothing we do ever injures anyone or anything.
- We must have the courage to 'go for it' – be bold and dream big dreams and forever hold a positive view of what lies ahead for us, never forgetting the need to embody the changes we wish to see occurring.

Chapter 23

Healing Evil

*If thou hast not seen the devil,
look at thine own self* – RUMI

*We create evil out of our highest ideals
and most noble aspirations* – SAM KEEN

The issue of evil

It is important that we understand the issue of evil – what it is and how we may best deal with it – as no matter what areas of the world we feel called upon to address, as activists, we will certainly come up against it in some form or other. Carl Jung saw it as a definite 'fact of life'. Writing at the time of the Second World War, he described evil as 'having become a determinant reality' that 'can no longer be dismissed from the world by a circumlocution', and therefore 'we must learn to handle it, since it is here to stay'. This is good advice. Evil has always been with us and will probably always be with us, even if a more compassionate culture comes into being, and it is perpetrated as much by those with overblown, wounded egos as by those with insufficient ego. Elisabet Sartouris defines it as ' utterly immoral behaviour perpetrated in ignorance of how the universe works'. It is closely aligned to what I earlier described as being our madness.

Three key things are necessary if we are to handle evil effectively. Firstly, we need to be able to recognise it for what it is and understand how, where and why it manifests. Secondly, we need to look inside our own hearts and see if there is anything about ourselves that may be evil. Lastly, remembering Edmund Burke's famous remark about evil being permitted 'when good men do nothing', we need to do something about it.

I see there being two kinds of evil in the world, both of whose tendrils reach into each other, but which are nonetheless quite distinct. One kind of evil is very obvious and I will call it 'obvious evil'. The other kind is not at all obvious, and is so prevalent that we often find it hard to recognise as evil, rendering it all the more dangerous. I will call it 'non-obvious evil'. It is closely affiliated with many aspects of the Shadow.

Obvious evil

Obvious evil is, well, obvious – it is out in the open! It is what transpired at Auschwitz. It is what took place at Darfur. Obvious evil is present in all acts of ethnic cleansing, intentional killing, torture, all uses of women and children as sex slaves. Hitler, Saddam, Gaddafi and Mugabe, who has bankrupted Zimbabwe for his own personal profit, are good examples of obviously evil human beings. The British serial killer Dr Harold Shipman, who intentionally killed more than two hundred patients by injecting them with morphine, is another example of obvious evil.

Interestingly, obviously evil people are all masters at negative Shadow projection. They never recognise their own evil. For example, Mugabe blames all the woes he has created for his country on the 'evil British colonialists'. Hitler believed he was a great leader, doing what was necessary for Germany's glory. One of the problems with obviously evil people is that we can often use them as smokescreens to conceal our own non-obvious evil, which we are often loath to take responsibility for. By this I mean that so long as Gadaffi remained the 'mad dog', so long as we recognise Mugabe's or Saddam's obvious vileness, we can feel self-righteously indignant and so not look at certain motes that might exist in our own eyes.

Non-obvious evil

Non-obvious evil is quite different. It doesn't initially appear to be evil, it exists within the provenance and landscape of many of caterpillar man's ordinary activities, and is an integral part of our 'mild psychopathology and crippling immaturity'. Hannah Arendt was referring to this evil when she coined the famous term the 'banality of evil', suggesting that 'it possesses neither depth nor any demonic dimension'. She also added that 'it can outgrow and lay waste the whole world precisely because it spreads like a fungus on the surface'. W. H. Auden understood this kind of evil and described it as 'unspectacular'; it 'shares our bed and eats at our own table'.[1]

Certain kinds of advertising are a good example of non-obvious evil. On the surface, they appear innocuous enough. What is wrong with suggesting we should buy this particular car or that brand of washing-up liquid? If we dig a bit deeper, however, all kinds of hidden facts begin to surface. We discover that many companies today employ neurobiologists to use ingenious methods of bypassing the conscious mind to find increasingly persuasive ways to sell us things, by subtly informing us that the way we currently are is not sufficient, but that we will look better, feel better and be better if we buy their products. Thus, already, we are made to feel inadequate unless we have something from 'outside ourselves' to bolster us.

But it goes deeper still. There is a link between advertising, consumer debt and the number of hours we work, and it has been found that people who see a lot of ads appear to save less, spend more and work harder to meet their rising material aspirations. In the light of our current economic crisis, these outcomes can have a terrible effect on family life and can even change the character of a nation. Burdened by debt, we are less free, less content, less resilient and, consequently, less endowed with the energy to be of service, as we feel continually compelled to buy products we can ill afford, do not really need and which do not, in the long run, make us feel any better. Sometimes this kind of non-obvious evil can do us more harm than obvious evil, because, being unaware of its capacity to harm us, we have fewer defences against it.

Indeed, if something clearly atrocious has been around for long enough, it somehow ends up becoming legitimised – becoming absorbed 'into our everyday scenery' and thus labelled 'normal'. World hunger falls into this category. What is so evil about our countenancing it is that it could be avoided totally if the world were only to organise itself more wisely, and, as I suggested earlier, if more of us haves were less greedy and shared our resources more wisely and generously.

'We kill at every step'

If all intentional killing is obviously evil (and we will look at this in more detail in the next chapter), Hermann Hesse suggested that we didn't just have to go to war to be a killer:

> *We kill at every step. Not only in wars, riots and executions. We kill when we close our eyes to poverty, suffering and shame. In the same way, all disrespect for life, all hardheartedness, all indifference, all contempt, is nothing more than killing. With just a little witty scepticism, we can kill a good deal of the future in a young person.*

In Hesse's eyes, then, many of us caterpillars are covert killers, and therefore participants in non-obvious evil. Whenever we engage in heartless behaviours that endarken, reduce or pathologise, whenever we fail to respect the humanity of another human being, we are engaging in a subtle form of killing and therefore being evil. The fact that we may be totally unaware of what we are doing and have no notion what close bedfellows evil, mild psychopathology and general unconsciousness are doesn't make our actions any less pernicious. Our lack of awareness that we are doing anything remotely evil — which I defined earlier as madness — is precisely what lies behind most non-obvious evil.

Arms-dealing

Most nations, if we explore their history, have a long list of both obvious and non-obvious evils which they have participated in. Britain is no exception. Over the years, we have propped up evil dictators and turned a blind eye to their callous behaviours because they gave us oil and served our strategic interests. We were responsible for making the slave trade into an international business. The international trade in opium was started and nurtured by us and we fought wars with China to ensure its health. We have always been ready to sell arms to almost anyone anywhere so long as we got well paid. (It was primarily the weapons we sold to Gaddafi that made it possible for him to gun down his own people.)

My point is that in none of these instances do politicians, British or other, ever believe that they are doing anything especially 'wrong', simply because every other country does the same thing. It's called realpolitik. In other words, in a brutal world — the so-called 'real world' out there — the loony logic goes that one needs to operate brutally in order to survive. This applies in particular to arms-dealing.

The thinking behind the selling of weapons is quite simple. Weapons are needed because countries fight wars, and as one can get a lot of money out of making and selling them, it is good to do so, as we need this money because we, too, need to fight wars, which is an expensive occupation. In addition, developing weapons also gives jobs to people, and shareholders who invest in those firms that manufacture them also get a good return, which also helps the economy and therefore is also seen as 'good'. As there is a lot of competition in this field, if you don't get in there first with your weapons, other countries will, and you will lose 'good business', which means your country's economy will go down, and so if you are a politician, you may not get re-elected. Therefore, you generally need to spend a lot of time pushing your arms brochures whenever you travel abroad, say, to attend peace conferences!

To a Setting Sun mindset, this all sounds perfectly logical, and if you were to meet an arms dealer (as I have done on several occasions), you would no doubt find out that he was no ghoulish fiend or serial killer, but in all probability a good father (his children are probably expensively educated on the proceeds of his business), and maybe a faithful husband. In all probability, he sees his job as simply 'business' – little different in many respects from manufacturing, say, kitchen equipment, except that it is more complicated, more fraught with risk and danger, and certainly much more lucrative, enabling one, if so inclined, to purchase a lot of costly toys!

This is why I have been stressing how important it is that our world leaders and our businessmen and those who are in positions of power be increasingly versed in the politics of Heart, as this hugely discourages a propensity to engage in certain activities, as the more we awaken to who we truly are, the more we come to understand how the universe works and the less blind we become as to what constitutes evil. Indeed, with Heart, we have access to a wholly different value system, one which allows us to stand up and say 'No. Just because thousands of people do something unethical that may be financially rewarding does not mean that I will do the same thing.' If suddenly all firms stopped producing weaponry, and all existing weapons were somehow eradicated, our world would change very radically.

Corporate evil

A great deal of non-obvious evil, and some obvious evil, gets perpetrated in the corporate world. In a recent correspondence with Elisabet Sartouris, I put to her the question of where she thought its evil primarily lay. I received the following response, which I would like to reproduce in full, only I will not name a particular corporation which she referred to, because it is known to be extremely litigious (this being part of its evil), and will simply refer to it as The Corporation. Those who are au fait with rogue multinationals may well be able to work out which one I am referring to.

> *I am opposed to pointing fingers at people (corporations are legally people in the US at least), rather than at the system permitting such*

utterly immoral practices to flourish. If you point fingers and hang the culprits, they will be quietly replaced by others and so the problem is never solved until the system is changed. That said, any names I do name herein, are to be considered immoral and ignorant of living in a loving universe rather than intentionally evil.

I believe bankers that trade third world debt or mortgages deliberately sold to people known not to have the means to repay them in order to make obscene profits are engaging in utterly immoral practices. Further, businesses such as The Corporation, with a boatload of practices ranging from engineering and selling dangerous foods, to hiding their dangers, taking organic farmers to court because its genetically modified pollen drifted into their fields, selling highly toxic herbicides etc., are equally reprehensible and should be boycotted and actively opposed. Companies that deliberately addict people to junk food with scientifically produced harmful 'flavour enhancers' are no better than cigarette companies, and possibly considerably worse. Many corporations have been identified as knowingly sacrificing ethics to profits (their names are not hard to come by); they do so in a fiercely competitive, biologically immature, capitalist growth economy that needs to be replaced by a maturely co-operative and sustainable economy based on loving human relationships.

I will give you one further example out of my own rather full dossier. Again, I won't give the name of the company, but it has a branch in Zambia. Its founder became a billionaire on the back of exposing thousands of Zambians to dangerous levels of sulphur dioxide emissions, which causes premature death from respiratory diseases and destroys crops by creating acid rain. Many children in the area around its huge plant wrote to him, asking him to do something to protect them. He did nothing and ignored all their requests.

While for the CEO, this may have implied being an 'astute businessman', for me, it is evil. It is particularly evil if a corporation makes a 'killing' (a very appropriate word) by doing their business in poor countries where they can get away with paying their employees a pittance, and where, as a result of elaborate tax avoidance schemes, the country itself not only never sees any of the benefits from the large profits which are made at its expense, but has its environment polluted in the process.

Evil and unconsciousness

A lot of non-obvious evil, then, is done unconsciously. It happens as a result of our lack of wakefulness. Heart-wise, we are too asleep to know what we are doing. This also is the case with much obvious evil. The aptly named Dr McDoom once embarked on a research project to see what it was that made people participate in the Rwandan massacres. He interviewed hundreds of people, a third of whom had been killers, and his conclusions were as follows:

> *I found that there were no significant differences in the background and belief systems between those who committed the atrocities, and the rest – except that the perpetrators were overwhelmingly men. Many were ordinary people caught up in extraordinary circumstances. I began to realise that what they did had less to do with unusual predispositions towards violence, and more to do with particular opportunities for violence.*

As we saw earlier, when we explored the Shadow, evil occurs when we get taken over by the collective shadow, which is clearly what happened in Rwanda. There, the men who did the killing were not all Hitlers or Saddam Husseins. They were just like you and me, only caught up in unusual circumstances. I stress once more: this is why our possessing Heart awareness is so important, as *with Heart, we have a powerful antidote against a propensity to commit evil*. It not only enables us to spot if evil is in the air, but also endows us with a greater amount of free will to choose not to engage in it. People whose Heart lives have begun opening up feel not only increasingly less inclined to participate in activities that harm life, but increasingly moved to engage in ones that enhance and sustain it.

Non-ordinary evil is primarily able to flourish, then, because we are mostly unaware of it and we think that doing certain things that come under the heading of 'normal' make them OK. Krishnamurti understood this only too well. 'The evil of our time', he said, 'is the loss of consciousness of evil.' One asks oneself if those pilots who dropped the bombs on Hiroshima and Nagasaki could have done so if, instead of having had numb and steely hearts – which they surely must have had – they had had hearts open to experiencing something of the enormity of the overkill and the pain and colossal suffering that their actions were about to unleash upon hundreds of thousands of innocent people. The same goes today for those who live in leafy suburban neighbourhoods and whose job is to guide the killer drones to their destinations.

Understanding non-obviously evil people

In an essay entitled *Healing Evil*, Scott Peck (referring to non-obvious evil) suggested:

> *Evil people may be rich or poor, educated or uneducated. There is little that is dramatic about them. They are not designated criminals. More often than not they will be 'solid citizens' – Sunday school teachers, policemen or bankers. They commit crimes against life and aliveness. Except in rare instances – such as the case of a Hitler – their 'crimes' are so subtle and covert that they cannot be designated as crimes. Evil people are destructive because they attempt to destroy evil, often in the name of self-righteousness instead of working it through inside themselves. They are utterly dedicated to preserving their self-image of perfection and moral purity. They dress well, go to work on time and are concerned with what others think of them. They intensely desire to appear good.*[3]

I think we all know several people who could fit into that category. Maybe we have a part of ourselves that fits as well! If so, we must own it. This is precisely why Shadow work is so very important, and why I have gone into it in such detail. Many non-obviously evil people are also to be found among the ranks of the fundamentalist religions of all denominations. They never like to own their dark sides but are forever self-righteously projecting it outside themselves. For them, the devil is always 'out there', inside others, never inside themselves. 'I am good and you are evil' is always how their thinking goes.

This mindset is of itself evil as it is inherently reductive and it emerges out of ego-woundedness, fear and narrow-mindedness. The problem with so many fundamentalists is that they arrogantly believe that they and they alone are beloved by, and will be saved by, their god, that they and they alone hold the keys to truth, and that anyone who does not agree with them and fails to see the world as they see it is not only wrong and bad, but is very often their enemy, and in certain instances (as with Muslim fundamentalism) deserve to die. This leads to a lot of obvious evil, as we will be seeing in the next chapter.

Non-obvious evil, then, is not created solely by a lack of awareness or consciousness; it is also connected to blinkered thinking, superficiality, stupidity and rigidity. This is why contemplation and continually asking ourselves deep questions as to the meaning of life are so important. In fact, the less willing we are to question our motives and actions, the greater our potential for being an instrument, in some way or other, of non-obvious evil.

What underlies obvious evil?

Obvious evil is a whole other issue. As distinct from non-obvious evil, it does have a distinctly dark or sinister dimension to it (which the actor Anthony Hopkins conveyed so chillingly when he played the part of the cannibalistic psychiatrist in *The Silence of the Lambs*). In the same way that we sense that many big-hearted people carry an aura of warmth about them, obviously evil people (possessed by the archetype of evil) generally radiate total coldness. This is because their humanity or their heart has never been activated. So how is it that certain people become *possessed* by this archetype? What is it that brings this about?

The spiritual teacher A. H. Almaas sees this kind of evil developing as a result of the absence of adequate 'holding' in early childhood, as a result of which the soul becomes estranged from divine love: 'Not only does the soul develop basic distrust, but she begins to lose the precognitive experience of holding, and the oceanic presence as her environment … She develops the position that there is no inherent benevolence in the world.'[4] As a result, when such a person connects in any way to love or goodness of any kind, they react with distrust, rejection and hatred, and

> *want to destroy it. Such a person cannot stand hearing about it, seeing it or feeling it, and feels venomous enmity and opposition towards it. He sees it as the enemy. This hatred of goodness typically manifests as hatred of God. The soul feels betrayed and abandoned.*

Almaas likened the person possessed by this kind of evil to the slobbery and hideous character of Jabba the Hutt in *Star Wars*:

> *Instead of the soul experiencing herself living in abundance, she feels deprived and empty. The boundless good is dismembered into*

material goods, to be attained, possessed and hoarded. [The evil person] loves excess, simply wants more of all material wealth, pleasure and power. It is selfish, self-centred, self-seeking, gross and primitive in its interests and aspirations.[5]

We can think of several kleptocratic and narcissistic tyrants to whom these words aptly apply. This ties in with what I was saying earlier about deficiency. Obviously evil people experience a vast sense of deficiency. Many have not yet evolved enough ego.

How do we address world evil?

Now that we understand a little more about both kinds of evil and how it manifests and what underlies it, what, as activists, do we do about it?

As I said at the start, we first need to look inside our own hearts and ask ourselves: is there evil inside us? Are we so outraged about it out in the world because it exists inside us? This self-examination is vital, for we cannot effectively deal with evil outside ourselves unless we first recognise that we might also have some kind of disposition towards it inside ourselves. However, even if we discover that this is the case, what we do about it may not be straightforward. Alexander Solzhenitsyn informs us why this is so:

If only it were all so simple! If only there were evil people somewhere insidiously committing evil deeds, and it were necessary only to separate them from the rest of us and destroy them. But the line dividing good and evil cuts through the heart of every human being. And who is willing to destroy a part of his own heart?[6]

His words only serve once more to reinforce the importance of Shadow work, where the darkness doesn't so much get 'cut out' as transformed or recycled inside the alchemical laboratory inside our hearts as we have the courage to confront our own evil and allow it to burn there. *This* is what transforms it. As we have seen earlier, some of us may be 'called' to work with species evil in this way.

A philosophical perspective on evil

However, before we are fully ready to embark on actually doing something about evil outside ourselves, there is one last question we need to ask ourselves: why does evil exist in the first place? Once asked this by a disciple, the great Indian saint Sri Ramakrishna wryly replied: 'To thicken the plot.' What did he mean? To answer this, we need to recall what I said earlier about the role of crisis, conflict and the 'oppositional forces' in the whole evolutionary process. Here, Stan Grof elaborates:

The existence of the shadow side of creation enhances its light aspects by providing contrast and gives extraordinary richness and depth to the universal drama. The conflict between good and evil in all the domains and on all the levels of existence, is an inexhaustible source of inspiration for fascinating stories ... Let us imagine for a moment that we can eliminate from the universal scheme anything that is generally considered bad or evil, all the elements that we feel should not be part of life. Initially, it might seem that this would create an ideal world, a true paradise on earth. However, as we proceed, we see that the situation is more complex. Suppose we start with the elimination of diseases ... We soon discover that this is not an isolated intervention but selectively eradicates an evil aspect of the world. This interference has a profound effect on many positive aspects of life and creation that we hold in great esteem.[7]

Grof believes that with diseases eliminated, the whole history of medicine is eliminated together with all the knowledge which it imparts. We lose all the great pioneers of modern medicine. Thus

there is also no need for the love and compassion of all those who take care of ailing people ... We lose Mother Teresa, all shamans and healers. And if there were no oppressive regimes and totalitarian systems, genocide and war, we lose all the heroic acts of freedom-fighters. There are no more triumphs of victory over evil empires and the intoxication of newly achieved freedom.[8]

We have seen how huge and courageous the heart of the Dissident grows as a result of their confronting and moving beyond fear. We also see that if, for example, the evils of the apartheid system had never existed, huge-hearted warrior activists such as Nelson Mandela would never have had the chance to emerge out of the woodwork. So we slowly begin to realise that there might even be a perverse kind of truth in the words spoken by Mephistopheles in Goethe's *Faust*, when he tells Faust that 'I am forever evil who does forever good'. In confronting evil, therefore, we need to do so in the recognition that it may serve a deeper evolutionary purpose and, at one level, exist to help us 'grow' bigger hearts.

There is an old myth that exists way back in all the great world religions. I will reduce it to one paragraph. Its gist is as follows:

> *Once upon a time, God reviewed his creation and saw that nothing was evolving. Everything was too comfortable. There was too much sunshine and goodness and milk and honey! So God realised that a further ingredient was required, and he contacted his 'good friend' (or his 'other half') the Devil, and asked if he would come along and participate in creation as things needed stirring up a bit. 'Nothing is evolving in my creation,' God said to his friend. 'If you could create some opposition and make things awkward for people, then maybe a sense of urgency would be restored and people would be moved to stretch themselves in order to deal with it.' And the Devil, who we can say represents the dark face of the divine, duly obliged!*

As Grof was suggesting, these 'devilish' or resistant forces of life which exist both inside us and outside in the world, and which oppose new life and do their best to damp a sacred culture trying to emerge – and we may call them the anti-life forces or the ultra-conservative forces or the dark or Antichrist forces – could therefore be said to have an important role to play. They exist to test our endeavours. They constitute the lifeblood of our initiations. How effectively we deal with these forces depends primarily on how courageous we are, how evolved our hearts are, and, of course, the nature of the particular situation which we happen to be encountering. Different kinds of evil need approaching in different ways. I will now suggest a few different concrete strategies that we might adopt.

Strategies for dealing with evil

Saying a resounding 'yes' to wholeness

We need to live as Heart-fully as we can, that is, with our Heart brain open all the time so as to ensure that the 'duping forces' don't pull the wool over our eyes and that we are never involved in any form of 'killing' as defined by Herman Hesse. In other words, the more aligned our lives are to our butterfly selves and the less we feel moved to engage with our world from the perspective of the mindset of the Setting Sun, the less energy we give to evil and hence the more we start playing our part in diminishing it.

This is very important to understand, as evil spreads only because in some way we subscribe to it. So if we consciously choose to surrender all our subscriptions and commit to living an ethical life where we respect everything and everyone – again I refer you to the wise advice given by the Shivapuri Baba – evil will have less and less to sustain it.

Not hating the darkness but lighting a light

This is the approach advocated by people like St Francis of Assisi in his famous 'Where there is darkness may I bring light' prayer. Here, we don't address evil head on, so much as build up our threshold of Heart light, so that it will starve evil out, in the same way that when we go into a dark room and turn on the light, the darkness vanishes. This is a wise approach, as not all of us are strong enough to confront certain kinds of evil, which are very powerful and might crush us were we to try. This approach won't work with obvious evil, since it is immune to most forms of subtle energy. During the Second World War, a few people thought that if they sent loving energy to Hitler, it would stop him. This had little effect, other than that Hitler was able to use the energy for his own purposes.

Exposing evil and naming and shaming it

Here, we bring evil out into the open – we smoke it out of its lair; we reveal it for what it is, by talking or writing about it or broadcasting information about it in some way, so that it has no place to hide. This approach can be powerful, as many kinds of evil thrive on lying low and pretending not to exist. Besides, sunlight is a powerful disinfectant. If we use this approach, however, we need to ensure that our own hearts are pure, that our facts are correct and that our defences are in place, as many kinds of evil have a very paranoid dimension to them and may use every trick in the book to fight back and do their best to harm those trying to 'out' them.

Cut out the offending evil with a scalpel

This is the approach that Barack Obama took when he ordered the night raid to 'take out' Osama bin Laden. Many will say that this is not a 'Heart approach' as it evolves killing. They may be right. However, I have thought about this a great deal and have come to the conclusion that bin

Laden was a kind of cancer on the planet, and one way of dealing with certain kinds of malignant tumour is surgically to remove them in order to ensure they do not spread. If this is done as non-invasively as possible, as this raid was done (sparing the lives of bin Laden's wives and young children), then, even though there is a killing, there can be a virtue to it, as the cancer of this particular organisation became weakened, and many lives may have been saved as a result. This approach is only to be used in very particular circumstances and is not to be seen as a general approach to evil as a whole.

Addressing evil in the areas in which we work
All areas that the activist works in contain their own kind of evil and when we see it, we need to address it. How we do so depends upon what kind of evil we are dealing with and where it is located. If, for example, we see it manifesting in the corporate world, we either say 'no' or we expose it or find ways to counteract or eliminate it.

Containing evil
In the face of very powerful forces of obvious evil, sometimes the best we can do is merely try to contain it. This is the strategy adopted by the very brave Morgan Tsvangirai in Zimbabwe, who heads the party working in opposition to President Mugabe (the apotheosis of Jabba the Hutt!). Aware that this dictator cannot be overthrown by force (he has rendered his people too weak to do this), Tsvangirai attempts to play a curbing role to try to calm the evil, so that the life of the average Zimbabwean might be a little more tolerable.

Making it difficult for evil to survive
At a political level, this may take the form of freezing the bank accounts of certain dictators and not allowing them to travel, or imposing sanctions upon particular nations that, for example, do not respect the human rights of their peoples. This approach is currently being used with Iran as a deterrent to stop her possessing a nuclear bomb. It only works so long as it hits the evildoers and not innocent people. As regards corporate evil, legislation can be passed to ensure that certain loopholes are plugged, rendering large firms less able to get away with their old shenanigans.

Concluding thoughts

The more we choose generally to stand for the values of the world of the Great Eastern Sun, the more we start creating a world that has increasingly less room for evil to grow and spread. That said, every situation involving evil needs to be dealt with individually, as what works in some situations may not do so in others. I do not suggest that we hate evil or ever try to attack it, nor that we go digging around to try and find it, rather that we only deal with it as and when it happens to show its face, and only once we have put a lot of thought into the wisest approach to adopt. If it manifests itself in an area where we feel we can be effective in doing something about it, then we should try and address it in the way we feel is best.

However, we need to tread very carefully. Certain kinds of obvious evil are extremely powerful and can subtly uncoil their tentacles inside us if we are not careful, which is why it is so important to work at centring and protecting ourselves spiritually and visualising ourselves surrounded by light. We should be especially careful about trying to take on obvious evil, unless we happen to possess the power, skills and courage of a Sharansky or an Aung San Suu Kyi. Certain kinds of evil are also very difficult to reach physically, as they are so hidden, and if we feel a strong desire to do something, it may be that the most potent weapon to use is that of prayer, requesting the 'help forces' to do the cleansing work on our behalf.

Chapter 24

Transforming War

> *Blessed are the peacemakers: for they shall be called the children of God* – MATTHEW 5:9
>
> *The power of change in the human heart is formidable. It can transform violent activists into peacemakers* – SCILLA ELWORTHY
>
> *If we use violence in order to reduce disagreements and conflicts, then we must expect violence every day* – THE DALAI LAMA

Understanding war

One of the prime ways that evil finds its expression in our society is through a predisposition on our part to wage war. As the need for peace is so important if we are to create a sustainable world for ourselves, and as it is also so dependent upon our having a greater understanding of the reason why we fight wars (we can't end them unless we know more about why we start them), I will firstly look at the psychology of war and then explore what, as activists of the heart, we might concretely do to find more appropriate ways of dealing with conflict. As terrorism is currently the world 'enemy number one', I will also look at a more Heart-centred way of approaching it.

As a species, we need to understand that we are extremely attached to violence, war and killing. Some have argued that war is innate – part of our nature. Von Clausewitz famously said that 'war is the continuation of politics by other means'. Certainly to the ancient Greeks, war was something to be gloried in, and Homer's account of the Trojan Wars in *The Iliad* used the words 'war-loving' to describe the Trojans.

The idea of war is therefore heavily imprinted into our species consciousness and it is not surprising that there is never a moment when we are not fighting a multitude of wars in different parts of the world. So prevalent is war, in fact, that many of us have come to see it as quite normal; horrible, yes, but like world hunger, a definite 'fact of life'. This is the problem.

The thesis I have been trying to put forward throughout this book is that if we want to create a more holistic society, we need to stop believing that because something has been with us for a long time and is therefore seen as normal, this means it is necessarily legitimate or sane. War is neither. Indeed, the whole idea of taking pride in killing – trying to resolve a conflict by obliterating your opposition – is a totally pathological activity. Not only is the whole war machine vastly expensive – and getting more so as it becomes more technical, with trillions of pounds being wasted on designing ever more subtle and ingenious ways to kill – but seldom does such an approach actually work in the long run. As we all know only too well, the emotional, social, political, financial and spiritual repercussions of war are hugely costly. Jesus understood this. That was why he suggested that we should 'put our sword back into its place: for all who take to the sword, will perish by the sword'.

It is interesting that Gaddafi, who waged war on his own people, vowing to 'hunt down and kill those cockroaches who oppose me, in every sewer in the land', ended up being himself hunted down like a cockroach. He was discovered emerging from a sewer, before being brutally put to death at the hands of those whom he had brutalised.

The psychology of 'enemy-creating'

If we look back at our history, we see that while wars have been fought with swords and spears, with bows and arrows and guns and germs and atomic bombs, and, more recently, with drones and in cyberspace, the mindset behind them has never wavered. It also doesn't matter if the war is hot or cold or long or short, or against a generalised or a specific enemy, or, indeed, against our own people as in civil wars. What all wars have in common is that they are evil, misinformation gets propagated, soldiers and civilians and children get killed, women get raped, people get tortured, a huge amount of suffering is created and it takes everyone involved a long time to recover. The other common factor which all wars share, is that instead of facing 'the enemy inside ourselves' – looking at the destructiveness inside our own hearts – we always create it to exist outside ourselves.

Underlying all wars, therefore, lies the projection of our individual and species Shadow. We are continually in search of convenient 'hooks' upon which to hang our hostility and destructiveness. It doesn't matter who the 'enemy of the moment' is – whether it is the Germans or the Japanese, the Vietnamese or the Chinese, communists or, more recently, terrorists. It doesn't matter whether the war is being fought over trade or water or land or oil or ideology or religion (Simon Sebag Montefiore's book Jerusalem is a horrifying account of the barbarous ways that Muslims, Jews and Christians butchered one another in the name of God); the enemy we have created always serves as an important embodiment of wrongness or evil. The insane logic goes like this: if we can put 'them' at the end of our shadow hook, then we de-skewer ourselves, we get ourselves off it, for now we have an enemy 'out there' to project all our hatred onto – to dump all our destructiveness into. Now that they have become the 'baddie', we are free to bask in the illusion of our own purity and goodness.

Politicians, attached to ideas of realpolitik, are safe in their ivory towers when they order their troops to go out and fight wars. They can be 'brave' because they don't have to go to the front line themselves. Again, it is primarily the poor people in every country – the have-nots – who march off as cannon fodder to get killed. Because war is popular (another of our insanities is that we think it a sign of a nation's 'virility' that it is prepared to fight), many world leaders have gained in popularity by initiating it. A prime example was Margaret Thatcher strategically engaging British troops in the Falklands, at a time when domestically things were not going well for her. Regrettably, it worked very much to her political advantage.

Wars are fought in order to eradicate evil

Because we don't properly understand evil (I hope a bit more clarity will have now emerged), at one level, we also fight wars in order to try to kill it off, in the belief that goodness will then reign supreme. The pattern goes like this: whomever we select to be the 'bad guys' at any time we then demonise or endarken (it is significant that all war posters depict the enemy as vermin, as sub-human, as 'Gooks', 'Huns' etc.) in the hope that if we can destroy the evil which we perceive them to embody – and which we have projected onto them – not only will goodness be restored, but there will be much more of it. In actuality, the opposite occurs. The power of evil grows bigger, and we ourselves turn into that very evil that we are seeking to eradicate. As I mentioned earlier, all the statistics show that the number of terrorist attacks in the world increased, not diminished, as a result of the invasion of Iraq in 2003.

What all nations love to do is to turn their wars into noble 'Holy Crusades' with both sides invoking God and believing God to be on their side (the 'just cause'); He will therefore help us eliminate the 'evil other'. Whether it is the Islamists fighting to rid the world of an 'evil, materialistic Western culture' so they may establish their 'godly Sharia law' (where women are denied all rights and may be stoned to death if suspected of being adulterous), or whether it was the Crusaders in the Middle Ages butchering and torturing the 'vile infidel' most horrendously in the name of Christ, the same monstrous delusions prevail. In war, all our repressed Mr Hydes are allowed out of their closets and given free rein to go on the rampage.

Wars kill hearts

Again remembering Hermann Hesse's words about killing, we see that wars not only destroy lives but they also traumatise and decimate hearts and souls in those who manage to survive them, and so a degree of emotional and spiritual 'killing' also occurs even if, physically, a person is still alive. Often, we find that people whose hearts have been badly traumatised through war lose all sense of connection to themselves and consequently, can become highly unstable and unable to think or function properly. As we saw in Chapter 18, when our hearts have been brutally murdered, often all we can think of is 'an eye for an eye and a tooth for a tooth'.

Many Palestinians today live in conditions where there is no possibility of finding work, and where members of their families have been assassinated and their properties bulldozed to the ground. The suffering and damage to their hearts can be so immense that some may totally lose the will to forgive. As I write this, Israel is talking about invading the Gaza Strip again, and the despair that this would bring may be summed up by this statement by a bereaved Palestinian, just before Israel invaded Gaza the last time: 'There is no purpose and no hope in this war that is about to swallow us in the flame of bereavement; there is no purpose to the mutual annihilation and to the approaching silence of death afterwards.'

'Look deeply into the truth of war,' the great peace activist Thích Nhat Hanh asks of us. 'Many people view it as moral, clean and liberating because they have not seen it with the eyes of heart. Show them the truth but don't be angry with them.' These words are very profound. We need to know that wars don't just happen because of 'them' (our war leaders) or for all the many political, social and economic reasons that we use to justify their necessity. *Wars also happen because of us.* Because of you and me and what lies unresolved in the darkness inside our personal and universal hearts. In Thích Nhat Hanh's words again, 'we all have war inside us, not just the soldiers'.

America: an example of a military juggernaut intent on world domination

America is no exception to this rule. While there is evidence that a great deal of change is beginning to happen and, I hope, may continue to happen under Obama, now that he has been re-elected (although I am deeply concerned by his use of drones), this is very recent. Up until a few years ago, American foreign policy had generally been embarked upon from a very aggressive perspective and had been focused primarily upon what was perceived to be in America's interest. Indeed, if we probe beneath the surface, we discover that for years she has been a master of the art of covert warfare and that in order to achieve her strategic objective of world domination, she had thought nothing of destabilising other regimes that proved obstructive. At the time of the Iraq War, John le Carré wrote an article entitled 'The United States has gone mad', in which he referred specifically to the belligerent doctrine of neo-conservatism which underlay the foreign policy of George W. Bush:

> *To be a member of the team (the neo-conservatives), you must believe in Absolute Good and Absolute Evil, and Bush is there to tell us which is which. What Bush won't tell us is the truth about why we're going to war. What is at stake is not an 'Axis of Evil' – but oil, money and people's lives. Saddam's misfortune is to sit on the biggest oilfield in the world. Bush wants it and whoever helps him will get a big slice of the cake. And who doesn't, won't. If Saddam didn't have oil, he could torture his citizens to his heart's delight. Other leaders do it every day – think Saudi Arabia, think Turkey, think Syria. What is at stake is not an imminent military or terrorist threat but the economic imperative of US growth. What is at stake is America's need to demonstrate its military power to all of us – to Europe and Russia and China and poor little mad North Korea, as well as the Middle East; to show who rules America at home and who is to be ruled by America abroad.*[1]

Many Americans had to wise up to the fact that for years, their country played the role of arrogant military juggernaut, focused on trying to dominate the world through her military power. Any country that did not fit in with her imperialistic ideals would get soundly bashed over the head. Put simply, it has been foreign policy operating at the level of the insecure and wounded ego.

Understanding terrorism

This bellicosity had resulted in America becoming extremely disliked by large segments of the global community – especially if they happened to have suffered at her hands. Also, her 'war against terror' sparked by 9/11 never worked. It actually brought many more terrorists out of the woodwork, and the terrorist constitutes a very different kind of enemy, one without any precise location. As Scilla Elworthy, director of Peace Direct, points out, 'terrorism is a tactic rather than a definable enemy. Their numbers are controlled by the level of anger and hate that drives people to join their ranks.'

Contrary to popular belief, not all suicide bombers are poor and illiterate. Many come from the ranks of the traumatised middle classes who have seen any sense of a meaningful life evaporate. To become a purveyor of death and destruction, therefore, is another example of the 'substitute unitive game' being played, endowing those whose emotional lives have been crushed with a new semblance of meaning, filling the empty hole inside their hearts.

In dealing with terrorism, we need to understand that militant Islam is much more a political ideology than it is a religion. What the Islamo-fascist desires is world domination, and death and destruction to those 'unbelievers' who don't see the world through their eyes. We are not seeing a 'clash of civilisations' as some believe (there is nothing remotely civilised about the aims of militant Islam), but a more extreme example of the same old struggle between those who wish to move forward into a new, modern, twenty-first century and those who want to stay rooted in a quasi-mythical past.

What breeds terrorism?

At one level, the terrorist has emerged in response to the injustice, materiality and heartlessness – I've called it madness – of many aspects of the world of the Setting Sun. He represents a particular fascistic facet of the species-wounded heart, acting it out in his 'holy war' of trying to kill off what he regards as evil with his own fanatical brand of what he deems to be 'goodness'. His extreme and fanatical puritanism (his worldview allows no joy, laughter or music, and women who dress provocatively, he believes, should be severely punished) represents the flip side of our decadent Western 'sex, drugs and rock 'n' roll' culture.

There are also more specific reasons behind the emergence of this militant mindset (which all moderate Muslims disassociate from and vow has nothing to do with the prophet's real teachings). 'Failed states' are prime breeding grounds. Many people also become terrorists because they live in very harsh environments, such as the Gaza Strip, where, as we just saw, there is a sense of abject hopelessness, which has the effect of closing people's hearts down, thus making them more susceptible to being brainwashed by fanatical ideas.

Ed Hussein, who was born in England and who, for some years, embraced radical Islam until he 'saw the light', recognised that there is also much about British society that has made it a fertile breeding ground for potential extremists. He felt that a toxic combination of politically correct policy, denial and fear had opened the way for hate to grow in our midst, and that no proper programmes existed to enable Muslims to become better integrated into our society – no way for immigrants arriving in England to learn about our English way of life. He also recognised that prisons served as powerful recruiting centres, that satellite TV channels transmitted distorted radical Islamic messages into many Muslim homes, justifying the use of killing in the name of one's religion, and that nothing was ever done about any of these things.

We also see how totalitarian societies – where people are routinely terrorised and denied their basic human rights – are also highly fertile breeding grounds for organisations such as al-Qa'ida, as those who have been terrorised are then moved to 'act out' their terror onto others. Many autocratic rulers also like to distract their subjects' attention away from the fact that it is they who are responsible for keeping them poor and miserable, by paying large sums to rogue imams to come and preach distorted messages, telling them that *all* their woes are due to the 'evil Americans' and their equally 'evil Israeli cronies'.

Handling terrorism at an inner level

Handling terrorism is not only the responsibility of our governments; it needs to be the responsibility of all of us. If we are to deal effectively with it, it is important that we stop thinking of a 'war against terror' – that is, playing the terrorist at his own game, which has not worked – and think of subtler and wiser approaches. We can begin by looking inside ourselves individually, exploring the contents of our own hearts and asking ourselves if we are guilty of Islamophobia in any way. Are we unconsciously playing our part in helping make Muslims feel unwelcome? Do we enshadow or 'kill' them in some way? The answer is probably, for many of us, yes. Ever since the fateful 9/11, a paranoia around Muslims has persisted, analogous to the way that many Americans used to feel about communists in the 1950s, when they believed there was a 'Red under every bed'.

This needs to stop. Indeed, the more each of us can reach out with our hearts in a befriending way towards Muslims and start 'walking in their shoes' and help with their integration into our society, the better. Remember: in the story of Frankenstein, what made the monster monstrous was the way he was treated. He wasn't born a monster; he became one, terrorising his creator because of the way he had been ostracised by him. The authorities can also take steps to ensure that prisons are no longer seedbeds for subversive ideas, that more effective steps are taken to ensure that Muslims arriving in England are integrated into our society and are made to learn English, and that radio stations that deal with fanatical material are closed down.

Integration is key. At a global level, the fewer rogue states or failed states on our planet (all of which are products of the have–have-not dichotomy), the fewer breeding grounds we will have for terrorists. Just as mosquitoes vanish when the fertile swamps where they breed are drained, so the number of terrorists will dwindle as the 'underworlds' on the planet become fewer. Deep down, we need to see terrorism as a cry for help. It is yet another symptom of an unsustainable system and the yawning gulf that exists between haves and have-nots, and in its violence and extremism, it mirrors this schism.

Islamists waking up and 'seeing the light'

Although I know that those who are hawkishly inclined and who believe that the only way to deal with terrorism is to use brute force will laugh at what I am now about to suggest, I nevertheless sense that the closer we get to the turning point, the more the new zeitgeist or spirit of our times will start playing an increasingly significant role both in the life of the terrorist and in the way in which the rest of the world relates to terrorism. The more the 'tide of love' begins to rise, the greater will be its dampening effect upon humanity's proclivity for violence and many terrorists may well feel moved to begin asking themselves serious questions as to what it truly means to be a committed Muslim.

I see the power of the awakening universal heart starting to influence other radicalised Muslims in the way that it did Ed Hussein, and believe that in the coming years, many will start to 'wake up' and see the light. I predict, therefore, that, species-wise, after we have gone through our 'dark night' and started moving into our 'new dawn' characterised by our world gradually becoming healthier and more unified, many terrorists will tire of living in thrall to such a violent mindset, and will be moved to start laying down their weapons and to feel inspired to attend training camps – not to be learn to be more efficient killers but to become more genuinely devout Muslims.

Yes, terrorists are right in that there is something inherently decadent and evil about the Western materialist worldview (today, as I write, the stock market in America is higher than it has ever been, yet more and more people are experiencing greater poverty than ever), but trying to combat one evil with another, as we have seen, is never any solution to a problem. As the old system begins to crumble, and as more and more people begin attuning to the power of the universal heart, many of these evils will start melting away and as they do so, the impulse behind terrorism will also begin to wane. For example, many of those who see their main *raison d'être* in life as being the destruction of the state of Israel and who consistently refuse to acknowledge her existence may well come to see that continuing to carry this old hatred inside their hearts all day is no way to live and that it also condemns them to a deathly existence. Increasingly, therefore, it will be recognised that to surrender such worldviews is not a loss but a victory, not a step backwards but a movement forward for all of humanity, one that heralds the possibility of real peace emerging in the world.

I am suggesting that there are far too many genuinely wise and Heartful young people all over the planet who want real freedom and who are prepared to work for it and whose combined Heart force (an idea whose time has come) has so much more potency than terrorism (an idea whose time will rapidly wane). Further, the numbers of these 'new world servers' or activists for a healthier world are ever increasing. I therefore predict that as the power of the new world of the Great Eastern Sun starts to grow, and as increasing numbers of have-nots become integrated into this new society, many of those who have been radicalised will come increasingly to realise how utterly morally bankrupt and insane their worldview really is.

All these changes, of course, will take time, so I am not saying the governments of the world should in any way relax their surveillance in this area, for, as I suggested earlier, the next few years may well be very challenging and difficult – and it may well seem as if things are only getting worse.

Terrorism and the Arab Spring

We are already seeing evidence of a shift along the lines I have been suggesting in the way the Arab Spring has now moved into its 'winter phase'. Among other things, it has shown Arab leaders that terrorism and repressive regimes go hand in hand, and that their war against terror has actually created more terrorists, while many Western world leaders have also had to learn how wrong they were – politically, socially and morally – to believe that propping up evil regimes which suppressed Islamic fundamentalism, would help them in their war against terror. In fact, it has been quite to the contrary. By assisting the Gaddafis and the Mubaraks, the West had actually been encouraging terrorism.

What the Arab Spring/Winter is starting to reveal is that the disaffected youth in the Arab world are already being given a powerful alternative to the murderous jihadism of Al-Qa'ida. There is currently much evidence to suggest that a kind of Islamism is emerging in many countries undergoing regime change that is much less fanatical. Even before Osama bin Laden's death, his organisation was in retreat. I believe that what many of the young people who today embrace terrorism *actually* want, in their heart of hearts, is what young people the world over truly want, namely freedom, respect, the opportunity to earn a decent living, the chance to hang out with friends and to enjoy life and better themselves – all things that were denied them under the old dictatorial regimes. Once they start to realise that it may be possible for them to have these things without all the trimmings of 'Western decadence' that quite rightly, they have reacted against, and that this may actually be much more liberating than a life dedicated to blowing up 'non-believers', a quantum shift will occur.

As more young men come into positions of power, the whole need for jihad, predicated on a position of feeling powerless, will start to diminish. The less fanatical Islamists being elected in countries that have recently overthrown tyrants are increasingly becoming aware that what most people want is more jobs and opportunities and that they will vote for those who give them these things, and not for those who offer more murderous extremism. We are therefore already starting to witness the rise of a more progressive Islam, and I believe that as the Western world also begins to make positive changes, we will see a whole new spirit of rapprochement between Islam and the West, which will result in greater numbers of those who currently feel disenfranchised being brought back into the fold.

In the years ahead, then, I see more and more young Muslims feeling impelled to become activists, not for the worldwide implementation of Sharia law, but to support Islam to continue to evolve in a wise and integrated way into the twenty-first century. The more our Western governments seek to address the many causes of terrorism and stop trying to attack its symptoms, the more these shifts will be empowered to take place. Also, our biggest allies in the struggle with terrorism lie in those many millions of moderate Muslims, many of whom already live in the West and who are shocked and embarrassed by the behaviours of their extremist brothers and sisters and in no way wish any kind of association with them.

Shifting away from war

So despite the fact that as I write, many wars are currently being waged and there is evidence aplenty of terrorist activity in different areas of the globe, my heart nevertheless feels hopeful as I look towards the long-term future. The wind of change beginning to blow on our planet is inducting a new spirit of realism not only inside the Islamist heart, but inside all of us. Species-wise, I believe we are all growing tired of war with all its debilitating economic, spiritual and moral costs.

Here too, our financial crises can also be a blessing, as most countries can no longer afford to fight wars and are focusing on reducing their military forces. (Even if America had another gung-ho George Bush in the White House, she can no longer afford to play the role of global bully/policeman, and this is to be celebrated, and I disagree with those who are critical of her, suggesting that America is now abnegating her responsibilities. I say she has just decided to stop interfering and trying to control the world so much!)

Just as in the Arab Spring, where the new, 'wised up' young took to the streets to protest against dictatorships, so I predict in the years ahead that more and more people from every country will take to the streets to march for peace, and that the peace movement will grow in strength and maturity and be a significant factor in the turning point. It is also my sense that use of the death-dealing drone, which is itself a terrifying weapon, and which has been killing many innocent people and so only serves to create new converts to terrorism, will be stopped sooner rather than later. Killing terrorists is never a solution.

Surrendering hostile attitudes

If we want peace in the world, all of us have a role to play, and here, what is vitally important is that we start surrendering the hostile attitudes which some of us may hold towards those nations which are in thrall to horrendous regimes, whereby we equate their citizens with their regimes. This is very unjust. Yes, agreed, 'we all have war inside us', some of us, perhaps, more so than others – and certainly the neo-cons in their brief outing gave America a very bad name – but the truth is that the vast majority of Americans are not neo-cons. I lived in the States for many years and found many to be fine world servers, deeply committed to making a difference and horrified by the warmongering of their leaders.

On a similar note, to call Russia evil because it is headed by Putin, or to see the Chinese people as being cast in the same mould as their democracy-averse leaders, is also to do both great nations a disservice. There are very many fine Russians and fine Chinese working tirelessly in very difficult conditions to try to move their countries into the twenty-first century. The same, of course, is true with Iran, which has the misfortune to be currently governed by a bunch of non-democratically elected, Islamic fundamentalist thugs who support terror around the world, and who in no way reflect the poetry and wisdom of the noble Iranian soul. Indeed, the desires of the majority of the Iranian people could not be further from the bellicose viciousness and paranoia of the ayatollahs controlling the show and terrified of losing their power and privileges, and the very last thing the average young Iranian wants is for their country to wipe half of Israel off the map and get obliterated in return.

The same is true about North Korea, which has also been described as an 'evil nation'. It is not. Its leadership is. Its people may be poor and uneducated, but they are essentially peace-loving. Unlike those who govern them, they don't have an inferiority complex about not being important enough on the world stage, and the last thing they are interested in is flexing their nuclear muscles in a macho way to prove how strong they are. This is the psychopathology of the leadership, which the new leader, the chubby-cheeked low-lifer Kim Jong-un, seems to have inherited from his father and predecessor, the totally weird Kim Jong-il. It is important, therefore, that we hold the peoples in those countries who are in thrall to despotic regimes tenderly inside our hearts and realise that they need all our love and prayers.

The war games which nations like to enact together are simply another expression of the various hostile and manipulative games that we individuals play out with one another when our egos are wounded and we lack sufficient Heart to be able to deal with our conflicts and differences in a mature way. Just as at a personal level, when our hearts emerge out of hiding, they enable us to bring the spirit of reconciliation into our lives, so the same thing holds true on the world stage, and I stress once more that the greatest antidote to war is the emergence of the universal heart in all its many reconciliatory capabilities. The more each of us is willing to work on behalf of the greater blossoming of this heart, the more we are doing for the cause of world peace.

Giving peace a chance

So, as John Lennon said all those years ago, let's 'give peace a chance'. Here is where we activists have an important role, as what transpires in the future is built out of what we all do today. No matter in what specific way we have chosen to be of service, all of us have a responsibility to work at building up the 'peace muscles' inside our hearts and to support others to do the same thing. As the Dalai Lama put it:

We talk about peace a great deal. But peace has a chance to flourish only when the atmosphere is congenial. We must create that atmosphere. In order to do that, we must adopt the right attitude. Peace therefore must basically first come from within ourselves.[3]

Ending war, therefore, needs to be a conscious choice. It has to manifest in how we live our everyday lives. We also need to change the consensus belief about war being normal and inevitable and debunk the myth that the only way to resolve certain problems is by brute force, and the way we do this is by working at opening our hearts to subtler and wiser ways of resolving conflicts. Above all, our politicians need to be made to understand, in no uncertain terms, that if they want our votes, they had better move away from their old belligerent stances.

Specific peace activists also have a role to play in helping military leaders shift their attitudes away from thinking war to believing peace, and investing more energy in soldiers' roles as peacekeepers. Most soldiers are naturally brave and committed people. If appropriately trained, they can do a huge amount of good. Here, I particularly think of those brave warriors who de-activate mines or who patrol the streets in dangerous areas to protect the local people, or who offer physical assistance when a country is hit by a natural disaster. We must not disband our armed forces. Rather, we need to campaign to see that they are employed in jobs other than killing. There is also a need for more people to be trained in the art of conflict resolution and for them to be sent out to troubled areas and work with the local troublemakers in 'hot spots'. The reason many peace initiatives initiated from the top down so often fail is that they are not effectively coordinated with similar ones orchestrated from the bottom up. This needs to change.

So too, must the myth that one cannot negotiate with terrorists. If this is the case with some terrorists, then one must find those whom one can dialogue with. After all, they are human beings just like ourselves, and we may need to take them out of the boxes labelled 'inhuman' that we may have put them into, and start seeing them through the eyes of our hearts. One can also think of strategies such as offering them work and paying them money, as in many instances the only way of financially surviving for many is to join, say, the Taliban. Indeed, it is always far more profitable to pay people not to fight than to spend money killing them, as the killing game is the most expensive of all options.

Peace initiatives created locally – that is, by men and women who actually live in those areas where conflict is breaking out – are generally the most effective. This is not surprising since local people understand much better than any outsider what is going on, and also have a greater incentive to wish to end hostilities. If ever a genuine and truly lasting peace does 'break out' between the Israelis and the Palestinians, it will undoubtedly owe a great deal to whatever both sides are doing at a grass-roots level to bring it about.

What can each of us do specifically to help end war?

There are eight main things.

1. We need to examine ourselves thoroughly and make sure that we work through all vestiges of 'war consciousness' that may exist inside our hearts, both at individual and at species levels. At the same time, we need to work at developing our 'peace muscles' along the lines we have already explored, remembering that being peaceful is a very active state. Thus, we need to be at peace with ourselves and with others, including, as we saw in the chapter on forgiveness, those whom we feel may have hurt us.

    We cannot stand for peace unless we are peace and it is embodied in all our relationships. We also remember that this does not mean we are against war, or indeed, against anyone or anything. The more we radiate peace into the world, the more powerfully this particular archetype becomes activated. Here, Radiator activists can play a key role.
2. We can put our money where our hearts are, by giving to organisations and individuals working on behalf of peace. Scilla Elworthy's Peace Direct, for example, raises money to train people in conflict resolution to go and work in trouble spots, and is a very fine cause to support. There are many important peace groups all over the world, and we need to find those that we most resonate with, and, if we feel inspired, we may even feel moved to work for them.
3. We can help educate people to be more open to ideas of peace through giving lectures and seminars on this subject.
4. We can organise peace groups, where people gather together regularly in order to demonstrate for peace.
5. We can keep abreast of any peace initiatives taking place and alert the media to give them greater coverage.
6. We can go on peaceful demonstrations.

7. We can ensure that we have no investments in any companies that are in any way connected with the war machine and, if possible, ensure that none of our taxes go to fund any war effort.
8. We can meditate on peace and can pray for peace (along the lines suggested earlier).

Conclusion

As those forces in the world responsible for unifying and integrating opposites gradually grow stronger, we will see evolutionary advances on every front. Those who have not yet developed a proper ego will start shifting from a pre-egoic state into an ego state while those still attached to their egocentricity will begin embracing Heart values. The United Nations will become much more effective, as it will start operating out of a 'higher order' planetary centre. War consciousness will gradually start winding down as a result of increasing numbers of top-down and bottom-up initiatives for peace being orchestrated all over the world, and as we move beyond our old win/lose model and increasingly start focusing on creating an environment that prevents violence, protects people and gives increasing support to the world's have-nots. I will leave the last word to Sam Keen:

> *We have to work at the tasks of creating psychological and political alternatives to war, changing the structure of* Homo hostilis *and the structures of international relations. This requires both a heroic journey into the self and a new form of compassionate politics. We have no chance of lessening warfare unless we look at the psychological roots of paranoia, projection and propaganda, nor if we ignore the harsh, child-rearing practices, the injustice, the special interests of power elites, the historic racial, economical and religious conflicts and population pressures that sustain the war system. If we desire peace, each of us must begin to demythologise the enemy, cease politicising psychological events, re-own our shadows and be conscious of how we have unconsciously created a warrior psyche and have perpetuated warfare in its many different modes.*[4]

Chapter 25

Awakening the Corporate Heart

We believe that if the corporate world does not play an active role in redefining its own operations and moving towards sustainability, the world as a whole will not succeed in that task – FRITJOF CAPRA

Businesses, because they wield unparalleled wealth and power, are a key factor in the equations that decide the human future – ERVIN LASZLO

The importance of the corporate world

Innovation is inordinately expensive. If a new culture – if the world of the Great Eastern Sun – is to come fully into being, many, many trillions of pounds are going to be needed to finance it. And where is this money to come from? Certainly not from activists, most of whom do not devote their lives to becoming rich. We also cannot depend on the philanthropy of a few generous wealthy individuals. Nor can we rely on governments, many of which at this time of financial crisis are strapped for cash and are doing their utmost to cut costs.

Most of the money has to come from the corporate world, not only because this is where the money resides, but also because it possesses the enterprise and capability to get things done. And a lot of things need doing – and doing well – if a new and better world is to come into being. Therefore, the more that those who run businesses work at finding their heart and souls, and in so doing, discover what the true or 'deeper' purpose for their businesses is (we cannot discover the corporate heart unless we first discover our own hearts), the greater the possibility that changes for the good will occur. The IBM founder, Thomas J. Watson Sr, understood this: 'Companies were not created just to make money but to knit together the whole fabric of civilisation.' The fact that in recent decades, many companies have been doing the very opposite does not mean that this trend is bound to continue and that many important changes are not also taking place in the corporate world. For they are. Bill Clinton is optimistic:

> *Charity alone will not solve the world's problems. Capitalism can help and at the same time, put people back to work. As our world and our economies evolve, we have an opportunity and a responsibility to reconsider how to rethink the relationship between economic and social challenges, so that benefits and opportunities are available to more people.*[1]

And this is precisely the challenge confronting businesses today. All sorts of new initiatives, born of a vision of a better society, need to come into being. Many of these new 'cultural strategies' require financial support if they are to get off the ground. To give one small example, following the publication of this book, I intend to start the Institute for Spiritual Activism.

The Institute of Spiritual Activism

Unfortunately, my earnings from my consulting practice and lectures and seminars are not sufficient to fund this enterprise. So I am going to approach certain people in the corporate world and request their support, as I know that the 'wind of change' that has been blowing into other areas of life is also starting to blow into the business world. I know from my own work with corporations that the universal heart is beginning to come alive in many executives today, and that they are starting to ask serious questions as to the deeper purpose of their lives and their businesses. Indeed, I never fail to be moved by just how many executives are open to self-exploration and to connecting more deeply with dimensions of themselves that are tender and vulnerable. Many show a genuine willingness to think outside the box and to confront their own and their corporation's Shadow sides; they are increasingly recognising that to continue in their old ways is not only to guarantee failure, but in many instances, is also morally repugnant.

I celebrate this fact and I only intend to approach those in the corporate world who I feel are kindred spirits and share a similar vision, and might like to be part of this project, because they would like their lives to be about making a difference and are prepared to put some money and ingenuity where their hearts are. I trust in the 'help forces' to support me in my endeavour and that if there is anything worthwhile in this initiative, exactly the right people and right resources required for this project to succeed will be drawn to me. Should you be in any way interested in participating with your ideas or even perhaps joining up in some way – I plan to have key activists in all the different fields come and give talks and share their know-how – I would ask that you get in touch with me.

The emergence of the corporate activist

Just as I feel positive that a new 'rising tide of love' is starting to enter the way we 'do' relationships and is making many of us grow tired of war and long for peace, I also see much evidence of it impacting upon the corporate arena, as with my own eyes, I have been seeing enormous changes taking place, particularly over the last five years. Even as the dark side of corporate life is emerging more and more into the light and we are becoming increasingly aware of corporate evil as never before, so a whole new quality of corporate Heart is also starting to come to the fore. In many instances, it has been crisis that has served as the catalytic trigger. To give you one example of how this can occur, I enclose, in full, an email which I received a few months ago from a middle-aged 'high flyer' (or, more accurately, an ex-high flyer), who had attended one of my spiritual retreats some years before. It is an excellent example of how a material loss at one level can result in a huge gain of heart at another. It deeply touched me.

> *Hey, Serge, I just wanted to let you know what has been going on with me since I last saw you and tell you that when I first attended your seminar in 2007, I thought you were a bit of a crackpot, one of those 'new age' cuckoo guys talking a load of codswallop, and thus something in me would not allow me properly to hear your message. Or perhaps I just didn't want to, as I was too flush with all my success as I was making large amounts of money at that time.*
>
> *Well, what has happened to me over the last years since I saw you, is that, primarily due to my greed and my speculating going awry, I have lost almost all the assets that I had, and what this is awakening in me, is not only a sense of financial loss but, much more importantly, a sense of the spiritual loss I have been suffering all those years, where I realise that all I was really interested in was making money and the power and status that having plenty of it gave me.*
>
> *And curiously, it is this second loss that I now recognise has been*

with me for so long, that I find the most devastating. I now realise how shallow my life has been and how much, while being feted as a financial success, I had lost my way as a human being. Now that I don't have all those 'things' that I once had to distract me from myself — I have had to sell all my 'toys' — I no longer need to feel superior to others poorer than me.

Actually, it is a relief to tell you this. What I am now asking myself is: what were all my things or possessions really for, other than to ensure my heart stayed closed so I could feel superior to people like you, who, unlike myself, didn't devote all their waking moments to thinking how they could make more money in order to impress people! How sad and pathetic. What a loser I was from a human viewpoint.

Serge, now that I have very little and not much work, I guess I have time for another, much more important kind of work — to discover what it means to be a human being. I really have lost my heart and I want to find it again. I know it must be around somewhere, as from time to time, it gives me little fluttery reminders of its presence. I feel it a tiny bit now as I write to you. I also understand what Jesus meant when he said that it was harder for a rich man to discover himself — or find his heart — than for a camel to go through the eye of the needle. Having far more money than we really need can be so seductive, unless one is a very wise and enlightened person and knows how to use it to bring good things to the world, to help others — and I certainly wasn't that person. I used it all for me — to bolster up my sad little ego. I feel so ashamed. May I come back now and work with you again, and get your help to birth a new me that I feel is desperately wanting to be born?

If that isn't the voice of a huge, humble, honest heart speaking, I don't know what is. It is so true what he says. Unless we are wise and know how to use our surplus funds to help others less fortunate than ourselves, having too much money can be a terrible obstacle to our becoming a genuine human being. As Ervin Laszlo points out, many business leaders are increasingly realising that

today, it is not enough to 'do good' as additional philanthropy while focussing single-mindedly on 'doing well' in the marketplace. The need is for those major companies who have the wealth and power, *to become forces for the public good not by philanthropy but by re-orienting their companies.*²

This is slowly starting to happen. As Fritjof Capra expressed it in his recent book *Steering Business towards Sustainability*, 'if business does not change its strategy, business itself may well be at stake'. Many business leaders are increasingly coming to see this. They are recognising that if their firms are to have any chance of surviving, the way they approach their work must radically change and that doing good and being successful do not necessarily have to exist on opposing sides of the fence. They are becoming aware, too, that their shareholders are also starting to 'wise up' and are capable of distinguishing between companies that make an effort genuinely to be of service to their local community and those that still like to play it close to the wind, and that they are much more likely to invest in those whom they trust and see as behaving ethically.

In my own work with organisations, I find that many executives value an approach that puts an emphasis on the *'being'* side of their nature, instead of what they were always being told in their business schools: the main things that are of importance are to *know* more and *do* more and think more strategically and rationally. Many welcome my programme that stresses that if they wish to 'do better', they also need to 'feel better' and 'be better', and that there are other ways to measure success than financial.

In this context, I am finding that increasing numbers of senior executives today are feeling moved to reflect deeply on the meaning of 'sustainability' and are becoming increasingly aware of how important it is to steer their businesses in that direction. Many are also learning that the technologies of many so-called 'primitive cultures' are actually highly advanced and Heart centred, and that these cultures' knowledge of social interaction and communal relations embodies a wisdom that is urgently needed in the corporate world. Therefore they are starting to visit those areas of the planet where this knowledge is available. I find this very positive. For far too long, we have enshadowed indigenous people and believed that because we were more sophisticated, we were superior. We are consequently discovering what an illusion this is.

Why can 'big business' be so important?

While you and I might talk about the terribleness of toxic waste or burning too many fossil fuels, as individuals we are limited as to what concretely we can do about it. Big business, on the other hand, can do a lot and can also start creating products that are truly needed. In Richard Branson's words:

> *If I go and live on a farm in Scotland and grow organic vegetables and have a little wind-powered plant, I'm not going to feed two million people in the UK or make much of a contribution to reduce global carbon. But industry with its massive resources, can and must, do this. It is up to big companies like Virgin to lead the way with a holistic approach, which, while creating and maintaining successful, entrepreneurial companies, also help maintain the balance of nature and do as little harm as possible.*[3]

This is pure Stradivarius speak. While in all probability there may be one or two areas in which Virgin is not yet 'totally holistic' in everything it does, and critics could no doubt find one or two inconsistencies were they to dig around, I don't think this matters. What matters is the direction that an organisation as a whole is intending to go, and where the CEO's heart is focused, and everything I read about Branson about how he approaches his work, and the way he works hard and has fun with it (and also makes space to have fun outside work), tells me that his heart is very much in the right place and that he is wholly committed to helping save the planet. Happily, there are also many other wealthy 'visionary entrepreneurs' who, like him, are emerging out of the woodwork, and this is to be greatly celebrated. If one happens to have a good heart as well as a few spare million on hand, one is capable of making a very considerable difference indeed.

The unacceptable face of capitalism

What I believe has gone so wrong with capitalism is not the system itself, but the low level at which people have engaged with it. What we call capitalism's dark, 'unacceptable face', symbolised by a well-known merchant bank recently described as a 'giant vampire squid, eager to get its tentacles around anything smelling of money', is created by the wounded ego or the deficient Heart state of normal man, wholly disconnected from experiencing the beneficence of the universe. This mindset, we remind ourselves, is inherently non-compassionate; it is overly materialistic and insecure, feels separate from the world, is not interested in doing good (unless the good can be seen and acknowledged), can never see life in terms of larger wholes, and consequently uses capitalism solely to serve its own self-centred, deficient and neurotic agendas. That is why capitalism has an evil face to it. What is needed, which I argue is now slowly starting to emerge, is a *'capitalism with Heart'*, where the spirit of free enterprise can instead be touched by the rising tide of love – a shift from caterpillar capitalism to butterfly capitalism.

Capitalism with Heart

Again, Richard Branson is one of many entrepreneurs starting to think along these new lines. He likes to use the term 'Gaia capitalism', because he recognises that since he is part of Gaia's self-regulatory mechanism, as a businessman he must assume responsibility for the health of the planet. Paul Hawken explores this idea more fully. In his book *Natural Capitalism*, he suggests applying market principles to all sources of material value and most importantly, to all natural resources. He argues that a new kind of capitalism needs to emerge which must include all the familiar resources used by us, that is, water, minerals, oil, trees, fish, soil, air and so on.

This 'natural capitalism' must also encompass living systems, which includes grasslands, savannahs, wetlands, estuaries, coral reefs and rainforests. He believes that there is a vast array of ecologically smart options available to businesses, and that it is possible for society and industry to adopt them. The following words, with which he opens his book, paint a picture of how our new society might look, if businesses began operating according to these principles:

> *A world where cities have become peaceful – cars and buses are whisper quiet, parks and greenways have replaced unneeded urban freeways. OPEC has ceased to function because the price of oil has fallen to $5 a barrel, but there are few buyers for it because cheaper and better ways now exist to get the services people once turned to oil to provide. Involuntary unemployment no longer exists and income taxes have been largely eliminated. Houses, even low income housing units, can pay part of the mortgage costs by the energy they produce. Atmospheric CO2 levels are decreasing for the first time in 200 years, and industrialised countries have reduced resource use by 80%, while improving the*

quality of life. With the exception of family-wage jobs, welfare demand has fallen. A progressive and active union movement has taken the lead to work with business, environmentalists and government, to create 'just transitions', as society phases out coal, nuclear energy and oil. In communities and towns, churches, corporations and labour groups promote a new, living wage social contract as the least expensive way to ensure the growth and preservation of valuable social capital. Is this the vision of a Utopia? In fact the changes described here, could come about in the decades to come as a result of economic and technological trends already in place.[4]

I find this hugely inspiring. As someone once said, 'we have the know-how to create a better world. What we don't yet have is the willingness to implement it.' Perhaps this is about to shift. Hawken suggests that what is needed in the world is 'a new type of industrialism, one that differs from the system that is the standard today', and that as the human population doubles,

a remarkable transformation of industry and commerce can occur through this transformation, and our society will be able to create a vital economy that uses radically less material and energy ... This economy can free up resources, reduce taxes on personal income, increase per capita spending on social ills (while simultaneously reducing those ills) and begin to restore the damaged environment of the earth. These necessary changes done properly, can promote economic efficiency, ecological conservation and social equity.[5]

If you are interested in learning more about his evolutionary ideas for addressing our environmental and economic ills, I recommend you read his very important book.

Three examples of truly Heart-centred businesses

I will now give you three examples of sustainable businesses that have been started by three remarkably wise and visionary individuals, each of which utilises our planetary capital in a slightly different way.

Example One
A large factory in Brazil had for many years spent a fortune burying its waste in huge pits, polluting the environment. A new boss came to run it and the first

thing he did was to connect it up with a waste management company, which processed its waste, turned it into fertiliser and other products for organic farming and sold it to a network of organic farmers. As a result, there was no more environmental degradation, the factory saved a huge amount of money, and 99 per cent of the processed waste got sold. This waste-processing involved low technology, was labour intensive and gave many local people full-time jobs. The owner also runs a landscaping company and therefore created a park right on the factory site. Instead of waste dumps, there are now fish ponds with reeds and an abundance of birds. The whole park is now a thriving ecosystem, wrapped around the factory.

Example Two
In Nepal, one of the poorest countries in the world, Sulo Shah was born into privilege but shunned a promising career in government to initiate a carpet-weaving business that would employ women. In spite of early teething difficulties, the business took off. Thirty women were employed in the first year, thirty more the following year. All were from the poorest levels of society. Sulo Shah refused to employ children, as is common in Nepal, but realised that sending them home when their mothers were working in the factory was not the solution. By slightly raising the price of her carpets, she was able to build a school alongside her factory that eventually allowed two thousand children to be taken off the streets and receive an education. Before she started her work, half the carpet makers in Nepal had been children. After her initiative, the numbers fell to 5 per cent.

To give an example of her human solidarity work, in a difficult year when sales to Europe were down, she was obliged to lay off some of her workers. To her immense surprise, the slightly better-off employees volunteered to be laid off, so that the very poorest ones would stay in work. Good years then ensued and they were all called back, but a wonderful spirit of solidarity had been established in the company. Sulo Shah managed to duplicate her model of operation in textiles and created a huge holding company.

Example Three
In 2007, Mohammad Yunus founded the Grameen Bank, and was awarded the Nobel Peace Prize for his invention. It specialises in making small loans ('microcredits') to poor people, mainly women, without requiring collateral. It embodies what Yunus calls 'social business' – a way to use the power of

business to tackle a wide spectrum of social problems, from poverty and pollution to inadequate health care, lack of education and hunger. Yunus foresees a world becoming increasingly transformed by thousands of social businesses created along similar lines.

It is my belief that in twenty years' time, these imaginative and essentially compassionate ways of approaching business are going to be the norm instead of the exception, and that we will find many similar, visionary enterprises emerging all over the world.

Traditional corporations moving towards sustainability

What is also very positive is that emerging out of corporate evil are increasing numbers of traditional organisations making definite attempts to move in more life-enhancing and sustainable directions. Some firms are trying to design production processes that provide a greater livelihood for the local workforce, while using the fewest possible non-renewable materials in their products. They are also learning to honour the human needs of their employees, as opposed to trying to squeeze every last bit of juice out of them. In this instance, I will name a few names.

The large blue-chip insurance firm RSA (whose stocks are among the most reliable and high yielding on the FTSE 100) has gone into partnership with the World Wide Fund for Nature, to sponsor a series of environmental projects. It is taking particular interest in the future of the polar bear. Its CEO realises that with huge losses due to climate change, it can in no way afford to neglect awareness of the environment. Rio Tinto is currently investing in solar and wind projects, while Coca-Cola, Nestlé and Pepsico are all trying to improve their environmental records, becoming increasingly convinced about the benefits of sustainability. Unilever has succeeded in reducing its CO_2 emissions by 44 per cent, while Canon, the Japanese maker of cameras and photocopiers, has shifted away from using batteries, which are an environmental hazard, and is currently testing flexible, amorphous solar cells which could provide energy without affecting the environment. As metals are hard to recycle when combined with plastics, they have been eliminated from Canon cameras, which are being redesigned with parts that can be reused, and all lead has been eliminated because of its known toxicity. I could give many more examples.

Sceptics may say that these organisations are only making these changes because they have seen the writing on the wall and are basically the same old wolves, only now they are trying to reinvent themselves and pretend to be sheep. Whether or not there is any truth to this argument with some firms, we need to acknowledge that the changes that are happening are positive ones (one has to begin somewhere) and seem to be moving in the right direction. Just as in our personal development, our hearts need to open gradually and we can't progress from closed-heartedness to huge-heartedness overnight, so this holds true at a corporate level. Interestingly, if an organisation starts making external shifts, they often begin to percolate down into its inner culture as well. I recently consulted with an organisation that was starting to move into new, more sustainable waters. While I discovered that this was initially being done from an ulterior motive – that is, to 'look progressive' – it nonetheless transpired that the entire firm began thinking along new lines, and quite spontaneously stopped manufacturing a particular product, which, while financially lucrative, was deemed detrimental to the environment and therefore not in alignment with the new direction in which the organisation now found itself headed.

The challenges facing the business community

All businesses today are therefore confronted with the same kinds of challenge which we have seen apply in all other areas of life, namely, to shift from doing things in caterpillar ways to embracing more of a butterfly approach. Given the crises that I have suggested might lie ahead if these changes do not occur, it is in all businesses' interest to try to transform themselves as comprehensively and as imaginatively as possible. Included in this is how they view and utilise money. Greed has to go out of the window along with undeserved gargantuan bonuses. Greater generosity is also required.

It is not as if many 'old style' organisations don't give money to charities or don't extend their support to outside causes. For they do. However, all too often, the funds are not directed to those areas where there is most need. Many large firms are willing to support a cause only if there is something in it for them. Thus, they tend to sponsor glamorous sporting events or give money to some cultural happening that is in the public eye, in the hopes that their 'generosity' will enable them to secure new business. Thus, no real Heart ever enters the transaction.

While of course sponsoring sporting or cultural events is no sin (certainly they need their sponsors), it is nonetheless evidence of an inherent 'bottom line' culture where everything has to be about financial profit and where every year a business has to grow financially. From a perspective of Heart, this is ludicrous and from the perspective of today's increasingly uncertain financial climate, it is a condition that is becoming more and more untenable. Often, in such organisations, employees work in highly repressive environments where they continually need to meet goals and targets regardless of how those objectives are obtained. Thus, the entire workforce is under constant pressure to perform better and better, which not only creates huge stress but gradually kills off any potential for Heart and soul to emerge, as they are forever forced to compete with one another. Over the years, I have worked with many people who have sought my help to recover from the battering they have received in such cultures (which are also prime breeding grounds for institutional racism, ageism, sexism and homophobia) and generally the damage done to them has been pretty severe.

The financial system as weapon of mass destruction

It is this same normal 'insane' mindset that lies behind the craziness of the way our current financial system operates, which yearly grows ever more convoluted with its vast array of incomprehensible financial products. If we bear in mind that the cost of bailing out the large banks in 2008 was estimated by Bloomberg to be an astronomical $7.8 trillion – more than the sum of the Marshall Plan, the Korean, Vietnam and Iraq wars and the total cost of NASA all put together – and that worldwide, the loss of wealth, including stock market losses, came to $26 trillion, and if we realise that billions get invested solely on more elaborate ways to make more money, and that people can make gargantuan profits by betting on the collapse of currencies and stock markets (if the euro finally goes kaput, many people will become very rich indeed), there is no doubt that *our financial system is perhaps the greatest weapon of mass destruction on our planet.*

People continue to protest and may they keep up the good work. A few years ago, thousands of activists took to the streets from Seattle to Sydney, building upon the success of the Arab Spring. Whether they were inspired by the Occupy Wall Street movement in New York or by the Indignados in Madrid, they burned with dissatisfaction about the state of the economy, and the unfair way that it is always the poor who end up paying for the greed and the often obscene risk-taking of many of the rich.

Playing the business game at a new level

If we engage in capitalistic enterprises in the kind of holistic 'Gaia spirit' that Branson and Hawken advocate, and so start opening our hearts to the true 'spirit of business', the whole nature of the way we play the corporate game begins to undergo a radical metamorphosis. In our new model, 'doing business' becomes synonymous with serving the local and global communities, as we begin operating in terms of thinking globally and acting locally. It is not that making a profit is not important, it is just that it is no longer the prime determinant of what constitutes success.

In our new model, a business may be deemed successful if it also fosters joy, if it gives work to local people who need work, if the culture in which the employees operate is an enheartening one, if the product or products being created in some way enhance life or support the emergence of a better world, and if surplus funds are able to be channelled into some 'difference-making' venture. The new business game, then, is a win/win one. Executives no longer feel motivated to operate out of a 'war model' where you try to discredit or 'kill off' your competitors or work your employees to the bone. Heartless practices such as 'creative destruction', whereby you buy a company, slice it up, bankrupt it, restructure it and sell it at a big profit, creating profits for the shareholders at the expense of destroying a workforce's livelihood, need to be totally eliminated.

Just as in the area of the 'new relationships', we established that there is no one model that is the correct one – couples need to work out between themselves what works best – so the same holds true at a corporate level. Each organisation will need to be guided by its own heart, and by the integrity and wisdom of those who run it, to find those structures and strategies that work best for it. In Bill Clinton's words again:

I am hopeful for the future. The problems we face are solvable; we have the means. What we need is innovation, imagination and commitment. The most effective global citizens will be those who succeed in merging their business and philanthropic missions to build a future of shared prosperity and shared responsibility.[6]

Guidelines for the corporate activist

If we see ourselves as advocates of a capitalism of Heart, we are challenged to operate our business according to the following guidelines.

- We need to be willing to work on ourselves and ensure that it is Heart and not wounded or deficient ego that is driving us. It is not enough simply to hold a new vision inside our heads. It needs to have percolated down to our hearts whereby we actually are – in our blood and bones and cells – the change we want to see take place in our society. Only from this place can we truly run our business out of the realisation that all of nature is life's capital and that the deeper purpose of what we are doing is to play our part in 'knitting together the whole fabric of civilisation', and in so doing, serve the emergence of a healthier society.
- We must ensure that the values that underlie our work come from our heart or from the world of the Great Eastern Sun, and that we follow our heart at all times and are never in business solely to make money.
- We must be aware of world need at all times and especially be conscious of how our business might in some way be angled either to help support those less privileged than ourselves or to help finance particular initiatives or cultural strategies that we deem are worthy and in need of assistance.
- We must ensure that our business is ethical and sustainable, that we never do business with firms which we deem to be unethical and non-sustainable, and that nothing we ever engage in comes under the heading of evil in any shape or form.
- We must only produce products that contribute to making a positive difference to life, and the way we produce them must always be environmentally friendly.
- We need to be open to new ideas and new technologies and to thinking 'outside the box', and particularly to the prospect of working with alternative forms of energy and of potentially generating more out of less.
- If we make any messes of any kind anywhere, we must ensure that they are fully laundered and recycled, and that we take great care that no damage is ever done either to other people or to any other company or to the environment. We also need to take care to be aware of and work creatively with the Shadow side of our organisation, if and when it ever rears its head.

- We must ensure that the culture we create for our workforce is one that encourages them to be in their full humanity, enabling them to experience their work (as David Spangler put it) as 'love in action.'
- Even though we may be in competition with other businesses, we need to respect our competitors, learn from them, even at times cooperate with them, and never regard ourselves as being 'at war' with them.
- We need to be open, direct and fully transparent in our business practices and never try to avoid paying tax. (It has been suggested that if all the very rich Greeks that have recently taken much of their money out of Greece had paid their taxes honestly, Greece would not now be in her current financial predicament.)
- We must ensure that no forms of discrimination are ever present, and that all employees and all we encounter in the course of our work, are treated with all the grace and reverence with which we would ourselves wish to be treated.
- If our business has branches in different countries, we must ensure that those countries also participate in whatever success we may experience and that we always regard success from a qualitative as well as from a quantitative perspective.

Epilogue

We are all 'in it' together

We now come to the end of our journey. While it has been long, I hope you feel it has been worthwhile, and that it may have opened your eyes and your hearts in some new ways and perhaps helped you fine-tune some of your life-skills and supported you to look at the world through a different lens. I hope too, that it is now crystal clear that the only true antidote against humanity's proclivity for abusing power and being greedy and destructive is to have an open heart, and that possessing such a precious commodity is no given but needs to be worked at in many different ways. When we have established a genuine connection with the universal heart, or when it has become fully embodied inside us, it will be our natural inclination to respect and honour our fellow human beings, to want our lives to contribute to the well-being of the larger whole, to want justice for all peoples. Love and integrity will flow out of us as naturally as water out of a spring.

Remember: the cosmos has assigned each of us with a different mission. What is important is that we find what that mission is, and then try to accomplish it in as full-hearted a way as we are able. Whether we choose to be an activist for a cleaner environment, for holistic health or animal rights, or to work to try to end war or poverty – whatever it is, the important thing is that we carry our cause with *fervour*. Wherever we go, we are continually challenged to radiate our stand passionately out into our environment through our thoughts, our words and our deeds, never forgetting that the more strongly we hold a positive image of the future inside our hearts, the more we enable such a future to come into being. The more care each of us specifically puts towards addressing those ingredients of our world which we personally feel moved to champion, and the more we ensure that we also stand for Heart in the way we choose to live, the more those three evils of inequality, instability and non-sustainability will start to fade.

Dark Night of the Soul?

Times of crisis, as we have seen, are times of opening up, when thinking that was consigned to the fringes begins moving to centre stage. Therefore, the more we open up our hearts to the new zeitgeist, the more we will start to live our lives from that new centre, and the more too we will come to understand that 'we are all in it together'. If our air or our earth or our oceans are polluted, if there is a severe financial or ecological crisis or food or water shortages, we will all be affected and caught up in it, regardless of whether we are rich or poor. This is why we are all being challenged to embrace our multi-cellular/butterfly/ Stradivarius selves, as this will enable us much more successfully to make virtues out of our necessities as we learn to group together and support one another more effectively.

In moving towards a new and better world, whether or not we do actually have to enter a species 'dark night' of suffering, and if so, exactly when, or how long our trials might last, or what form or forms they may take, I don't wish to speculate on. I simply want to remind you once more that many of us still require something monumental to confront if we are truly to burn through our complacency and sense of isolation and awaken the compassion of our hearts sufficiently to enable individuals, communities and nations to fuse into a cohesive and organised global community. So if this particular crisis *does* lie ahead for us, we need to remember that whatever pain we may go through will be immeasurably lessened if we have already started embarking upon the work of opening our hearts and aligning ourselves with the world of the Great Eastern Sun. It will mean that instead of our feeling moved to fight and resist what we may have to confront, we will be much more able to accept what is taking place. It will also be much easier for us to go with the flow, since we will be far more adept at learning whatever lessons we may be called upon to learn.

The importance of integrating the world Shadow

I also remind you again that just as in our personal lives we cannot effectively move forward without also needing to go backwards and work at integrating those parts of ourselves that we have ignored or cut ourselves off from (if we don't, they will sabotage us), exactly the same thing holds true at a societal level. Therefore, unless we commit to trying to integrate into our new society those people and those interest groups, tribes or nations which, for one reason or another, have become alienated or cut off from the whole, we will also not be free to move forward en masse into the twenty-first century, since whatever is left behind will fight a rearguard action to try and prevent us from advancing.

We therefore recognise that not only are we 'all in it' together but we all have to evolve together. In other words, *all* 'underworlds' of every shape and size need lifting up and integrating into the newly emerging world. The more this happens, the more the world of the Great Eastern Sun will come into its own. The Buddha understood this, which was why he proclaimed that we needed to work for the liberation of all peoples and that so long as *all* peoples are not free, then we also are not free.

A culture of Heart as a caring culture

If there is one central thing that must characterise the emerging world of the Great Eastern Sun, it is that it be a *caring world*, caring not only for our fellow human beings in general, but especially for our most vulnerable elements – for all our down-and-outs and outcasts, as well as for those who suffer from any kind of emotional or physical deformity. From a Heart perspective, all of us are equally valuable and have an equal right to be. All of us are impregnated with divinity. None of us is more important than anyone else. The autistic child or the little baby dying of malnutrition in Africa has as much right to a full life as a duke or a king or a multi-millionaire or some world leader. Only if our hearts are open can we truly experience this.

I have talked a great deal about the power and significance of youth in the world today. Old people must also be permitted a voice, and in our Western culture, they often get badly enshadowed and are either left to fend for themselves, or conversely, shunted into loveless care homes. Why we do this is because we don't want to be reminded that we too, will one day grow wrinkly and die. As there are more old people around on the planet than ever, many of whom still have a huge amount to contribute to life, this situation urgently needs remedying. In many tribal cultures, which in so many ways are much more mature than our own, the contribution of the elderly is always recognised and many are openly venerated for their wisdom. The West needs to follow their example.

It is also important that this same kind of inclusion occur for the many millions of drug addicts all over the world, so many of whom also live at the peripheries of society. Again, this sense of being excluded is painful. Instead of being criminalised, instead of our conducting a war against drugs, which, as with our war against terror, has not only failed miserably but has been inordinately expensive (it would have been much wiser to have spent the money on rehabilitation), addicts need to be seen for what they are, namely, casualties of an unstable system, exhibiting particular symptoms of the wounded species heart, and therefore in need of our compassion and support.

Heart as our greatest weapon of self-construction

And of course we don't have to be fully enheartened before we start doing our activism out in the world. We can – and we must – begin right now. As we have seen, what will often propel us forward is our indignation or our outrage. These are powerful motivators and we should always allow for these feelings. As I mentioned in Chapter 25, I plan to start an institute that will run a variety of training programmes focusing on teaching activist skills, hopefully in different countries. If you feel you would like to participate in some way – partake in some of the programmes, or even consider training to be a trainer – or if you want to lend your support, skills and vision to the creation of this venture, which I wish to be a collaborative effort (I cannot do it all on my own and do not intend to), I would be delighted to hear from you. I may be contacted at www.spiritual-activism.com.

I am also not going to try to speculate as to what specific forms our new culture will take, or exactly how long it might be before the ideas we have been exploring here begin to occupy centre stage. I only know that there is enormous goodness in the world and that this goodness is continually growing in strength, and that when the universal heart truly does come of age, a new and kinder world will increasingly open up for *all of us*. In this new world, there will be more of all the Heart virtues present, cultural differences will be respected, many more people will find many more opportunities to thrive, blossom and celebrate the magnificence of what it means to be human, and evil, if not fully overcome, will at least be drastically reduced.

Notes

Invitation
1. Albert Schweitzer, *The Teaching of Reverence for Life* (New York: Holt, Rinehart & Winston, 1965).

1: The Significance of the Heart
1. John O'Donohue, *To Bless the Space between Us: A Book of Blessings* (New York: Doubleday, 2008).
2. Osho, *The Book of the Secrets* (London: Thames & Hudson, 1974).
3. Daniel Goleman, *Emotional Intelligence: Why It Can Matter More than IQ* (London: Bloomsbury, 1996).
4. *The Times*, 30 October 2008.
5. Rumi: *The Ruins of the Heart* (Putney, VT: Threshold, 1981).
6. Ian McGilchrist, *The Master and His Emissary: The Divided Brain and the Making of the Western World* (New Haven: Yale University Press, 2009).

Chapter 2: The Treasures of the Heart
1. Thomas à Kempis: *The Imitation of Christ*.
2. Thomas Merton: *Disputed Questions* (New York: Farrar, Straus & Cudahy, 1960).
3. Tarthang Tulku: *Skillful Means* (Berkeley, CA: Dharma, 1978).
4. Chögyam Trungpa: *Shambhala: The Sacred Path of the Warrior* (Boulder, CO: Shambhala, 1984).

Chapter 3: Understanding the Wounded Heart
1. William Wordsworth: 'Ode: Imitations of Immortality' (1807).

Chapter 5: The Challenges of Being an Activist
1. Zbigniew Brzezinski, 'The Global Political Awakening', *New York Times*, 16 December 2008.
2. David Lorimer (ed.): *Prophet for Our Times: The Life and Teachings of Peter Deunov* (Shaftesbury: Element, 1991).

Chapter 6: Eastern and Western Perspectives on Self-healing
1. Carl Jung: *The Meaning of Individualism*.
2. Robert Johnson: *Inner Work: Using Dreams and Active Imagination for Personal Growth* (San Francisco: Harper & Row, 1986).
3. A. H. Almaas: *Essence: The Diamond Approach to Inner Realization* (York Beach, ME: Weiser, 1986).

Chapter 8: Healing the Universal Heart
1. Thích Nhat Hanh: *Being Peace* (Berkeley, CA: Parallax, 1987).
2. Christopher M. Bache: *Dark Night, Early Dawn: Steps to a Deep Ecology of Mind* (Albany: State University of New York Press, 2000).
3. Thích Nhat Hanh: *Call Me by My True Names: The Collected Poems of Thích Nhat Hanh* (Berkeley, CA: Parallax, 1999).
4. Roger Woolger: *Other Lives, Other Selves: A Jungian Psychotherapist Discovers Past Lives* (New York: Doubleday, 1987).
5. Jack Kornfield: *After the Ecstasy, the Laundry: How the Heart Grows Wise on the Spiritual Path* (New York: Bantam, 2000).

Chapter 11: Opening to the Spiritual Heart
1. Graf Karlfried von Dürckheim: *The Way of Transformation: Daily Life as a Spiritual Exercise* (London: Allen & Unwin, 1971).
2. Christopher M. Bache: *Dark Night, Early Dawn: Steps to a Deep Ecology of Mind* (Albany: State University of New York Press, 2000).

3. Ken Wilber: *One Taste: Daily Reflections on Integral Spirituality* (Boston: Shambhala, 2000).
4. Ibid.
5. J. G. Bennett: Long Pilgrimage: *The Life and Teaching of Sri Govindananda Bharati, Known as the Shivapuri Baba* (London: Hodder & Stoughton, 1965).

Chapter 12: Opening to the Meditative Heart
1. Tarthang Tulku: *Openness Mind* (Emeryville, CA: Dharma, 1978).
2. Osho: Meditation: *The Art of Ecstasy* (New York: Harper & Row, 1976).
3. Ken Wilber: *One Taste: Daily Reflections on Integral Spirituality* (Boston: Shambhala, 2000).
4. Ibid.

Chapter 13: Awakening the Heart of Prayer
1. Thomas Merton: *Contemplation in a World of Action* (London: Allen & Unwin, 1971).
2. Ibid.
3. Peter Deunov: *Gems of Love: Prayers and Formulas by Beinsa Douno (Peter Deunov)*, compiled by David Lorimer (Grain of Wheat Trust, 1994).
4. Emphasis added.
5. Merton: *Contemplation in a World of Action*.

Chapter 14: Cultivating the Heart of Love
1. Pitirim A. Sorokin: *The Ways and Power of Love: Types, Factors, and Techniques of Moral Transformation* (Boston: Beacon Press, 1954).
2. Kahlil Gibran: *The Prophet* (1923).
3. Ibid.
4. Tarthang Tulku: *Skillful Means* (Berkeley, CA: Dharma, 1978).
5. Dag Hammarskjöld: *Markings* (London: Faber & Faber, 1964).

Chapter 15: Embracing the Virtues of the Heart
1. David Spangler: 'What Is Peace?'

Chapter 16: Entering into the Heart of Relationship
1. John Welwood: *Journey of the Heart: Intimate Relationship and the Path of Love* (New York: HarperCollins, 1990).
2. Susan Campbell: *The Couple's Journey: Intimacy as a Path to Wholeness* (San Luis Obispo, CA: Impact, 1980).

Chapter 17: Working with the Sacred 'Help Forces'
1. John G. Bennett: *Transformation* (Sherborne: Coombe Springs Press, 1978).
2. Aldous Huxley: *The Doors of Perception* (London: Chatto & Windus, 1954).
3. John G. Bennett: *Witness: The Autobiography of John G. Bennett* (London: Turnstone, 1975).
4. Ibid.
5. Hafiz: 'The Jeweler', in *I Heard God Laughing: Poems of Hope and Joy* (New York: Penguin, 2006).
6. Romain Rolland: *The Life of Ramakrishna* (1929).
7. Lorna St Aubyn: *Rituals for Everyday Living: Special Ways of Marking Important Events in Your Life* (London: Piatkus, 1994).
8. Charles Leadbeater: *The Hidden Side of Christian Festivals* (Los Angeles: St Alban Press, 1920).
9. St Aubyn: *Rituals for Everyday Living*.
10. Ralph Metzner: 'Hallucinogenic Drugs and Plants in Psychotherapy and Shamanism', *Journal of Psychoactive Drugs*, vol. 30, no. 4 (1998).
11. Ibid.
12. *A Course in Miracles*, 2nd edition (Miraclevision.com, 1976), Lesson 24.

NOTES

Chapter 19: Understanding the Crises of the Heart
1. Alice Bailey: *A Treatise on White Magic* (New York: Lucis, 1934).
2. Roberto Assagioli: *Psychosynthesis: A Manual of Principles and Techniques* (New York: Hobbs, Dorman, 1965).
3. Martin Luther: *Ninety-five Theses* (1517).

Chapter 20: Looking to the Future
1. John G. Bennett: *Deeper Man* (London: Turnstone, 1978).
2 Sri Nisargadatta Maharaj: *I Am That* (Bombay: Chetana, 1973).

Chapter 21: Exploring the Path of the Spiritual Activist
1. Andrew Harvey: *Radical Passion: Sacred Love and Wisdom in Action* (Berkeley, CA: North Atlantic, 2012).
2. Alice Bailey: *A Treatise on White Magic* (New York: Lucis, 1934).
3. Martin Luther King: *Strength to Love* (New York: Harper & Row, 1963).

Chapter 22: The Many Faces of the Activist of Heart
1. 'The Passing of Arthur', *Idylls of the King* (1859).
2. Aung San Suu Kyi: *Freedom From Fear and Other Writings* (London: Viking, 1991).
3. Ibid.
4. Natan Sharansky: 'Why Dictatorships are Terrified of Dissidents', *The Times*, 10 December 2010.
5. Martin Luther King: *Strength to Love* (New York: Harper & Row, 1963).

Chapter 23: Healing Evil
1. W. H. Auden: 'Herman Melville' (1939).
2. Ideas here are taken from an article by George Monbiot in *The Guardian*.
3. M. Scott Peck: 'Healing Evil'.
4. A. H. Almaas: *The Inner Journey home: Soul's Realization of the Unity of Reality* (Boston: Shambhala, 2004).
5. Ibid.
6. Alexander Solzhenitsyn: *The Gulag Archipelago* (London: Collins Harvill, 1974).
7. Stan Grof: *The Cosmic Game: Explorations of the Frontiers of Human Consciousness* (Albany: State University of New York Press, 1998).
8. Ibid.

Chapter 24: Transforming War
1. John le Carré: 'The United Sates has gone mad', *The Times*, 15 January 2003.
2. Scilla Elworthy: *Making Terrorism History* (London: Rider, 2006).
3. Dalai Lama: *Ocean of Wisdom: Guidelines for Living* (Santa Fe: Clear Light, 1989).
4. Sam Keen: *Faces of the Enemy: Reflections of the Hostile Imagination* (San Francisco: Harper & Row, 1986).

Chapter 25: Awakening the Corporate Heart
1. *Financial Times*, 21 January 2012.
2. Ervin Laszlo: *You Can Change the World : The Global Citizen's Handbook for Living on Planet Earth* (New York: Select, 2003).
3. Richard Branson: *Let's Not Screw It, Let's Just Do It* (New York: Random House, 2007).
4. Paul Hawken, Amory Lovins and Hunter Lovins: *Natural Capitalism: Creating the Next Industrial Revolution* (Boston: Little, Brown, 1999).
5. Ibid.
6. *Financial Times*, 21 January 2012.

Index

activism
    Agitator activists 275–6
    awakening of sacred heart 61–3
    being an 1–2
    challenges for 55–66
    commentary on paths 279–82
    and danger 267–8
    Dissident activists 276–9
    Educator activists 274
    and evolution of new humans 64–5
    forms of 261–2, 263–4
    and freedom 59
    in the future 251–3
    guidelines for 282
    and heart-centred politics 267
    and higher purpose 262–3
    in times of change 55–66
    in times of crisis 58–9
    Infiltrator activists 271–2
    and initiations of the heart 55–6
    Initiator activists 270–1
    Innovator activists 272–3
    Investigator activists 273
    move from individuality 63–4
    primary activism 264
    Proclaimer activists 272
    Protestor activists 274–5
    Radiator activists 269
    resistance to 65–6
    testing 56
    and women's rights 265–6
    as world servers 260–1
Adi Da 195, 230, 237
Agitator activists 275–6
alchemy of heart 41–2
Almaas, A. H. 77, 291–2
ancestors
    as source of wounded heart 36
Aquarius, Age of 55, 56–7
Arab Spring 307–8
Arendt, Hannah 284
Assadourian, Erik 1
Assagioli, Roberto 227
Attar, Farid u–din 29
Auden, W. H. 284
Aurobindo, Sri
    as divine madman 237
    on higher possibilities 124
ayahuasca 202–5
Baba, Shivapuri 125, 129–30, 295
Bache, Chris 39
    on species wounds 88–9
    on spiritual practice 125
Baez, Joan 263–4, 265
beauty 23
    cultivating 170–1
    as treasure of the heart 22

Bennett, John G.
    on Gurdjieff 193–4
    on the future 257
    on help forces 189, 192–3
birth trauma 37
Blair, Tony 239
Bloom, William 98
Branson, Sir Richard 319, 320
Brzezinski, Zbigniew 58–9
Burke, Edmund 283
Campbell, Susan 186–7
Capra, Fritjof 318
Carré, John le 302
Chardin, Pierre Teilhard de
    on joy 25–6
    on strength of the heart 9
Childre, Doc 10
Clapton, Eric 5
Clinton, Bill 315, 326
Colvin, Marie 273
compassion 21–2
conflict resolution 43–4
contemplative awareness 150–2
corporate heart
    and big business 319
    business challenges 324–5
    and corporate activist 316–18, 327–8
    and financial system 325–6
    guidelines for 327–8
    heart–centred businesses 321–3
    importance of 314–15
    and sustainability 323–4
    and unacceptable face of capitalism 319–20
Couple's Journey, The (Campbell) 186–7
courage
    cultivating 173–4
    as treasure of the heart 24–5
crises
    from abundance 230–1
    activism in 58–9
    and dark night of suffering 332
    and death 225–7
    fear of the sublime 232–4
    in the future 247–9, 250–1
    as a gift 223–4, 235–6
    and the Shadow 224
    significance of 22–3
    and spirituality 227–33, 234–5
    as universal heart trigger 5
curses 82–4
Dalai Lama
    on importance of the heart 28
    and kindness 22, 175
    on peace 310
    on spirituality 5, 125
    on violence 298
Daskalos 208

INDEX

Dass, Ram
    on need for open heart 54
    on healthy ego 79
death 225–7
Deunov, Peter
    on importance of love 21, 154
    on prayer 149–50
    on times of change 62
Diana, Princess 50–1
Dissident activists 276–9
Doors of Perception, The (Huxley) 190
Dossey, Larry 144
Dürkheim, Karlfried von
    on garden of the heart 123
    and species heart 60–1
Dylan, Bob 263–4, 265
dysfunctional relationships 31–2
early childhood 37–8
Educator activists 274
ego
    healthy 78–9
    and madness 239–40
    need for integration 77–8
    problems of 76–7
    and spirituality 80
    unhealthy 78
ego wounds
    curses on 82–4
    and listening heart 81–2
    and negative belief systems 86–7
    psychic mines 84–5
    and wounded inner child 85–6
Eliade, Mircea 55–6
Elworthy, Scilla 298
emotional heart
    working with 69–70
emotional intelligence 10
enhearteners 4
Ennis, Jessica 48
evil
    corporate evil 287–8
    non-obvious evil 284–7
    obvious evil 284
    philosophical perspective 292–4
    responding on 294–6
    and unconsciousness 289–90
    understanding of 283–4
    and war 300–3
Farah, Mo 48
fasting of the heart 133–4
feminine principle 126
forgiveness
    challenges of 210–11
    and forgiveness committees 221
    and God 216–17
    importance of 209
    international 217–21
    and Palestinian/Israeli conflict 219–20
    process of 215–16
    requirements for 212–13
    self forgiveness 213–15
    and victimhood 211–12
freedom
    and activism 59
    and the future 243
future, looking to the
    activists in 251–3
    in autocratic countries 253–4
    as breakthrough 245–6, 247
    and crises 247–9, 250–1
    and critical mass 254–5, 256–7
    and freedom 243
    and help forces 250
    and inequality 257–9
    positive image of 246–7
    preparing for 255–6
    terrorism in 306–7
    and world situation 244–6
Fry, Christopher 59
Gandhi, Mahatma 2, 209
Gbowee, Leymah 266
Geldof, Bob 275
George, James 243
Gibran, Kahlil 161
Goethe, Johann Wolfgang von 177
Goleman, Daniel 10
Gore, Al 241
gratitude 24
Grof, Stan 6, 293, 294
Gurdjieff, George 193–4, 247–8
gurus as help forces 193–7
Hafiz 194
Hammarskjöld, Dag 167
Hanh, Thích Nhat
    on species wounds 88, 89–90
    on war 301
Harvey, Andrew 260
Hawken, Paul 241, 251–2, 320–1
healing
    Buddhist perspectives of 72–4
    and power of prayer 142–5
    in relationships 178–80
    rituals for 200
    Western perspectives of 72
Healing Evil (Peck) 290
healing heart
    activating 45–6
    alchemy of 41–2
    and conflict resolution 43–4
    Jesus as embodiment of 52–4
    and living appropriately 42–3
    living in the present 47–8
    mundane adventures 46–8
    and universal heart 48–52
heart
    and caring culture 331–2
    different levels of 127
    importance of 9–11
    integration with mind 14–15, 26–7
    loss of 11–13

power of 17–18
and self-construction 332
and war 301–2
working with 13–14
help forces
 and ayahuasca 202–5
 forms of 190
 and the future 250
 gurus 193–7
 and miracles 207–8
 rituals as 197–201
 sacred sites 205–7
 in supportive universe 189–90
 synchronistic 191–2
 unusual forms of 190
Hesse, Hermann 285–6
higher-order heart 75–6
Hussein, Ed 304, 306
Hussein, Saddam 35
Huston, Jean 123–4
Huxley, Aldous 190
I Am That (Maharaj) 151
Imaginal Journey of Peace, An (White) 64–5
individuality 63–4
Infiltrator activists 271–2
initiations of the heart 55–6
Initiator activists 270–1
Innovator activists 272–3
international forgiveness 217–21
Investigator activists 273
Jesus
 as embodiment of healing heart 52–4
 and importance of prayer 141
 and the Shadow 107
Johnson, Robert 70
Joplin, Janis 146, 147
joy
 cultivating 171–2
 as treasure of the heart 25–6
Jung, Carl
 on evil 283
 on repression of unconsciousness 69–70
 on the Shadow 99, 108
justice 27
Kabir 60
Keats, John 23
Keen, Sam 283, 313
Kempis, Thomas à 21
Kennedy, J. F. 19
Keshavadas, Sant 60
Khul, Dwaj
 on activism 269
 on crises 223
 on higher purpose of humanity 263
 on initiations 56
 on importance of rituals 198
kindness
 cultivating 175
 as treasure of the heart 22–3
King, Martin Luther 24, 54, 114, 209, 268, 271

Kornfield, Jack 94–5
Krishnamurti, Jiddu 289
Kundalini energy 229
Kyi, Aung San Suu 276–7
Lao Tzu
 on desire 131
 on healing ego wounds 81
'Last Night' (Machado) 41
Laszlo, Ervin 243, 317–18
Leadbeater, Charles 198
Lennon, John 310
listening heart 81–2
Liu Xiaobo 267–8
loss of heart 11–13
love
 appropriate love 164
 conscious love 163
 description of 154–5
 forms of 155–6
 loving children 164–5
 loving ourselves 157–9
 loving work 166–7
 romantic love 159–61
 and the Shadow 161–3
 and spiritual love 156–7
 as treasure of the heart 20–1
Luther, Martin 231
Maathai, Wangari 266
MacArthur, Ellen 270
Machado, Antonio 41
Maharaj, Sri Misargadatta 151
Maharshi, Ramana 195, 237, 269
Mandela, Nelson 17, 221
Mann, Thomas 30
McCann, Madeleine 214
McDoom, Dr 289
McGilchrist, Ian 15
madness
 divine madness 237–8
 and ego 239–40
 as normality 238
meditation
 and fasting of the heart 133–4
 forms of 139–40
 importance of 131–5
 practising 136–7
 and presence 135–6
 stages of 137–8
Meera, Mother 142–3
memories
 and healing universal heart 91–4
 and world suffering 94–5
Merton, Thomas
 on contemplative awareness 152
 on loss of heart 11
 on love 21
 on prayer 146
Metzner, Ralph 204–5
mind 14–15, 26–7
morphogenetic field resonance theory 39–40

338

INDEX

Mtetwa, Beatrice 266
Muller, Robert 3–4
mundane adventures 46–8
Natural Capitalism (Hawken) 320–1
negative belief systems 86–7
non-obvious evil 284–7, 290–1
Obama, Barack 217, 243, 272, 295–6
obvious evil 284, 291–2
'Ode: Intimations of Immortality' (Wordsworth) 43–4
O'Donohue, John 9
Okri, Ben 11
Osho
    on importance of the heart 9–10
    on meditation 137
P'ang, Layman 131
Papaji 195–7, 237
past lives
    and healing the universal heart 90–1
    as source of wounded heart 38–9
    and species heart 94
peace
    cultivating 172–3
    as treasure of the heart 26
    and war 310–12
Peck, Scott 290
prayer
    in action 148
    and comtemplative awareness 150–2
    healing power of 142–5
    impersonal 148
    importance of 141–2
    interpersonal 147–8
    personal 146–7
    set prayers 148–9
    spontaneous prayers 149
    timing of 145–6
prejudice 111–12
Prigogine, Ilya 249
Proclaimer activists 272
Protestor activists 274–5
psychic mines 84–5
Radhakrishnan, Sarvepalli 241
Radiator activists 269
Ramakrishna, Sri 131, 194, 293
relationships
    ending 184–5
    guidelines for 187–8
    healing power of 178–80
    importance of 177–8
    modern-day 181–3
    problems as allies 180
    and sexuality 183–4
    and the wounded heart 31–5, 183
Rilke, Rainer Maria
    on healing ego wounds 81
    on relationships 177–8
Ring, Kenneth 248
Rinpoche, Chögyam Trungpa
    on challenge of activism 55

    on courage 24
    on two states of consciousness 61
rituals as help force 197–201
Roerich, Nicholas 23
romantic love 159–61
Rumi
    on evil 283
    on the healing heart 41
    on importance of the heart 13, 119, 121
    on love 185
    on the wounded heart 29
sacred heart 61–3
sacred sites 205–7
St Aubyn, Lorna 197–8, 199
Sanai 119
Sartouris, Elisabet 63–4, 287–8
sexuality 183–4
Shadow
    and ayahuasca 203–4
    and blaming others 101
    conflicts in 110
    and crises 224
    dark side of 104–5, 106–7
    and death 104
    description of 99–100
    in different environments 113–14
    explorations of 101–2
    identifying 108–9
    in families 105–6
    gifts from 104–5
    and love 161–3
    in opening hearts 102–3
    and prejudice 111–12
    projections 114–15
    and Shadow projection 100–1
    in society 103
    and wealth inequality 115–16
    working with 108–9
    world Shadow 116–17, 330–1
Shamabala: The Sacred Heart of the Warrior (Rinpoche) 61
Sharansky, Natan 278
Sheldrake, Rupert 39
Sleep of Prisoners, A (Fry) 59
Solzhenitsyn, Alexander 292
Sorokin, Pitirim A. 154–5
sources of wounded hearts
    ancestors 36
    birth trauma 37
    early childhood 37–8
    past lives 38–9
    spirit attachments 36–7
Spangler, David 63
species heart
    and past lives 94
    suffering of 60–1
    working with 95–6
    wounds in 88–90
spiritual activism see activism
spirit attachments 36–7

spiritual heart
    and crises 227–33
    and enlightenment 129–30
    and feminine principle 126
    as a garden 123
    growing requirements 124–5
    and image of higher possibilities 123–4
    and substitute transcendence 121–2
spiritual love 156–7
spirituality
    and crises 227–33, 234–5
    deeper stages of 128
    early stages of seeking 127–8
    and ego 80
    and the heart 4–5, 6
    translative 127, 129
Steering Business towards Sustainabilty (Capra) 318
sublime 227–33
substitute transcendence 121–2
suffering 97–8
Tarnas, Richard 55–7
Teresa, Mother 17–18
    on the healing heart 41
    on love 21
terrorism
    and the Arab Spring 307–8
    causes of 303–4
    in the future 306–7
    at inner level 305
    understanding 303
therapeutic support 70–2, 74
Toynbee, Arnold 7
translative spirituality 127, 129
treasures of the heart
    beauty 23
    comments on 27–8
    compassion 21–2
    courage 24–5
    gratitude 24
    joy 25–6
    justice 27
    kindness 22–3
    love 20–1
    peace 26
    vision 23–4
    wisdom 26–7
Trevelyan, Sir George 63
truth 176
tsunami of 2004 51–2
Tulku, Tarthang
    on compassion 22
    on loving work 166
    on meditation 135
Tzu, Chuang 133
Ulanov, Ann Belford 99
universal heart
    definition of 3–4
    crises as trigger 52
    engaging with suffering 97–8
    experience of 48–9
    and past lives 90–1
    Princess Diana's death as trigger 50–1
    and healing heart 48–52
    and memories 91–4
    and species heart 88–90, 95–6
    tsunami as trigger 51–2
    and world suffering 94–5
Up From Eden (Wilber) 121, 140
virtues of the heart
    beauty 170–1
    courage 173–4
    development of 168–9
    joy 171–2
    kindness 175
    peace 172–3
    truth 176
    vision 170
    wisdom 169–70
vision
    cultivating 170
    as treasure of the heart 23–4
war
    ending 312–13
    and enemy-creating 299–300
    and eradication of evil 300–3
    and the heart 301–2
    and hostile attitudes 309–10
    moving away from 308–9
    and peace 310–12
    understanding 298–9
Watson, Thomas J. 314
Way of Transformation, The (Dürkheim) 60–1
Ways and Power of Love, The (Sorokin) 154–5
Welwood, John
    on relationships 179–80
    on spiritual by passing 127
White, Michael 64–5
whole-heartedness 16–17
Wilber, Ken
    as Innovator activist 272
    on meditation 137–8, 140
    on spirituality 121, 122, 127, 128
Williamson, Marianne 260
wisdom
    cultivating 169–70
    as treasure of the heart 26–7
Woolger, Roger 90–1, 92
Wordsworth, William 38, 43–4
world suffering 94–5
wounded heart
    and dysfunctional relationships 31–2
    and relationships 31–5, 183
    responses to 31
    sources of 35–9
    understanding 29–30
wounded inner child 85–6
wu wei 152–3
Yeats, W. B. 247
Yousufzai, Malala 266
Yunus, Mohammed 322–3